THE COMPLETE WORKS OF HARTMANN VON AUE

Arthurian Romances, Tales, and Lyric Poetry

THE COMPLETE WORKS OF HARTMANN VON AUE

translated with commentary by

FRANK TOBIN   KIM VIVIAN   RICHARD H. LAWSON

THE PENNSYLVANIA STATE UNIVERSITY PRESS
UNIVERSITY PARK, PENNSYLVANIA

LIBRARY OF CONGRESS CATALOGING-IN-PUBLICATION DATA

Hartmann, von Aue, 12th cent.
[Works. English. 2001]
Arthurian romances, tales, and lyric poetry : the complete works of
Hartmann von Aue / translated with commentary by
Frank Tobin, Kim Vivian, Richard H. Lawson.
p.   cm.
Includes bibliographical references.
Contents: The lament—Lyric poetry—Erec—Gregorious—
Poor Henirich—Iwein.
ISBN 0-271-02111-X (cloth : alk. paper)
ISBN 0-271-02112-8 (pbk. : alk. paper)
1. Hartmann, von Aue, 12th cent.—Translations into English.
I. Tobin, Frank J.   II. Vivian, Kim.   III. Lawson, Richard H.   IV. Title.

PT1534.A3 A14 2001
831'.21—dc21
2001021481

It is the policy of The Pennsylvania State University Press to use acid-free paper for the
first printing of all clothbound books. Publications on uncoated stock satisfy the
minimum requirements of American National Standard for Information Sciences—
Permanence of Paper for Printed Library Materials, ANSI Z39.48–1992.

CONTENTS

Acknowledgments   vii
Introduction   ix

The Lament   1
       translated with an introduction by Frank Tobin

Lyric Poetry   29
       translated with an introduction by Frank Tobin
     1. "Because I have endured"   30
     2. "If a man takes his delight"   32
     3. "I said I wanted to live always for her"   33
     4. "My service to my lady"   35
     5. "Taking the cross"   35
     6. "If a woman sends off her beloved"   38
     7. "He who is sad in good times"   38
     8. "Mighty God"   39
     9. "If one can save one's soul by lying"   40
    10. "I have little reason to complain"   41
    11. "No one in this world is a happy man"   42
    12. "Noble lady"   42
    13. "By rights I must ever hold dear the day"   44
    14. "Those who reap joy from summer's flowers"   45
    15. "Many a person hails me"   46
    16. "These would be wonderful days"   47
    17. "By your leave I depart"   48
    18. "Alas, why are we so sad?"   49

Erec   51
       translated with an introduction by Kim Vivian

Gregorius   165
       translated with an introduction by Kim Vivian

Poor Heinrich   215
     translated with an introduction by Frank Tobin

Iwein   235
     translated with an introduction by Richard H. Lawson

Bibliography   323

ACKNOWLEDGMENTS

The editors wish to express their deep gratitude to the following persons: Ed Haymes, Jim Walter, and Frank Gentry, for their readings of the manuscript and for their insightful commentary; Dr. Armin Schlechter, director of the Department of Manuscripts at the University of Heidelberg, for his help in obtaining a reproduction of the portrait of Hartmann von Aue in the Manesse manuscript; Stefanie Bluemle, for assistance with the bibliography; Christine Vivian, for her assistance with every stage of the manuscript; and Peter J. Potter of Penn State University Press, for his support of the project.

INTRODUCTION

One of the most enduring legacies of the Middle Ages is the storybook world of bold knights and incomparably fair ladies, a world first and best described by the poets of the age. Their greathearted heroes ride off fearlessly in search of adventure and, though severely tried in the process, nevertheless show their mettle and emerge ultimately victorious, whether the enemy be an evil knight, a wild beast, or a monstrous and magical creature. Yet these same knights, who display great virility in such encounters and on the jousting fields at their tournaments, have hearts and minds enthralled by love. They strive in all they do to attain the love of a woman so fair and virtuous that she embodies all one could hope for in a soul mate. How did this idealized world come into being? What were the social and cultural conditions that gave rise to it?

For a variety of reasons—among others, innovations in farming methods, relative peace, and possibly a change in climate—living conditions improved in most of Europe from about the year 1000 onward. As basic survival became less and less a major concern, people, at least many of those who were above the class of the unfree serf, began to devote much of their attention to what we generally term *culture*. In the church this led to an increase in intellectual activity and artistic expression. Scholasticism, the pursuit of philosophical and theological knowledge through rational inquiry, replaced the earlier monastic theology with its greater reliance on church authorities, such as Augustine (354–430). The movement culminated in the founding and flourishing of universities. In art we owe to these times the marvels of high Romanesque and early Gothic architecture and sculpture which we find embodied in the medieval cathedral.

During this same period, the lay nobility consolidated itself into a class with its own self-awareness and self-confidence. Though throughout the Middle Ages all segments of society remained permeated with religious values and were greatly influenced by theological points of view, here was an island of secular culture with its own values and viewpoints that could not simply be reduced to seeing things *sub specie aeternitatis* (in the light of eternity). This knightly-courtly culture often allied itself with religious goals and ideals, as happened, for example, in the

Crusades. In other ways, however, this culture existed in tension with the religious point of view. It saw the world in a more positive light and found that it offered many things that were of value in their own right, such as the beauty of women, human love relationships, and the valorous and unselfish deeds of knights. How to reconcile these two value systems became the preoccupation of those endowed with powers of insight and reflection.

This new secular attitude found expression chiefly in literature, especially in the narrative and lyric genres. But we must not imagine that this literature presents us with a realistic view of the everyday lives and experiences of the knights and ladies of the feudal court any more than a Hollywood western depicts the daily lives of people in the Old West. It is hard to imagine that knights really spent most of their time off in search of adventure, at tourneys, or pining away for some lady sadly and definitively out of their reach. It is the ideals and values of this society that we see reflected in the actions and attitudes expressed in this literature.

This knightly-courtly culture and the literature resulting from it first arose in France. Though some love lyrics in German poetry existed previous to and probably independent of French influence, the poetry expressing "courtly love" in the more proper and restricted sense of the term entered the German-speaking world from its neighbor to the west. Middle High German Arthurian romances show an even greater debt to France, more particularly to the narratives of Chrétien de Troyes (fl. c. 1170). Most of the construct of the world of King Arthur as it appears in German literature was his creation, and the plots and structure of the individual German Arthurian romances are in large part reworkings of his narratives.

The classical period of medieval German literature spans the relatively brief time from 1170 to 1250. Those with even a nodding acquaintance with medieval literature should be familiar with its greatest poets and their chief accomplishments. Narrative masterpieces include the anonymous *Nibelungenlied*, Wolfram von Eschenbach's *Parzival*, and Gottfried von Strassburg's incomplete *Tristan*, while Walther von der Vogelweide is generally recognized as the greatest German lyric poet of the age.

It is Hartmann von Aue, however, whose poetry served as the model and standard against which these and other poets of the age were measured. Hartmann preceded slightly most other major German-speaking poets, and for many of them his work served as a model for theirs. Gottfried von Strassburg expressly praises Hartmann's poetic talents above those of all others. Hartmann's lyric poetry consists of finely fashioned verse and expresses the themes of love current at the time. His *Lament*, which, in contrast to his other works, may have lost much of its original appeal, is, nonetheless, an excellent example of a form popular at the time, the dialogue treating human love. In his version, the disputants are, not Body and Soul, but Body and Heart.

Though this dialogue and his lyric poetry put him in the ranks of the age's worthy poets, Hartmann's reputation, then and now, rests mainly on his narratives. Two of them, *Erec* and *Iwein*, are classic Arthurian courtly romances. Though these stories reflect the world and ideas of their times, their continuing appeal rests on their ability to speak to the spirit of adventure in all of us. The knights Erec and Iwein inhabit the never-never-land of pure fiction, which as Aristotle remarks, has more relevance for us than historical reality because in that land the characters face situations that, though unreal, paradoxically touch everyone (*Poetics*, chap. 9). Like the classic films about the Old West, these stories present us with a world that never really existed and yet tell us in an imaginative way who we are and who we want to be.

Many critics suggest that Hartmann has deepened the relevance of the stories he adapts from Chrétien by focusing more directly on the universal human issues inherent in the plots. Hartmann is also often credited with a remarkable and almost modern insight into the psychology of his characters. And his female figures—especially the servant girl Lunete in *Iwein* and Enite in *Erec*—are some of the most appealing created before the time of Shakespeare.

Both of Hartmann's Arthurian tales tell the story of a knight who is privileged to be one of an illustrious group of knights gathered around Arthur. The famed Round Table at which they gather symbolizes in its form their equality as members of the knightly class. Erec and Iwein, like their peers, must ride out on quests to prove themselves. Arthur is *primus inter pares* (the first among equals), different from the rest only in that his reputation rests securely on his past deeds. This court is the arbiter of courtly values, and from it knights venture forth seeking encounters. If they triumph, they return to Arthur's court to reap the fruits of their prowess and toils—the esteem of Arthur and his knights, and the love and admiration of the ladies. Though the Arthurian world forms the backdrop of both stories, Erec and Iwein are each more concerned with a court other than Arthur's—Erec with the court he is to inherit from his father, and Iwein with the court whose lord he becomes by marrying Laudine. Before they can take their rightful places at these courts, each must set off on a series of adventures that function to correct some flaw or flaws in his relationship with his wife. Thus both stories focus on achieving the ideal relationship between a knight and his lady.

Hartmann's other two narratives, *Gregorius* and *Poor Heinrich*, are religious or theological in nature. Their heroes, knights though they be, misunderstand their place in the ultimate scheme of things, and because of that find themselves at odds with God. Like Oedipus, Gregorius sets out to discover who he is; and like Oedipus, the success of his quest ironically crushes him but at the same time redeems and elevates him above all humanity. Like Gregorius, Heinrich, too, sees his life disintegrate, but the tone of the story is lighthearted in spite of this, and he is miraculously given a chance to relive his best years with the opportunity to avoid his old mistakes.

All four narratives follow a basic pattern of courtly romances: the hero starts out on a quest and, after facing challenges that severely try him, achieves a goal that seems to be everything he could wish for. Then something happens to disturb the happiness which he thought was securely his. (In *Poor Heinrich*, as the story begins, the protagonist is portrayed as having reached this supposedly ideal state. He is then stricken with leprosy and topples from his lofty perch.) The happiness attained was vulnerable because it rested on false values. What seemed real reveals itself as illusion. To gain insight and reorient himself the hero must embark upon another series of adventures. Only when the goal is reached a second time can he and his lady "live happily ever after," because their happiness is now well grounded. They have overcome their disorientation, and thus their lives now rest on a true understanding of the world and their place in it.

Our factual knowledge about Hartmann is scant. He was born between 1160 and 1165. His *Iwein*, generally considered to be his last work and his masterpiece, was completed about 1200. He is mentioned as still living in a document from about 1210 and as dead in another shortly after 1220. He describes himself in his works as a *dienestman*, or ministerial, serving the house of Aue in Swabia. Ministerials were those who by their abilities were able to rise above serfdom and held some administrative post in the service of a lord. Though still considered unfree servants, they could attain considerable power and influence, sometimes ruling over several castles for their lord. Some even married into noble families. Thus their social standing was ambiguous. Usually they were knights who were ranked among the lower echelons of the nobility. Since Aue is a frequent geographical designation in southwest Germany, it is difficult to determine more exactly Hartmann's place of origin or which house of Aue he served. He proudly tells us that he can read books, which implies that he knew Latin. Because of the detailed description in his *Gregorius* of education as it existed in the monasteries, some have surmised that Hartmann received his schooling in a monastic environment and was perhaps in his youth a member of a monastic community. But this remains at best an educated guess. Little more can be said of his life.

We have chosen to offer the reader all of Hartmann's poetry in a single volume not just because of its intrinsic quality. Because it is Hartmann we have chosen, we are able to present the reader with examples of most of the kinds of literature produced by the principal poets of the age. Hartmann tried his hand at Arthurian tales; several variations of love poetry, including one of the most important crusading songs; an allegorical dialogue on the nature of courtly love; and two narratives—one somberly Augustinian and one light-hearted, mirroring the emerging optimism of the times—that probe the conflict between the values of courtly society and the absolute demands of God represented in the theology of the times. Thus in reading Hartmann one is able to become familiar with a broad spectrum of high medieval literature and thought.

We have endeavored to capture some of the flavor of the medieval way of viewing and expressing things without resorting to obsolete and antiquated formulations foreign to our intended audience. Hartmann's language sounded fresh and vigorous to his contemporaries. We hope we have been able to catch some of this in our translations. Though only one translator is listed for each individual piece or section, ours has been a truly collaborative effort. We have reviewed one another's translations thoroughly and exchanged helpful suggestions and emendations. We based our translations on the editions of the Middle High German originals listed in the bibliography.

The introduction to each work is intended to provide the reader with some background material and with some points concerning critical discussion of the work. The introductions are not meant as exhaustive interpretations. Readers are advised to consult the bibliography for lengthier interpretive analyses.

The notes have been provided to point out mythological and biblical references, to explain aspects of medieval culture, be they in matters of clothing, warfare, religion, contemporary events, etc., that are now obscure, and to show the interdependence of Hartmann's works. We have not assumed that readers will read Hartmann's works in the order presented, or that readers will read the entire anthology. Thus we deem it important that readers see how Hartmann reuses or varies words, phrases, scenes, and ideas.

THE LAMENT

Introduction

Though a few of Hartmann's extant lyric poems may have preceded *The Lament*, scholars agree that it was most likely his first longer work and that it lacks the polish and maturity of his later works. For the modern reader it may prove difficult reading because it is neither narrative nor lyric poetry but belongs, rather, to a genre that has generally gone out of style. It is a dialogue or dispute between the knight's body and his heart on the nature and practice of courtly love.[1] The origins of courtly love are obscure, but it arrived in Germany by way of the troubadour love poetry from the south of France. The most famous "theoretician" of courtly love was Andreas Capellanus, a chaplain at the French court of Marie de Champagne. Sometime between 1174 and 1186 he wrote his treatise *The Art of Courtly Love* (*De arte honeste amandi*). Though dialogues on courtly love existed in France before Hartmann's work, the *Lament* is the first such dialogue known in the German vernacular, and Hartmann is unique in choosing the body and the heart as the participants in place of the traditional body and soul. The extent of his dependence on French antecedents is a matter of dispute. Another point of contention is whether Hartmann borrows from the scholastic *disputatio*, a practice of the emerging universities in which two professors dispute some thorny problem of philosophy or theology, or whether he looked to legal disputes for his model.

After a brief introduction (lines 1–32), the body begins the dialogue with a long speech blaming his heart for all the suffering the body has had to endure because it has followed the heart's advice to enter the service of a lady as her courtly lover (lines 33–484). The heart defends its advice, maintaining that in all it undertakes it has the best interests of the body at heart, and it begins to instruct the body in

---

1. To avoid needless repetition here, we suggest readers consult the introduction to Hartmann's lyric poetry for a brief explanation of courtly love.

the proper conduct of courtly love (lines 485–972). The body continues its complaints of being mistreated by the heart but softens its attitude by admitting that it is indeed completely devoted to the lady and recognizes the good that comes from this (lines 973–1125). The heart, too, then strikes a more conciliatory tone and praises the body for its change of attitude (lines 1126–68). There follow a hundred lines of stichomythic exchanges between the two in which the body abandons its defensive posture and begins to accept the heart's criticism of it (lines 1168–1268). In the longer exchanges that then follow, the heart explains what qualities the body must develop to be a successful courtly lover, whereas the body comes to see the wisdom of the heart's advice and ends up defending the lady against criticism leveled at her by the heart (lines 1269–1644). In a line of argument typical of Hartmann the heart places its instruction of courtly love in the context of one's ultimate goal of practicing Christian virtues and pleasing God. Finally, the body, now fully reconciled to its heart, addresses the lady and pleads their case in exemplary fashion (lines 1645–1914).

The Lament has survived in only one manuscript, the so-called *Ambraser Heldenbuch*, compiled with care by Hans Ried for Emperor Maximilian I about 1517, in other words more than three centuries after its composition. It is not surprising therefore that there are many problems with some individual lines and words. We are not infrequently dependent on editors' attempts to establish what this or that line or word originally was. With a few exceptions we have followed the emendations of Arno Schirokauer and Petrus Tax. These occasional uncertainties do not, however, seriously affect our ability to understand the overall meaning of the text. It is rather the meaning Hartmann attaches to individual words that may cause difficulty. Foremost among these, of course, are *heart* and *body*, and readers are urged to work out for themselves what aspects of the man each represents as well as their relationship to each other.

Text

[Prologue] Love commands great power; it conquers the foolish and the wise, the young and the old, the poor and the rich. Overwhelmingly did it force a young man to surrender everything he had to its power and live according to its commands. And thus he began with proper moderation to love a woman for her beauty in both mind and body. But she did not accept his service, telling him he should let her be.

[17] Nevertheless he continued to pursue the matter, not daring to mention this distressing conflict to anyone, preferring to endure it alone with the idea that if he were to be successful in his request and she did what he wanted, it might remain a secret. He complained of his misery only to himself and saw to it, as best he could, that no one find it out. It was Hartmann von Aue who began this lament. Because of this unspoken distress his body said to his heart:

[33] "Alas, thinking heart, if you were at all something separate from me, you would have well deserved from me that I complain about you to all whom I trust to feel sorrow at my misfortune, so that they might take revenge on you for me. And if I had the opportunity, I would indeed kill you and pay you back with such afflictions as you often bring to me; alas, with your great strength you force me to do whatever you want. The power you have been given over me is so great that no man's ingenuity can gain peace for me in the face of it. I am forced to live in your power. That I cannot escape it causes me many an unhappy day. For it's not enough for you to inflict piercing sorrow on me. Since you have taken up dwelling within me and are carrying on your affairs in me, this is an act of disloyalty that has no place among friends, for it robs me of joy utterly.

[61] "Indeed, it's your ruin if you are of no use to me. Don't let yourself feel joyful about that. You are firmly locked within my breast; you will reap no benefit from that. Believe me when I tell you that rather than bear this misery any longer I shall take my revenge on you, thrust a knife into you, and die along with you. That is better for me than to continue suffering this wretched business unwillingly. That would make my life much too long.

[75] "God knows, you are quite the deceiver. Often you have lied to me to the point that your evil suggestions have caused my wretched self under your spell to be hopelessly attracted to a woman. Your reasoning bids me serve her for the sake of love. You told me much of her goodness, as one does who wants to deceive another, saying how well things would turn out for me if she were to grant me her favor. Alas, she is too good for that. That is the cause of my misfortune. For there is no chance for me to benefit from it.

[90] "For so many a day I have heard so much of her goodness. Now I have come to a full understanding of things. Ever since she has rightly known that all my joy rests on receiving her favor, she doesn't care one bit how I feel. That is the attitude of a forceful woman. I don't know why I displease her.

[99] "All the while I kept my thoughts and feelings secret from her. I bowed often at receiving her greeting and considered myself the kind of man upon whom a woman bestows her favor. I imagined I could improve my chances of success, but then my lot worsened. I imagined I could approach her when I had made it

clear to her that I had chosen no other woman in the whole world but her to be mistress over me. That is what caused me to lose her. May a man of good fortune benefit from this. Her attitude is a strange one: she pays back my good with evil. Justice is thus not well served. If she would consider me the same as she did before, I would ask for no other favor. Since I now have lost that which should benefit those who are rewarded according to their actions, my well-being concerns me not a bit.

[121] "Friend, if it were not for the fact that I should not revile a woman whom all the world speaks well of, I would say openly that she is the worst I have ever heard of, because she begrudges me the kindness—with no harm to her—of being relieved of my heavy burden and of taking me into her service, as would well befit a refined woman, that I might, by her leave, make her the object of my thoughts. Now thoughts are so free that she cannot keep me from being close to her, as a man in his thoughts can very well be to a woman. For whatever can happen in deeds I have already accomplished in thought, whatever, that is, well befits her honor. My intentions go no further than that. That is, after all, the total content of my joy: that I dare think of her. There is no greater joy than this. But now she wants to have the honor that I perish at her hands and in utter joylessness press my suit. Oh heart, it is your advice that keeps me from turning away from her.

[149] "Since I shall not be rewarded and cannot successfully escape suffering, I often try to imagine how good women are spoken of by those who know them. When these then name the best ones, describing what virtue this one has and criticizing the faults of that one, I keep perfectly silent. And if it were my wish that someone take revenge on her for me by speaking evil of her, so that I would hear something about her unbefitting a woman—some tales that would make her cheap in my eyes and make her my enemy—that person is not doing what I want. For I hear them speaking with a single voice: a better woman is not known to them. The only gain I have from this is that I am worse off than before. Before I had a state of mind that I now have lost because of my suffering.[2]

[173] "Heart, if only your power would release me so that I, too, might be able to recognize a good woman as other men can. God knows, I can see nothing but good in her. If only she would abandon that single attitude she has had toward me for so long a time. Heart, speak, what is your counsel?

[181] "You bade me serve her always. That I would gladly do if I knew how. If only she were so well disposed toward me—but unfortunately she is not—that she

---

2. That is, because she has rejected me, hearing her praised causes me suffering.

were to speak thus to me: 'I want you in my service.' No matter how this service were to be—pleasant or arduous—even if it were to last until death, it would seem to me a sweet distress. Never was there a peril so great that anyone was required to conquer that I would not be ready to face for her sake. Alas, that she does not tell me what she would have me do. If she would only test my constancy! But this, alas, is not to be. Indeed you know, my heart, what I suffer at your bidding. Now call to mind God, the Almighty, and tell me whether you know what purpose it serves—whether it is yet going to do me any good and turn out to be to my advantage. Do not keep me waiting any longer. From your response I shall have profit and honor.

[207] "And yet so good is she, God knows, if she really knew me—even if I were a heathen, cut off from Christianity—she would not act wrongly because of anyone's counsels, and once she perceived that she had never left my mind, even for half a day, she would express to me some gratitude for it.

[216] "Now it is, alas, a blow that a woman cannot know who sincerely loves her. Frequently, too, they are exposed at the hands of men to such trickery that quite rightly does us harm: men's solemnly swearing a promise that they have no intention of fulfilling. And so a woman is hesitant to risk committing her honor totally in the face of such uncertainty. Such misgivings do men harm because the woman fears that she will experience what befell many a woman before her who also, in the hope of a constant love, yet with much trepidation, gave in to the desires of a lover who considered himself worthy of such a reward. But then, when his wishes had been fulfilled, her reward from him was rude hostility. Then she thought it would have been better left undone.

[239] "His pleading of former times turned into spite, for it was not love of her that had driven him to toil so intensely in pursuit of her. As still happens to many, it was an ignoble attitude prompted by a morally dissolute heart that bade him play her honor false, so that he might boast about it. If many men find out about it, he considers this an honor and an advantage. May such a man and all like him, whether poor or rich, fall under the power of the devil, his forefather, even if I have to do penance for cursing him. Whether they be dead or alive, I shall hand them over to their master, so that he can well reward his servants as they deserve; and may God take from them the hope of ever being delivered from the pit of hell. Whatever blessings I may be able to bestow, I would gladly be their intercessor in this matter because I willingly grant them their due.[3] May anyone who takes up this way of

---

3. This is said, of course, ironically, since the speaker wishes hell to be their reward.

acting never find reward for it. So many have taken it as a model that deception seems appropriate to them. Such a man thinks himself a mighty lover when he seduces a woman, especially if he is able to deceive her.

[272] "Someone who had never previously learned to lie suddenly knows how to do so quite well when he sets out to bedazzle a woman. He calls it practicing a skill. May God make him suffer! They hinder many of life's joys and rob love of many a sweet playful encounter. Because of this, women lose heart, and no matter what someone says to them, they are ready to swear an oath that it is a complete falsehood and then pursue the matter no further. This causes us harm among women, since many lovers then go without a reward who rightfully deserved one. Day after day I hear the hearts of many men, who simply could not be of higher quality, lamenting this very thing.

[290] "My own care increases because of it, for I fear that she will treat me the same way. Come, Death, it is not too early. For, when I ponder the joys I have ever attained, they are completely extinguished and I lose all color; and as sudden as a thunderclap a mood grabs hold of me that is very hard on me. I don't rightly know what has happened to me or how, or what I should say to the person next to me when he asks what is wrong with me. I tell him simply this: 'Friend, I am sick at heart.' I do so with this in mind: that no one find out what is the matter with me. I don't dare tell anyone. My heart has commanded me to endure it alone. This is the most telling point. I don't know what I am supposed to thank you for.[4]

[313] "If I were to find the man who knew how to advise me, I would dare risk asking for advice. But that I may not lament my anguish among my relations—O heart, that is not nice of you, since you give me no help either. And so I would often reach out to where you lie and would willingly come to you with my lament. But as things stand, it is good for me to keep silent, because in this whole matter you behave—and this I call a lack of love—as cheerfully as a little bird. Now how could you be more faithless? You are supposed to be my refuge; and if it were not a breach of propriety, I would raise a cry 'to arms' against you. Why, then, are you trying to kill me?

[331] "To my misfortune God has given me in you an unproductive life, though I know well how to conceal it. I am a joyless man. For only rarely during the day does this suffering leave me. But when it does forsake me—which, alas, seldom happens—and I give myself over to happy pursuits for other people's sake, my good humor lacks any real sincerity because it does not proceed from the heart. My dis-

---

4. That is, heart, I don't know why you think bearing this suffering alone is such a good idea.

position is such when I am so listless that all those who knew me previously are starting to say that I have lost my good sense and have become silly.

[350] "But they do not understand what is going on inside me and that my moods change just like the tides of the sea. When the steady wind stops and a calm prevails, it is good to be on the water. It can also easily happen suddenly—as all well know who have been in that situation—that the bottom of the sea moves and a wind rises up from the depths. They call this a tidal swell, and it causes huge crashing waves that have sent many to their death—a poor exchange for their life—and sunk many a sturdy ship into the maw of the sea. This is exactly how my life is. Whenever I think I'm in the midst of joy, the cares which I bear secretly move me and I heave a sigh from the depths with my mouth smiling, but my eyes grow dull. The facts cannot be denied: I could not keep from weeping except that it is not proper for a man.

[377] "But as things stand, I am in such anguish that I dare not spend more time among people. And so I make my way all alone to where there is no one but me (otherwise, I would have to be everybody's object of ridicule) until the sadness leaves me that till then held me in its clutches.

[385] "Heart, if you were a man—something that God in no way grants me—and if I had struck your father dead, which no one can bear lightly; and if I had robbed you of all your friends, I would have paid dearly;[5] but you deprive me of all pleasure and rob me of everything that can be called joy. And yet I must endure your blows and live in such misery that it would be better for me to have died with honor than to bear this never-ending anguish that you, heart, have brought upon me. For what purpose have you so contrived to want to keep me here alive in order to torture me? If I could now discover why I first earned your ill will, I would be more than happy to beg you for God's sake to stop and not destroy us both. For it will cause you harm when the end comes for me. Who shall settle the conflict between the two of us? Why don't you do it for God's sake, but don't take excessive vengeance on me. If I have harmed you in any way, let me make amends to you. You shall judge me yourself. Thus you shall bring honor to yourself. You can well afford to accept me. Don't despise my service and my friendship, and consider what strength I have, entrusting me with those things that I am able to accomplish. Thus I shall serve you as I should and it will be to the advantage of us both.

[427] "But as things stand, I am sorely wounded. My well-being has declined in incredible ways. And so cares must of necessity oppress me. It is joy you should

5. That is, heart, you are treating me as though I had done something terrible to you.

be giving me, but you make my life miserable and prevent me from being happy. And yet, as long as I live, I have to wonder—and I would like to hear from you, dear heart of mine, whether you are so utterly indifferent to my pain that you feel it not at all. But I would never dare ask this because it might offend you. From morning till night you provoke me to ask, but I have only asked because of this: that I have reflected on the fact that you, as is your right, live in comfort, dwelling in my breast, as does the nut under the shell. I can well count us as one.

[451] "A nut hangs on the tree under the leaves and the shell protects it from all kinds of weather. This is the way things should be—that it provide protection to the nut as long as it is around it and shielding it. But the nut is not at all free. If the weather is as the shell expects, the nut thrives very well because of this arrangement. The kinds of weather that are bad for the shell are not good for the nut either. It must pay for it, too. It never turns out otherwise.

[465] "If someone puts a kettle full of water on the coals and then it froze, this would be unbelievable, because the heat which the water receives from the kettle forces it to boil up inside it. I think I am burning in this way because of someone, however it may come about. Since you lie inside me, I would like to hear whether you are secure against such harm and it does not oppress you. I often use these two images as examples, and yet I still don't understand how things really are. Heart, it is this very uncertainty, as you well know, that causes me to suffer. Why should it disturb you to reveal this to me?"

[485] "Body, I shall be happy to tell you. It could be that I, too, have been silent too long. Body, I beg you for God's sake that you quit your derisive contempt and bid your mouth here to cease talking now and leave complaining to someone who has a just cause for it. That you twist things so pains me greatly. You cause me suffering of many kinds. It is certainly true what one tells me: wherever harm is to be found, one finds a contemptuous derisive spirit there as well. This is quite obviously the case here. But enough about that.

[501] "You behave like a guilty man who is skilled at extricating himself once he has done the damage. His cunning convinces him that it often works to his advantage that he be the first to appear before the court. He well knows how to pass over his own guilt in silence and begins making accusations against the person he has harmed. This person is then required to make recompense to him. In this way then the innocent man suffers two kinds of harm: he loses his innocence and the favor of his lord is denied him, thus adding to his harm. My own miserable state is similar to that of such a person.

[517] "Since I suffer cares because of you, you should certainly quit your com-

plaining and your insolent threats; it does not seem to me that I am happy. I don't know why you are leaving it at this,[6] since you have said that you wanted to take vengeance on me and stick a knife into me. You claim I quite rightly deserve this. But you ought to believe me when I say this: if I had such power over you as you have over me; if I had hands, your life would not be safe. I would soon make it clear to you that I am guiltless of the cares I have because of you. They must be reckoned as troubles caused by you.

[535] "You claim your troubles come from my advice. You know well enough what the situation really is—that I cannot even know whether it's night or day, that I cannot distinguish evil from good, that I cannot be happy or unhappy unless it is transmitted to me by you. You have not carefully considered the arguments you are making—that you are blaming me for things that are not my fault. Use your eyes, for it cannot be denied that you have used them to look upon evil and good day in and day out and to scrutinize for me without my involvement what things are known to me. For this reason I call the eyes 'spies for the heart.' But I would gladly do without their spying. I know absolutely nothing of what goes on in the world except what you present to me through them.

[558] "For my part I have a fine faculty of discernment; you ought to let me have the benefit of that which I have had to pay you dearly for. Since you have chosen me to give advice and do not free me from this obligation, you well know that I have never allowed you to love base things. I have always pointed you toward good things. I kept you away from all duplicity. That is why I am suffering your animosity. Nevertheless, I am willing to put up with it in good humor: no matter what may happen to me because of it, I shall never give you anything but the right advice. My guilt is only that I counseled you to do whatever I knew was good and would redound to your honor, and I always strove to prevent you from engaging in any wrongdoing. It is because of me that you had to avoid it. You must put up with my instruction: do what is good and avoid evil. Conduct yourself as seems good to you. I advise you to act only from a noble spirit.

[581] "Vile body, you accuse me of recommending this woman to you. God knows, I did so. I know for certain that when I saw her through your eyes my own intelligence declared there could be no one better. My advice was given in your best interest. Why are you blaming me for this? How could I better award you honor? Take action accordingly. It has to turn out to your advantage if your service brings about your success with her. Then you will become the happiest man

6. That is, that you just complain and threaten, and do not act on your threats.

who ever attained love in the world. You can readily dare to seek helpful advice in such matters where it is right for you to be granted your wish—you, and I as well, your own heart.

[603] "You are complaining excessively for no good reason. Granted, it's not child's play for someone to gain the favor of women. He who takes aim at gaining love is in great need of refined sensibilities. And if someone is going to cultivate love's teaching at all, he must put aside everything that is not good and embrace the proper attitude for a man. This requires constant toil and that one have her frequently in his thoughts. Love does not free one to enjoy great comforts. These are the very things with which one should serve her, for she shall reward them generously.

[621] "If one wants to be in her retinue, one needs a goodly amount of the right attitude. Such a man should consider how to *do* more good and not just talk about it. Let him not break faith on anyone's account. Generosity and courage do not hurt in her service. He should cultivate proper bearing in pursuit of love. He should be high-spirited and courtly.

[632] "I have enumerated for you the good qualities through which you can bring it about that women be favorably disposed toward you. You must struggle for their favor by employing extreme measures. One has to risk body and soul for the sake of women if one wishes to be rewarded by them. It won't be granted otherwise. This is what custom demands. Also, you have certainly heard that your heart will not turn you out. Whatever disgrace befalls you, you may not attribute it to me. For I shall make it quite clear to you that if you follow my instruction, you will never take a false step. Rather, you will receive all honors.

[650] "You complain about great misery and drag on your life in dejection. But the cares we bear are not in the least comparable. You have reason to be silent. Let me express my complaints. Dear me, what great cares you have! Compared to mine they are child's play if it were a question of weighing their gravity. That I bear mine with great patience is a great benefit to me and provides me with help for my cares. My attitude is such that I am never satisfied unless I am striving night and day to see how I can arrange things for you so that you might rightly be content in a way honorable for us both. What joy beyond this could we have? And if this same woman were to accept you, you would be happy.

[671] "You can well come to grips with whatever misery accrues to you because of this. You have many diversions which I shall now enumerate for you so that you may not forget them. Night brings you the comforts of sleep. You certainly have complete repose then. This accounts for half the year. The day you can easily spend

occupied with enjoyable things. You listen to songs and tales. You can hunt and engage in falconry, play and shoot, dance and prance about. How can you find all this tiresome? Your life is hardly a struggle. There are a thousand other things that distract you constantly from your love pangs. These diversions will keep you cheerful. But this is hardly the case with me. Morning and evening I am ever struggling with cares, and in between as well, since without a doubt care has conquered me without a struggle.

[695] "When you are lying in your bed and have put aside all your cares, I am still awake, occupying myself intensely with thoughts about the many ways I might bring it about that she might do as you wish. The whole time she is present to me. Even though I am still here at home, I never leave her. That is why it happens that she appears to you in a dream. Listen to the substance of what I am saying. Whatever you experience in dreams is nothing else but the result of my efforts alone. You say that you are suffering. Alas, how happy you are! I know of no plan for dealing with cares except this one, which is really good: that I turn my whole attention to nothing else but to devising ways that you might gain love. The toil involved matters little to me. Yet no matter how great the injury is to me, you are safe from all of it. No one ever heard me complain because you, given your mindlessness, never let me do so; and I have chosen to endure this injury with patience for the honor of us both. My intent is always fixed on nothing other than how I might arrange to bring you the joyful bliss that will satisfy you.

[730] "May He who created all humankind and holds it in His power give us assistance and the good fortune that I might yet succeed in my struggle to win her. As long as I live, I shall never allow you to turn away from this striving. And therefore, take heed, body; here is what you must do. Take action like a man, for I'll not excuse you from any of it. Whatever cares befall you because of this, just realize that two-thirds of them are mine. This is, you see, the way things are with success. It does not readily give itself to anyone who does not earn it. It enjoys making you chase after it, and it escapes the weak-willed. Whenever it meets a half-hearted hunter, it eludes capture. It is wily and well versed in escaping its pursuer. One must give chase and never give up. One must drive it into a corner, confidently overtake it, catch up to it, and pay dearly for it with distress.

[755] "Then, too, there are many men in the world whose thoughts were never focused on honor. Yet they have had more success than those who are intelligent and who in thought and feeling side with virtue. God has portioned this out to them and we should not be envious of them. For whatever good things may happen to them, if they ever claim that it was due to their own abilities, they are to be

sharply contradicted. Let them not themselves express gratitude to themselves for their success. I shall mete out to them feeble joy.[7]

[769] "If a person is so inclined—indeed, there are many who find this quite enough—that the help of a friend and his own wealth are what make him content, I am happy to grant him generously of this. But it is a false idea of honor and a childish illusion. Having said this, I can well explain to you what a man should find pleasurable: virtue and intelligence. Then love will be pure. And so whoever finds that success flees from him and he must earn its greeting through virtue alone—as, body, is the case with you—such a person must realize for what reason people hold him in esteem. If he achieves anything of what he desires, he can thank himself for it and feel exhilaration because of it.

[791] "I am convinced that no man ever gained love without enduring misery.[8] We have more often heard of someone who was exemplary in all his intentions, who in hopes of love served with constancy and yet remained poorly rewarded, than of someone who was successful without really earning it. Body, consider this carefully and act as a man should. Stop acting like the faint of heart. Quit your inane complaining. Look ahead, be happy, and act accordingly. God is as good as He always has been. He never leaves one of his own in the lurch. Watch out for meanness. May God make one suffer for it. Brush your shaggy hair from your eyes. Let's keep this whole business between us. You know very well that you have always been an inveterate sneak. I've wasted a lot of time trying to teach you. I could just as easily beget you without a mother![9] My, my! What a courtly figure you cut! By what sort of devil would a woman have to be possessed that, seeing you, she would offer you her love?

[821] "Look here, body, I am suffering just like a flower under the snow that blossoms in March. Because it does not get enough help yet from summer, it suffers many a fierce onslaught from the force of winter, which often makes it too cold. Yet it would be beautiful except for its domination by winter. Winter robs it of its vigor and banishes it from its rightful place; winter, that is, and its lackeys, frost and wind, which are the bane of flowers. Then, too, snow often weighs them down. And yet the damage I suffer is greater, because a flower has certain defenses against damage. It can have strong sunlight at midday and can look forward to the solace of May when it will then be saved from the hand of winter. And then it breaks its fetters and thrives in its beauty all summer long, undisturbed by any force.

7. That is, if they take credit for their success, I'll reward them with appropriate, i.e., weak, joy.
8. See *Gregorius*, note 26.
9. That is, it is impossible to teach you anything.

[849] "But what comfort I have is very small because you allow me no hope of achieving love. The joys I think about night and day, going over them carefully in my mind, I have to leave aside because I have not a bit of help, and it all remains unfulfilled when your mean attitude pulls me away from it. Unfortunately, you have no sense at all. You think about nothing but easy living, which I do not approve of in the least. Since I can't discover any good quality in you at all and am not able to improve you through instruction, nothing would suit me better than to give up pursuing all honor, just as you do. Immediately my life would be one of ease. For despite my thoughtful planning, I achieve nothing but misery and hardship. Alas, that I ever said that! Certainly I shall forever regret it. How can a heart lose heart? Indeed, I must ever more bemoan the fact that a shameful doubt has entered my thoughts. If I possessed virtue, I would remain unswerving. But early on constancy became such a part of me that I practice it again and again. In thinking it over, I know that everyone will despise me unless I strive for honor, quite apart from how much of it I am able to achieve.

[887] "I hope I have put this idea out of your head. You can just forget the thought that any control you have over me could rob me of my strength, so that through wayward advice I might consider committing an evil deed. My intelligence is very keen, much better than yours. You should obey me. To the extent that you do not do this, you must realize that you will experience many a hard time. An unending struggle will arise. Therefore, be quick to follow my good advice and remember my instruction.

[904] "In the time since I began beseeching you to look to your honor, I could have persuaded a peasant to harm himself.[10] We are not joined together as we should be; we don't pull evenly.[11] Indeed, one should separate us. That would be the right thing for us both. If it were in my power—and not in yours, which is unfortunately not the case—to bring matters to a close, you would have to live according to your given word, though it be against your will. But my power lies only in the will and in thinking freely.[12] Alas, no more power than this has been given to me. This causes us both great harm because I should be your adviser in all things. But you are not obedient to me.

[926] "I know very well that I have never heard of someone acting so wrongly against the advice of his heart. This has always been out of the ordinary. Hence I

10.   Since peasants were considered both slow-witted and self-serving, this is a very cutting remark.
11.   The image is of oxen pulling a wagon or plow.
12.   That is, I, the heart, have only the power to will and to think, and cannot on my own bring about the effects of these spiritual activities in the physical world.

do not know why a person takes it out on me by always speaking up when he sees you doing something wrong, claiming that a false heart is doing it. This simply amazes me. If people would not blame me for any shame you experience, I would soon stop my complaining. Yet whatever anyone now says, our dear Lord Christ knows that I am without fault and am being treated unjustly, even if no one says so. The same way of thinking does not benefit us both. What harms me most of all is that no one believes me the least little bit. What good does my refined perceptivity do me, when the whole world thinks of me as the wolf in the fable? As a defense against this I quickly adopted an attitude that I shall regularly use against my troubles: that I at least believe myself. A man who earns his daily bread by robbery and has no sense at all receives more justice than I do.

[960] "Body, I assign to you the blame for this because without you I cannot accomplish any intentions I've ever had. If your help is not forthcoming, we shall not share in honor and possessions. But if you join me with the proper frame of mind, we shall accomplish whatever we set out to do. I am asking you to do nothing more than to follow my instruction. You shall yet win renown from so doing. Tell me if you intend to do so."

[973] "Heart, I don't know what to say to you. I can only complain to God that you should be severely mistreating me utterly without cause, as though I had committed some incredible offense. This should not happen among friends. Besides, it would be more fitting for a teacher educating someone in virtue and honor to transmit his teachings with refinement. That would certainly be appropriate. But you are punishing me as you would a servant. It has always been the right way of acting among friends to avoid invective and, in a refined manner, approaching each other, to clasp each other by the hand. The one tells the other person exactly what he has against him and asks him to avoid it. A friend would be able to accept this; and if he were a man with good sense, he would take it in the spirit given and consider it as a show of his friend's trust in him that he had spoken his mind without ill will.

[1000] "This same way of acting would also be more proper for you than threats and vituperation. What are you making me pay for? I have to ask you for help. If you want to quarrel about all this, that is not the way you should act because then you will never ever be happy. You are well acquainted with the idea that it is the nature of the body to receive help and advice from the heart. Hence it would befit us both to live together without quarreling all the time because your senseless anger is pointless from the start. If anybody were to come now and hear it, he could only laugh at you. And so, for heaven's sake let's stop it, keeping in mind that the two of us make up one person. What good would I be without you, or what can you accomplish without me?

[1025] "If from now on you stop all your abuse of me, I'll forget about the whole matter. You, too, should be happy to have me let you off. You be good to me as I will be to you. Without each other we cannot survive for a minute. We always have to remain together. We cannot be separated. To the two of us God has given only one soul. Without it we could not have life.[13] God shall take it from us whenever He wishes, and so we have no knowledge of how long we shall live. Besides, He has commanded us under dire threats that He will deny the soul His blessing if we do not treat it as we should. If we do conduct ourselves properly, its reward is assured. If we take care of it in such a way that we keep His commandments, He will reward us in heaven with a bright crown. If, by exercising our free will, we refuse, He will turn us over to the children of hell to serve at the devil's court. In that case, we were born for damnation and are lost forever, you and I both. Heart, with this in mind, tell me how you want me to act and do not lead me on the wrong path where we both will be lost. For my well-being is yours as well. My will shall not shirk whatever service is required. Whatever I can and should do, I shall accomplish, and it will do me good. Whatever suffering it is my lot to endure, whether it turns out well or not, I shall persevere as long as I live. May it be God who gives us success. But if it turns out that failure overwhelms me, that I shall not triumph, it does me still very much good to continue serving such a fair woman. I willingly devote to her all the years of my life. Indeed, I truly receive more solace from the uncertain hope I have of her love than I would from some trifling success that might bring me some pleasure.

[1081] "Besides, I gain more by doing whatever I can or am equipped to do by striving for love of her to act well and as I should, and to avoid for her sake any falseness. Very willingly shall I turn all my thoughts to what is good and be in every situation constantly watchful against my doing wrong, unless I am led astray because I did not know any better. May He who can grant me success then punish me for the sake of His honor. Then I shall never repeat the offense. I shall back up my works with deeds for all to see. Thus shall she be served. And whatever good I am able to accomplish will be done expressly for her. If I never receive a reward for this from her, it is nevertheless profitable for me in that the world will recognize the good in it and look upon me the more kindly.

---

13.   The spiritual soul is what gives a human being its life. Separation of the soul from the rest of the human being is death.

[1103] "This[14] is for me small consolation, for it does not free me from suffering. If she wants to ignore me in my loneliness, I still don't value the world in the least, whichever of the two courses she takes: speak well or badly of me, I still don't value the world in the least. For my way of thinking is this: that the benevolence of all other women would not bring me any joy if I were to have no success with her.

[1113] "Heart, I have come to the decision that I shall not pursue happiness in hopes of love with any other woman. Whatever reward I may or may not receive from it, I intend to stand ready in her service. Whatever anyone has ever suffered for love of a woman, I have no reason to reject any of it. Except for magic, murder, and what offends against loyalty, there is no plan I would refuse to carry out in her honor. In this regard you shall never discover any base wavering in me."

[1126] "Body, I am grateful for what you have said. It is hardly surprising that a man who doesn't know better behaves badly for a time. If he has the will to improve—even if out of shame he does not put this into action—whenever he becomes aware of his misconduct and does not intentionally act wrongly but rather allows someone to restrain him; and if he sees fit to seek help, thinking it a good thing that he accept help, such a man can certainly be given good help. But he whose attitude is such that he despises help and rushes off to action rashly will be played false by his thoughts. Unless my mentors have lied to me, he is deceived in his understanding and the world will make sport of his conduct.

[1148] "Body, this is why I praise God for what I have heard you say. For quite some time you caused me to have grave misgivings. But now you have thought better of it—that continuing on that path you would fail. I have now sensed in you a very good change. That shall yet work to your benefit. Do not reject my advice, knowing that things will turn out well for you. And if you truly accomplish what you have promised me, we shall with no trace of ill will forget about the harm you caused us many a day when we were enjoying good times without a care, as should be our right.[15]

[1167] "Body, it is your laziness that bothers us."

"Heart, I shall always regret this and shall make up for it wherever I may."

"Body, I like how you are talking now."

"Really, is that a fact?"

"Yes, this is truly the case."

14. That is, the world's good opinion.
15. For about the next hundred lines Hartmann employs a rhetorical device called stichomythia, in which partners alternate lines. (Here, occasionally, heart and body will share a line or one of them might speak two lines.) To help capture the effect, the line breaks of the original text have been retained.

"Now I shall willingly do whatever you wish."

"Then I shall send many pleasant things your way."

"Heart, what gave you this power?"

"Body, your senseless question gives me gray hair."

"Don't be angry, be nice to me."

"What is it that irritates you?"

"You should certainly know that yourself."

[1180] [Heart:] "If it were explained to me, I would understand it better."

[Body:] "I never had need of help more than now."

"Tell me, body, what do you mean by that?"

"My life is filled with misery."

"Are you ill?" "No, I am not."

"If I knew how, body, I would help you."

"You should help me anyway."

"What is wrong with you? Tell me."

"You know as well as I do."

"My guess is you fear death."

[1190] [Body:] "No, it is a different concern."

"Has it to do with the soul or the body?"

"With both." "Get rid of it!"

"Teach me how." "Does it have some sort of a name?"

"Heart, you should really be ashamed, the way you are laughing at me."

"Why is it that you won't let me know about it?"

"I am in pain, though I am healthy."

"I don't understand how that can be."

"Heart, you know it all quite well."

[1200] "No, I don't. Not before you tell me."

"Heart, do you have anything weighing on you?"

"Yes, I do. I would like to be rid of it."

"Where did it come from?"

"You have heard of that often enough."

"And is it just one thing that weighs on you?"

"If there were any more of them, it would be the death of me."

"Where then does this distress come from?"

"It is indeed my lady who oppresses me."

"Then believe me all the more."

[1210] "Body, is that what distresses you, too?"

"Well, where else do you think my pain would come from?"
"Then take steps yourself to get rid of it."
"How?" "I've already told you."
"Alas, I still don't know how."
"It's a lot of hard work."
"So what is it that you bid me do?"
"Serve her with great courtliness."
"How long?" "Until she rewards you.
Whatever I do means your happiness."
[1220] [Body:] "But perhaps my service is unwelcome to her."
"You should persuade her to abandon such an attitude."
"Tell me, by what means?"
"By your service, if you perform it properly."
"That is what you must explain to me."
"Well, be honest and good."
"What if she doesn't notice?"
"Then she would not be a refined woman."
"She is refined. If only I were a happy person."
"You shall make yourself happy."
[1230] [Body:] "I don't know by what means."
"You must buy your success by using your head."
"That is my weak suit."
"That is why happiness must be a stranger to you."
"Her favor has always been lacking to me."
"You have not served her well enough."
"Why do I deserve her ill will as well?"
"Body, that is obvious just by looking at you."
"Heart, I have as much success as a scoundrel does."
"Body, you are very pleased with yourself."
[1240] "Not more than I by rights should be."
"In one respect fools have it good."
"In what respect?" "They think themselves wise."
"Heart, you think that fits me?"
"Yes, body, I really do."
"What have I done to deserve this from you?"
"That I know well." "Then tell me."
"It's that you lack insight."

"I would like to change that for the better."

"That is where I shall help you."

[1250] [Body:] "If I knew how to change, I would certainly do it."

"Then follow those who are wiser."

"Teach me then. I am your child."

"And I am your trustworthy counselor."

"Then I'll follow you as willingly as I live."

"Then you shall experience pleasant things."

"May this be the case for us both."

"Your wishing it doesn't help you in the least."

"Heart, that is certainly true enough."

"Just wishing has always been inappropriate for a man."

[1260] [Body:] "Then I, too, shall renounce it on the spot."

"Do you languish for her love?"

"Oh, if she doesn't love me, I'll die."

"Then let her know your serious intent."

"I shall do just as you bid me, dear heart."

"Inexperienced though I be myself,

I shall provide you with very sensible advice."

"I shall listen to it willingly

So that I can learn it."

[1269] "Body, you should now follow my bidding. That will profit no one as much as you. Earlier I heard you forswear magic. This is a vow you must break. If you ever want to achieve success or partake of any sweetness, then learn the craft of magic. It is definitely something valuable. If you can gain full possession of all that one should have of it, you will have to succeed. I have brought it from Karlingen.[16]

[1281] "Now see to it that you keep it quiet. Then again, I don't care whom you tell. Here is what it's all about: whoever is to use it properly must have three herbs that will make him lovable and loving. But you should not expect to find them in any man's garden; nor are they for sale. Unless one has the good fortune of obtaining them by having a lofty spirit from the One Who has them under His control, no help will be of any use to him. He will probably always be without them. God is the keeper of the herbs. He alone grows them. His storeroom is spotless. From it He takes them and gives them to whomever He wants. That person always has great success.

16.   That is, from France. Compare *Erec*, line 1547 and note 45.

[1301 "You are unacquainted with these herbs. These are their names: gen-erosity, courtliness, and humility. No other magic is as good. Anyone fortunate enough to know how to mix these herbs in the proper prescribed amounts—that is the real craft of magic. Other spices must be added as well before one does it as one should: loyalty and constancy. If one does not add these, the magic will fail. Also, you must mix in chasteness and modesty. One herb still must be mentioned: dependable manly courage. Then the magic is fully prepared. And whoever has successfully collected these herbs must then pour them into a jar. This is a heart free of ill will. He should put them all inside it. Then I can say to you in truth that he is well prepared for happiness as long as he has them along with him.

[1327] "Body, if only you had at your disposal the herbs that I have just listed for you! Look, I'll lend you the jar. I know that I am the jar. As things stand, there is a great lack of them in you. But if you can gradually acquire them, body, then do so. That's my advice to you. Don't spare yourself; for if you are ever to have true happiness with a woman, you much possess this magic. One more thing is good to remember: one should do all this without shame and serious sin. Happy the man who is well versed in these herbs! That leads to happiness in this world and does not offend God. It is a twofold gain. Both God and the world love this man. He who knows this kind of magic is a happy man in the world.

[1349] "I advise you to use this one kind of magic and no other, for it would be a wrong kind of success if a woman were conquered by other kinds of magic. You must not count on other magic. I simply won't hear of it. If someone gets love from it, he has an ill-gotten joy. This is something that the lowly servant and the pow-erful lord have in common: that it can certainly spoil true happiness for a man. May God make the man suffer who first started this, because many men and women as well have lost body and soul. This is why we should avoid such magic. A curse upon it! If you are going to be successful, then do it by the proper means. I don't know what I should tell you other than to conduct yourself properly and well, and may you profit from good things said about you. If these ideas are too difficult for you, then I know that you are doomed to remain unhappy."

[1376] "No, heart, that is not the case. These ideas make me a much better man. They shall please me more and more. I shall eagerly put them into practice con-stantly if I can, and I would gladly live to see the day when I was a magician accord-ing to your instructions, if only for the good chance that I might gain a bit of her[17]

---

17.   Schirokauer and Tax have *dir*, which would refer to heart and mean "favor (or thanks) to you, heart." Since the body goes on to speak of the woman, *ir* (her) seems to make more sense and is adopted by other editors.

favor, for, without a doubt, I shall have to take leave of my senses unless I am prevented by receiving her gracious greeting, which I am still doing without completely. Without her greeting joy must remain a stranger to me. And yet I no longer need to be puzzled about whose fault it is that she bears my heavy sufferings of the heart so lightly.

[1397] "Since my thoughts and feelings have remained so hidden from her that she is aware of nothing more than that I, as has always been the custom, express them in words, she does not know whether or not I am really sincere about them with the genuine intent of being true to her. And so she begins to fear that she is being played false. Women are so often lied to that she indeed has to fear it. And since, in addition, I have not earned her greeting, I could well give up my lamenting.

[1411] "Since you yourself are inflicting suffering on me and yet shall recover together with me, and since you are the keeper of my intelligence and know all my wishes, that is why my life is so difficult. You scarcely believe me that I am in dead earnest about this. Well, I know of no better way than this of convincing you: I have raised my hand and swear an oath to you about it:

[1423] "So help me God, may I never again be happy or never gain love in this world or honor, but rather may I carry on my life in anguish and end it badly; and may my poor soul eternally be the companion of Judas in the depths of hell (There no one experiences any joy up until the last day. Even then one is not free of the bonds of the devil): I swear that I have never had thoughts toward her or feelings of disloyalty by which many men in their duplicity wrong women.

[1443] "Ever since her power overwhelmed me, I have constantly had but one thought: if things were to turn out so well for me that she accepted my favors, I would want to live so completely at her bidding that, aside from God, I would prefer nothing else to this. If I were ever to waver in this, no one but me would be the loser. I am not, after all, my own enemy. If she should give me her love, I would not willingly throw away something that good. It increases in value if carefully protected.

[1457] "Alas, what have I done! I think I have acted too hastily in speaking of such intimate matters. If she were to grant me my wishes and if I were worth such bliss as my inner being indeed longs for, what I have just said could by rights move her to anger. For if God had lost an angel from His kingdom, she indeed would be its equal and she could fill the gap in the heavenly hosts with great honor. Truly, she could fittingly take the place of an angel.

[1470] "Also, I have hopes of perhaps being granted what a man may properly desire. One thought should be to my advantage. I have the firmness of will and intent that if God wants to grant it to me, I shall bring things to the point that people begin to say of me that I deserve to have things go well for me. And in those respects in which I am as yet unworthy—since I lack full virtue and wisdom—no one will demand that of me already. It would be far too early to expect that of me. Men of my age are not those to whom people attribute great wisdom. No matter how things turn out for me, no matter what the state of my happiness may be, may God repay the one who gives sweet advice; advice, that is, resulting in unstinting praise from insightful people. My mind advised me to pursue her, no matter what difficulties this might entail for me. The more fine women I notice in the world, and as I learn to judge their worth, it turns out that she rightfully pleases me more and more because of her great perfection. For her noble qualities enhance her person above all others, just as the sparkle of a deep red garnet does—as I have heard tell. I haven't seen it myself. Many have told me that this stone lights up a dark night and that it alone extinguishes the light of other stones when it is placed near them.

[1509] "All women now alive should take these words of praise with no ill will. I give her the prize because of this: no other woman strikes me as being as good. I don't know what others think of her. But if someone says, 'Look how he raves on, praising her out of all proportion,' that person is himself lacking in good sense, unless I am a complete fool. She pleases me very much. I don't know how she strikes others. But if no one thought her pleasing, that would indeed make me happy. For if no one were to esteem her as I do, she would remain free for me. I have said all this in a playful spirit and will be happy to take it all back. I don't know why it would be important to me that no one wanted or looked with favor upon what I was seeking. Because, as I have seen and heard, she is perfect in virtue, no obstacle—aside from death, that everyone must endure—can thwart my will nor deflect my intentions about her from this time forward."

[1536] "Body, I thank you for these sentiments. Not until now have I heard that we are joining together well and that we are equally serious. Now don't delay for a minute and take stock of what you are to do. Be ever on the alert for an advantage, as one is who wants to strengthen his resolve until the goal is attained. Do not approach her rashly, so that your advances in her presence are not capricious. Such conduct will prove to her your steadfastness. The noble woman shall repay you for it. Unjustifiable haste will only waste your time. Body, this is how I recognize those who are overly eager. Like a gust of wind they burst upon a person full tilt, and then they soon collapse. This is not the way a man acts who is constant and of good temperament. He sets off at a moderate pace, as constancy requires of him, holding back a bit, but he soon overtakes the overly eager suitor. The latter then gives up and loses, though his spurs are bloody.

[1565] "I still have more to tell you, but you shouldn't lose heart because of that. If for a time she is not disposed to have you in her service, even though your efforts show good sense, you may well have more success later on if she is really refined. Let me tell you about the mind of women: they have one trait especially that causes them often to do needless harm to themselves. The man they pick as a companion and choose as an object of their affection, they keep putting him off till the whole world becomes aware of the situation. And even if nothing ever really happens, everyone is convinced that it has. This is the result of poor advice. The benefit amounts to no more than harm and loss of honor. It's certainly a mystery to me what joy a woman gets out of letting her friend languish so long in agitation and uncertainty. It is a senseless way of acting. She ruins her friend by so doing and misses out on genuine love. That is all they get out of it."

[1593] "Heart, I hear you complaining about something that you could well pass over in silence. You will grow old dealing with other people's problems. What you have just been telling me about the foolish behavior of women, I'll let the man who is harmed by it deal with the problem. Unfortunately, this is not our situation. That is the distress of those who are blessed. We certainly have never yet had this happen to us. This is what many are longing for.[18] You have not been so indulged. That could be a very pleasant life for you. Men in that situation are not going to choose you as their adviser. Indeed, as a judge you have very little value to them. And so stop your criticism and, if you wish, tell me more that contributes to valuable instruction."

[1613] "Body, I am giving you the best instruction I know. Be steadfast; that is the best plan. Notice that no matter how hard a stone is, if it is lying somewhere where water repeatedly and regularly drips upon it, even if the power of the drops is very slight, they do make a hole in the stone. Body, that is not due to the power of the drop. It happens because of the persistent regularity with which it drips. You should realize from this example that if you want to enjoy the reward, you must not grow impatient but should continue in her service until she becomes aware of it. If she is indeed a noble woman, look, body, she will reward you.

[1633] "Also, keep your sense of what is appropriate, so that she never hear you speak a word, whether seriously or in jest that she might take as an expression of

18.   That is, men you have just described have at least in some sense the affection of a woman. You and I, heart, have not even made it that far.

ill will. Try to discover her every wish whenever you can if you do not begrudge yourself some success and happiness. Now, tarry no longer. I commend our honor to you. Our chance of success is in your hands. Body, you shall go to her now and plead our case."

[1643] "That I shall be happy to do, dear heart of mine."[19]

[1645] [Body to the Lady:] "Whatever cares I have endured till now from the time when I began to be in anguish, that was a pleasant occupation up to the present. Love has always eluded me; she was unknown to me. But now she has let me feel her power, for she robs me of my pleasure as though it would be no concern of hers if I were to disappear completely. She attacks me so fiercely that my heart has been set on fire. For love of you, fair lady, it burns from its depths. And thus you should accept my oath, trust what I say. My thoughts about you are vast. If your graciousness would allow me to do so, I would be ever poised to serve you in whatever way I could. He who would eagerly devour Christianity envies me that the anguish my heart endures might come to an end.[20] No one talks of misfortune who never has known it. Failure crosses my path like a dog. I gallop after it too intently. That makes me ill. Its fangs have sunk deep into me. The wound is bleeding still.

[1677] "When I felt the wound, it was the end of my joy. My pleasures nearly disappeared in the face of suffering. Who is it who will make the suffering disappear? Cares fill my life. Lady, make that change. Certainly the devil is scheming to destroy my happiness. You are called to be my bliss, however things turn out for me. For God's sake you should realize how your virtue has conquered me, even if I were from the East.[21] Therefore, courage! Or I shall live like an extinguished fire, while other fires blaze away. No other bond can help me but your bond.[22] No one's hand heals me but one of your hands. If you do not send me solace, I don't know who will send it to me. So remember to be gracious so that I may revel in it before uncertainty takes what I owe and demands from me my life. Such is the frame of mind I have taken

---

19. In this final section of the poem in which the body addresses the lady, Hartmann no longer employs simple couplets (aa, bb, cc, etc.) for his verse but adopts rather an alternating rhyme scheme (ababab) that can continue for over thirty lines before another rhyme (e.g., cdcdcd) is employed. This tour de force of rhyme often makes the translating more difficult, since it seems that Hartmann often subordinates fulfilling the substantive requirements of the content to fulfilling the formal requirements of the rhyme scheme.

20. That is, the devil, whose punishment shall never end, envies the lover, who might receive love from his lady.

21. That is, even if I were a pagan.

22. The second *bond* in this sentence (*gebende*) is probably meant as a play on words, since it means both bond or fetter as well as a woman's hairdo.

on that, no matter how I look at things, without you all lands are foreign to me.[23]

[1706] "I have always struggled to attain the favor of success. If only one could count on gaining its reward. It kept me from all other kinds of happiness. That I have always failed to accomplish this displeases me. Failure was setting traps for me. Hence I've seldom sung in triumphant tones in order to make this clear. Because of its evil will toward me I almost went under, and would have, too; but what helped me keep from drowning was the hope of good news. This consolation would always force a laugh from me, since I was still hardy enough that, if for the love of the Creator, you would let me experience your good will—a sweet embrace by your lovely white arms—it would bring me peace from care. Then I would be free of worry. And if I waver from what I have said, may I be worthless in God's eyes. My thoughts center on you with loyalty, but my distress moves you not at all. A mountain would be too weak an image for my distress if I think of its weight. My life would be too long, so that I would prefer to give it up.

[1735] "Ever since I first became aware of you, it has been you, and only you, that I wished for as my lady. Now you are very slow to praise me for it. Very often I, a man bereft of joy, weep in my heart shackled by the anguish of this thought, and I know of no way of making it disappear. Because I began to love this one woman among them all, for whom my heart and mind were so inflamed, as I made known to her who begrudged me the least bit of joy (we share nothing that brings pleasure)—because of this I am subjected to strict exile. A stone would be moved to pity. Unless God yet comes to my aid, I shall lose my equanimity completely. To cheer myself up I still rely on my hopes that have never deserted me. I am without any falseness toward you. My love for you is true. For the sake of your pure goodness do not let me be disappointed in it.

[1761] "What should work to my advantage often causes me great harm. I live as though I were swimming in a deep sea and one has a long way to shore. A man could think that luck had visited him if God let him reach land. If someone were to say this was a good thing, his lies would cut like a sharp edge. If my service is of no use, I give my soul as a pledge that my devotion will not slip away, for the harm of it would bring shame. The way I am thinking now, I would like to work hard at it. I imagine it would be easier to burn up all the water in the Po,[24] so that nowhere in the land was there one drop of the river left, than for me to guess what

---

23. Again a play on words: "all lands" = *alliu lande*, and "foreign" = *ellende*. *Ellende* can mean both "foreign" and "miserable."

24. A river in northern Italy.

you are really like. This is why I feel so bad, fearing that you will withhold your consolation and I shall not be freed from such bonds. This is the most serious wrong that I have ever seen you do.

[1785] "As to joy, I endure, poor in great poverty. I am unshielded from cares— may God protect me from them. What good are the summer's flowers to me with their motley blossoms?[25] I don't care if the tree turns green in ever greater green-ness if you do not show me favor and are not nice to me in feminine kindness. I've gone crazy over you. Help me before I go completely mad.[26] . . . in flames. Rather than face this anguish I would wade through the floods of the deep ocean with its tides, though no one has ever made it.

[1807] "I am wounded beyond measure. I feel the damage, beaten to the depths of my heart, and I cannot overcome it. I am sick as to joy, in the retinue of death, if your mercy does not offer me help to make my suffering disappear. No doctor's bandage, no matter how well he wraps it, will do me any good, even if I paid a thousand pounds to find relief. But if your rosy mouth would bid me do so, I would recover very quickly. May happiness receive me at once.[27] . . . that he still go blind.

[1827] "Hope makes me often bold. But, as I begin hoping, doubt turns my heart cold again to my great loss. I imagine that water and the woods and the earth would burn up (this is reserved for the Day of Judgment), and our days will pass by fleetingly—if I am able to get so old—before I turn my thoughts from you. However little it has meant till now, I am serving for love of you. Because of this, lady, as I keep my thoughts fixed on you, keep your many virtues for me. I don't know where to escape to. Because of this receive my cares into your power, for you are my goddess.

[1842] "Lady, consider, before your comfort arrives too late, that I have never forgotten you in my able steadfastness. Now do not let base ill will toward me do harm, nor evil counsels. There is many an untrustworthy vessel[28] that wants noth-ing else except, rather than its own portion, to ruin the joy of others. No bliss in this world would give it more pleasure than this. Such a person is always slow to all virtue and quick to vice. He sprouts up—something that has always horrified me—where no one has planted him.

---

25.   Here and in his comments on the trees turning green Hartmann seems to be making fun of the usual use of nature in courtly love poetry, where flowers and trees function as a mirror of the mood of the speaker of the poem.

26.   Here there is a gap of a few lines in the manuscript.

27.   Again there is a gap of about four lines in the manuscript.

28.   That is, an evil person.

[1861] "If I ever achieve my long-enduring fantasy of succeeding in gaining your love, as I hope in God, then He has done well for me through His graciousness and I shall owe Him a reward that I shall proclaim in words and song. Then, too, I must always remain in a state of sorrow unless I succeed. Now you should act toward me in a way that will ennoble you a little. And let your heart feel pity that I am struggling with cares.

[1875] "Lady, your campaign against me has been sinful ever since I began; since then you have never received me into your favor. That someone brings joy to good friends—who is going to be offended by that? He certainly spends his time far better than someone who lies around, a fearful captive. If someone's envy harms me then let him be hanged! If I were born to succeed, I would enjoy it. The lady I have chosen—whatever her words would command me do, I would not put off at all. If my deeds were wanting, I would endure the anger of my heart. I shall free my heart. I have sworn this at its command. I shall not regret it.

[1897] "Now I desire that your goodness honor its name in me, that favor be shown to me. Lady, do not let my thoughts and feelings struggle any longer so intensely to reach you. Certainly my body must be yours according to the teaching of a loyal heart.

[1905] "I am taking part in your amusement in such a way that I shall yet attain what will bring happiness to my heart or—die utterly without joy. That is a dire threat for me if you wish me to go to ruin. Into your power I have surrendered both soul and body. Take them. They shall live for you and for no other woman."

LYRIC POETRY

Introduction

Hartmann's surviving lyric poems, all of which we have translated here, including some of doubtful authorship, treat the themes of what is commonly known as courtly love. The poetry of courtly love is conventional poetry in the sense that in its vocabulary, imagery, and ideas it presupposes a set of meanings and rules which readers must be familiar with if they are to understand what the poet is trying to convey.

The conventional situation of the poet/speaker of the poem is this: He is a knight at the court of a feudal lord and loves at a distance a lady of the court (usually married), who is of higher social standing than he. He wishes to devote himself to her service, but he has no idea how she feels about him, since his feelings for her, being basically adulterous, must be kept secret. Thus he is condemned to lament his hopeless lot in his poetry. The substance of this love consists in longing and separation from the beloved. Though desired, physical union is out of the question. At best the knight can hope to receive some sign from the lady acknowledging his love and devotion.

An important social function of this strange phenomenon of courtly love is that it is meant to refine courtly life and to raise ethical standards. The lady in these poems is more symbol than reality. To be a worthy object of this love she must be the embodiment of all the physical, moral, and cultural qualities of the ideal noblewoman. The knight who yearns for her love must strive to improve himself in order to be worthy of even hoping for some indication that his service is acceptable.

As a consequence of this stereotypical point of departure, the vocabulary in the poems is limited, with some basic words serving almost as a kind of shorthand or code. The knight is a *man*, which denotes both his sex and his subordinate social standing at court. The woman (*wîp*) is addressed as lady (*frouwe*), which is the female equivalent of *lord* and indicates her high social standing. Perhaps she is mistress of the castle. The knight laments (*klagen*) his cares and sufferings (*kumber, sorge*) and his pangs of longing (*senende nôt*). He wants to be her intimate friend or lover (*vriunt*) and to be in her service (*dienest*). His hope or consolation (*trôst*) would be a sign (*gruoz*) from the lady acknowledging her favor (*genâde*) toward him. This would be his reward (*lôn*). Alas, in his thoughts and feelings (*muot*) he is without joy (*vreude*) or good fortune (*saelde*). Still, he must remain steadfast or constant (*staete*) and continue to serve her faithfully with loyal devotion (*triuwe*). This increases the honor (*êre*) of them both. Familiarity with this vocabulary and the conventions they express should help the reader to understand Hartmann's *Lament* as well.

Besides poems devoted specifically to the situation described above, one finds among Hartmann's lyric efforts examples of two other kinds of poems related to courtly love but having different points of departure. One is the lady's lament (*Frauenklage*) in which it is the woman who complains about having lost the service and affection of her friend. The other is the crusading song (*Kreuzlied*) in which the knight speaks of the necessity or value of going on a crusade and relates this in some fashion to courtly love.

The Poems

1. "Because I have endured"

This poem is a good example of a lament (*klage*) of the courtly lover who concludes that his service was rejected by the lady, not because of any lack of perfection in her, but rather because of his own shortcomings. It is worth noting that in the first stanza the poet plays with the stereotypical functions of the seasons. Summer usually signifies a joyful mood in the poet, while winter symbolizes sadness. Here, however, summer has been a winter of discontent for him. The mention of the death of the poet's feudal lord as a cause of sadness, which most commentators consider a real biographical event felt very deeply by Hartmann and which motivates him to go on a crusade, is a jarring note very unusual in a love poem.

> Because I have endured sorrow and misery all summer long,
> My hopes of joy are not very good.
> My songs shall bear winter's coat of arms.
> The longing I feel is wintry as well.
> How little pleasure does my fidelity bring me![1]   5

1. That is, fidelity in the service of his lady.

For I have utterly wasted on her my time, my service,
And—what is worse—years of misplaced hopes.
For the rest, I shall not revile her,
Except to say: She did not treat me well.

If I wanted to hate the person who harms me,   10
Then I would have to recognize that I am my own enemy.
Both in body and spirit I am sorely lacking in steadfastness.
That is what has become evident in my misfortune.
My lady wants nothing to do with me. The fault is mine.
Because sensible conduct makes a man happy   15
And impulsive behavior has never brought anyone lasting happiness,
I, and I alone, am the one at fault
If I do not know how to serve her in a thoughtful manner.

That I am unhappy is as it should be
Since strong pangs of longing oppress me.   20
Whatever joys I have experienced throughout life
Have been dearly paid for, as God has willed it.
The death of my lord has deeply saddened me.
The usual troubles plague me as well:
A woman has denied me her favor,   25
Though I have served her steadfastly
Since the time when I was still riding my hobbyhorse.

Since my service was not able to touch her heart,
It seemed to me that it was because of her shrewd judgment
That she was withdrawing her precious person from me.   30
In so doing she thought the matter through quite rightly.
If I am moved to anger, it only makes her laugh and me grow old.
My lack of constancy was enormous; when this startled her,
She began avoiding me—this is my conviction—
More to preserve her honor than out of hostility toward me.   35
She thinks that, by acting thus, her reputation will be improved.

When she first allowed me to enter her service,
She misjudged me in her first impression.
When she then discovered how unreliable I was,
It was this that made her wisely reject me.   40
She kept her promise to me:

She granted me what she owed me.
It is indeed a foolish man who expects anything else.
She rewarded me according to what I seemed worth to her.
It is my own sword, and nothing else, with which I've been struck.   45

2. "If a man takes his delight"

A standard poem of courtly love expressing typical thoughts: the long and unsuc-
cessful service to a lady who remains distant; the wish to approach her directly or
to send her a messenger; and the momentary entertainment of, followed by the
rejection as unthinkable the idea of leaving the "battle."

If a man takes his delight in the company of noble women,
He should speak well of them
And be ready to serve them.
This is my practice and my advice as well.
True devotion requires this.   5
Yet this does me no good
With regard to a woman
With whom I have long been seeking to find favor.
I have surrendered myself to her utterly
And shall live always with her as my goal.   10

If I could express to this fair woman, as I would like to do,
What I am thinking and feeling,
I would give up courtly song.
But I have not had such good fortune,
And so I must complain to her of my distress   15
In the form of song; and this disheartens me.
Far distant from her though I might be,
I shall send her a messenger
Whom she shall surely harken to and receive in private.
He will not betray me.   20

It is with a lament and not in song
That I express my suffering yet again
To this noble lady.
The oppressive days have lasted far too long
Throughout which I have begged for her favor;   25
Yet she continues to reject me.

If a person could give up such a battle
That brings nothing but misery and not one whit of joy—
Which, alas, I can never do—
He would indeed be a fortunate man.   30

3. "I said I wanted to live always for her"

A poetic formulation of the ideals of courtly love and its power to refine the person of the lover.

I said I wanted to live always for her.
I let this be known far and wide.
I had given my heart to her.
Now I have taken it back from her.
If a person takes an ill-considered vow,   5
Let him renounce it in time
Before the battle robs him
Of his days and years completely.
That is what I did.
Let the victory be hers.   10
From this time on
I'll serve some other lady.

I have always detested those with no sense of loyalty.
But now I would rather be disloyal.
I would live much better disloyal to her   15
Than if my loyalty to her
That bade me serve her
Would not let me leave her.
Yet it does cause me pain
That she intends to let me go unrewarded.   20
I shall speak only well of her.
Rather than cause her distress,
I shall accept the blame
As well as the loss.
What fault could I find with her   25
Of whom I have always spoken so well?
I can duly lament my misery
Without thereby embarrassing her by my entreaties.

Still, she did accept my service
For many a year.   30
I sought her love
And have found her displeasure.
That I never had any success with her—
That was my own fault.
If she were to think me deserving,   35
She would have given me a better reward.

Though I must go without a reward from her
Whom I have served so many a year,
May God nonetheless grant me my wish
That this beloved woman   40
Live happily and with honor.
But since I must take revenge,
Then so be it—
But in this way and no other:
That I wish her well, better   45
Than does any other man,
And that in so doing
I grieve at her distress and am glad when she is happy.

The years I have devoted to her
Are in no way lost.   50
Though the reward of her love has eluded me,
One pleasing thought lifts up my spirit:
I would wish for nothing more
But that I might say, as I have till now,
That she is my lady.   55
It ultimately turns out for many men
That they never experience any happiness
Other than that they believe
It might happen some day,
And this hope is their happiness.   60
She whom I have served till now
Shall be the source of my joy,
Even though my service has done me little good.
I know well that my lady
Conducts herself honorably.   65

If a man leaves the service of his lady,
Let him do so.
He deeply regrets his years in her service.
Yet a man who only knows how to love in this way
Is a man without honor.   70
I have nobler thoughts and feelings:
I shall never cease serving her.

4. "My service to my lady"

A typical lover's lament.

My service to my lady has gone on much too long,
While I remain uncertain of her feelings toward me.
She, who has ever been the goal of my heart's striving,
Lets me go on with no grounds for hope.
I could complain to her   5
And tell her
Of the long oppressive hours I've spent
Since I realized how she is treating me.
Truly, since that time an hour seems to me
Like a day, a day like a week, a week like a whole year.   10

Alas! What would she do to a man
Who was really her enemy,
Since she knows how to ruin
The life of a friend with so much misery.
It would be easier for me   15
To bear the enmity of the whole empire.
Then, at least, I could flee
And hide somewhere from its armies.
This anguish is ever present to me
And takes sums from my joy as though it were my landlord.   20

5. "Taking the cross"

Though the subject matter of this poem is going off on a crusade, it is not a cru-
sading song (*Kreuzlied*) in the usual sense of the term because it does not treat the
standard theme of the knight's being torn between the obligation of going on a cru-

sade and the desire to remain in the service of his lady. Here, rather, Hartmann
emphasizes the pure motives one should have for "taking the cross" and the rewards
that a crusade promises. The only woman in the poem is the seductress Lady World.
Though the speaker of the poem has served her in the past, the death of his feu-
dal lord has effected a spiritual conversion in him which motivates him to join the
crusade.

Taking the cross demands that one have
Purely spiritual intentions and a blameless personal life.
Then it can gain a man happiness
And all good things.
What's more, it is no little support   5
For the unseasoned man
Who has not achieved
Mastery over himself.
It does not allow a man
To avoid the deeds it demands.   10
What good does it do to wear the cross on one's garment[2]
If there is no trace of it in one's heart.

O knight, now pay to redeem your life
And your thoughts and hopes
For His sake who has given you   15
Both life and possessions.
A man whose shield was ever prepared
To pursue great fame in the world—
If he now refuses to fight for God,
He is foolish indeed.   20
For he to whom it is granted
To return hale and hearty
Attains a twofold reward:
Honor in this world and salvation for his soul.

The world smiles at me and nods,   25
Hoping to seduce me.
In my naïveté

___

2. As a knight did who had taken a vow to go on a crusade.

I followed her.
Many is the time
I ran after the wanton woman;   30
I hurried on to where
No one can find constancy.
Now help me, Lord Christ,
With the symbol that I wear[3]
That I may renounce him   35
Who waits to ambush me.[4]

Since the time when death
Robbed me of my lord,
I have taken no part in
What goes on in the world.   40
The best of my joy
He took with him.
If I might now attain salvation for my soul,
That would give life meaning.
If I can come to his aid,[5]   45
I promise to him half the benefit
Of the journey I have taken upon myself.
May God grant that I see him myself again.[6]

My joy was never free of cares
Until the day   50
I chose for myself the flowers[7] of Christ
That I now wear.
They foretell a summertime
That shall fill our eyes with precious beauty.
May God lead us   55
To the tenth choir[8]

3. That is, the cross that the crusader wears.
4. That is, the devil.
5. That is, if my going on a crusade can shorten my lord's time in purgatory.
6. That is, in heaven.
7. Probably a reference to the cross.
8. A reference to the popular medieval notion, which may have originated in *The Celestial Harmonies* by Pseudo-Dionysius, that Lucifer and his minions fell from the highest (tenth) choir of angels and that the faithful on earth are destined to take their places.

From which perversity
Caused the dark one of hell
To be driven out
And which lies open for good souls.   60

I have adopted an attitude
Toward the world that makes me
Have very little desire for her.
This is certainly good for me.
As things now stand,   65
God has treated me very well.
I have been freed from worldly concerns
That bind
The feet of many,
Forcing them to stay at home,   70
While I in the army of Christ
Depart in blissful joy.

6. "If a woman sends off her beloved"

This poem, another variation on the theme of crusades, emphasizes the woman's
role and the rewards both for her and for her knight.

If a woman sends off her beloved
On a crusade with the right intention,
She receives half the reward for it
If she so conducts herself at home
That she deserves to have chaste words spoken of her.   5
Let her pray for them both here
As he goes off to fight for them both there.

7. "He who is sad in good times"

A light-hearted lament stressing the speaker's failings as the cause of unrequited
love and courtly love's role in refining the speaker's person.

He who is sad in good times
Never becomes merry and in good spirits when things turn bad.
But I have a scheme for coping with sadness:

Whenever something bad happens to me, I take it in the following way:
Let it be; it was supposed to happen to you.   5
Soon something will happen
That will be good for you.
This is how a person should expect the best for himself.

Whoever says something other than that a man must gain the love of a
    steadfast woman
Through his own steadfastness, he speaks not the truth.   10
This is how my inconstancy cost me
The favor of a steadfast woman who treated me with such friendliness
That she presented me with hopes of love.
When she realized
That I was unreliable,   15
Then her favor toward me also had to end.

It is in the long run a good thing
That my lack of constancy caused me to fail with women.
Now I am devoting myself to being constant,
And I shall be successful in getting help for my misfortune.   20
I am in the service of a steadfast woman.
With regard to her my steadfastness
Shall become manifest
And that in steadfastness no one is my master.

8. "Mighty God, what will her greeting be like"

Hartmann treats here the theme of constancy to the absent loved one that true
courtly love demands. He contrasts this with gaining the favor of a woman through
flattery. In the final two lines he uses *gah* (quick, quickly) four times to stress how,
in contrast to the long service required for true courtly love, the quick success won
by flattery quickly fades.

Mighty God, what will her greeting be like
When I see the woman from whom I have been away so long a time?
Even someone who stays at home has to fear a change of heart
Though he can greet his beloved often enough.
I shall put my trust in her good judgment   5
And that she knows full well why I have been away.

Then she does well and my hopes rest on the fact
That a heart that is true can never turn false to a friend.

No one alive, who sees his loved one so often,
Can help but think of the loved one, even against his will.   10
That is not how love from the heart manifests itself.
Some of us stay away so long
That a woman is able to show her constancy toward us.
A lady should realize that inconstancy is a terrible blow.
If I receive her fair greeting after a long absence,   15
With what increased careful attention must I then serve her!
If it is true, as I hear many claim,
That flattery is the best approach to women,
Alas, what success can a man hope to gain
Who avoids it as well as all falseness because of his sincerity?   20
Let him remain constant in his irreproachable conduct.
By so doing he shall gain constant success,
Just as he who is quick to flatter sees his quick success trickle away
That he quickly had with her who quickly succumbed to flattery.

9. "If one can save one's soul by lying"

This poem is a lady's lament (*Frauenklage*). The speaker is a woman who com-
plains about the consequences of having chosen a false lover.

If one can save one's soul by lying,
Then I know someone who is holy.
He has often sworn false oaths to me.
His shrewd cunning overwhelmed me
And I chose him as a friend.   5
I thought I had found in him constancy.
But my own good sense deserted me,
As I now announce to the world:
He is as free of duplicity
As the sea is free of waves.   10

Why should I seek help from others
Since it was my own heart that deceived me?
It led me to the one
Who is worthless to me or to any good woman.

It hardly honors men   15
How this man conducts himself with regard to women.
He is so well versed in uttering sweet phrases
That one could write them down.
I followed them even onto slippery ice.
Now I am suffering the harm they caused.   20

If I were now to begin to detest all men,
I would do so out of hatred of him alone.
But how are they all at fault for this?
Many men show better gratitude to their ladies.
One lady, by using her good sense,   25
Chose a friend who makes her happy.
She is laughing while I am sad.
Our lives play themselves out quite differently.
I have begun with suffering.
May God, the mighty One, ease my pain.   30

10. "I have little reason to complain"

The first stanza of this poem expresses the paradox of the knight's suffering in the
presence of his lady. The second praises all women.

I have little reason to complain
That I hardly ever see the woman
Of whom I have spoken only good
All my days and shall continue to do so.
I never feel worse   5
Than in her presence.
My life is in danger
Unless I can bring it about
That she might see fit
To declare me her friend.   10
Otherwise, it would be better for me not to see her.

The happiness of good women
Has always caused my heart to rejoice.
No one is more ready to serve them,
And that shall always be the case.   15
I shall be happy when they are happy,

All my days,
And shall lament their sufferings by suffering.
No one should cease to praise them.
Whatever we achieve that is valuable,   20
And that we have not yet gone entirely to ruin,
For this we should express our thanks to them.

11. "No one in this world is a happy man"

This poet laments the suffering that is at the essence of courtly love.

No one in this world is a happy man
But he alone
Who has never experienced love,
And, what's more, has never given the matter a thought.
His heart is free of the pains of longing   5
That bring many to the point of death
Who have well deserved success in love
And yet must continue on without it.
Nothing touches me so much.
I am very sensitive to such suffering,   10
For I am afflicted with this same misery.

To be met with this misfortune
Is worse than all other kinds of misery:
That I must part from friends
With whom I would ever like to remain.   15
This distress arises out of my sense of loyalty.
I don't know if it is of any benefit to the soul.
As for my body, the only reward it gets
Is to feel sadness all day long.
My steadfast loyalty often causes me suffering.   20
For I cannot get over the loss of the fine woman
Who once treated me so well.

12. "Noble lady"

Only a few commentators attribute this poem to Hartmann. Most consider
Hartmann's contemporary, Walther von der Vogelweide, to be the author. Another

point in dispute is whether it is one poem or two (stanzas 1–3 and 4–5). The poem begins as a messenger's song (*Botenlied*). The first stanza is spoken by the knight's messenger; the second is the lady's response. The final three stanzas seem to be spoken by the knight.

"Noble lady, a knight who wants
The best for you has offered you his service.
He will most eagerly do
The best his heart can achieve.
Because of you he wants to be   5
In high spirits all this summer in hopes of your favor.
You should accept this with a friendly spirit
So that I can return to him with the good news.
Then I shall be welcome to him there."

"Please tell him that I am obliged by his offer.   10
No one who has never seen him
Could be better pleased than I
At whatever good things might happen to him.
And ask him to engage his noble efforts
Where he may be rewarded. I am not a woman   15
In a position to accept the kind of proposals he has made.
Whatever else he desires, I shall willingly fulfill,
For he is worthy of it."

My first message, which she heard,
Was, I thought, well received by her—   20
Until she succeeded in getting me close to her.
Then suddenly a different attitude took hold of her.
No matter how much I might want to, I cannot get away from her.
My great love for her has increased to such an extent
That she never lets me go free.   25
I shall have to be her serf forever.
But I don't care. It's what I want, too.

Since I shall be subject to her
Like a serf as long as I live,
And she can easily pay me back   30
For the cares that I have suffered because of her—and must always suf-
     fer—No one can lighten my heart

Unless it be she.
She should then accept my service
And thereby save me   35
And thus not neglect her obligations toward me.

Whoever says that love is a sin,
Should beforehand carefully consider this:
There is much honor connected with it
That one can legitimately enjoy.   40
And it results in much constancy and even happiness.
That someone ever abuses it causes me pain.
I do not mean false love.
That could better be called un-love.
I shall ever despise it.   45

13. "By rights I must ever hold dear the day"

This straightforward hymn of praise to a lady is generally considered to be one of
Hartmann's early efforts.

By rights I must ever hold dear the day
When I first saw the noble lady
With her charming refinement and feminine insight.
Lucky for me that I ever made her the object of my longing.
She suffers no harm because of it, and it improves me ever and again.   5
It is because of her that I give
More thought and good will to God and the world.
And so I hope to increase my joy still more.

My body is able to be far away from this fair lady.
My heart, my will have to remain near her.   10
She is well able to turn my life and my joy into misery,
Yet at the same time drive all my cares away:
She is the source of both my joy and my sorrow.
Whatever she wants of me, I am ever ready to do.
If ever I was happy, it happened only through her kindness.   15
May God protect her life and honor.

I parted from her unable to express to her
What she meant to me in my heart.

Since then it chanced to happen in an hour of bliss
That I found her to my great good fortune unaccompanied.[9]   20
When I, acting with proper etiquette, saw the noble woman
And spoke to her openly of my wishes,
She responded to me in such a way—may God ever reward her for it.
She always was and ever shall be the crown of my life.

14. "Those who reap joy from summer's flowers"

Hartmann's authorship of this poem is disputed by several critics. Those who consider it authentic place it among his early poems. The poem is certainly not without charm, but the woman who speaks expresses attitudes toward love not typical of Hartmann's authenticated poems.

Those who reap joy from summer's flowers
Must soon feel sadness as gloomy wintertime draws near.
Still a woman who during the long nights
Lies by a man she loves has something to help her.
This is how I shall shorten the long winter   5
When no birds sing.
If I must do without the latter, I do not do so willingly.

My family has proposed a game
In which I have two choices, but I lose either way.
But I shall choose between them anyway,   10
Though if I make the wrong choice, it would be better to have left it
    undone.
They say: If I choose love
I must give them up.
But my plan is to pursue both paths.

If I were to follow the advice of my family,   15
Dear Lord, what gratitude should I then expect from him?
Because he has well earned it
It seems to me that his wait for a reward has been much too long.
Because it is my intention to risk
My honor, and my whole being—body and mind—for him,   20

---

9. Ladies of the court were to be in the constant company of other women.

I shall succeed, if luck is with me.

He is well worth receiving
Everything that a man desires in a woman—
If I wish to remain faithful to him.
Indeed, no honor would be excessive for him.   25
He is such a refined and sensitive man.
I hope I can keep him that way.
If I give him my love, nothing can go wrong for me.

15. "Many a person hails me"

This poem gets its charm from the playful manner with which it treats the serious matter of courtly love, a love by nature unrequited. The poet philosophizes about his lack of success with courtly ladies and proposes to try his luck with less noble women—an idea that appears again in the poetry of Walther von der Vogelweide. The irony is that the poet's distress and doubt about where he should direct his affections is not caused by high-flown musings about his unworthiness but rather by a deflating snub he experienced from a lady of the court.

Many a person hails me with the following proposal—
A proposal that adds little to my cheer:
"Hartmann, let's go feast our eyes
On the ladies at court."
He can just leave me in peace   5
And dart off to the ladies himself!
Standing before ladies protesting my loyal devotion
Reaps me only this: weariness.

This is my way of dealing with ladies:
As they treat me, so do I treat them.   10
For I can better spend my time
With poor women.
No matter where I go, there are plenty of them.
Among them I shall find one who wants me around.
She shall be the delight of my heart, too.   15
What good is it for me to chase after too lofty a goal?

In my folly it happened
That, addressing a lady, I said:

"Lady, I have turned my attention
To winning your love." 20
She just gave me a weird look.
And so, let me assure you,
I shall confine my gawking at women
To those who don't put me through anything like that.

16. "These would be wonderful days"

Most commentators today accept the poem as Hartmann's, but there is no consensus on the nature of the poem. Some believe it to be a lament for a dead lover or husband, while others, arguing that nothing in the poem points to the man as being dead, see it as a lament for a knight off on a crusade. Still others consider it simply the lament of a lady whose lover has left her.

These would be wonderful days
For someone who could live them in a carefree spirit.
But God has visited on me a lamentable distress
In these fair days
From which I shall never recover. 5
I have lost a man
And, if the truth be told,
No woman ever gained a dearer friend.
The while I nurtured our friendship, he was my joy.
But now may God watch over him. He can care for him better than I. 10

No one can rightly see what I have lost
Without thinking that my bitter lament is appropriate.
I found him to be always faithful and honorable,
And everything that a woman desires in a man
Was taken from me all too suddenly. 15
Never shall I get over it
Till I die
But must suffer the pains of longing.
Any woman who has had a more pleasant time of it—
Let her show it through her demeanor. 20

Since the joys of love end in such suffering,
God has treated a woman quite well

Who has spared herself both of them.
Such a woman spends her time in good cheer,
While I spend many a bright day lamenting   25
And she is in such a frame of mind
That she finds my lot incomprehensible.
I have been made happy by love.
If I should live to be very old,
The cost in suffering will be a thousandfold.   30

17. "By your leave I depart"

This poem, probably the most famous of Hartmann's lyric poems, plays with the
conventions of the *Kreuzlied* (crusading song). The usual theme of the crusading
song is the pain the crusader feels in separating from the lady he loves. Hartmann
exploits the genre to contrast courtly love with divine love.

By your leave I depart, lords and kinsmen,
May the land and its people be blessed.
There is no need to ask about my journey:
I'll say straight out where I'm going.
Love captured me and, receiving my word of honor, let me go free.[10]   5
Now she has bid me go for love of her.
It is irreversible: I am firmly obligated to go there.
What little chance there is of my proving disloyal and breaking my oath!

Many boast of what they would do for love's sake.
Where are their deeds? I hear their fine words quite clearly.   10
But I would like to see her bid some of them
To serve her as I shall serve her.
Love is genuine if one must set out for strange lands for love's sake.
See how she draws me forth from the sounds of my mother tongue and
    across the sea.
If my lord still lived, Saladin[11] and all his army   15

10. After knightly combat the vanquished knight swore an oath to carry out whatever charge his van-
quisher commanded. For further examples of this, see *Erec*, lines 1014–19 and 1078–85.
11. Saladin was the fabled and respected leader of the Islamic forces fighting against the crusaders dur-
ing the Third Crusade.

Would not budge me one foot from Franconia.[12]

You minnesingers, you are often doomed to fail.
What brings you harm is illusion.[13]
I can boast that I sing well of love
Because love possesses me and I possess her. 20
That which I want to have is just as eager to have me.
But you often lose much because of illusion.
You struggle for a love that wants nothing to do with you.
When will you poor unfortunates love such a love as I do?

18. "Alas, why are we so sad?"

This poem is considered by most commentators to be falsely attributed to
Hartmann. The reasons for this view are drawn from considerations of both form
and content. The poem is perhaps best taken as a parody of the high-minded atti-
tude expected of the knight in his lady's service.

Alas, why are we so sad?
It certainly isn't appropriate for anyone to be so.
I shall gladly give up such a burden
That gives me no pleasure.
Just look how beautiful the countryside is all around, 5
Dressed in green
When the pleasing days of summer have arrived.

It is right that a lucky man achieve
With little effort whatever he wishes,
For he understands how to use praise.[14] 10
I would be very pleased if I had that talent.

12.   These two lines are the cause of some controversy. As translated here they take Hartmann to be
saying that he is obligating himself to "taking the cross" in connection with the death of his feudal lord.
This could be a reference to the crusade of 1189. However, the lines can also be construed as follows: "If
my lord Saladin were alive, even his whole army would not budge me." Since Saladin died in 1193, the
reference might be to the crusade of 1197. The translation given in the text seems more likely to be
Hartmann's meaning.
13.   That is, given the conventions of courtly love, the love celebrated in courtly poetry may exist only
in the mind of the lover.
14.   That is, he knows how to get what he wants through flattery.

He receives the charming attention
Of the most noble women now alive.
It's a pain if you have to wait long.[15]

That a woman be true in her love   15
Is something I need very much,
Since I am rarely in her presence.
I should not have to make amends for this
Because I stay away from her with good intentions.
If I were not doing it[16] to preserve her honor,   20
I would never go farther than a foot from her.
She does not want to grant me the favor
Of lying with her.
And yet, as she tells me,
She does not want to give me up as a friend.   25
Clearly she does not hate me.
But if she were to grant me no favor,
I would be better off with an agreeable enemy.

She wants to see me rewarded.
Well, I want the same as she wants.   30
I must consider this as something good.
Otherwise,[17] she would consider it excessive
To let me serve her.
Look, not even a heathen would do that.
It is certainly already much if she does not sin in the matter.[18]   35

15.   That is, if you have to wait long to get the attention of the ladies.
16.   That is, keeping my distance from her.
17.   That is, if she does not reward me.
18.   If this poem is, as it seems to be, a parody of courtly love, this confusing final line is perhaps best
interpreted thus: I will be happy if she does not sin by taking back her promise to reward me.

EREC

Introduction

In the third decade of the twelfth century the Welsh (or possibly, Breton) teacher and poet Geoffrey of Monmouth incorporated his earlier *Prophetiae Merlini* (*Prophecies of Merlin*) into the expansive, and largely fictional, *Historia Regum Britanniae* (*History of the Kings of Britain*). One of the kings Geoffrey wrote about was Arthur, a quasi-historical figure who led the indigenous seventh-century Britons against the invading barbarian Saxons. Much as medieval illustrations provide biblical and classical scenes with a medieval backdrop, so does Geoffrey have Arthur preside over what looks like a twelfth-century court. With the names of Guinevere, Merlin, Caerleon, Mordred, and Avalon, among others, Geoffrey set up the Arthurian court, which over time would accrue figures and places and endure to the present day without losing popularity.

In the second half of the twelfth century, the French poet Chrétien de Troyes took up what he had read and heard of Arthur and his court and covered it with the golden patina of French courtly society, then at the apex of power and resplendence. Chrétien wrote five Arthurian romances and two lyric poems on Arthurian subjects. Two of these works, *Erec et Enide* and *Yvain*, were adapted by Hartmann.

As their titles imply, King Arthur is not the major character in Chrétien's romances. Rather, Arthur's court, in all its transposed twelfth-century splendor and with its chivalric code, serves as the meeting place of the present and future knights of the round table (the invention of the Norman poet Wace in his 1155 *Roman de Brut*) as they set out and return from their knightly "adventures."

Chrétien's *Erec et Enide* must have immediately and decisively influenced the young poet Hartmann, who probably from an early age had been surrounded by the flowering courtly culture of the Hohenstaufen era. Hartmann most likely composed *Erec* between 1175 and 1190, when he was in his twenties, some short time after the *Lament*, and contemporaneously with some of his lyric poetry. While the legend surrounding King Arthur had to a large degree a nationalistic underpinning in England and France, mirroring the court of Henry II Plantagenet, king of England and also of large parts of western France through his marriage to Eleanor of Aquitaine, this nationalism gave way to a focus on the external and internal trappings of courtly society itself and of chivalry when Hartmann introduced the large-scale Arthurian romance in Germany.

While Hartmann obviously based *Erec* to a large degree on Chrétien's *Erec et Enide*—though he may have also used other sources, written and oral—and acknowledges the fact in line 4629[12],[1] it would be more appropriate to call *Erec* a reworking or an adaptation rather than a translation, for Hartmann took great liberties with his French model, among other things expanding it by over three thousand lines (10,192 versus 6,958). The differences between the two *Erecs*, which can be used very well as an interpretive tool, are too numerous to be recounted here.

What might strike the reader of both works is Hartmann's focus on courtly society, and the concomitant etiquette of chivalry, and on the relationship between Erec and Enite. The development of these two themes goes toward making Hartmann a great writer and not just a narrator of entertaining knightly adventures. To be sure, Hartmann was an entertainer, as a court poet had to be, but in *Erec* he rises high above the typical minstrel. One can justifiably call Hartmann didactic, moralistic, and possibly even preachy—and not just in regard to *Erec*—for behind the Arthurian façade he had a point to make.

Hartmann lived in a courtly society and wanted to show how a young knight ought to comport himself within that society, and how deviations from the right path, as Hartmann saw it, could lead to trouble. When Hartmann looked around, he must have seen examples of both exemplary and not-so-exemplary knightly behavior. While one cannot call *Erec* a *Fürstenspiegel* (a sort of primer for the education of a prince), one has to believe that Hartmann would not have been disappointed had all knights turned out like Erec.

Readers of Hartmann's *Erec* can enjoy the trappings of an Arthurian court, the knightly contests and prowess, the unusual characters, the irony and humor, but they can also appreciate how a medieval writer understood the primacy of the relationship between a man and a woman, and how the couple's understanding of that relationship in society, and their individual growth, was the underpinning of a society that fascinated the poet Hartmann.

Gottfried von Strassburg, in his *Tristan* (c. 1210), was the first to praise Hartmann for the purity of his writing, singling out his elder contemporary for "sîn kristal-

---

1. The superscript on this line number indicates a variant that does not appear in every manuscript, but which has become, since the nineteenth century, a part of the printed tradition and is included in all modern editions.

lîniu wortelîn" (line 4627—"his crystalline words"). Not only is Hartmann a gifted storyteller, a master of psychological insight, a humorist, a moralist, but he excels in the use of language, in simile, metaphor, and symbol, in rhetoric, in lovely verbal imagery, and this sets him apart from most of his contemporaries, as Gottfried rightly noted.

What is less appreciated, perhaps, about Hartmann is his skill at building the structure of a story. In *Erec*, Hartmann begins with Arthur's court and ends with it and Erec's homeland, thus showing how Erec has come full circle. Erec's "resurrection" forms the dénouement of the epic, while on either side of the narrative climax, Erec undergoes a series of adventures, several shorter ones before and one major one after. Even within the number of adventures prior to his "awakening," Hartmann skillfully marks the progress Erec makes by having him overcome first three robbers, then five, and then six followers of the "faithless count." It is fitting that Erec begin with robbers whose lack of knightly dress and comportment is underscored, then deals with a count, and finally a king, the dwarf-like Guivreiz. Similarly, the "faithless count" and Count Oringles serve as parallel figures to Erec, for both are initially described as decent, chivalrous men, yet both are undone by behavior that mirrors flaws in Erec. And in the last major scene, "Joie de la curt" at Brandigan, Hartmann presents readers with a married couple who to some degree parallel Erec and Enite at the beginning of their marriage, and who also must come to see the flaws in their relationship. Gottfried was correct in singing the praise of Hartmann's language, but later generations of readers have also come to appreciate Hartmann for being a writer who is completely in charge of his material.

Text

. . . with her and the ladies of the court.[2] This was Erec, fil de roi Lac,[3] who was brave and favored with good fortune, and with whom this story begins. Now they

2. The opening of Hartmann's *Erec* is missing. Approximately one hundred lines precede this point in Chrétien de Troyes's *Erec et Enide*. On Easter Day (see note 65), King Arthur has his court gathered at Cardigan. Arthur announces his desire to hunt for the white stag. Gawein opposes Arthur's suggestion, saying that the custom of allowing the killer of the stag to kiss the most beautiful maiden at court could cause trouble, since there are five hundred maidens and their knights present. Arthur insists, and at daybreak the hunting party sets out. Erec ("although not yet twenty-five, he was noble, brave, and becoming") catches up to the queen, who is also accompanied by a "beautiful lady in waiting." The three fall behind the hunting party, which has spotted the white stag, and stop in a clearing to listen for the hunting horns.

3. Old French, "Son of King Lac," an epithet used for Erec throughout medieval epics. The mention

both had been riding not too long a time next to one another when they saw at a distance across the heath a knight with two companions riding up in great haste: in front was a dwarf and in between a lovely maiden, fair and well dressed.

[14] Now the queen was eager to know who the knight might be. He was well armed,[4] as a good warrior should be. Erec, the young man, asked his lady whether he should find this out. The lady did not desire this and asked him to stay with her. She chose a lady in waiting whom she could send over. She said, "Ride over and find out who the knight might be, and his companion, the maiden."

[28] The lady in waiting set out, as she had been ordered, to where she saw the dwarf riding. Courteously she spoke to him, "God's greetings, friend. Hear what I desire. My lady has sent me over here. She is the queen of the realm. She commanded me, out of courtesy, that I greet you in her name. She would gladly like to know who this knight is, and this beautiful maiden. If you can let me know that, you do so without risking any harm. My lady asks only with good intentions."

[44] The dwarf did not want to tell her and ordered her to be quiet and to stay away from him, stating that he did not know what she had come riding over for. The maiden did not let that keep her from wanting to ride further and asking the knight himself who he was. The dwarf blocked her way. The queen and Erec saw how he struck her about the head and hands with a whip he carried in his hand, such that, to his disgrace, she received welts from it.

[59] With such an answer she then parted and went back to her lady and let her see how badly she had been struck. The queen lamented greatly that such a thing had happened so near her that she was forced to witness it. Erec considered the knight to be no honorable man, since he allowed the dwarf to strike the maiden in his presence. He said, "I shall ride over there and get the information for you." The lady replied, "Ride then."

[73] Immediately Erec set out until he came so close to them that the dwarf could hear his words, "Can you tell me, little fellow, why you struck the maiden? You have done a great wrong. Out of courtesy you should not have done it. You should tell me the name of your lord. My lady wishes to know who he is, and the fair maiden."

[83] The dwarf replied, "Enough of your twaddle. I shall tell you nothing but that the same thing will happen to you. Why did she wish to know who my lord

---

of the king underscores erec's noble heritage but also distinguishes him from others with the name of Erec, at a time when family names had not yet become commonplace.

4. A reference to both his arms and his armor, or chain mail.

is? You two are idiots for inquiring so much about my lord today. It might well bring you trouble. If you want me to spare you, then be on your way, you commonplace scourge."

[95] Erec too wanted to ride on, but the dwarf did not let him. With his whip he struck him as he had the maiden. Erec wanted to avenge himself but wisely was able to control his anger. The knight would have taken his life, since Erec was as unarmed as a woman. Never had he experienced a more sorrowful day than the one caused by the lash of the whip, and never had he been so ashamed than by the fact that the queen and her lady in waiting had seen this dishonor.

[109] After he had been struck by the whip he rode back in great shame. He lamented his grief thus—red with shame were his cheeks—"My lady, I cannot deny, for you have seen it yourself, that great disgrace has been inflicted on me in your presence, the likes of which someone in my position has never suffered in the least. That such a little man struck me so disgracefully, and that I had to endure it from him, shames me so much that never again shall I dare see you and these ladies. And I don't know what use life is to me unless it be to make good what has happened to me in your presence. Unless I die soon I must try. My lady, deign to let me part by your leave. May God in heaven preserve your honor, my lady. You will never see me again unless I take revenge on this man whose dwarf has inflicted these welts on me. If God so honors me by increasing my good fortune such that I succeed, as my heart truly hopes, I shall return in three days, if illness does not hinder me."

[144] The queen was very troubled that he, such a young man, was riding into such great danger. She begged him to forgo the journey. But he so persisted in asking for leave that she at last granted it to him.

[150] The young knight reflected that it would be too far for him to ride back now to where he kept his armor, and that he could never get it fast enough—however quickly he might return, they would surely have ridden away—and thus he hurried after them, unarmed.

[160] As he hurriedly pursued them, he straightway came upon the tracks of the ones who had caused him harm. Very quickly he caught sight of them; he was in no hurry to reach them. He rode behind them at such a distance that he could see them but they could not see him. He acted as one does who has suffered grief: he makes every effort to set things right again. All day long he never lost sight of them along the way until night fell. Before him he now caught sight of a castle called Tulmein, whose lord was Duke Imain. The knight who was ahead of him rode into it and was well received there, as one should be in a friend's castle, in a manner befitting the lord of the place.

[181] I shall tell you why he had come there with his lady friend. Duke Imain had held a festival there the last two years. If my sources speak truthfully,[5] he was now holding one a third time. In the middle of a meadow on a high stand he had set a sparrow hawk on a silver pole. This event took place yearly for the entertainment of his subjects. He excluded no one from the event: all of them, poor and rich, old and young, came when they heard about it, to be entertained on account of the great hospitality. Whoever's lady friend won the contest at his festival, thereby designating her the most beautiful, claimed the sparrow hawk. The knight had claimed it twice and had come to claim it a third time, and if it were to happen thus, he would keep it, to his great honor, uncontested, forever. The story was told that many a woman there was more beautiful than the knight's lady friend. But here his superiority in knightly skills was obvious: he was so feared that he took the hawk by force. No one dared challenge him. He did not even have to fight.

[218] Now Erec knew nothing of these things. Only because of his troubles had he ridden after him in search of adventure.[6] The day drew to a close. Before the castle there was a market town.[7] He rode off toward it. The castle he avoided with the thought that he would not be noticed by the knight he had followed there.

[228] As he now rode in search of someone who out of kindness might put him up for the night, he encountered along the way a great swarm of people. The houses everywhere were quite full with lodgers. Nowhere could he find someone who would take him in as a guest. He was also completely without means. He had not provided himself with anything because this journey had come upon him so suddenly, as I told you earlier. He had nothing more than his horse and his clothes—this worried him greatly. He was also unknown there, so that no one spoke to him or looked at him kindly. The lanes were full of activities as is fitting at a festival.

[250] He rode on aimlessly until he noticed far ahead of him an old building. Since finding lodging had been so difficult for him, he took a path that led him to it because he intended to spend the night there, since he could not elsewhere. He inspected the house and did not think that he would find anyone in it. He was glad about that. He thought: now things are going well for me because I can stay in a corner until day comes, since this is the best I can do. Certainly no one will begrudge me that, for I can see well that it is abandoned.

---

5. A topos in medieval epics, whether the "sources" are real or not. Originality was not essential for medieval poets. Harking back to a source, however questionable, gave a story authenticity.

6. *Âventiure* encompasses more than just "adventure." It is the raison d'être of the knight on a quest.

7. A market town was a small community that had been given the right to hold a regular market, an important economic right in the High Middle Ages.

[270] When he entered the house and inspected the corners as to which would best be suited for his staying in it, he saw sitting there an old man. His hair was snow white with age. Nevertheless, he had taken great pains to take care of it according to good etiquette: it lay smoothly combed down over his shoulders.[8] According to my sources this same old man had on a sheepskin coat and a cap of the same.[9] Both were as good as his circumstances allowed. Riches he did not have. His appearance was very lordly, like that of a nobleman. The man who sat there had a crutch for support.

[292] Erec was upset at this because he feared the same old thing: the old man would turn him away as he had been before. He tied up his horse; on it he laid his cloak. His hands he held out in front of him, as a well-bred man should,[10] and walked over to the old man. Hesitantly he said to him, "My lord, I am in need of lodging." The request made him turn red with shame. When the old man had heard what he said, he replied, "You are welcome to whatever I might have." Erec fil de roi Lac thanked him.

[308] To run his household he had only one child—this was the most beautiful maiden we have ever heard of—and the lady of the house. One could see that his way of thinking was that of a rich man in that he had taken in such a poor guest. He called his daughter over and said, "Daughter, go and take care of the horse of this lord who deigns to be our guest, and take good care of it so that I do not have to rebuke you." She replied, "My lord, this I shall do."

[323] The girl's figure was praiseworthy. Her dress was green,[11] completely tattered, and worn thin everywhere. Her blouse underneath was dirty and also torn here and there. Thus her body shone through, white as a swan.[12] It is said that never had a maiden a body so completely conforming to what one would have wished.[13] And had she been rich, nothing would have been lacking in her as a praiseworthy wife. Her body shone through her dirty clothing like a lily, when it stands white among black thorns.[14] It seems to me that God had taken great care with her regarding beauty and grace.

---

8. Longish hair was sometimes worn by the nobility, not the peasantry.

9. Such clothing would immediately point out to Erec the man's impoverishment. Thus the contrast with his noble appearance, on which great stress was laid in the Middle Ages.

10. A sign of a friendly greeting is hands held open with no weapon.

11. In Chrétien, Enite's dress is white. Color symbolism played an important role in medieval literature and painting. Green is the color of hope and a new beginning.

12. Hartmann has a fondness for "peeping." Compare *Poor Heinrich*, lines 1187–96ff.

13. Hyperbole is a literary device frequently used by medieval writers. For just one example, compare *Poor Heinrich*, lines 678–83.

14. "As a lily among brambles, / so is my love among maidens." The Song of Solomon 2:2.

[342] Erec was sorry about the trouble he caused her. To her father he said, "We should spare the young lady this. It seems to me she has seldom done such things. It is much more appropriate for me." Then the old man replied, "One should let the host have his way. That is only proper. We have no servants. Therefore it is right for her to do it."

[352] The young lady did not fail to do what her father had ordered. Her very white hands diligently cared for the horse, and if God were to ride here on earth, it seems to me He would be satisfied with having such a groom. However she looked in poor clothing, I know that no one ever had a more charming squire than had Erec fil de roi Lac when she took care of his horse. It was by rights pleased to get its feed from such a stablehand.

[366] Here the guest was provided for as their conditions permitted: beautiful rugs spread out, such rich bedding laid on it, the best in the world, covered with samite[15] interwoven with gold, such that one person could never move the bed, and even four would have to lay it out. Spread out over it, in the magnificence of great lords, a cover of sendal,[16] rich and colorfully ornamented—but on this evening these things were rare indeed by the fire.[17] They did, however, provide clean straw. Over it they were satisfied with simple bedding covered with a white sheet. There was knightly fare as well: whatever a very intelligent man can imagine as being good, they had in abundance, with complete hospitality—however, it was not put on the table. The good will that was at home there had to suffice, because that is the pledge of all goodness.

[396] Now you may hear the story of who this old man was, that he received his guest so well, and had not avoided it, though impoverished. Earlier he had possessed more wealth and esteem than now. He had been a powerful count[18] who through absolutely no fault of his own had been robbed of his inheritance by those more powerful than he. No dishonorable deeds had plunged him into this poverty. It had come about from a feud. Superior force had taken from him everything he had ever owned. So little was left the once powerful man of his great standing that he could not keep even one servant.

[414] Now he and his excellent wife bore this poverty in their old age cleverly, and wherever they were lacking in possessions they covered their need with courtesy, as best they could so that no one noticed it. That poverty had fully gained the

15. A heavy silk fabric sometimes interwoven with gold thread.
16. A light silk fabric.
17. A literary device frequently used by Hartmann. See *Gregorius*, lines 3379–402.
18. An elevation in rank over Chrétien's lord. This rank makes Enite worthy of the princely Erec.

upper hand over them—no one at all knew that. The hardships the lord suffered because of his great poverty were on the other hand as sweet as mead when compared with the shame he felt. The aged host was named Koralus, his wife Karsinefite, and their daughter Enite. Whoever would not take pity on these noble, poor people was harder than stone. The uncle of the maiden was Duke Imain, the lord of the land, who had arranged the festivities. Her birth was without shame.[19]

[440] Now we shall go back to the story we had begun. When the horse had been taken care of, the host said to his guest, "Let us while away the time."[20] Erec was greatly troubled by the harm he had suffered earlier. He asked his host what the swarm of people he had seen in the marketplace signified. His host explained what it was all about, as I have already told you: both about the festival and the contest for the sparrow hawk.

[456] When the host had told him all of that, Erec asked him further about the knight: whether he knew who the man was who had ridden ahead of him into the castle, as I have already told you; Erec concealed his troubles from him. The old man replied, "The entire land knows him: his name is Iders fil Niut,"[21] and he explained fully to Erec the purpose of his journey: that he had come there with his lady to take the sparrow hawk. As soon as Erec had heard this, he kept asking further questions until the lord had revealed to him the circumstances of his own life.

[474] When he had explained things entirely, Erec stood up and said, "Please, my host and lord, allow this request of mine. Since your situation is such, I seek your help and advice. Trusting in your favor, I can tell you this: I have suffered from this knight a wrong that I shall always lament unless I make amends for it. His dwarf struck me very severely. Out of necessity I had to bear it. He was armed and I was not, which his dwarf knowingly took advantage of. From this I had to endure great humiliation. My heart will always lament this until God grants me the day that I might avenge it. In hope of such adventure, as I have already told you, I rode after him here. I must ask for your assistance. Both help and my good fortune rest absolutely, my lord, in your hands. If you could somehow provide me with armor—I shall tell you what I have in mind—he will not escape a fight. I have a good mount. Thus you should let me ride to these very festivities with your daughter Enite. I would prove in the contest that she is more beautiful than the knight's lady friend, and thus take the sparrow hawk. Consider whether that might be pos-

19. That is, she was of noble birth.
20. It was the responsibility of the host to entertain a guest and provide for his needs. Koralus may sense Erec's troubled state but may misinterpret it.
21. Iders, son of Niut.

sible, and do so with this promise from me: if I succeed in gaining victory, I shall take her as my wife. You should not reject my offer, thinking she might have a bad match in me. This is an honorable affair. I shall tell you who my father is: he is King Lac. I shall make subject to your daughter both land and people, my life, and everything I have, so that she shall rule over them."

[525] Then the old man's eyes grew dim from hidden misery. His heart was so immediately moved to tears at these words that he could hardly bring forth the words he had in mind. He said, "My lord, you should, for God's sake, refrain from making sport of me. Your words are very insolent. God has now imposed on me what He willed. My life is now different than it should be. I accept this from God. His power is so great: that He can make a rich man like a poor man whenever He desires, and can make the poor man rich. I am an example of what His power can do. You should, for God's sake, stop this joking. You can well do without my daughter as your wife, since she possesses no wealth. However much want I now suffer, you can well believe me that I once knew a time when your father, King Lac, called me his equal. We were knighted together in his land.[22] The fact that you now ask for my daughter must be a joke, unless my mind is deceiving me."

[560] Erec blushed at these words, saying, "My lord, what gives you the idea that I did this as a joke? Drive that from your mind and consider my words seriously. What good is derision to me right now? As truly as I ask God to help me, body and soul, so truly do I want your daughter as my wife. In this regard I shall give you a date no later than when the contest at this very festival is over, if your help aids my cause to be successful. I hear you lamenting your poverty. You should be silent regarding that. It does not harm you in my eyes, since I can easily forgo her dowry. Besides, I would be thinking basely if instead of what I said I want I preferred the acquisition of property. Reflect on this now. Since the contest will take place early tomorrow, let us delay no longer. My honor depends completely on you. Rest assured: I shall fulfill what I have promised."

[588] These words pleased the old man. He replied, "Since this is what you intend, then we have right here a magnificent suit of armor, both light and strong. Poverty could never force me, nor bring me to such despair, to be without it. I kept it in the hope that a friend of mine might have need of it—for this reason I was willing to lend it to him. As long as God wished, I was always disposed to don it

---

22. Contemporary documents and illustrations show that it was often the custom for young men raised together to be knighted at the same time. This would be a further indication that Enite would be a good match.

myself, very willingly, and be at His service, until old age won out. That has indeed sapped all my strength. Now it is of use to us so that we do not have to ask strangers and are thus spared the degradation. Up till now I have also kept together both a shield and a lance." Erec thanked the old man for that.

[614] He asked him to show him the armor so that he could see if it fit him and were neither too tight nor too heavy. It turned out to be light and strong. This gave him, Erec fil de roi Lac, a sense of exaltation. Very soon the day dawned when they were to ride to the festivities.

[624] When day appeared in full they rode to Tulmein castle. There Duke Imain heartily bade them welcome. Their arrival astonished him. They took him aside and told him the purpose of their journey, why Erec had come there and asked him for his help. He replied, "I'll tell you what I shall do. My life, wealth, and a willing heart are at your service, my honored guest, because of your courage and my niece's honor. Take my advice and let me clothe her better." Erec rejected the offer, saying, "That must not be done. Whoever might judge a lady solely by her clothes would not be seeing her in the right way. One should judge whether a woman is worthy of praise by the beauty of her person and not by her clothing. Today I shall show knights and ladies that even if she were as naked as my hand and blacker than coal, my lance and my sword would ensure for me full praise of her, or I shall lose my life."

[657] "May God grant you good fortune," replied Duke Imain. "You can also rest assured that your manly courage will provide you with everything that is good." With these words they went to hear a mass of the Holy Spirit. This is the custom most of all among those who are thinking of knightly deeds and who love participating in tournaments. Then a meal was prepared; they were served with great care. When the meal was over each pursued the pleasure he felt like, and which came to mind. The entertainment took place near to where the sparrow hawk sat perched.

[676] All were paying special attention to when Iders fil Niut would arrive with his lady love and take the sparrow hawk, as he had done before. Now they saw Erec approaching with Lady Enite. He led her at his side to where he saw the sparrow hawk. Within hearing range of the knight he said, "My lady, untie the bands and take the sparrow hawk on your hand, for it is incontestably true that there is no one here more beautiful than you."

[690] That vexed the knight. Very contemptuously he said, "Leave the sparrow hawk alone! You will not fare so well, you beggar! What could you be thinking? Leave it for her whom it befits more and who has the right to take it. That is my lady friend here. It belongs to her by rights."

[700] Erec replied, "My lord, brave knight, these past two years you have taken the sparrow hawk without any right. Rest assured, this can happen no more unless the people accord it to you. This must be decided between us by knightly combat."

[708] The knight answered, "Young man, if you value your life at all, then abandon in good time your childish contest, because you will have to abandon it soon under worse circumstances when your life is at stake. I shall tell you in advance what will happen to you. I shall have no pity on you. When I defeat you, which I do not doubt in the least, my mind is made up that I shall then not accept any ransom for your life. Whoever advised you in these matters will be happy about your misfortune."

[724] Erec replied, "My lord, I have said all I wish to say. I shall not change anything." Immediately they parted and armed themselves, the knight as suited him best, and Erec as well as he could.

[732] Iders was well prepared, since he had equipped himself as one should for knightly combat. His lances were beautifully painted, he was well emblazoned, and his charger was decorated with a magnificent caparison,[23] which Erec lacked. His tabard[24] was just as magnificent, of samite green as grass, trimmed with a luxurious braid. Our sources tell us that his suit of armor was worthy of praise. He himself looked like a distinguished knight.

[746] Erec, too, rode up. His shield was old, heavy, long, and wide, his lance unwieldy and too thick, he and his charger half unprotected, as the furnishings were those that his old father-in-law[25] had lent him. Good fortune did not refuse him its help. Among all the people one voice spoke in common, "May God grant you success today."

[755] At once the way to a large ring was cleared for them. Erec's knightly bearing befitted the young man very well; his courage gave him great strength. Great anger drove them both. They spurred on their horses, their thighs slapping against them. The knight's arrogant attitude deceived him: he thought he was challenging a boy. They clashed together. Then he observed in truth that Erec bore a hero's courage. In the joust Erec struck the knight's shield back against his head. He was so stunned by this that he could hardly stay seated. Never before had that happened to him. The joust grew so violent that the horses reared up on their hind legs. Up to this moment the knight Iders had not known such courage; now he

---

23. Ornamental trappings for a horse, often hanging well down.
24. A short tunic worn over the suit of armor.
25. Once agreement had been given for a couple's marriage, they were considered as good as married. Thus Koralus is already in essence Erec's father-in-law.

learned its full extent. Their lances flew splintered over the edge of their shields.[26]

[782] When both of them, in very praiseworthy fashion, had ridden the fifth joust, such that neither of them missed, but struck their lances against each other causing them to splinter, Erec then had no more lances. That hindered him greatly. But he had kept in reserve until the final charge the old lance of his father-in-law. He had saved it for the following reason: the shaft was thick and solid. He had also carefully and completely kept his strength in reserve until then.

[798] When he had taken the lance in his hand—his shield sat well tucked up under his chin—he rode a short distance away from the ring toward Lady Enite, where he saw her weeping. He spoke over the edge of his shield, "Be of good cheer, noble lady and maiden, I have not lost my courage in the least. Your worries will come to an end." He turned his charger so that it carried him toward the knight. His lance he slapped under his arm. The knight rode toward him, likewise well equipped. They charged at each other with as much force as they knew their horses to be capable of. They clashed together so violently that both of the knight's saddle girths broke: the surcingle and the breastplate straps—never had he experienced such distress. However much courage he might have had, Erec threw him from his charger, to the derision of all the people.

[824] When Erec had succeeded so well in striking the knight from his horse, he stopped at some distance from him. He did that so that no one could say that he had acted so disgracefully as to kill the fallen man. He wanted to gain a better name for himself. He dismounted and ordered the knight to get up. They came at each other.[27]

[834] One saw them fight like two brave knights. Sparks flew from their helmets. They fought as is fitting for people forced by bitter necessity, for they had placed a very high stake on victory. It was a question of giving on the spot no more and no less than life and honor. They acted accordingly; they fought like men. They went at it this long and hard until Iders struck Erec on the helmet with a blow that brought him to his knees.

[850] When Lady Enite saw that, she was greatly troubled. She lamented her companion. She thought he had been struck down dead and would remain there from the blow. But Erec sprang up, quickly rotated his shield around to his back, took his sword with both hands, full of rage, and fought on furiously. He stripped

---

26. A topos in the description of knightly jousts. Compare *Gregorius*, lines 2116ff.

27. The second stage of the contest, once all lances had been splintered, or one rider unhorsed but still capable of fighting, was the swordfight on foot.

the knight of his shield, striking it from his hand. The knight stood for none of that and countered blow with blow. If he borrowed something from him, he paid it back as one does who wants to take more. They both played a game that could easily rob a man of fifteen pieces up to the king.[28] And sometimes they were given both from the front and from the side. In fury they threw the dice and wagered it all. Whoever wanted to collect on his loan might have well received in return a wound a yard long. Many an offer was made and a counterproposal offered. Neither wanted to give up, because for him both honor and life would have been destroyed. Thus the game continued, with many a fiery blow, from early until after midday until the blows they offered started losing force so much that the two men started to grow weary. They were incapable of and could not make a forceful offer, and could not even move their arms as they had done earlier.

[891] Now they had spent themselves so much in anger and by fighting that they were incapable of continuing. Their blows tapered off, becoming like those of a woman. They were so exhausted that they could not inflict any harm. Then Iders said to Erec, "Stop, brave and noble knight! We are both disgracing chivalry with what we are doing now. It is not praiseworthy and brings no fame. Our weak fighting does not befit brave knights. Our blows are not manly. We are fighting disgracefully. If you do not consider it cowardice, my advice is that we end this weak fighting and rest a while."

[910] These words pleased Erec. They sat down to rest and they loosened their helmets. And when they felt that they had rested, they faced each other again and continued their old game, as I shall tell you now. With great skill and renewed strength and with very equal ability they kept playing. They went at it a long time such that those standing around, whether knowledgeable or ignorant, could not discern at all whether one or the other had one spot more than his foe.[29] Things remained like this for a long time. They were uncertain who would gain the victory until Erec, the young man, recalled what disgrace and grief had been inflicted on him by the dwarf in the meadow. And when, in addition, he looked at beautiful Lady Enite, that helped him fight mightily, for because of that his strength actually doubled. With a determined hand he rolled it all at the knight's helmet. Though Erec threw the highest number any player has need of, the knight was helped by the fact that he never let Erec escape his blows, and because of his great zeal started winning after a while, until, however, the knight lost the game and lay defeated at Erec's feet. Thus he avenged the whipping.

---

28. A chess metaphor, the king being the sixteenth piece.
29. That is, one point more on a die.

[951] When he had ripped off the knight's helmet, he also removed his coif as though the knight were to be killed, except that the knight saw fit to beg for mercy, "In the name of God, have mercy on me, noble knight. Honor in me all women and let me live,[30] and take into consideration that I never caused you, gallant man, such heartfelt grief that you could not let me live."

[964] Erec answered him thus, "How can you speak like this? You mock me for no reason. You wanted nothing but my death. Shall you get off so lightly with your confidence and your excessive pride? You would have accepted no ransom in this contest in exchange for my life. Now God has granted me the good fortune that the matter has been reversed. Look, now I can forgo having to offer any ransom for my life. No matter how God protects me elsewhere, I am now very safe from you. If you had held in check a little your arrogance toward me, you see, that would now serve you well. But now your pride has brought about your fall here today and has put you in harm's company."

[986] The knight countered, "What do you mean? I have never deserved your animosity, for I have never seen you before."

[989] But Erec then replied, "Now you shall be shamed at my command as I was yesterday when I, because of you, had to suffer shame that cut me to the heart. I can also foretell here and now regarding you that your dwarf's use of force and his great ill breeding will never serve you as well as they have caused you disgrace today."

[1000] But then the knight answered, "If you have suffered distress through any fault of mine, I am sorry. In addition, your knightly prowess has caused me, on this very spot, to atone for this fault. Deign now to spare my life. And if I have done something for which I should by rights make amends, I shall make up for it completely."

[1010] Erec took pity on him. To the knight he said, "I shall spare you your life, which you would not have done for me." Now the knight gave him his pledge that he was prepared to carry out whatever Erec ordered, since he spared his life.

[1018] When the pledge was given, Erec ordered him to get up. And when they both had then taken off their helmets, Erec said, "Now you must guarantee me this. I insist on it. My lady the queen must be honored to make up for the humiliation she has suffered. You have vexed her greatly, such that she has never experienced anything more painful. You have done great harm to her, and you should atone for this because she greatly laments what happened. Your dwarf struck her maiden yesterday around this time. What's more, he then struck me as well, so that

---

30. In a contest to determine the fairest lady, it would do dishonor to ladies if Erec killed Iders.

I have these marks to show for it. See, it is I, the very same man. I would have ridden after you forever rather than let you escape my revenge. I shall not tolerate being thus flayed here about the face—you cannot deny this—and that your dwarf displayed such ill breeding as to strike the maiden. By rights he must pay for that. I shall tell you why: his ill breeding pleased him so much that he deserves payment for it. I shall not even speak about me. He should not have done that to the maiden. From this dog I shall get a lovely token: nothing less than his hand, so that in the future he honors ladies better."

[1056] Good Erec did not have in mind to actually do this, but really just wanted to warn the dwarf so that he would avoid doing it again. And it did not take much pleading for him to do nothing of the sort. But he did avenge it justly: he ordered two servants to lay him out on a table and thrash him soundly with two sturdy switches so that it showed on his back a good twelve weeks later. His ill breeding was avenged in that blood ran off of him. Everyone alike agreed that he got what he deserved, since he displayed such ill breeding. His name was Maliclisier.[31]

[1078] Erec then said to the knight—his tarrying vexed him—"I don't know why you are waiting and not riding to my lady the queen. You should have left by now. You are to place yourself at her command and act at her behest. Tell her exactly who you are, and about our contest, and who has sent you to her. This is my name: Erec fil de roi Lac. I shall come tomorrow if I can. I shall ride at my leisure, for it is only seven miles[32] there. Think about your pledge." The knight then rode away, he and his lady friend and the little dwarf, in the direction of King Arthur's court.

[1099] Now the king had departed again for his castle in the countryside—the castle was called Karadigan—where the stag was hunted, as I told you earlier.[33] Now it had turned out that King Arthur had caught the white stag by his own hand. The privilege belonging to it now fell to him: that from among all the maidens he should kiss whichever one he wanted.

[1112] When they had returned to Karadigan, the king wanted to make use of the privilege, as was custom. When it had been acknowledged as his right, the queen asked him to postpone it until she had informed him what had happened

31. Perhaps a "speaking name"—a proper name made up of a word or words that mean something in themselves and thus describe a character—since *mal* means bad or evil in Old French.

32. A mile (*mîle*) at this time was more than the modern mile, but a widely variable unit of measurement.

33. This refers to a scene from the missing introduction (see note 2). The annual hunt for the white stag seems to belong to the cycle of spring, when life is renewed, knights set out on adventure, and armies are readied for the summer campaigns.

and what grief had been caused her by the knight in the meadow, and until she had told him exactly how she had fared that very day.

[1124] She said, "Companion of mine, I must lament my troubles to you. My maiden was beaten this way and that, as was Erec, fil de roi Lac. Distressed by this whipping, he took leave from me in the meadow, saying: 'Believe me, my lady, I shall always be a stranger[34] to you in Britanje[35] until I have avenged this disgrace. And if I can get revenge, I shall return in three days.' My lord, tomorrow is the third day. I have both hope and worries regarding the young man and how things are now going with him. I was not able to dissuade him. May God send him back to us. Companion of mine, I now ask of you, for his and my sake, that you not make use of this privilege until you have heard how things have turned out for him. I would like for him to be present too. Wait then only until tomorrow morning. If he is successful, he will come to the ceremony."

[1150] This request was made at the court of Karadigan. Walwan[36] and his friend, Kei the seneschal,[37] had taken each other by the hand[38] and had just left the ladies to keep a lookout from the castle. Both of them saw this knight galloping from afar, out of the forest. They quickly reported this to the queen. She stood up at once, gathered her ladies around her, and went to a window so that she could see who it was who came riding. She and the knights stood there next to one another, uncertain who the knight might be. Then the queen said, "It is surely the man Erec rode after, as far as I can discern at this distance, and as my heart tells me. Look now, there are three of them. The dwarf and the knight's lady friend are riding along with him; it is none other than he. He is coming as though he were riding from a contest. You can see that his shield has been hacked right down to his hand, and that there is blood all over his armor. I must declare to you, either he has killed Erec and is coming here to boast that he gained the victory, or Erec has sent the

---

34. Strong family ties, feudal associations, and friendships were very important in the Middle Ages. The idea of being a "stranger" or "foreigner," not belonging, would be unwelcome. The concept of "stranger" appears frequently in Hartmann and much of medieval literature. See *Gregorius*, note 62.

35. "Britanje" has been translated by some as "Britain," the original home of King Arthur. In some French epics, Arthur's world has been transferred to Britanny, in northwestern France, which shares a historical bond with Britain. In Britanny today there are sites still identified with scenes from Arthurian legend. See lines 9281–82 and *Iwein*, note 6.

36. Walwan has been equated with Gawein. The name *Gawein* is used later in the text (line 1512).

37. The seneschal was one of the five administrative offices of a lord, somewhat equivalent to a chief of staff. The other offices were butler, in charge of the kitchen; the marshal, reponsible for military matters; the chamberlain, who oversaw the lord's finances; and the cupbearer, who attended to the king at table.

38. A common practice in medieval epics. For further examples, see lines 1372 and 9925, and *Gregorius*, line 1929.

defeated knight into this land to the honor of our court. I truly hope it's the latter." They all agreed with the queen that one of the two must be the case.

[1196] Before they had finished speaking, Iders was at that moment riding into the courtyard at Karadigan, up to a stone that was broad and stood raised a bit next to the steps. It had been placed there at the castle so that King Arthur could dismount or mount there. The knight decided he could dismount nowhere better than there, and thus he dismounted quickly at the stone.

[1208] When their horses had been taken away, the knight, with his lady friend and the dwarf, stepped up courteously before the queen. She bade him heartily welcome. He knelt at her feet and said, "Noble lady, receive mercifully into your command a man upon whom God has bestowed no honor. The one I mean is myself. I have acted rashly toward you. No necessity compelled me to do that other than the bidding of my own baseness. And so I shall do penance to you because I have followed the advice of my foolish heart. Too late did I regret it. I did not take heed in time, like the hare caught in the net. My regret at this is great. It is just as people say: pride comes before a fall. I realize this after great disgrace to myself, and it is now clear to me, for he almost took my life along with my honor. I surrender myself as the guilty one. You have suffered grief because of me. I am the one you encountered yesterday in the meadow. It has been to my grief that I allowed my dwarf, in violation of all courtly behavior, to strike the maiden.

[1244] "Erec fil de roi Lac has made me atone well for the insolence of the whipping, as my true guilt demanded of him. He defeated me with his own hand and has sent me here, my lady, so that I might gain your favor for this guilt, and place myself at your service. I have yet more to say. Do not worry about him. He will come himself to see you tomorrow and will bring with him a maiden. No one can say, if he speaks the truth, that he has ever seen one more beautiful."

[1260] Arthur and the queen were heartily pleased at this news and praised our Lord that Erec, although so young, had already had such great success, and that his first knightly deed had turned out so praiseworthy and so completely successful, since he had never undertaken such a thing before. No one bore him any animosity. Only an envious person could do that. Never was one better liked by the people at court, because from childhood on[39] he had served them so well that all were now pleased about his success. The queen said to the knight, "Your penance

---

39. It was customary in the Middle Ages for aristocratic families to send their sons to the castle or court of a higher-placed nobleman. Since Erec's father is a king in his own right, he would send Erec to the court of King Arthur, the most powerful king. Such sons left home at an early age. Compare lines 2866–69.

will be less than you actually deserve. I want you to stay here and be part of our courtly retinue." The knight couldn't argue with that.

[1284] After these words the king said to the knights, "As Erec's reward we should receive him in the proper fashion. By rights we should grant every honor to a man who has served so well. He has begun so well that he is deserving of praise." All the knights agreed with that.

[1294] When things had thus transpired, as you heard earlier, that Erec was successful at Tulmein castle in defeating Iders, who had always been a true hero, and that Lady Enite's position had been proven in a contest, everyone, rich and poor, was very heartily pleased by his good fortune, and all said alike there was no doubt that Erec was the most outstanding man who had ever come to that land. There was no one present who was vexed by his victory. They praised his manly courage. They increased their festivities in his honor.

[1314] A great *buhurt* began,[40] and elsewhere there was dancing. Duke Imain removed Erec's armor, and the maiden, Lady Enite, had him lie down, his head in her lap, so that he could rest after the contest. Her comportment was very shy, like a maiden. She hardly said a word to him because that is the etiquette among maidens. They are at first bashful and shy like children. Later they gain good sense and know well what is good for them, and that something might please them that now seems difficult, and that they would take, wherever they could get it, a sweet kiss over a slap and a good night over a bad day.

[1334] Then Duke Imain requested that he, along with his lady friend, do him the honor of spending the night with him. He asked his niece the same. Erec declined. He answered him thus, "My lord, how could I do this? Should I abandon my host who has done so much good for me? He received me yesterday, he and your sister, although I was completely unknown to him, and in such a way that I must repay him. I know well that he could not do more. He gave me his daughter. Do not, therefore, think badly of me. I shall not abandon him. If I should now turn away from him, he might certainly think he was paying the price for his poverty, which is not the case, God knows. I am very happy to stay with him. I shall let him see that I am true to him. And if we should only live half a year, I shall make him rich, truly, unless I don't have the means. I shall not change my mind, and I shall arrange it that he was never richer."

---

40. A *buhurt* was a mock battle and was normally held outside the castle. The jousting in a *buhurt* was done with blunted lances; it was not, however, without some danger. Monastic sources in particular were quick to criticize the practice. See *Gregorius*, line 1585 and note 71.

[1364] Then Duke Imain replied, "Since you do not wish to stay with me, then we shall remain with you and accompany you to your quarters." Erec, the lord, thanked him very sincerely for this, as did Erec's father-in-law. They then stood up, took each other by the hand, and went to their quarters, leading Lady Enite at their sides, between them. She felt great joy, because on her hand she carried the sparrow hawk that had been won. That was indeed a cause for joy. Thus the maiden had happily won praise and great honor. But she had greater joy, as well she should, because of her beloved husband, whom she had won there this day.

[1386] For anyone who did not find pleasure annoying, there was entertainment aplenty. By their quarters there was a great swarm of people. There that evening Erec saw innumerable guests, knights and ladies, because they invited all who came there to the festivities. Lady Enite's father could not have covered the costs. The duke took care of that. Food enough was brought in from his castle.

[1400] When the next day came, Erec fil de roi Lac did not want to tarry there any longer. He felt the time pressing and said he had to ride on and take Lady Enite with him. Her uncle, the duke of Tulmein, asked that he be allowed to clothe her better. Erec rejected that. The duke offered him gold and silver. Erec said he had no need of that. He refused both war horses and clothing, except that he accepted from a cousin of hers—a maiden who lived with the duke, it was said, and was his relative—a palfrey suitable for her to ride.[41] The cousin beseeched him, in such a friendly manner and for so long, to take it, that he took it from her. And mark this well: never before in the world had anyone received a more beautiful palfrey.

[1426] It was neither too strong nor too weak, its color as white as ermine, its mane thick and wavy, [its chest strong and broad,][42] and its build neither too large nor too small. It carried its head at the right height, and was gentle and well-dispositioned, with long flanks. One could ride it well. Its back and feet were just fine. Oh, how very gently it carried its rider! It galloped fast across the field in a beautiful fashion, gliding like a ship. In addition it went gently and never stumbled. The saddle was such that it suited the palfrey very well. The metalwork was as it should be: of red gold. What good would a long story be of how it was crafted? I must keep silent about much of that, because if I were to tell you everything, the story would be much too long. I shall end my praise with very few words: the saddle girths were embroidered.

41. There is a distinction between the horses Erec says he does not need, the war horse, or *ros*, being a large horse capable of carrying a knight, and the *pherit*, or palfrey, Erec accepts from Enite's cousin.

42. Here and following, lines in brackets are questionable in the manuscript tradition but are retained to preserve the customary numbering.

[1454] When these were tightened on it,[43] the journey was delayed no longer. With many hot tears lady Enite took leave as befits a daughter who is riding off to a strange land away from her beloved mother. Her mother said, "Almighty, merciful God, deign to take care of my daughter." Solemn declarations made the blessing longer. The parting caused many tears from both of them, and also from Enite's father. He asked our Lord God to watch over her. Erec said to the old man that when his messenger came to him he should do whatever he was asked by him, because he, Erec, intended to help him out of his poverty. The old man knelt down at his feet and was pleased at the hope of it. They then took leave of all the household there, parted quickly, and rode away. Erec did not allow anyone to ride with him. Wishing them good fortune he asked them to remain there.

[1484] When they both came out to the open meadow, Erec gazed at his intended. She too looked quite often and shyly at her betrothed. Quite often they exchanged loving glances. Their hearts were full of love. They pleased each other very well and more and more. Hate and envy gained no footing there. Loyalty and constancy took hold of them.

[1498] Now they rode very fast because he had promised to arrive that same day. From the queen's story all the noble knights knew exactly what time he was expected to come. They had also heard this from the knight who had come and whom he had defeated. Their horses were ready. That was the reward for his knightly prowess. Together with King Arthur there rode out from the castle[44] Gawein and Persevaus, a lord with the name King Iels of Galoes, and Estorz fil roi Ares. Lucans the cupbearer appeared in the company, as well as the entire retinue, so that all could receive him amicably and well, with knightly revelry, as one should a dear friend who was lost and found again. At the same time, my lady the queen crossed the courtyard toward him to receive him. She bade him welcome. She was happy about his adventure. She took Lady Enite aside and said to her, "My lovely maiden and lady, you should have a change of clothes."

[1532] The noble queen led her into her private chambers. A bath was prepared for her there, and she was bathed most lavishly after her hardships. The lady with the crown dressed her dear guest, for a very expensive dress lay there ready. With

43. This line has been interpreted in various ways. The German reads: *alz ez im gezogen wart*. The neuter pronoun *ez* could refer to the *phert* and thus its being led out (*gezogen*) for Erec (*im*), and thus for Enite. But if one believes that the horse has already been brought out by the cousin (thus the description), then *ez* could refer to the saddle girths (a plural noun not requiring a plural pronoun in Middle High German) and their being cinched (*gezogen*) and made ready for Enite.

44. A customary show of respect. The greater the distance, the greater the homage. For another example, see further line 2896 and *Gregorius*, note 117.

her own hands she laced the maiden into a shift made of white silk. She covered the shift—that brought about praise—with a gown of fine cut, in the French style,[45] neither too tight nor too loose. It was of green samite with wide borders with which she adorned her, with spun gold on both sides, as is fitting, on each of the edges. In addition, Lady Enite was also belted around her waist with a belt from Hibernia,[46] which ladies like to wear. On her bosom was set a broach as wide as a hand. It was a bright ruby. Yet the maiden completely surpassed its radiance with her glowing coloring. The gown was surrounded and covered with a mantle that fit well. The lining was ermine, the outer material a rich ciclatoun.[47] This majestic clothing was trimmed at the wrists with sable. A ribbon held her hair together. It was an appropriate width and was laid crosswise across her head. So great was the radiance of her headdress that there could not have been a better ribbon. Her clothing was rich, she herself distinguished.

[1579] Now Lady Poverty covered her head in great shame, for she had been very boldly robbed of her dwelling. She had to withdraw then and flee from her house. Wealth moved into her home. As beautiful as the maiden had looked in poor clothes, it is said that she now, in rich clothing, was very worthy of praise. I would like to praise her very gladly, as I should, but I am not so clever a man. I am lacking, and have no knowledge of such skills. Besides, many a clever mouth has taken upon itself the praise of women, so that I would not know what kind of praise I might invent that had not been said better to women before now. She must remain without her deserved praise from me, because, fool that I am, I am lacking the ability to do it. Yet I shall relate matters as best I can and as I heard them: there can be no doubt that it was Lady Enite who, it is said, was the most beautiful maiden ever to come to the king's court.

[1611] The queen took her amicably by the hand and went to where she found the king sitting in his rightful place with many a brave knight at the Round Table. Of those who sat there then or later, one of them had, without dispute, the greatest claim to fame. All of them said this, because by all accounts he had never committed a thoughtless act and had such numerous virtues that still today he is reckoned among the most outstanding men ever to have had a place there. Thus he had every right to his seat there, did Gawein the brave knight.

45. The German is *kerlingisch*, Carolingian, referring here to the western part of the former Carolingian empire, the cultural and literary model for Hohenstaufen (eastern) Germany. Compare *The Lament*, line 1280.

46. That is, Ireland. Artistic imports (e.g., jewelry, illustrations) from Ireland were numerous and greatly prized.

47. A silk material interwoven with gold thread.

[1630] Also there were Erec fil de roi Lac, and Lanzelot von Arlac and Gornemanz von Groharz, and li bels Coharz,[48] and Lais hardiz,[49] and Meljanz von Liz, and Maldwiz li sages,[50] and the impetuous Dodines, and brave Gandelus. Next to him sat Esus, then the knight Brien, and Iwein fil li roi Urien, and Iwan von Lonel, who was quick to seek every kind of honor.

[1644] More of them sat there too: Iwan von Lafultere, and Onam von Galiot, and Gasosin von Strangot. Sitting right next to him was the one called The Knight with the Golden Bow, and Tristram and Garel, Bliobleherin and Titurel, Garedeas von Brebas, Gues von Strauz, and Baulas, Gaueros von Rabedic, and the son of the King von Ganedic, Lis von quinte carous,[51] and Isdex von mun dolerous,[52] Ither von Gaheviez, Maunis, and Galez the Bald, Grangodoans and Gareles, and Estorz fil Ares, Galagaundris and Galoes, and fil Dou Giloles,[53] Lohut fil roi Arthur,[54] Segremors and Praueraus, Blerios and Garredoinechschin, Los and Troimar lo mechschin,[55] Brien lingo mathel,[56] and Equinot fil cont Haterel,[57] Lernfras fil Gain, and Henec suctellois fil Gawin,[58] Le and Gahillet, Maneset von Hochturasch, and Batewain fil roy Cabcaflir,[59] [. . .][60] Galopamur, this is true, fil Isabon, and Schonebar, Lanfal and Brantrivier, Malivliot von Katelange,[61] and Barcinier, loyal Gothardelen, Gangier von Neranden, and Scos, his brother, bold Lespin, and Machmerit Parcefal von Glois, and Seckmur von Rois, Inpripalenot and Estravagaot, Pehpimerot and Lamendragot, Oruogodelet, and Affibla delet,[62] Arderoch Amander, and Ganatulander, Lermebion von Jarbes, fil Mur defemius a quater bardes.[63] Now I have named for you the entire gallant company. Their exact number was forty and a hundred overall.[64]

48. Coharz the Beautiful.
49. Lais the Bold.
50. Maldwiz the Wise.
51. Lis of the Five Broad Swords.
52. Isdex of Pain Mountain.
53. Son of Duke Giloles.
54. This is Arthur's son from a prior relationship.
55. Troimar the Boy.
56. Brien Quick Tongue.
57. Son of Count Haterel.
58. Henec the Skillful, son of Gawin.
59. Son of King Cabcaflir.
60. There is a lacuna in the manuscript at this point.
61. Perhaps Catalonia, an area in northeastern Spain and southeastern France.
62. Affibla the Merry.
63. Son of Mur of the Fourfold Armor.
64. Only seventy-five are named due to the lacuna.

[1698] Now the queen led Enite toward the group. She was completely the embodiment of beauty. If the red of roses were poured among the whiteness of lilies, and were that to flow together, and were a mouth entirely the color of roses, thus was her appearance. Never had been seen a lady more fitting for a knight.

[1708] When she first walked over to them from the door and saw them sitting there, she was uncomfortable and embarrassed. Her rose color faded. First red and then pale she grew in turns at the sight, in such a way as I shall tell you: when the sun on a bright day has its full radiance, and suddenly in front of it a thin, narrow cloud passes, then its radiance is no longer so great as it was before. Thus for a moment the maiden Enite felt slightly troubled because she was embarrassed.

[1726] When she stepped in through the door, her beautiful face regained its magnificent color and was more beautiful than before. How well it became her when her coloring changed! That came from great embarrassment, because she had never seen sitting together so many heroes, the elite of gallant men.

[1736] When the maiden entered, those who sat at the Round Table were startled by her beauty, such that they forgot themselves and stared at the maiden. There was no one who would not have considered her the most beautiful maiden he had ever seen. The king went to meet her. He took her, Lady Enite, by the hand, and had her sit next to him, and on the other side the virtuous queen.

[1750] Now it also seemed to the king that the time had come for him to quickly end the knightly dispute. You know—you have already heard that—that he was to exercise his privilege, because things had turned out so well for him in capturing the white stag, of kissing on the mouth the lady who by common aclaim was the most beautiful there. Up to now he had put this off at the queen's request. Now there was no argument among them that Enite was the most beautiful lady there, and anywhere in the world. And I can tell you exactly how her beauty surpassed that of the others: it was as though on a dark night the stars were unobstructed so that one could see them well and had to honestly say that they were very lovely as long as nothing more beautiful appeared. But when the time at night comes for the moon to rise, then one considers their beauty to be nothing when compared with the moon. They would seem praiseworthy if the moon were not there, and if it had not extinguished them with its shining brightness. Thus did her coloring completely dim that of the other ladies. The king hurried unbidden to observe the custom, as his father had bequeathed him—his father was Utpandragon—of taking the kiss there and from nowhere else than where the brave knights had granted it to him as his right. The king rose and quickly claimed the right from his nephew's lady friend. That could pass without any animosity, for Erec was his relative.

[1797] Now a great joy arose at the castle of Karadigan. That was done for Erec's sake and for his lady friend. Where could there be greater joy than what one had there at all times? All those present vied with each other in merriment.

[1806] Then the gallant and very chivalrous Erec thought of the poverty of his father-in-law, and through a messenger sent to his home riches that King Arthur had given him: two pack animals with a very heavy load. They carried silver and gold—for Erec loved Koralus's daughter—so that Koralus could clothe himself elegantly and equip himself well in order to ride to the land of Erec's father. It was called Destrigales. Through his messenger he asked his father, King Lac, to place under his aged father-in-law's rule two castles that he named in his land so that they might become Koralus's own property. He designated them by name: Montrevel and Roadan. That all was carried out. When he had taken possession of the castles, the noble man was compensated for whatever had plagued him. He was completely without need. He was made so wealthy that he could live with them in distinguished fashion, as befitted his nobility.

[1838] Now we shall again take up the story we had already begun. When Erec had come to the court and the king had claimed his right, Lady Enite, who sat there like an angel, through her beauty and goodness aroused Erec's heart to yearn very longingly for her. The days seemed to him too long to wait any longer than the next night for her love. She too privately harbored for him similar feelings so that they probably would have ended in some kind of loving play, had no one seen it.

[1857] Truly, I can tell you, Lady Love was the victor there. Love ruled them both and troubled them greatly. When one looked at the other, it was no different for the two of them than for a hawk that by chance catches sight of its prey when hunger drives it. And if the prey is shown to it and it cannot do without it, then that is worse for the hawk than if it had never seen the prey. Waiting pained them just like that and even more. The thoughts of both of them went like this: indeed, I shall never be happy unless I lie with you two or three nights. Their senses desired a different kind of love—measured to fit them—than when a child who has been left alone longs for its mother who has accustomed it to good things whenever she greets him, and who holds her hands in front of him to protect him from harm. It was no small thing they desired, which they later did gain.

[1887] Now the wedding day arrived, which made them both happy. Gallant King Arthur insisted that he should have the wedding at his castle for the enjoyment of his land. Immediately he sent out, wherever he could, letters and invitations so that the princes and all those who heard the news would come from far and wide to the festivities. The wedding date was set for the week of Pentecost.[65]

[1902] Now I shall name for you all the counts and also the company of princes who came to the festivities when Erec took Enite as his wife. There were mighty guests: Count Brandes von Doleceste—he brought in his company five hundred men whose fittings were praiseworthy and who were all dressed as he was—and Count Margon, born in Glufion; the lords of Alte Montanje[66]—which is near Britanje—and Count Libers von Treverin with one hundred men; the mighty Count Gundregoas, and Lord Maheloas, called The Knight from Glass Island, because his land was such that no storm actually ever occurred there. Then, too, it was very pleasant there because no one ever saw vermin there. It was neither cold nor hot, and this is the truth. Gresmurs Fine Posterne—whom one was glad to see there—and his brother by the name of Gimoers—the island of Avalon was his land. His good fortune was hardly slight for he loved a fairy by the name of Marguel. Davit von Luntaguel came too. Duke Guelguezins came there with a magnificent company; his realm was called Hohe Bois.[67] Now I have enumerated for you all the dukes and counts.

[1941] Listen as well now to the number of kings. There were ten of them in number, five young and five old, all powerful and rich. They had joined together in knightly fashion: the young with their kind, the old with the old; moderation[68] was preserved. The young had, it is said, like mounts and like clothing; the old were likewise, accordingly as befitted them. Now I shall describe the clothing of the young: velvet and ciclatoun were together in various colors and lined with different kinds of fur, cut exactly in accordance with their wishes, neither too tight nor too loose. [The horses that the young rode] were completely black as a raven and went at a trot. These rode out ahead into the land. Each of them carried on his arm a falcon that had molted four times.[69] This group was praiseworthy. Each

---

65. In Arthurian literature Pentecost is a favorite time for celebrations, as spring in general in the Middle Ages had great significance, as the end of a long, cold winter and the beginning of the agricultural and military seasons. It is the setting for much of medieval love poetry. The Old French prose *Lancelot of the Lake* (c. 1225) describes when Arthur held court, "Il ne tenoit cort esforciee de porter corone que cinq foiz l'an: ce estoit a Pasques, a l'Encension, a Pantecoste, a la feste Toz Sainz et a Noel" (chap. 18) [He held plenary court, where he wore the crown, only five times a year: Easter, Ascension Day, Pentecost, All Saints' Day, and Christmas]. See note 2. In Wolfram von Eschenbach's *Parzival* (trans. Helen M. Mustard and Charles E. Passage [New York: Random House, 1961]), Arthur is called "the man of May" (6.281).

66. Old mountain region.

67. Timber forest.

68. Moderation (*mâze*) is one of the key elements of the knightly ethos.

69. That is, four years old. A bird that had molted more often was more valuable. Compare line 2032.

of them brought there three hundred men in his company. Great care had been taken with their clothing. The first was King Carniz—his land was called Schorces—and the King of Scotland, Angwisiez, with his two sons—the one was Coin and the other Goasilroet; and King Beals von Gomoret.[70] These were the young knights.

[1979] Now came in their majesty five old and powerful kings. They too had like mounts and clothing. They had put on an attire that befitted their age. It was, as one heard regarding them, the best brunet[71] that could be found in all of England. The fur lining was gray, such that no one could find better anywhere, neither in Russia nor in Poland. Their clothing was long and full. Sewn everywhere on it was wide gold leaf. The work was as it was supposed to be: beautiful and elegant and so artful that one must praise it fully. The cuffs were finished in wide sable. The sable was such that no one ever found better or more precious in all of Connelant.[72] The sultan rules this land, for it is subject to him. It is long and wide. Conne lies locked between the lands of the Greeks[73] and the heathens. The best sable the world has ever seen comes from there. That was the outer clothing of the princes. Underneath they had also put on rich furs that went well with their outer attire. The hats of each were made of very fine sable. They had magnificent mounts, as I shall tell you. Their horses were snow white. Great care was taken with them as befits powerful old kings. Their harnesses were also magnificent, radiant from the fine gold. The metalwork, as it should be, was inlaid with silver and bright gold plate; the saddle girths had wide bands of silk.

[2029] When this company rode into the land of Britanje, a beautiful falcon of six moultings or more sat on the hand of each. They were entertained well on the three-mile journey. They found good hawking there: both creeks and ponds were full of ducks. They found plenty of whatever falcons catch. Never had one seen hunting birds undertake so many beautiful flights.

[2043] They saw rise up in front of them ducks and partridges and herons and pheasants, and cranes on the meadows, and wild geese. On this day their squires had their saddles hanging full of bustards, because everything that had been flushed was caught. The fields were entirely cleared [of birds and game]. Wherever a rabbit was flushed, that was its last run. When they had ridden on after hawking and

---

70. We might count the kings differently. There are three kings and two princes, that is, (possible) future kings, who, however, might have already been crowned during their fathers' lifetimes.

71. A dark woolen cloth.

72. Iconium in Asia Minor. An example of the influences of the Crusades.

73. That is, of Byzantium.

were arguing in a friendly fashion, a certain quarrel arose among them: each one maintained, just as one still does today, that his falcon had flown the best there.

[2064] Now King Arthur, with his entire retinue, rode toward them from his castle and received the splendid company with great honor. He was very glad at their coming. The noble knights were received as was their right and were lodged even better. I shall name for you the old kings: there was King Jernis von Riel, distinguished and wise. He brought with him there a praiseworthy company of three hundred men. Now hear about their age: the hair of their heads and their beards was completely snow-white and had grown so long that it hung down to their belts. The youngest of all—this is true—was one hundred and forty years old.

[2086] Hear now about the rest: the dwarf king Bilei and his brother, Brians by name. Their land was called Antipodes. No children of one mother, who are called brothers, could be more dissimilar than Brians and Bilei. Our truthful source tells us that Brians was taller by one and a half spans[74] than anyone at that time in all the lands far and wide. In addition, we are told that there never was, nor is now, a dwarf shorter than Bilei. What he lacked in size the small guest made up in courage. Regarding wealth one could not find someone equally rich. He arrived in magnificent fashion. His entourage was large. He also brought there two friends who were also lords of lands of dwarfs. These two were called Grigoras and Glecidolan. I have finished naming the kings. King Arthur, at his castle in Karadigan, received these mighty guests as best he could.

[2118] Now the day had come when Erec fil de roi Lac was to take Lady Enite as his wife. Why should they wait any longer, for both were happy about it. They were given in marriage by the bishop of Canterbury from England. Festivities then began that were accorded great praise. No poverty appeared there. There were so many brave knights there that I can tell you but little about their gluttony, for they paid more attention to honorable comportment than to gorging themselves. Therefore I shall only speak briefly about the service. There was an abundance of everything that men and horses live on. This was offered them without measure, but each took only as much as befits a man.

[2142] A *buhurt* and dancing began as soon as the meal was finished, and lasted until night. Sadness was hidden away. If they had been troubled, they now had joy as great. They went to the ladies who received them properly. The hospitality there was good. In addition, their hearts were delighted by very sweet string music and

74. A span was the length of the hand, when extended, between the tip of the thumb and the tip of the little finger, about nine inches.

many other kinds of entertainment such as storytelling, singing, and lively acrobatics.[75] Skill in all these arts could be found there, and masters in every field. Present were three thousand minstrels and more who were the very best the world had ever seen and who were called masters. Never was there greater honor, neither before nor since, than at these festivities.[76]

[2166] No matter who came there from among the people and was paid for their words of praise, no one was turned away. Vagabonds have the following behavior: when someone gives one of them a lot and another one nothing, they become spiteful because of this and curse the festivities. Nobody there got caught up in this squabble because all were equally wealthy. People gave very generously. Thirty gold marks[77] were given to many a man who previously had never received as much as half a pound. All were given so much that it will probably never happen again.

[2183] Both horses and clothing were given to the poor people for whom no one had earlier had any concern. Great care was thus taken so that no one grew envious of anyone else's possessions. They were all given enough. Nobody had any cause to be ashamed; all were immediately given something. They kept on receiving things until the festivities ended on the fourteenth day. Thus Erec fil de roi Lac was married.

[2196] When the wedding came to an end, many an eloquent minstrel parted joyfully with hands full. All spoke with one loud voice about the festivities: they wished Erec and Lady Enite all good fortune. This was their prospect for a long time and many a year to come. This wish was fulfilled completely, for never were two people more in love until it was ended by death, which turns all love to sorrow[78] when it separates love from love. The princes who had come there also wanted to take their leave. The host extended the festivities a further fourteen days. He did this for Erec's sake, since Erec lay close to his heart, and also for Lady Enite. At the second festivities they had pleasures as before, not less, but more.

[2222] Now many said it would not be proper if such a brave man were to take leave without a tournament being held, since they had come to their land of

75. Minstrels often performed all three skills.
76. It is possible that Hartmann has in mind here the great festival held by Friedrich Barbarossa, Holy Roman Emperor, in 1184 (at Pentecost) to celebrate the knighting of his two sons Heinrich (later Heinrich VI) and Friedrich. Although other medieval poets make specific reference to the events of the festival, Hartmann's presence cannot be proven, and it is not certain if *Erec* was composed before or after the famous celebration. Hartmann's description of the festivities resembles accounts of other celebrations in other epics. It is true, however, that medieval nobles sometimes modeled their feasts after those described in literature, so one can ask who is imitating whom? Compare also *Iwein*, lines 31ff.
77. A vast sum of money. Compare *Gregorius*, line 715.
78. See *Gregorius*, note 26.

Britanje for this pleasure. Gawein replied at once that they should have their tournament there as well. He then quickly arranged for one against these four companions whose names you will now hear: Entreferich and Tenebroc and Meliz and Meljadoc.[79] The tournament was set for three weeks from the following Monday. According to my source, the tournament was to take place between Tarebron and Prurin, which was equidistant to them, halfway in between. These four men now took their leave so that they might prepare themselves, for it was not too early for them.

[2247] Erec fil de roi Lac deliberated long how he might go there and do his name proud, because before this time he had never entered a tournament. He thought a lot about how the reputation a young man acquires in the first years may easily be kept forever. He feared long-lasting reproach, and his thoughts took even greater care as to how he might do well there. He was not rich enough to satisfy completely his desires concerning wealth. Whatever he lacked, however—this was because he was a stranger there, far from his land—Arthur, his lord, provided him with all that he asked for. Yet Erec was considerate toward him and did not ask for too much from him. He bade the king, whenever he could, to be sparing in his generosity, as befitted his sense of modesty. He would have worked miracles had he had a free hand to do what he wished. He made up his mind according to what his circumstances now were. Neither his armor nor his entourage were as good as they would have been had he had wealth. He started out according to his means.

[2285] Now the young man readied three similar shields as well as three sets of riding equipment, all with the same coat of arms yet different in color. The one shield was suitable for the charge, on the outside shiny like a mirror—its reflection gleamed far in the distance—the inside out of gold. On it hung a golden sleeve in the right proportion.[80] The second shield was bright red. He ordered fixed to it a sleeve of shining silver that had been fashioned so carefully that a better one could not be produced in such a short time. On the inside it was like the first one. It was very knightly. The third shield was completely golden in color inside and out. On it was a sleeve of sable that could not be better, and a boss was laid over it. The clasps, of silver, spread beautifully, neither too broad nor too narrow, encompassed the entire frame. The sleeve was attached to this. On the inside a lady was depicted on the upper edge. The shield's strap was a cord with precious stones. This was not the only one; on the inside the straps were all alike.

---

79. These are place-names in Chrétien.
80. This was usually a token of affection given by a lady.

[2320] Now he readied with care, as quickly as he could, three similar banners, each like one of the shields. In addition, young Erec acquired with the help of Arthur, king of Britanje, five Spanish chargers, helmets from Poitiers, hauberks from Schamliers, and greaves[81] from Glenis. The lord, young and prudent, carried with each charger ten lances from Lofanige—the shafts being from Etelburc[82]—painted for the tournament. His helmet was magnificently decorated: an angel appeared in a crown wrought in gold.[83] His tabard and caparison matched exactly. They were of green velvet blended with costly silk and decorated with embroidery. He obtained fifteen squires,[84] so agile that no one ever found better in the entire land of Britanje. The outfitting of each was excellent: armor and an iron helmet and a finely studded truncheon. A cart carried his lances to where the tournament was to take place, between Tarebron and Prurin, before Erec was finished getting ready. As I told you earlier, the time for the tournament had come, and many brave knights were arriving there.

[2358] When Erec was about to set out and part from Lady Enite, there took place between the two beloved an exchange of loyalty, and I shall tell you exactly what kind: the man in true devotion took her heart with him, and his remained with his wife, locked away in her body.[85]

[2368] On Saturday night King Arthur arrived there with his entire force of warriors. He brought his entire retinue. The best were fed and housed along the way. They engaged in knightly revelry. Everywhere the lodgings were decked out in lights, in fact, all through the night.

[2378] Erec lodged there at a place away from the others. He did not engage in revelry. He lived as a very thrifty man, not wasteful, and did not want to act like a great knight, and rightly so. Extravagance was allowable for those who, unlike him, had often tourneyed before. He did not think he had come fully to that point, nor had his manly courage been so tested that he could allow himself such things. If one of his companions sought out his lodgings for friendship's sake, he was received there warmly and bidden more welcome there than anywhere else. If Erec was not

81. Leg armor covering the shins.
82. A mixture of real (Poitiers) and fictional places.
83. The great collection of medieval German poetry, *Die Manessische Liederhandschrift*, does indeed, in the accompanying portrayals of the poets, display similarly fantastical helmets. It dates, however, from some one hundred years after *Erec*.
84. Some of the squires' duties were to transport lances and other equipment, take captured horses, and protect a fallen knight.
85. For a similar image when lovers part, see *Gregorius*, lines 651–54, and the poem "By rights I must ever hold dear the day," lines 9–10.

able to offer other things, his good will was so obvious that everyone was happy whenever they could praise him. All who saw him loved him. He acted like a child of Good Fortune. Otherwise one would not have spoken so well of him.

[2404] Now these knights led a life with the usual abundance of pleasures, as is customary at tournaments. On Sunday morning they did what was necessary: they ordered their chain mail to be polished and fitted with straps. There was no one at all who was not worthy of tourneying.

[2413] When midday had scarcely arrived, Erec fil de roi Lac armed himself quickly before anyone else so that he could participate in the first joust and get ahead of the others wherever he might find the opportunity. Now, at the same time, two companions of his, brave knights having the same desire, had ridden out, and when they had seen him they started riding toward him full of confidence. The one jousted with him. Erec knocked him off his charger. The same thing happened to the other knight. Erec did not concern himself with their horses,[86] but instead sought further knightly activity. He received honor and praise for jousting five times, so well that no knight was better. This happened because of two favors he had: Good Fortune and the great esteem that God had bestowed on him.

[2440] These jousts he had undertaken before anyone had come out onto the jousting field, for it had been very early. But now they rode out toward him from every side. To his great renown everyone saw the horses galloping back and forth, after he had knocked the knights from them. They all said, "By God, who could have relieved these horses of their riders? Surely it was Erec." He was greatly praised for this.

[2453] Now the vesper tournament,[87] in all its splendor, began quickly in the middle of the jousting field. The knightly contest was especially good because the strength on both sides was completely equal.[88] There was plenty of knightly jousting and the clashing together of lances and the striking of swords. As long as the tournament lasted, Erec fil de roi Lac was constantly active. Whoever wanted to watch him could never let his eyes rest. He was seen here and there. Never had a knight tourneyed better. All attention was on him alone. He was always the first one there and then the last to leave. On this evening Erec gained praise from both sides. They affirmed this without dispute.

[2476] He rode until night stopped him. When all had returned to their quarters, no other talk was heard than, "Erec fil de roi Lac is the most capable man of

86. The victor gained the vanquished opponent's horse, a valuable commodity.

87. The "vesper" (from the Latin, meaning "eve") tournament was the preamble to the larger tournament the next day.

88. Two sides, two "armies," would be drawn up for the *mêlée*, a tumultuous affair.

his years that our land has ever had. He could not have conducted himself better." This was said emphatically. He gained great fame from what was said about him that evening.

[2487] When the next day dawned Erec arose. His first step was chivalrous: he went to church[89] and commended himself to the One Whose abundance of mercy has never run dry. Never has there been a truly upright man who was denied His help, because whoever has Him before his eyes in all his affairs can count on succeeding. Erec trusted in Him completely for his knightly honor that He might deign to preserve it.

[2501] When the benediction had been given, his shield and charger were made ready. His boldness seemed to me very noteworthy in that he came out to the jousting field without armor and companions, except that he brought five squires with him. Each of them carried three lances. These he used up in regular jousts, with no armor, without anyone from his side noticing it. After this success he stole back to them as though nothing had happened.

[2516] Now Lady Rumor[90] had sent a page out early to the jousting field to observe what had happened to Erec to increase his honor and praise. The well-spoken page reported this to King Arthur. Those Arthur found still lying in bed he chastised and scolded for being asleep. He said, "Why are you lying here? Who has ever won honor by sleeping? Erec has used his lance and sword very well today. May God grant him success whenever he desires it. I shall always speak well of him. I have seen him do such manly deeds that he will always be honored for them." Thus Erec won more friends for himself and was praised more than ever.

[2538] Erec then took only a short rest, for as soon as he returned to them they all came out and heard mass as those should do who want to take part in a tournament. He ate and drank a little. The thought of getting back to the contest did not allow him to eat or drink much. They all armed themselves in an amazingly quick fashion; Erec did the same. That had hardly happened when they saw their four companions, Entreferich, Tenebroc, Meliz, and Meljadoc, speed across the jousting field with their banners. They exhibited great strength and bold, knightly bearing, and had many costly banners of various colors.

[2560] Erec and Gawein and whatever knights were there sallied forth at once. A number of battle cries could be heard in front of the banners. Erec engaged them first as befits a knight. Tabard and crown distinguished him readily such that no

---

89. Exemplary behavior for a knight. Compare *Gregorius*, lines 2080ff.
90. In Roman mythology Fama (Rumor) was the daughter of Terra, the earth deified.

other knight was recognizable at such a distance. Sir Erec rode out ahead just so far that he had room to joust.[91] A brave man rode at him. The proud Lando held the others back from jousting. Without a doubt he had earlier proven himself so often that he was considered one of the best in his land. Erec succeeded so well that he knocked him from his charger. He distinguished himself very well in that he used up twelve more lances in contests between the two groups. His great ability kept him from any harm.

[2589] He did this so long until his shield was hacked up and so pierced with blows that it was no good to him. As carefully as he could, he withdrew from them. He put down his shield, got off his charger, mounted another one, and equipped himself with a new shield and with a new banner. He had just finished doing that when he saw his side riding toward him. He could no longer joust alone between the two groups. Now there were many sword blows and lance thrusts and many a lance splintered when the knights on both sides clashed together with such unbridled fury. The din of the lances could only be compared to a forest falling from the power of the wind. Erec fil de roi Lac distinguished himself before all others, because on this Monday he had freed many a charger from its rider. He quickly turned them loose and took none of them because he had not come there for booty. His intention was solely to win honor. I can also assure you that he spared himself little. Now that the tournament had begun, he was often seen nowhere else but in the mêlée, where he had to receive and give blows. He was seen fighting bravely.

[2630] When Erec had jousted long and hard and had struck with his sword until he grew tired, he left them to go rest up. When he dismounted, a hireling took his charger and humbly thanked him. His rest did not last long. By the time he had untied his helmet, his squires were immediately on the spot and loosened his head covering[92] so that he could cool off. But he had no opportunity to do so, since he saw his own side draw back in retreat, yet slowly. They yielded more and more. It seemed to him they were being put to shame.

[2649] So quickly did he rush for his charger that he forgot his helmet. He mounted with his head bare. By chance he grabbed both shield and lance. He waited no longer and went riding toward them smartly with his banner. If he had not come quickly to the aid of his side, they would have had to suffer a loss and been put to shame. This was evident from the fact that they all retreated. From his entire side no one put up a fight except for these three men: noble Sir Gawein,

---

91. That is, had enough room to take his jousting run.
92. The tight-fitting head covering worn under the helmet.

who had truly never suffered humiliation and who enjoyed every virtue. Fil Dou Gilules[93] and Segremors stayed by him. These three stood firm against them. You should know that they battled better than three knights ever did, because neither with thrusts nor blows could they be budged from the spot. Yet they would have been captured, and that would have happened because of the others' superior strength—the master of all things against which no one can do anything—if Erec fil de roi Lac had not come galloping up boldly like the roaring wind, as befits a friend in time of need. His manly courage was so great that he quickly turned them all to flight. Once more he had to struggle fiercely with his own hands or things would have turned out differently for him.

[2691] When his side had seen this, they turned around on the spot. Boidurant jousted against Erec. Erec also unseated this noble knight with his lance. For this he won much praise. In a short time he alone put the opponents to shame, driving them back a good third of a mile. His companions came to his aid with their force and pushed them back without resistance almost to their boundary. He gave away his third charger. His companions profited handsomely, which would not have happened without him. Many a man enjoyed his presence that day and won much because of him. Their booty was great. He was thanked for this, and it was all the more appropriate for them to speak of his honor. They considered it a great deed that Erec, though his head was bare, did not avoid an unprotected situation and rode to their aid so magnificently, and so boldly put the opponent to flight.

[2720] Gawein battled that day as bravely as ever, as was his custom. It was such, they say, that no one ever heard say of him—in whatever he did where one distinguished oneself with knightly deeds—that someone had outdone him. For this reason he is still renowned. He was chivalrous in spirit. In him there appeared nothing but good. He was sufficiently rich and noble. His heart bore no one ill will. He was loyal and generous without regretting it later, steadfast and well bred, his words without deceit; he was strong, handsome, and manly. He possessed the strength of all virtues; he was cheerful and very courteous. Perfection had made him so—as we have truthfully heard—that never had such a perfect man come to the court of King Arthur. How well he fit in with Arthur's retinue! He made every effort to gain honor. That day he demonstrated exceptionally great manly courage. Except for Erec fil de roi Lac no one won more there, for he won both possessions and honor.

[2752] He had immediately captured two knights: the one was called Ginses, the other Gaudin de Montein. Gawein had captured them. On this one day I place

---

93. The son of Duke Gilules.

Erec fil de roi Lac higher. I dare not do it for any longer period, because it is said that Gawein's equal never came to Britanje. But if one were ever to come, that could well be Erec. This was apparent from his knightly abilities.

[2764] When their opponents had then been driven to their boundary, as I told you, Erec asked whether anyone still wished to come forth to joust, for the honor of his lady. Immediately a knight called Roiderodes said that he wished to joust if it were a friendly joust.[94] This pleased Erec greatly. He swore the joust would be friendly. Erec rode out toward him on the jousting field, for his manly courage was undaunted. He had often shown this.

[2780] They were eager to get at each other. They both used up twelve lances, never missing the mark. Gallant Erec now quickly sprang from his steed and gave it away. He mounted a fifth that stood ready for him. It was his earnest intention to end the matter. He did not want them to wait any longer. He asked that the course be cleared. He slapped his lance up under his arm. An able will drove them together. Erec struck him such that Roiderodes felt the four nails of his shield against his hand.[95] He stuck him so hard that the horse's breastplate straps broke. Cinch and surcingle snapped as if they were rotten bast. Roiderodes was left with a miserable token: broken reins in his hand. At this mishap he fell a good three lengths of a lance behind his steed. Erec was praised greatly for staying in his saddle; he gained honor for that. There was no more to be done.

[2808] The tournament now came to an end. The king's retinue took its leave without any misfortune. Gallant Erec was accorded full praise. He had won renown, and so completely that his wisdom was compared to Solomon's, his handsomeness to Absalom's, and his strength to Samson's.[96] His generosity seemed so great to them that it seemed comparable to none other than that of generous Alexander.[97] His shield was broken apart and had been so struck by lances that a fist could have been thrust through it. Thus had Erec earned his praise.

[2826] When the news spread, and Lady Enite heard tell of the heroism of her companion Erec, his manly courage caused her both joy and sorrow. That she felt joy was because good things were said of Erec. That she had sorrow was because she knew well that her husband was of such a temperament that she feared she

---

94. A joust with blunted weapons. Nevertheless, medieval chronicles are replete with stories of knights being killed in "friendly jousts."

95. The studs in the center of the shield that fastened the handhold. Compare *Gregorius*, line 1620.

96. For Solomon, see 1 Kings 4:29, for Absalom, 2 Samuel 14:25, for Samson, Judges 14–16. For similar biblical references, see *Gregorius*, lines 2623.

97. Alexander the Great (356–323 B.C.) was a very popular figure in the Middle Ages and the hero of a number of epics.

would not have him long unless God wished to stand mercifully by him with His protection, since Erec would readily risk his life for honor's sake and would try where a coward would lose heart, whether good or bad were said about him. But her mind quickly decided on one of two possibilities: that she preferred as a husband a hero rather than a worthless coward, and she ceased her slight lamenting and was both proud and happy about his manly courage.

[2852] When the tournament had ended, the king rode to Karadigan with his retinue. Each lady received her knight with joy; Lady Enite did the same. They did not stay at court very long. Erec quickly asked King Arthur for leave to ride home to his father's land, which was called Destrigales. It seemed to him high time, for he had not been there since he was a child.[98] What better time could there be to return?

[2870] When he had made up his mind to journey home, he took along sixty men, whom he dressed like himself and outfitted well. The gallant warrior took them along as his entourage. He sent his messenger ahead into his land to announce his arrival to his father. The messenger immediately hurried to Karnant—that was the name of the capital—found the king there, and told him quickly what his son had ordered him to say. For this he received a rich reward because King Lac had never experienced a more joyful day than when he heard that his dear son was coming. He rejoiced and was happy. He quickly sent for both relatives and vassals, of whom he gathered five hundred, and rode for three days to meet him. According to the account of my source, they all received Erec and his wife most cordially. Never could a lady have been greeted better than she was when they received her.

[2904] Old King Lac felt exceptionally great joy, for they both, Erec and Lady Enite, were such a beautiful sight for his eyes. No matter to which side of himself he looked, he was happy, for both of them were a joy to look at. He was very pleased with his son, as a man should be with his child who has been endowed with great beauty and is thus very worthy of praise. And yet Lady Enite pleased him even better. He demonstrated this to them very clearly: he escorted them home to Karnant and handed over his land to their rule so that Erec would be counted among kings, and so that she would be queen. He relinquished rulership to them both.

[2924] Erec was upstanding and good. His mind was set on chivalry before he took a wife and returned home. But now after coming home he turned all his thoughts to Lady Enite's love. His mind was occupied with how he might arrange everything for his comfort. He changed. He spent the day as though he had never

---

98. In other words, Erec had been at court, as mentioned above (note 39), since childhood.

become a man. In the morning he lay down to make love to his wife until the time for mass was sounded. Then both got up in a hurry, took each other by the hand, and went to the chapel. They remained there only long enough to hear mass sung. That was the most difficult thing for him. By then a meal had been prepared. As soon as the table was removed, he hurried off to bed with his wife, away from everyone. Then the lovemaking began again. He did not leave there until he went to the evening meal.

[2954] When Erec fil de roi Lac withdrew from the knightly way of life, he nevertheless kept one virtue to which he held fast: although he himself did not seek out a tournament, he did provide for all of his companions so that they, on their own, could ride to tournaments. He ordered that they be so well equipped as though he himself were riding along. I commend his conduct.

[2966] Because of his wife, Erec grew accustomed to great comfort. He loved her so much that because of her alone he no longer concerned himself with his honor. It reached the point that he spent so much of his time lying around[99] that no one held him in esteem. This, quite rightly, displeased the knights and squires at court. Those who earlier had been happy were now very displeased there and left him quickly, for no one had any doubt that he had ruined himself. This was the reputation he had acquired. A change had occurred in him: the good that people had earlier said of him turned into disgrace for those who knew him. The whole world insulted him. His court was bereft of all joy and was disgraced. No one from a foreign land bothered seeking it out for entertainment. Those who were his subjects and who were well disposed toward him cursed him, all saying, "Woe is the hour when we met my lady! Because of her our lord is going to ruin."

[2999] Such talk was so widespread that it reached the lady. When she heard the reproach, she was greatly troubled, for she was upstanding and good, and thought of many ways how she might avert this general animosity. She also started to recognize that she was at fault. She bore this pain in a womanly fashion. She did not dare complain about it to Erec. She feared she might lose him.

[3013] Now it happened that around midday he was lying in her arms, as was their custom. The sunshine found it very appropriate to be at their service, for it shone on the loving couple through a window and had filled the chamber with bright light so that they could see each other. She began to think how she had been

---

99. The MHG verb *sich verligen*, a central concept in *Erec*, literally means to lie around inactive, thereby neglecting one's duties, e.g., one's knightly duties. For similar situations, see *Gregorius*, line 1683, and *Iwein*, lines 2763–98.

cursed. Suddenly she pulled away from him. She thought that he was asleep. She let out a deep sigh and looked at him intently, saying, "Alas for you, you poor man, and for me, miserable woman, that I must hear so many curses."

[3033] Erec heard her words clearly. When she had finished speaking, he asked, "Lady Enite, tell me, what are your worries that you lament in secret?" She tried to deny everything. Erec responded, "Stand by your words. It should be clear to you that I want to know what you were talking about. You must by all means tell me what it was I heard you lamenting, what you have not told me." She feared that she would be accused by him of other things and told him on the condition that he promise her not to get angry.

[3050] When he had heard what she told him, he said, "Enough of that." He immediately ordered her to get up, dress well, and to put on the best garment she had. He told his squires to ready his steed and Lady Enite's palfrey. He said he wanted to go out for a ride. They hastened to the task. He armed himself secretly and wore his armor hidden under his clothes.[100] His helmet he tied on over his bare head. He made every effort to conceal his actions. He acted as a clever man should. He said, "Something is wrong with my helmet. I'm glad I noticed that, for if I had needed it, I would have been very bad off. I shall tell you what it lacks: it needs to have better straps." There was no one, however, who could have understood what he had in mind. From the wall he took both a shield and a lance and let out a battle cry as though he wanted to ride in a *buhurt*. The knights and squires wanted, as is fitting, to ride out with their lord, but he ordered them to wait behind. To the kitchen he at once sent word that the cooks be informed that they should arrange to have a meal ready for them as soon as they returned.

[3093] With such instructions he rode out, ordering his wife, the beautiful Lady Enite, upon penalty of death, to ride out ahead, and he ordered her at the same time not to open her mouth to speak during the journey, no matter what she heard or what she saw. She had to pledge to follow these capricious, disturbing orders, for she feared his threats.

[3106] Now they both rode through nothing but unforested fields until daylight left them. When night came, the moon shone magnificently. The brave knight

---

100. While at first reading it seems unrealistic to be able to "hide" armor under clothing, it must be remembered that the massive suits of armor typically thought of as medieval and typically on display in museums are products of later centuries. "Armor" here could be chain mail. Later (lines 3510ff.), however, a squire notes that Erec has been riding in full armor (see also line 4155). Either Erec has removed his outer clothing, or the armor is so conspicuous. "Full armor," though, still does not necessarily mean the suit of armor we have come to envision. The helmet, however, as opposed to the head covering that went underneath it (mentioned above, line 2640) is another matter, and would seem hard to disguise.

Erec rode in hopes of a quest. The road led them into a thick forest. Three robbers had it in their power. In fact, they were watching the road at that time for anyone who might come riding toward them whom they could defeat, and whose honor and life they could take in order to have his possessions. Lady Enite saw them first because she was riding far in front.

[3125] This was the first heartfelt grief to overcome her on the journey, because she saw from their actions that they were robbers. She tried to inform Erec of this through some kind of signals, but he was not able to understand, for he had not seen them. Because of this he almost suffered harm. Lady Enite was both grieved and distressed because she saw the danger and thus feared losing the dearest husband a woman ever had, for things looked bad for him. What could compare with the deep-felt anguish she suffered because of her loyal love for her husband?

[3145] As she rode along so uncertain whether she dared say anything to him or should keep silent, she said to herself, "Almighty, merciful God, I seek help through Your mercy. You alone know how things stand with me. My worries are many, for I shall very soon be dealt an unpleasant hand that I shall have to play too quickly. Now I cannot see what the best decision is. What will happen to poor me? No matter what I choose I shall surely lose. If I warn my dear husband, I shall suffer harm, for I shall lose my life. If, however, no warning is given, then my beloved will die. Indeed, a woman's heart is too weak for such a distressful situation."

[3167] Then this conviction came to her: better for me to lose my life—as a woman whom no one would lament—than for such an excellent man to lose his, for many would lose thereby. He is noble and rich. Our value is not weighed equally. I shall die for him before I see him perish, let happen to me what God wills. My beloved shall not lose his life in such a way so long as I can prevent it.

[3180] She looked over at him fearfully and said, "Look up, my dear lord. Believing in your future mercy I shall tell you in all sincerity—I cannot keep silent about what harm could come to you—there are riders nearby who will harm you if they can unless our Lord saves you." Erec prepared to defend himself.

[3190] Now one of the robbers spoke [to his companions], "I have good news for you that will be to our benefit"—he had seen Erec and Enite first—"I see a man riding there. As far as I can tell at this distance, he has a lady with him. You can tell clearly from their appearance that they are rich. Their clothing is magnificent. Our poverty is at an end. I imagine they are carrying great wealth with them. Now let me remind you gentlemen to honor what we vowed among ourselves: that you give me first choice of this booty, and that you allow me, before the two of you, to ride the first joust that is undertaken against this knight, for I saw them first. If I take his life, I want only the woman. I do not desire any of his possessions." This honor they granted him.

[3216] His shield he raised up to his neck. When Erec approached him, he spurred on his steed. He said, "My lord, you have lost both your life and your possessions." Erec in his anger offered him no answer and struck him dead from his steed. His companions tried to avenge him. The same happened to them. Their legs and arms were not protected. This was to Erec's advantage in gaining victory. They were poorly armed, as robbers usually are. This suited Erec well. Each of them had on an iron helmet in addition to a breastplate. Thus Erec quickly laid them low on the same spot.

[3235] When he had succeeded because of his knightly prowess, he said to Lady Enite, "How now, you strange woman? Did I not command you upon pain of death not to speak? Who ordered you to disobey? What I have heard about women is true. It has become clear to me here: whatever one has ever very strictly forbidden them, afterward they felt the strong need to try it. It is absolutely time lost to order you to refrain from anything, because that only intrigues you so that you cannot avoid doing it. For this you deserve to suffer humiliation. Whatever a woman would never do, as long as it were not forbidden her, she can no longer refrain from doing as soon as it is forbidden her. She simply can no longer resist."

[3259] Enite replied, "My lord, if I had not done it for your safety, I would never have said anything to you. I did it out of loyal devotion. If you want me to be sorry, then forgive me for the sake of your honor. It will never happen again."

[3266] He answered, "My lady, so be it. I shall let it go unpunished. But if it ever happens again, I shall not spare you. However, you will not get off completely. I shall punish you a little. I insist that on the way you take full and proper charge of the horses. On this journey I shall not do without you as my squire."

[3277] "My lord, so be it," said the noble lady, for it did not bother her. In a most womanly manner she endured this unaccustomed hardship and, in addition, whatever else troubled her heart. She took charge of the horses. She took the reins in her hand and rode out ahead on the road, as Erec had ordered. She took care of the horses as well as a woman can. She could do no better.

[3291] Immediately thereafter—hardly any time at all—they had ridden only three miles when worries again caused her grief, for she saw in front of her five robbers lying in wait. It is said they were members of the same band, and that they shared their booty with those whom Erec had slain. The one group would keep in touch with the other. These five men and the three I told you about earlier controlled the forest and lay in wait along the road so that whoever escaped the one group would fall into the hands of the other.

[3310] Erec had come away from the other three with honor, as you have heard. He then came so close to these five that the one robber, who lay in wait far ahead of the others and manned the watch, caught sight of him and was pleased about his arrival. He spoke to his companions thus, "Good news! We shall all be rich. I see people riding up whom we shall easily take care of. It is only one man as far as I can tell. He has with him a noble lady who must be distressed. She is leading by the hand three horses and is, if I judge things correctly, not up to the task. I wonder where he got such a strange squire. She ought to be taken from him, as is only proper. As far as I can see from a distance, I have never seen a more beautiful woman. Gentlemen, you should leave her for me, for I saw her first." They all spoke, agreeing that she was by rights his. "Listen," said his one companion, "what I want from the booty: just his armor." The others immediately divided the five horses among them. That was impudent, for the armor served by rights the brave knight Erec. He could make good use of it. Besides, their distribution was for nothing.

[3348] Erec was unaware of their words. Now one of them readied himself at once to ride against Erec where he had seen him. This caused Lady Enite great worry and distress. She thought: if I warn my husband, I shall again break his command. Neither honor nor God will prevent him from taking my life. Alas, what an unfortunate woman am I! If only I were dead now, I would prefer that to this plight. Things would then go much better for me. If I were to watch the man be killed who lifted me out of great poverty to a lady of great wealth, by which I am highly honored — people say I am a powerful queen — I would regret that, because out of disloyalty my soul would go to ruin and rightly die, along with my body. May God advise me, poor woman, how to begin, so that I do not do the wrong thing. I think I should keep quiet. No, certainly not! I should tell him. Whatever the plight facing me, I shall risk it as before. Very quickly she looked around and said timorously to Erec, "My lord, hear me, for God's sake. Watch out or you will be struck dead. I see five fellows who want to kill you." As soon as she spoke to him he prepared to defend himself.

[3386] One of the robbers had split off and had ridden out ahead of the others so that he could joust with Erec, to his own loss, because Erec fil de roi Lac struck him in such a way that he lay dead beneath his horse. There were still four of them. Erec quickly struck the one dead from his horse, breaking his lance in the process. He then turned things over to his sword. The fight did not last long. He knocked down the three of them next to their companion.

[3400] When he had now single-handedly defeated the five men, and was about to ride on, he said to Lady Enite, "Tell me, you ill-bred woman, why have you lied yet again? Since I tolerated it the first time, you thought that was not enough and had to do it again. If a man could gain any honor by fighting a woman, you would not get off so lightly. I would take your life on the spot."

[3413] "Mercy, my lord!" the woman replied. "You should be lenient toward me, since I have acted out of loyal devotion. I would prefer to bear your anger than for you to lose your life, no matter what you might do to me. If I had waited any longer, my lord, you would have been killed. From now on I shall gladly keep quiet. Now forgive me, for God's sake. If I disobey your command in the future, then punish me at once."

[3425] Erec said, "My lady, I can tell you this: your arguments will only cause you trouble. You will not go without punishment. You will have to put up with whatever I think of for you. I shall keep you as a squire as long as we are on this journey. Take, now, these horses into your care and tend them properly so that your payment will not be something bad. And if one of them gets lost, you will have to suffer wrath that you would gladly do without, if you were smart."

[3440] Lady Enite then took the horses. Earlier there had been three; now there were eight in all. She led them as well as she could but was unable to manage them easily. However much it was against a lady's nature, and against the rights of her station, she suffered it without complaint and good-naturedly. Her goodness taught her that. The lady suffered great affliction, but in her heart she turned her sorrow to joy, as her humility taught her. Whoever considers this matter correctly knows that four squires would have had a hard time in leading and tending eight horses, if they were to do it correctly, whereas she had to ride all by herself. Had Lady Fortune not helped her, and had not God's courtliness hovered above my lady and made every effort that no great trouble should happen to her from the horses, her journey would have been distressing. The lady was well spared this. Moreover, because of such a squire the horses willingly and rightly ceased surging ahead impetuously and went gently at her side.

[3472] Now they quickly rode out of the forest. The day dawned beautifully. As night left them, Erec saw in front of him that the road led to a castle not far away, where the lord of the land, a powerful count, resided. Both of them had ridden the entire night without food and had suffered affliction. They were glad to see the castle, for they intended to rest there during the day in the market town below the castle. They hurried in that direction when they saw the market town.

Meet squire from the count (margin note)

[3490] Along the way they encountered a squire who had in his possession cooked ham and bread, wrapped in a white cloth and carefully guarded, as he had been ordered. In his hand he carried a jug of wine. To whom this was being sent I was not told.

[3499] As the squire rode nearer, he observed closely the troubled lady. He wondered at her circumstances. When he rode up to her, she greeted him in a very proper manner. He bowed to her in thanks. His way led him further. Now Erec greeted him, furtively from under his helmet, with a "good morning."

[3510] The squire saw clearly by looking at him that he had endured great distress during the night and had been riding in full armor. Their hardships moved him. He said, "My lord, if it does not offend you, I would like to ask you what your intentions are. Be so kind as to tell me. I ask only with good intentions. It seems to me that you are a stranger here. I have always lived in this land and am the count's squire. It seems to me right and proper, and I beseech you moreover that my lord be honored by your presence, and that you stop in at his castle and rest after your hardships. There you will have people at your service. And I further beseech you, for the honor of God: it seems to me that you have ridden and have suffered great hardships, and that you are hungry. I am carrying with me here ham and bread and a quantity of delicious wine. Now be so kind and bid the lady as well to stop and to ride back and have a bite to eat here."

[3541] Erec did as the squire requested. This pleased the squire. He hurried up to the lady in order to take the horses from her. She returned to her companion. The squire tied up the horses together, then laid down his cloak there, took his hat in hand, and went to find some water. He brought back enough for both of them to wash their hands. He spread some cloths out on the grass, and on it the food he had: meat, bread, and wine. There was nothing more.

[3556] When they had eaten enough and had mounted their horses again, Erec said to the squire, "Lad, you should by rights receive some reward for what you have done for us. You have well earned our affection. Now I have neither silver nor gold with which I could reward you. Friend, do then what I request and choose from among the horses one that pleases you the best. And rest assured that if the day ever comes when I can treat you better, you will not go wanting on my account. You should take the horse as we have requested." The lad did that very gladly. Erec would have given them all to him except that the lady's life would thereby have been made easier. He refrained from this in order to make her life burdensome.

[3580] When the squire had taken the horse that suited him best, he thanked Erec warmly, and said, "My dear lord, grant me now what I request. You will be

doing me a great favor. The lady is suffering hardship from the burden of these horses. May I take them? This would be a sweet service for me."

[3590] Erec said, "Lad, let that be. This is not being done completely without cause. At this time she must live with this distress."

[3595] The squire replied, "I shall ride on then."

[3596] Erec answered, "May God repay you with kindness and wealth. May your honor be under His protection so that you can live in good fortune. Lad, ride then in God's name." The squire was pleased with his gift. He rode off in the direction he had come. Joy made him hurry. Erec rode leisurely behind him.

[3604] Now the squire's lord spotted him and recognized him from afar, for he had gone out in front of the castle gate; there he sat. He was very astonished that he was returning so soon, and he asked him whose horse it was he was leading by the hand. The squire quickly told him the entire story. He said, "My lord, see, they are riding this way. I don't know why you're waiting and not going down to the road. You will be acting impolitely if you don't. In the person of the lady you can see the most beautiful woman we have ever seen. [You should receive her properly.]" The count then went down to the road and received them with a friendly greeting.

[3626] When the count saw them riding up, he went toward them and said, "Welcome, my lady, welcome, my lord," and entreated them very sincerely to show him the honor of stopping in at his castle and staying there. "My lord, you will have to excuse us," replied the knight Erec, "but the long way has made us unfit for court. We are overwhelmed by exhaustion. We bow before your graciousness, but decline with thanks. At this time you should let us ride on to a place where we can find rest." They begged for leave until he had to grant it to them.

[3644] Erec then asked that a squire show them to the best inn in the town.
5 There he removed his armor. Lady Enite was very pleased with the rest she got
6 there when the horses were taken off her hands. She felt like a soul saved by St.
7 Michael's help from hell's fire, where it had long resided.[101] Erec ordered a bath
8 prepared, for he was sweaty and dirty from the hardships of wearing armor on the
9 journey. He cleansed his body of this. By the time he and his wife had bathed, a
so meal had been prepared. When he was told this, he ordered the table to be set.
1 He did not allow Lady Enite to eat with him, rather he sat apart on one end and
2 she on the other, where they had washed their hands.[102]

101. As early as the second-century pseudepigraphal *Testament of Abraham*, Saint Michael was characterized as the rescuer of souls from hell (*The Oxford Dictionary of Saints*).

102. It was customary, even though Erec and Enite had just bathed, to wash one's hands in a bowl set on the table and to dry them with an accompanying towel.

[3668] Now the count harbored thoughts contrary to honorable deportment and began to regret having let the lady go and not having ordered her taken from Erec. His thoughts as to how he might win her—since the lady's beauty compelled him—were many. Deceit drove his mind to the point of thinking that he could take her from him. It was surely against the law that he wanted to take the wife of the brave knight who had come into his land and whom he should have guaranteed peace if anyone wanted to harm him.

[3684] This way of thinking had come about on account of Love, for we heard tell of the count that he was truly both upstanding, good, and mindful of honorable comportment—up to this very moment. But powerful Love taught him deceit and robbed him of good sense, for the snares of Love can very often capture a clever man who otherwise could not be taken. The world knows of many a man who would never lift a finger to do something wrong, if Love would leave him be. And if Love did not cause such exhilaration, then nothing would be so beneficial to the world and so truly just as to give it up. But no one has such strength, if she has taken control of him, that he can evade her. But whoever could serve her faithfully and in the right way, she would not abandon him along the way and would have a reward ready for him so that he would not regret his hardships, provided that he maintain his honorable comportment better than the count. The count was not steadfast in this, for Lady Love compelled him to dishonorable thoughts, so that he decided to take the good man's wife.

[3722] He took four knights with him. When he came to the inn, he found Erec and Enite sitting at the table. He took off his cloak and went and stood before them, offering his greetings. Erec had no idea that he wanted to harm him, which was his intention. The count was greatly astonished that they sat so far apart at the table and did not eat together. He said slyly, "My lord, if you do not mind, you should tell me why this is thus. Is this woman not your wife? She is very beautiful and so well-pleasing that it would suit her better to sit next to you than over there. Why have you had her sit far away from you? Erec answered him thus, "My lord, I simply felt like it." The count asked him further not to be offended if he sat down by her while they ate. Erec answered him thus, "If you deign to do so, my lord, it is fine with me."

[3752] The count said, when he had sat down next to Enite, "I shall tell you, lady, why I have come here to see you: partially to turn matters to your advantage, but actually because of your honor. Never have I pitied anyone so much as you, lovely lady. When I saw you suffering such unfitting distress today, as has never been proper for a lady, it touched my heart so much and still pains me greatly. I do not rebuke you out of meanness for your great poverty. On the contrary, it pains me. You would truly be a fitting lady for the emperor. Who gave you, poor woman, to such a man who has neither the desire nor the ability to want you as one should by rights? He keeps you as a squire. This companion of yours—may God strike him dead—is only concerned with whatever suffering he can cause you. If God had given you to me, you would be worthy of more respect. If you wish, everything will turn out all right for you. I shall tell you, lady, what my thoughts are, and if you are smart you will not object to anything. I shall alleviate your hardships. I shall tell you how things stand with me: I am the lord of this land. Neither near nor far have I ever found the woman [—I swear on my life!—] who would suit me such that I would want to take her as my wife. You, however, please me so well that I would gladly make you the lady of this land. Thus you will have changed your life without disgrace."

[3797] "May God give you a wife," said the virtuous woman, "who would indeed better grace your land and you. You would by rights very quickly regret having me, and it would be unfaithful of me. If the world were to hear of it and to know about it, it would only bring you ridicule. Therefore stop talking like that, for God's sake, for by rights you deserve better. I am not worthy of being a countess. I am neither of noble birth nor do I have wealth. Whatever my companion does to me, I am suffering it justly. Whether he wants me as a wife, a squire, or whatever, I will be subservient to him in every regard. My lord, what more can I say? I would rather be burned alive to ashes on the spot and scattered to the winds than do what you desire. Our positions are similar. Neither of us is wealthy. We are well suited for each other. May God preserve his life for my sake!"

[3826] When he had heard this answer and had seen at the same time what her intentions were, he said, "I shall tell you what I desire. Consider that and act accordingly. If you do not want to submit to my request amicably, then it will happen against your will. Your defense against me here is too weak. Your companion may ride wherever he wishes. You must stay here with me. This is my final word."

[3838] When she saw that he was serious and that he spoke with heartfelt conviction, she looked amicably at him, the very false man, and smiled very cunningly. She said, "I think you are serious. My lord, do not be angry, for you do not need to speak like that. I truly thought you were speaking in jest, for it is the nature of you men to like to deceive us poor women—if I dare say, even 'lie' to us—by promising us a lot of good things against your real desire. I have often seen women suffer much grief because of this. If I had not feared that, I would have given you a better answer, for I, my lord, am not so foolish as to act if I could improve my situation and make it comfortable, for my life is so miserable, as you have seen yourself. I shall tell you exactly how my husband first took me as his wife: he is not my equal. He took me from my father who is truly noble and rich. He often came to us at court. As children do, I used to run around there. One day he played with us. There it is obvious that children are easy to deceive. With trickery he lured me outside the gate. He snatched me up and abducted me and has had me ever since.[103] Many a miserable hour he has let me suffer, and for this reason he must avoid being in his own land. I, poor woman, suffer harm and disgrace all the time. If a better man were to free me honorably, I would gladly follow him. May God reward him for that. I thought your words were derisive. If you prove to me with some surety that you mean what you say, I am ready to follow your request."

[3896] The count was pleased at these words. Laughing, he answered her thus, "You cannot resist any longer, for I shall swear my loyalty to you." He raised his fingers, and the lady recited him the oath he was to repeat. She, too, immediately swore to carry out what he requested. An unreliable pledge was the loyalty she swore by placing her hand in his.

[3906] When the pledge had been given, Enite said cunningly, "My lord, I now advise you, as one friend to another—for I now wish no man so well as I do you— to follow my advice. It will not be a burden to you. Since you want to take me, I advise you to wait until tomorrow morning. That way you can take me without any trouble and without a fight. When he is lying in bed, come into the room, for he will not be able to harm you then, and you will be able to do with me as you desire, with no difficulty, for tonight I shall steal his sword."

[3926] She continued, "I love you now, for you have well earned that, and it will trouble me if you suffer harm on my account, which will surely be the case if you do not do as I have said. For if you take me with you right now, things stand so with us that he will not let me go willingly. He has his sword with him. I know well that he can do harm with it."

[3937] The count replied, "Your advice is good. It pleases me so well that I shall gladly do as you say."

[3940] With fine female cunning she had saved her honor and her husband's life. Lady Enite was a loyal wife. Thus she persuaded the man to take his leave through her deception, as I have told you.

[3948] When they had eaten, Erec ordered that beds for them both be prepared

---

103. Early medieval Germanic law codes deal often with abduction, which must have been frequent. By the end of the twelfth century the prevalence of such abductions seems less, but one still reads of such incidents among the nobility.

in a chamber, but that they be apart. He did not want to let her lie by him. Then they went to bed.

[3954] Now they were lying apart. It was certainly strange that he had made up his mind in a fit of anger to avoid such a beautiful woman. Because of her loyalty and goodness, affliction troubled the lady's heart greatly about how she could inform him of what had been said, for he had forbidden her to open her mouth to speak, no matter what she heard, as I told you earlier. Yet had she not disobeyed, she would have lost him, but consequently he in his anger would not keep company with her, but ate and lay apart from her.

[3972] Now the good woman was thinking to herself: things have reached the point that the dearest man a woman ever had will surely be taken from me unless I warn him. I also know that I shall pay for it if I break his command again. Advise me now, almighty Lord God! I have never needed Your advice so much. I know well that this means my death, for he has twice put up with it. But why does it matter if I am struck down and he takes my life? There will still be many fine ladies alive. Besides, I am not to be lamented. However, he, my dear lord, is noble and rich. Before anything causes him trouble I shall choose death. Her loyalty commanded her to go to his bed and to kneel down before him and tell him the entire story. She was pale from fright.

[3998] When he had heard it all, he immediately stood up and had the innkeeper awakened. He prepared to leave. He told the innkeeper's servant to have his horses readied. This was done quickly. He requested that the innkeeper come see him and told him when he came, "You have treated us properly and well in your house; I owe you some money. Hear now what you will get: I have here neither silver nor gold with which to pay you. Do then as I request: take these seven horses as payment from me." The innkeeper bowed deeply before him. Like any man who makes a profit, he was heartily pleased. To ensure Erec's good fortune he immediately offered him a cup in memory of Saint Gertrude's love.[104] Thus Erec, the stranger, rode away in the night and, with his wife, quickly left the land. She had deceived the count and had lied without sinning.

[4028] Before Erec had set out on his way, the very faithless count had been thinking about how Erec might have already taken Enite away before he could come get her. As he lay in bed he awoke from his sleep with a start, for he feared coming too late. Very loudly he cried out, "To arms! We have overslept. Get up,

---

104. Saint Gertrude, abbess of Nivelles (d. 659), was the patron saint of travelers and pilgrims, who drank a stirrup cup (a farewell drink) in her honor before setting out.

my friends, if you want to help me!" In total there were nineteen of them, and he was the twentieth.

[4044] When he had gathered them around him and had come to the inn, with an uncouth greeting he kicked down the door so that it broke into pieces. That vexed the innkeeper who wanted to cry out for help. "You can see that it is us," said the faithless count. "Don't be afraid, and tell me what these lights here mean?" They were the ones that gallant Erec had left when he set out on his way.

[4058] The count did not know that. "Where are your guests sleeping?" "My lord, they have ridden off." Angrily the count retorted, "They have not!" "If I were to lie, my lord, I would be a fool." "You are certainly mocking me." "No, my lord, so help me God." "You are. Show me to them." "Check yourself then." "I'll certainly do that." "I gladly give you my permission." "How long shall I keep on asking you questions?" "Now you can see for yourself where they were lying; why should I deny to you that they were here?" Making a gesture to strike him dead, the count said, "I think you are trying to put me on the false track." "My lord, Christ knows they have ridden off." "That is your fault." "Indeed not, by your grace." "Otherwise they would have waited for day." ["My lord, they just rode off."] "Tell me, have they gotten far?" "No, certainly not, my lord. They rode off this very hour." "Where are they off to?" "I don't know."

[4084] Thus his deceit brought him great heartfelt sorrow. He mightily cursed his sleeping. He said, "Honor was not mine to have, since I have lost, because I tended to my own comfort, the most beautiful woman my eyes have ever seen, either here at home or abroad. Cursed be the hour when I fell asleep tonight." He called for the horses and said, "Whoever turns his attention to comfort, as I have done tonight, must lose all honor and be disgraced. Whoever gained anything worthwhile without hardship? I got what I deserved." Now the squires came riding up with the horses. There was no further delay. "Let us be off, gentlemen," he said. Only lance and shield had they taken along as weapons. That was due to their haste.

[4110] Day began to break so that they could clearly see hoofprints and a trail. They hurried and followed it. In the meantime Erec had ridden about three miles. Because he feared for his wife [and not for himself], he was in a hurry to leave the land. He knew well that they would be followed. As soon as he had a chance, because of their haste, to speak on the way, he said, "Lady Enite, you have been too strong in your defiance of me. What I asked you not to do, and forbade under penalty of death, distresses me greatly because you do it all the more. Now I shall tell you what I think: I shall not tolerate this, and if you do not stop, it will surely cost you your life.

[4133] "Have mercy, my lord," said the woman. "You should be lenient toward me, for if I had not done it, you would have lost your life. Therefore it would not have been good to do nothing. In the future I shall heed your wishes." Now Enite heard the others approaching, fuming with rage. However recently the good woman had sworn not to warn him, the vow did not last long, for she broke it immediately as the bonds of loyalty compelled her to do. The others were still far away. She said, "My dear lord, a large party is riding after you. They want to harm you. They are hurrying so."

[4150] Now no one should ask, "How did it come about that the lady could hear and see them better?" I shall tell you how that happened: the lady was riding without any armor. He on the other hand was in full armor, as a good knight should be. Therefore he could neither see nor hear as well through his armor as he could have without it. Therefore he was in need of a warning, and that saved him from death. Even though it made him angry, he would well have lost his life because of his inability to see, if his wife had not warned him.

[4166] Enite had not yet finished speaking when the count rode up, and when he saw Erec he said, very unchivalrously, in unjustified anger and in an unfriendly voice, "Look around, you worthless thief! Who can be happy about your leading around in our land, to the disgrace of us all, such a noble, sweet lady? And you should know that you are going to lose your life to me right now. If you did not enjoy the privilege of being called a knight, I would have you hanged here on the spot.[105] You are detaining her against the will of her relatives. Indeed, it was a very nasty trick to ride off in the night. One can tell clearly from your actions that you have taken her from her father. How else would you have gotten her? Even a fool can see that this lady is not appropriate for you. If you want me to spare your life, you worthless knave, then let the woman go. I want to return her to her relatives. She should no longer lead such a miserable life. Now let her go and be off."

[4197] "You are acting very unchivalrously toward me," said Erec. "Who has taught you to insult a man who has the status of knight? You have been raised at a vulgar court. Shame on you. You have lied. I am more noble than you."

[4205] Then the fight began. There was no further delay. Angrily they rode at each other, whereby the faithless man got the reward for his treachery: a lance thrust in the side, which for some time afterward did not heal over, for he wore no armor beneath his shield; in addition, his arm was broken. When Erec had struck him from his horse, the count's followers were very concerned about him. They

---

105. Hanging was normally reserved for commoners.

fell over their lord so that no harm might come to him. There were several there who quickly wanted to avenge him with their swords. They could not ward Erec off for long. Six of them Erec struck dead. They had had enough fighting. The others were all cowards. They fled, although no one chased after them. That was the end of the fight. Without suffering harm the knight Erec very quickly rode on his way.

[4232] Erec said, "Merciful Lord God, keep me in your protection and help me leave this land without dishonor. If the people here find out about this, they will at once all follow me [and kill me in a moment]." This thought, however, was unnecessary, for no one heard anything about it until he was well out of the forest. That was his great good fortune. For the following reasons things went unreported: of the knights who remained alive and stayed with their lord, no one, from whom one would have heard about it, wanted to leave his lord. The cowards who fled did not dare speak of their disgrace before Sir Erec had ridden far away from their land. The knights dressed the count's wounds and with heartfelt sorrow carried him, as well as the dead, home on a litter. That was the reward for his deceit.

[4258] When Erec had ridden to safety, where he no longer had to fear the count, he reproached Lady Enite for breaking his command so often. His anger was great and distressing and more severe than before. Enite now swore that in the future she would never again do it, but she did not keep her word.

[4268] Whatever hardships Erec had suffered up to now were hardly any effort, and even child's play, when compared to what he still had to suffer, about which I shall now tell you. Both distress and trouble were his lot. He was not spared this. He suffered more than enough.

[4277] The road immediately led him to a strange land whose lord was unknown to him. Of the lord's manly courage we have heard wondrous things. He was a very small man—unless I was told lies—almost the equal of a dwarf, except that his arms and legs were very big. In addition, his chest was powerful and broad. Within it he carried a heart full of manly courage. It gave him his strength, because that is really what it is all about. Know this for a fact: if a man were twelve klafters tall[106] and had a timorous heart that was from birth cowardly, his hulking body would be lost. This was not the case with this lord. We cannot relate much of his story. Much could be said about him, except that this story would then become too long. Therefore I shall shorten it for you. The brave lord had good fortune and an exalted frame of mind and had courageously gained victory against many

---

106. A *klafter* was the length of a man's outstretched arm.

a man. Therefore one still says about him that his manly courage has never failed
him to this very day. Whoever encountered him with evil intentions, be he strong
or weak, the little man always gained the victory. During his lifetime he never
missed any knightly combat within riding distance, and no one ever did better at
one.[107]

[4318] When Erec encountered this new battle, Enite again proved her loyalty
to him. When she had warned him, they watched the little man ride up quickly.
He greeted Lady Enite. When he had ridden close enough to Erec so that he could
hear his words, he said, "Welcome, my lord. Whether you have ridden from near
or far into this land, I have no doubt that you are a warrior. That is apparent from
two things: you are leading, by my life, the most beautiful woman I have ever heard
tell of. Who would give her to an ignoble man? In addition, you are well armed,
as befits a brave knight, who at no time desires to be met defenseless, and who
seeks adventure. If God deigns so, you will find plenty of it here. And if good for-
tune falls to your lot, I can tell you truly that you can gain victory for which you
will have great fame. Now defend yourself, knight, it is time."

[4348] Jokingly, Erec answered him, "God forbid, brave and distinguished knight,
that you should ever act against your sense of loyalty. You would regret that later.
You did indeed offer me your greeting. How could you ever make up for the humil-
iation if after that you were to attack me? That would be too precipitous, and you
would gain no fame from it. Act in God's name and leave me in peace, for I have
done nothing to you. I have ridden far and have suffered such hardship that every
bit of advice my heart gives me is not to fight."

[4366] The lord thought: he is a coward, since he complains about his hardships.
He replied, "You refuse unnecessarily simply because I offered you my service. I only
did that because I was in hopes of knightly combat. Whatever happens to you on my
account, you should not doubt my loyalty, which I shall never violate. Defend your-
self for the sake of your beautiful wife if you want to save your life."

[4378] When Erec saw that he had to fight, he turned his steed as his courage
had taught him. Two men, neither of whom had ever shown any sign of cowardice,
rode at each other. Strength and good fortune had to decide the victory between
them. Their lances clashed so hard that they splintered. The joust was so violent
that their steeds sat back on their hind quarters. Both men had to let the reins go
from their hands, and it became a different kind of struggle for them. They dis-
mounted at the same time, very quickly, and drew their swords. Each received in

---

107. There appears to be a lacuna here regarding the encounter between Erec and Guivreiz.

full measure at this place here what he had long prayed to God for: that He send him a man against whom he could test himself.

[4404] Now they fought like two brave knights. This began at midday. Erec fil de roi Lac feared humiliation and death. His shield he held out against his opponent and cleverly began to hold himself back without offering any sword blows. The other knight did not understand Erec's intentions and struck the shield away from his hand, right down to the straps. Because no one separated them there on the heath, he struck Erec in the side, wounding him. He thought he had found a coward in the stranger.

[4421] For her part, Lady Enite despaired greatly when his side started to bleed so profusely. The good lady cried out loudly, "Alas, my dear lord, if I could only be in your place! I think I have lost you."

[4428] "Lady, your thoughts deceive you," spoke the courageous man, "for I would then lose even more." This he clearly proved to her. He stepped forward a bit and no longer put up with what was happening. He struck the little man a blow on the helmet such that he was wounded and lay before him.

[4439] Erec fil de roi Lac almost committed a misdeed, for he was about to kill him. "No, brave knight," said the little man, "for the sake of your virtuous nature and your beautiful wife, spare my life and honor God in me. I gladly pledge you my security. Receive me now as your vassal, and know that I have never been beholden to any other lord. If you had not gained this honor through your manly courage, I would rather die than let this happen. No nobleman would pledge himself to you otherwise. Therefore it does not matter to me who your father is, for your virtue ennobles you such that I am glad to have you as my lord."

[4460] Now this battle had lasted until around three o'clock in the afternoon, an entire long summer day. When Erec had gained victory, he showed him mercy in that he let him live. He pulled him up by the hand and untied his helmet, saying, "I desire of you no other sign of honor than that you, with no shame implied, tell me your name. I desire nothing of you at the moment but to know who you are." He answered, "My lord, so be it; I shall tell you: I am the king of Ireland and am called Guivreiz le pitiz."[108]

[4478] Erec did not accept him as his vassal. Both lamented the other's distress. Erec then quickly tore off a bandage from his tabard. Where else at that time could he have found a more friendly bandage? Guivreiz le pitiz likewise tore one from

108. Guivreiz the Small.

his tabard. They bandaged each other's wounds that they had inflicted with their hands. This was done in a friendly enough fashion.

[4492] Enite, as was her nature, helped out with much kindness. The two knights took each other by the hand, being happy for each other, and sat down together in the grass, for they needed to rest. The battle had made them very hot. Both blood and sweat ran down the two of them. Lady Enite went over to them. She was happy and sorrowful, as I shall tell you: she was pleased about her husband's victory, but she wept because of his wounds. With the edge of her wide sleeve the good lady now cleaned them of sweat and blood.

[4509] In friendly conversation these two lords sat on the heath and cooled off in order to be comfortable. The king said to the foreigner, "My lord, do not take too seriously what I now tell you and do not let it bother you. Your manly courage made me want to become your vassal. You have succeeded well. Your courage is so apparent that I would like to be your vassal even more if I could know whether your family is just as good, and if you could tell me this, my honor would be even greater. What happened to me at your hands has never, up to this moment, been forced upon me, yet I have had success and shall not complain, but be forever happy if a man of noble birth has done this to me."

[4535] Erec answered him thus, "I shall tell you of my family: I think it is indeed of noble birth. My father is King Lac. My name is Erec." The king was pleased. As soon as he had heard who he was, he did not remain sitting very long. He jumped up with joy and fell at Erec's feet, saying, "How happily I would be your loyal vassal forever, in whatever way I can be of service. I know your father well. Both my life and my land will be subject to you. You should also let me have the honor of swearing to you, without regret, for as long as I live, my constant loyalty. I beseech you to grant me one favor. Where could there ever be greater loyalty than a friend owes a friend where both trust each other? In the name of this loyalty I beseech you that you ride with me for my sake to my castle and stay there till such a time as you have recovered. Let there be no argument about this. Thereby you will be treating me so graciously that I shall always be at your service."

[4570] Erec replied, "I shall grant you this, but you should not desire it for too long a time. You must not get angry over this. I cannot stay here any longer than until tomorrow morning, and I shall tell you why I am doing this. I am not traveling out of pleasure, and whatever pleasure does arise, I pay little attention to it, for I am not seeking it."

[4580] The king was pleased regarding his guest. He went over to the horses and said, "We should go." He now helped Lady Enite mount her horse. He did that with great courtesy. He led her out ahead to the road. Erec rode behind. When they had ridden up to the castle, his squires no longer restrained themselves but ran out through the castle gate toward their lord. There they received him with joyful tumult, for they were happy at the thought that he, as usual, had captured the knight. He said, "Things have not gone as you think they have," and he told them in great detail the story of what had happened. He added, "Whoever loves me should turn his attention to receiving properly the most outstanding man I have ever met. For this I shall forever reward you." They did that gladly. Erec was never treated better anywhere than there that night.

[4614] When they had eaten that night and had afterward sat down together, the host said, "My lord, my advice is that you allow a doctor to tend to our wounds. If you leave now before you have healed, that strikes me as harmful. Unfortunately, you are severely wounded. Besides, you are unfamiliar with the land, and things might go badly for you." Erec replied, "Let us not speak of this, for I can only stay until daybreak."

[4628] All honor was shown Erec for the night, [4629¹] for Guivreiz le pitiz made every effort to care for him properly until the next day.

[4629⁵] When he [left there] in the morning [. . .] [as our sources tell us] of the virtuous man, he rode into a magnificent forest into which, according to Chrétien,[109] King Arthur, coming from his castle Tintajol[110] with his splendid retinue, had ridden for the hunt. He and his company of knights were camped near the road, about a quarter mile away. At the same time, Lord Walwan[111] had come riding up and had tied his steed Wintwalite next to his tent. Kei had found it there. He mounted it to go for a ride, Lord Walwan having given him his permission. Both his shield and spear stood leaning there. He took them and rode off alone out to the road. Sir Erec came riding toward him. Kei caught sight of him from far away. When he could see him clearly, he noticed that he had suffered hardships along the way and had ridden far and was covered with blood. He decided to ride toward him, and he spoke deceitfully, "Welcome, my lord, to this land." He took the reins in his hand. He did not dare confront him any other way. In this way he acted as though he had defeated him, and he asked [who he was.][112] [. . .] "There is no cause to be angry. I wanted

---

109. See the discussion of Chrétien in the introduction.

110. The now ruined coastal castle of Tintagel in Cornwall, England, is from the twelfth century. According to legend, King Arthur was born at Tintagel.

111. Walwan/Gawein is the exemplary knight Erec encountered earlier at King Arthur's court (line 1152).

112. Taking the reins of someone's horse was a customary greeting, but could also be seen as a sign of

you to ride with me now so that you could rest. I can see clearly that you are badly wounded. My lord King Arthur is camped not far from here. In the name of the king and the queen you are requested to ride with me now and to rest there with them from your suffering. Both will be glad to see you."

[4629[56]] Kei was thinking thus: if he brought him to court [4630] he would then say that he had caused his wounds and had captured him. From this it was perfectly apparent that the world had never seen a stranger man. His heart was divided into four parts: sometimes adorned with very great loyalty so that he regretted all the unjust acts he had ever done. Thus he was freer of deceit than a mirror and took care in his deeds and thoughts never to commit a misdeed. But he was inconstant, for afterward the time came when he did not trouble himself with any kind of loyalty. Then he was not satisfied with whatever deceit he could very zealously commit with his actions or his words. Every desire aimed at this. In addition, on some days he was brave, on others the world's greatest coward. These were two sides lying at odds, and in this way he dishonored himself so that he displeased everyone, and no one considered him good. Because of his deceitfulness he was called Kei Bad Mouth.[113]

[4665] Now Erec noticed quite clearly what Kei had in mind, and let him know it. He said, "My lord, I must still ride far and cannot at this time part from my path. If I had time, I would ride a thousand miles to be greeted by the king. For the time being you should let me go on my way. May God keep you, my lord."

[4678] Then the deceitful Kei said, "My lord, don't talk like that. You cannot depart in this manner. That would not be fitting for either of us. I shall bring you to King Arthur if it lies in my power."

[4685] Erec fil de roi Lac was somewhat annoyed at this and replied, "I don't think you can. You would do well if you set your mind on it less, for if you want to take me there you will have to force me. But if you have the ability, you will be able to take me there, for you will have defeated me."

[4694] "I know quite well," said Kei, "that I am very capable. Long before you can convince me that you should leave without seeing my lord—for going there cannot harm you—I shall force you in a friendly manner. Therefore you should depart from your course and see my lord. Indeed, that must be done."

[4704] Then Erec got very angry. He spurred his steed on. "Take your hand away!" He threw open his cloak and drew out his sword. Because Kei had well

---

victory if Kei led Erec to Arthur's camp. Asking someone's name is done only after the other is defeated in battle (compare the preceding encounter with Guivreiz). Thus Erec's angry reaction, which is missing.

113. For further descriptions of and comments about Kei, see *Iwein*, lines 803–78 and 2557–642.

deserved it, Erec wanted to strike off the hand of the worthless coward. But Kei withdrew it in time and fled without a fight. Although Kei was riding Wintwalite, the best steed a knight ever owned, he headed back such that Erec caught up to him. And when Erec clearly saw—this was fortunate for Kei—that he was wearing no armor, how well did Kei gain from Erec's virtue. With amazing quickness Erec turned around his lance so that he would not wound him. He turned the shaft against him and jabbed him with such force that Kei lay like a sack beneath his steed, just as he deserved, unlike a brave knight. Erec led Kei's steed away.

[4735] Kei, the scoundrel, ran quickly after him. Loudly he called out to him, "No, brave knight! For the sake of your virtuous nature leave me the steed, or I shall be disgraced and ridiculed for ever more. It is, God knows, not mine."

[4744] The good man turned with a laugh and listened to his complaint. He said, "Knight, tell me then, what is your name? And let me know what lord owns this steed. You will not come to harm. I want to know your name. You do not need to feel ashamed. This has happened to many a man who was never a coward."

[4756] Kei said, "No, my lord! I sincerely beseech you. If you want to show me mercy, then do so fully by leaving off what you asked me: that I should tell you my name. My cowardice has brought such disgrace upon me that I would suffer heartfelt grief if I should tell you my name, for I have indeed earned your scorn. For God's sake, do not insist on it."

[4770] Erec replied, "Knight, tell me. There is no one here but you and me. There is no help for you. You will lose the steed." He spurred on his own steed as though he wanted to ride away.

[4777] Kei asked him to wait. He said, "I lament to God that I have to proclaim my humiliation. Now I shall tell you who I am. My name is Kei. King Arthur deigns to keep me as seneschal of his castle. One of his nephews, the noble knight Gawein, lent me this horse. It is too bad that he did not refuse me for I would be spared this dishonor that I now have to suffer. When my lord was eating today—I myself do not know why in the devil I could not live peacefully. I sought humiliation and have received my share—misfortune advised me to ask him to lend me his horse. He lent it to me on the spot. If he had not done that, I would have been spared the dishonor that has befallen me. No one can prevent what is to happen to him. Noble knight, be so good and give it back to me, for God's sake, or I shall be the scorn of everyone who sees me returning on foot."

[4807] Erec replied, "So be it. I shall give it to you on one condition: you should give it back to Lord Walwan in my name. You must promise me this upon your honor."

[4813] Kei answered, "That I shall do," and he did, for he was pleased with Erec's decision.

[4816] When Kei had taken back the horse, he said, "I beseech you, gallant man, since you have been so good to me, that you now complete your kindness by letting me know who you are. Please tell me your name. It will not harm you and will help me. I should like to know your name on account of your bravery. I would always be sorry if I had to take my leave thus, being ignorant of your name and not knowing how I should call you when I happen to think of you kindly. For God's sake tell me who you are." Erec replied, "No, not at the moment. Perhaps you will find out later."

[4833] Now they parted at once. Each rode his own way, Kei and Erec. Kei rode to court, and his honesty forced him not to keep quiet but to tell truthfully the shameful story of what had happened to him, and he told of his misfortune in such a pleasing way that his disgrace was taken as a joke and he was not ridiculed.

[4846] When those there were told of the knight's manly courage, they were all very curious who the knight might be. Kei then said, "I was not able to find that out. He did not want to give his name. I did hear his voice, for he spoke to me a lot, and as far as I can tell it is Erec fil de roi Lac." Then they all agreed that is was truly he.

[4860] Then King Arthur spoke, "I would be very happy and would reward with my affection the one who brought him to me. Gawein, I leave that up to Kei and you. Up to now you have brought me such honor that I can only speak well of you. If you do this now, I shall esteem that more highly than anything you have done to please me. Gawein, remember how things stand between us, that you are my closest friend, and do not delay a moment more, for my sake, and help me and the queen to see Erec. Nothing would please me more"

[4880] Gawein replied, "My lord, do not urge me so fervently, for I am willing to ride out. Indeed, there is no one living whom I would prefer now to see more than him. And if God grants me the good fortune of overtaking him, I can tell you, my lord, what I shall do: I shall bring him back, if I can persuade him."

[4889] Quickly they rode off. Kei brought Gawein right to the place where he had left Erec. With amazing quickness they both hurried after him, always on his track. And as soon as they had caught up with him as he rode, the gallant Gawein greeted him warmly, in a friendly tone, and not in anger. Thereby he showed him that he meant only good. He offered him a "good day." When Erec fil de roi Lac thanked him, Gawein realized who he was, and when he had recognized him he immediately called him by name.

[4910] Gawein embraced him firmly, compelled by joy and the pleasure that befell him at seeing him strong and well. He bade him and his lady welcome. He thanked him heartily for the friendly honor he had shown him regarding his horse, the loyalty that had compelled him to send it back to him. As soon as he had spoken his name, he said to the warrior, "At quite a pace have we ridden after you through the forest. If you ask, my lord and former companion, why we are in such a hurry or what I wish, that will not be kept from you. I beseech you, let it be seen if you love my lord. I shall tell you why: when our friend Kei returned my steed to me at court and told us his story, praising you for your great manly courage, we were all very curious who it could have been. But we surmised, with one voice, that it must be you. Then the queen and my lord at once urged us to hasten after you—that is why we were in such a hurry—and to bring you back to the king's court. If you have ever loved or esteemed King Arthur, see to it then that you do not refuse him and deign to go see him. If that now happens, then no one will experience greater joy than he will. Do this without any objections if you are willing to serve him. This will make us all happy."

[4959] Erec answered him thus, "The king fully deserves that I, in my heart, should always be subject to him, and wherever I must refuse him by not carrying out his command, it is not my own decision that averts me. I shall do everything he wants, but this I must refuse. I shall make apparent my devotion to him, if it ever comes about—which may perhaps happen—that I must risk both life and property for his sake. Then there will be no doubt. I shall indeed show him what he means to me. This time he should let me ride on with his blessing. At the moment I have completely renounced all comfort. Deign to let me be beholden to you wherever I ride. You should tell my lord and the queen that I am at their service and deflect any anger from me."

[4984] When Lord Gawein saw that Erec objected so strongly, he was very unhappy. He beckoned to his companion and whispered to him, "Noble knight, act virtuously and with good will, for which I, as well as my lord, shall be indebted to you. I suggest the following: ride quickly on your way and report that Erec will not turn back. Therefore, my friend, I have thought of a scheme regarding him that is most advantageous for us. Tell the king that if he wants to see Erec things must happen as I shall tell you. Ask him to move from where he is in the forest and to head out quickly to where the knight Erec will ride out on the other side of the forest. In the meantime I can surely hold him up with a ploy and delay him on the road from getting there ahead of the king."

[5013] "If that will help us," spoke the knight Kei, "then I shall gladly do it."

Immediately he rode off and did everything that was requested.

[5018] When King Arthur heard of this, the dining table was removed and they hurried out ahead, as Arthur's nephew had advised, and set up camp right by the road so that the knight Erec, if he should come anywhere near, would have to ride straight at them.

[5026] Gawein, the gallant knight, held Erec up with ploys, as best he could, until he had used up enough time entertaining him for the king to get well ahead of him. As often as Erec asked him to ride back, Gawein would answer, "right away," until by means of his nice deception he had ridden out with him to the edge of the forest where the king was camped along the road.

[5037] And when Erec fil de roi Lac saw all the tents, he was not at all happy about it, because the fields were completely covered. Also, he recognized them exactly, for he had seen them often. [He said, "How has this happened to me?] I think I have ridden in the wrong direction. You have not done right by me, Lord Gawein. This is your idea. I have never heard anything regarding such a wrong-doing on your part. It was certainly not my idea to come riding here. It was bad of you to bring me here. If one were to come to court and it did him no good, as is the case with me, he would do just as well staying home. Whoever is to be at court is suited better by being happy so that he can act properly. I cannot do that now and must forgo it like a crippled man. You can surely see that I am at present exhausted and wounded and so incapable of being at court that I would rather have avoided the court if you had allowed me to. You have not done well by me."

[5068] Gawein repaid Erec's anger with kindness. He drew him closer and said, "My lord, soften your anger. Certainly it is better to lose a friend for a good reason and in a good way than to keep his friendship in an unfitting way. If he is quickly angered a little, he will be understanding afterward and value the other more than before. What more can I say? For if I have troubled you, I only did it with good intentions. Judge me for yourself."

[5081] Thus Gawein, in a very virtuous manner, became reconciled with Erec, such that the latter gradually forgot his displeasure and distress. Never was a man shown greater esteem or more honor than was Erec at court. That people were pleased to see him was made apparent by Arthur and the queen and their entire retinue. They, Erec and Enite, who for some time had experienced disturbing events on unknown roads, were welcomed there, and were received with dignity, both of them in the same manner.

[5100] Guinevere, the queen, displayed her sweet nature when Lady Enite came up to her. She took her into her care and led her away from there, and from her husband, to her private chambers. There they both lamented matters, as women are wont to do, and there was much asking and telling about the unaccustomed hardships Lady Enite had suffered. For such afflictions the very noble queen compensated her with some comfort for as long as possible. Sir Erec too was led aside by the knights to where he, wounded as he was, could find rest from his exhaustion. The knights went up to him and quickly removed his armor. He was given many splendid squires, none of whom then begrudged the other his superiority. Their one thought aimed at being of whatever service to him they could be.

[5129] The queen soon came with all her ladies to see him and to express her sympathy. She brought along a bandage. I shall tell you how good it was for wounds: many a mortally wounded man was healed by it. Whoever had his wounds dressed with it felt no more pain, and the wounds did not heal too quickly, but just in the right way. No further affliction arose. It drove out all sickness. Whatever good was there remained, and those who were healed were freed from scarring, so that the body appeared smooth as though there had never been a wound. With her own hands the queen dressed the knight's side. At no time has the world ever seen a better bandage.

[5153] If anyone wonders, and would like to hear, where the bandage came from, Morgan le Fay, the king's sister, had left it a long time ago, when she died.[114] What great arts and strange knowledge perished with her! She was a goddess. One cannot tell of all the miracles this very lady brought about. One must pass over in silence most of them. But as best I can, I shall tell what she was capable of.

[5167] Whenever she began to perform her magic, she would fly around the world in a short time and come back quickly. I do not know who taught her. Before I could turn my hand over or blink an eye she would quickly travel back and forth. She lived in great splendor. She could hover and rest in the air as on the ground, and could live in the water or beneath it. It was also not unusual for her to live in fire as gently as she would on the dew. The lady could do all of these things. And if she wanted, she could turn a man into a bird or an animal. Afterward she quickly gave him back his original shape. She was indeed capable of magical powers.

[5190] She lived in great defiance of God, for the birds and wild animals in the woods and the fields obeyed her commands, and—what strikes me as the most powerful—the evil spirits called devils were all in her power. She could perform

---

114. Morgan le Fay (Morgain la Fée) is the Lady of Avalon who received the wounded Arthur after his last battle. Her reputation and the powers associated with her changed greatly in the course of the Middle Ages. She is further mentioned in *Iwein*, lines 3419ff.

miracles, for the dragons in the air had to support her deeds, and the fish in the water. She also had relatives deep in hell; the devil was her companion. He sent her as much support from the fire as she wanted. And whatever she desired from the earth, she took that in full measure without any fear. The earth possessed no herb whose power was not as known to her as my own hand is to me. Since Sibyl died and Erichto passed on (about whom Lucan tells us that her magical powers could command whomever she wanted, even if he had long been dead, so that he would rise up completely healthy)[115]—I shall not tell you any more about her at this time, for it would be too much—since then, rest assured, the earth has not seen a better mistress of magical powers than Morgain le Fay, about whom I have told you. Therefore, the man for whom she prepared a bandage would not be wise if he were greatly offended by this. Indeed, I believe one could find nowhere, however much one looked for magical powers in medical books, such powerful arts as she practiced, whenever she wanted, in defiance of Christ.

[5243] This was the very bandage—that Morgain le Fay had excellently made with all her knowledge—with which the queen dressed Erec's wound. Erec indeed felt the excellence of the bandage, for when his wound had been dressed, he again thought of his journey. He believed he was already healed and did not want to be there any longer, however much the knights and ladies who came to visit him beseeched him and talked to him. Nevertheless, that night they attended the worthy guests as best they could, and would gladly have done so further, if Erec had allowed it. He, however, did not do that. The requests of King Arthur and the queen were of no use, so that they were not able to delay him with ruses any longer than very early the next morning. No request did any good.

[5270] When morning came and he did not wish to forgo his journey for anyone, they all thought this was wrong. For his sake the king had eaten early. Afterward the horses were brought up. Erec, as befitted his courtliness, took his leave from the knights and the ladies. It was very obvious from the demeanor of all of them how fond they were of Erec and Enite, for they all wept with grief as they departed. The king was so distressed that he no longer wanted to remain in the forest. He left for Karadigan.

[5288] The knight Erec now rode wherever the road led him. He himself did not know where. His thoughts were directed only at a place where he might find

---

115. Sibyl—originally one, later there were many with the name—became a generic name for a prophetess in Greek and Roman mythology. Lucan (Marcus Annaeus Lucanus, A.D. 39–65) writes about Erichto in his epic *Bellum Civile*, also known as *Pharsalia*.

adventure. He had ridden a short time, hardly a mile, when he heard a voice from off the road crying out in misery and fury, a woman pitiably calling out for help. She was in distress. When he heard her crying out he wondered greatly what it was all about. His manly courage was apparent. He commanded Lady Enite to wait at that spot for him and had her dismount on the road. As he left her, she placed her concerns in God's care, as her heart instructed her.

[5313] Taking his direction solely from the woman's voice, he set off in that direction through dense, roadless forest on an uncleared path until he came right to the place where she, wailing, was suffering great sorrow in the wild forest. Her grieving hands had unsparingly ripped down her headdress. The half-dead woman had scratched and torn at herself such that her clothes and body were covered with blood. Her misery had caused her such pain that there could surely be no one with such a hard heart—if he had seen her pain at that time (since I must tell the truth)—that he would not have taken pity on her.

[5335] When he saw the poor woman in such a miserable state, Erec, the gallant man, close to tears, said, "Lady, tell me, for God's sake, why you are weeping? How is it that you are all alone in this forest? For God's sake, tell me quickly whether I can help you." The fury of bitter grief had almost robbed her of her voice. The sobbing of her heart broke off her words so that she could hardly speak. "I have good cause for weeping, my lord, for I have lost the dearest man a woman ever had."

[5354] Erec replied, "Lady, how did that come about?" "My lord, two giants have robbed me of him. They dragged him along the way in front of my eyes. My lord, they will not let him live, for they have been his enemy for a long time. Alas, I have good cause to weep!" "Lady, are they far from here?" "No, my dear lord." "Then show me which way they went." "My lord, they rode this way." With her finger she pointed out the direction he had taken. Erec said, "Lady, farewell, for I shall surely die with him or help him out of his trouble." With words and with her heart the good lady now commended him to our Lord's care. Her prayer was very long, and sincere was the blessing she said over the warrior.

[5378] He had now come upon their tracks and hurried quickly after them until he caught sight of them. The two huge men had neither shield nor lance nor sword as Erec did. That was to his advantage. They had no armor. What were their weapons? Two heavy clubs, big and long, whose shafts were plated with iron. A coward might grow weaker and weaker if he dared fight them. Then too, the evil men had two whips with finger-thick cords. With these they cruelly drove on the man they had captured. He rode without any clothing and was naked as the back of a hand. His hands were tied behind his back with fetters, and his feet were bound together beneath his horse. He had to suffer many lashes from the whip as he rode ahead of them. They struck him mercilessly, so much that the poor man's skin hung down in shreds from his head to his knees. They broke completely with knightly custom and treated the good knight in such a way that if he had been stealing and had been captured, such punishment would have been too severe. He had been beaten to the point that he had lost much blood, and he was now so weak that he could no longer cry out. The blood flowed like rain down the horse's flank. It was covered with blood. The knight suffered great anguish and such unheard-of hardship, that no one could suffer greater distress than he did unless one were dying.[116]

[5429] When Erec saw this, the knight's torment moved his heart so much, shown by the color of his face, that he would have preferred to be killed with him rather than allow this to go on. He said to the two, "My lords, both of you, I am not asking in order to offend you, but you should tell me, for God's sake, what has this man done to you whom you hold captive here? Tell me, what crime has he committed? An answer will not hurt you, and I would appreciate it. Is he a murderer or thief? Or how is it that he deserves at your hands the oppressive punishment he is suffering?"

[5446] One of them answered, showing contempt for Erec's question, "What matter is it of yours, fool, to ask what he has done to us? We shall not tell you what he has done. You great ape! Just see how you are disgracing yourself by asking about so many things that no one will tell you. Why then are you pursuing me?"

[5457] Erec answered, "My lord, I am not." But he continued to speak artfully with the thought of delaying him. "From afar I heard him cry out. Believe me, gentlemen, I did not follow you here with evil intentions. I wondered what was going on. You should not take that badly. But I want to tell you truthfully—I cannot be silent regarding this—that if this man is of knightly standing you should be forever ashamed that he gains no advantage from it, and that this great impropriety does not trouble you. Indeed, he has suffered enough punishment, whatever he has done. Do you not wish to release him, for God's sake?"

[5476] The huge man replied, "Your babbling annoys me. Stop all this questioning. You are putting your life at great risk. If I could gain any honor or any renown from defeating you, I would wring your neck like a chicken's. What good to him are your questions? Take up his cause as a relative and help him. He needs it."[117] Before

---

116. For another episode with an evil giant, see *Iwein*, lines 4914–51.
117. A familial bond would require Erec to fight for the knight's cause.

Erec's eyes the giant struck the knight and ordered Erec to be on his way. Erec still wanted to convince him through kindness to release the knight. The request was in vain, for it only provoked the giant's anger. Out of animosity toward Erec they tormented the knight worse than before, because they did not fear or believe that Erec would dare challenge them.

[5498] And when Erec, the bold warrior, saw that the knight was being punished because of him, that pained him greatly. He delayed no longer, but courageously slapped his lance up under his arm. He spurred on his steed. His anger drove him toward them. But that mattered little to them, except that the one was so careless in his disdain until a lance thrust was directed at his head that caused him to lose an eye. The thrust was so powerful that the shaft hung out an arm's length from his eye. However little the giant wanted to see it thus, Erec thrust him dead to the ground as God's courtliness[118] ordained.

[5518] When the giant's companion saw the heavy fall the huge man took, he turned around in anger and wielded his club, taking it in both hands. Erec dismounted. This pleased the giant, who thought he had already won. His thinking was dashed, as God willed. He struck as though he were crazy. Erec, however, was on his guard and was cleverly able to save himself or he would have been killed by the first blow. His quickness was able to take him out of reach. He held up his shield to him. It was the one to suffer distress. Where the giant struck the shield, the hard surface yielded so much that it broke into three pieces, and what had been securely fastened flew up like dust. The club was so heavy that as often as he struck with it, it bent him so far over that he could not [raise it again] in a short time, and before he had readied another blow, Erec's quickness had allowed him to reach the giant and spring back again.

[5549] Thus Erec had struck him four good blows in the leg. That did not bother the giant until finally Erec struck off the leg. When the uncouth fellow fell down on his knees, Erec quickly charged him. Still the devil fought on with a courageous hand. He struck so many enraged blows that it might amaze us that Erec came away alive, except that He, Who had given David the strength to be victorious over the giant Goliath, was with him. He helped Erec too gain victory, such that he with great strength threw the giant all the way down and cut off his head. Thus the fight ended.

[5570] By the time Erec had gained victory the prisoner's horse had carried him

---

118. "God" does not appear in the manuscript, but has been interpolated and appears in most editions and translations.

into the forest so that no one could say where he was to be found. But this put Erec on the right track. Everywhere the prisoner had ridden the trees and grass had become completely covered with his blood, wherever he touched, as his horse carried him, for he was bound so that at no time was he able to avoid the trees, and had to brush against them. Erec, the brave man, tracked him far using the blood until he found him. Then he untied the bonds from his feet and hands and brought the miserable fellow back to his wife just as he had found him, flayed with a whip. Though injured, he was nonetheless alive. But he had no reason to complain because he still had his life and recovered well from this pain.

[5600] When the good lady saw him, both joy and distress entered her heart's shrine. Yet they do not go together well. When she saw him covered with blood, her heart was saddened, for she was not accustomed to see him in such heartfelt misery. She had never seen him punished like this before. At the same time she also experienced joy, so that it gained a victory over grief. This was because he had returned alive. Now the sadness of the lady's heart was transformed like a piece of glass, well polished, which had been completely covered in black. When the color is wiped away, what once was dark becomes beautiful and clear. Thus her heart was like a pure piece of glass, scraped clean of earlier worries and elevated to the light with unfeigned joy as though she had never experienced grief.

[5628] The two lovers were happy. They expressed their thanks to Erec many times. They said, "My lord, we should place ourselves as serfs in your power, since we owe our lives to you."

[5634] Erec answered the knight, "My lord, had I served you in some useful way, I would be forever pleased. God willing, this may happen yet—in so far as I have not already been useful—for I have the good intention of doing so. At this time I ask of you as a reward no other kind of honor than to tell me who you are." He gave his name as Cadoc, from the land of Tafriol, and told Erec how it had happened that the two devils had captured him. From his land he had wanted to travel to Britanje so that he and his lady love could be introduced to the king's retinue. His way led through the forest. The giants had been told this beforehand. They had long been his enemies. I do not know for what reason they were against him. Anyway, at that moment they had lain in ambush for him along the road and had captured him as he rode by.

[5662] When Erec had heard how things had come about for the knight, he said in a very clever fashion in order to relieve the knight's suffering, "My lord, do not be unhappy regarding these things that the giants inflicted on you. No one who wants to exercise manly courage is spared things happening to him for which he might perhaps be ashamed. Afterward it will be made up to him. How often have I been treated worse!"

[5675] With these words Erec consoled him. He continued, "This is my advice: do not let anyone keep you from completing your journey to Britanje as you had intended. Things there are such, as I can truthfully tell you, that in no other land anywhere can a knight gain greater praise than there. Whoever can achieve success there will quickly become a fortunate man. Now I desire a token of honor from you and nothing more. When you arrive in the land, take your lady friend by the hand and go before the queen and tell her I am at her service. Inform her all about your affairs and that I have sent you there to her to join the retinue. My name is Erec. She knows me well."

[5699] He promised this, and they parted. Cadoc rode to court and did as Erec had requested. He paid the queen his respects properly, according to the instructions Erec had given him. He placed himself in her power. The lady with the crown, the most noble queen, wished for Erec all good fortune in return.

[5710] Gallant Erec very quickly rode out of the forest again and searched for the place where he had ordered Lady Enite to wait for him. He had fought so hard that his wounds could not stay closed; they had opened again. He had lost so much blood, and the blows had so exhausted him, that he lost all color, and his strength was so sapped that only with great effort did he ride back to where the lady was waiting for him. Had he needed to ride on further, he would have dropped dead. This was very apparent by what then transpired.

[5730] When the half-dead man began to lean over in order to dismount, for he needed to rest, he was so faint that he fell over head first. He took such a fall that he lay there as if dead. Now there rose up in Lady Enite's heart at this fall bitter distress and the gall of all her suffering. In her misery the good woman raised a pitiful, heart-wrenching lament. Her wailing was so loud that the forest reverberated from it. There was no one to help her lament her heartfelt misery save for the echo that the forest sent with equal loudness out to the field and back. There was no one else there to help her lament her heart's distress.

[5755] The good lady fell over him and kissed him. Then she struck her breast, kissed him again, and cried out. Every other word was "Woe, oh, woe is me!" She tore mightily at her hair and took revenge on her body, as women are wont to do, for this is how they take revenge. Whatever they suffer, the good ladies do nothing about it, but only set their eyes and hands to work at crying and beating themselves, for they can do nothing else. Therefore may he who causes harm to women suffer misfortune—this is what I wish him—for that is neither manly nor good.

[5774] Lady Enite vented her anger on God, "Lord, if this is Your will that such a brave knight lose his life because of his pure heart, then a strange kind of anger has robbed Your mercy of its compassion. I have heard about You that You are merciful. What a pitiful example of it You show to poor me! If You want to have mercy on me, look, now is the time. Look how my husband lies dead or half-dead. Have mercy. That is what I need, for my heart has died. See how sadly I stand here. Have mercy on me, Lord, for it is to be pitied if I, an orphaned woman, should live any longer in such lonely misery. Even if all Your works are without a flaw, Lord, I accuse You of a wrongdoing by letting me live any longer, since You have taken from me the one for whom alone I should live. If You can show, Lord, that the depths of all hearts are visible to You—for nothing can be hidden from You—then make that apparent through Your mercy. And if I, ever since gaining my husband, have brought any ruin whatever upon him through any thoughts or deeds that were not proper, I shall find it just if Your power takes him from me, for it is just that I do without him. But if I have not done that, then You should not punish me.

[5818] "Lord, have mercy on me then in Your goodness, and let him live for my sake. But if You do not want to give him back to me, then be reminded, Lord God, of a word You have spoken that is known to the entire world, and I beseech You that You let it be, that a man and his wife shall be one body.[119] Do not separate us, for otherwise I shall suffer unjust violence at Your hands. If Your mercy is boundless, then help me too find death here. Where are you now, hungry animals, both wolf and bear and lion? May one of you come here and devour us both, so that our bodies do not have to separate and go two ways! And may God deign to take care of our souls, which will truly not be separated, no matter what happens to our bodies."

[5842] Seeing none of these animals come, she called out to them again and said, "You stupid animals, you have already feasted on many sheep and swine, the livestock of poor people who neither begrudged you that nor could overcome the loss. If you were smart, you would fill your mouths with food here, for I willingly give myself to you. That would certainly have to please you. Come then, you can gladly take me. Where are you now? I am right here."

[5856] The invitation did not help her a bit, for no animal heard it or came there. But if one were to come and clearly see her sad bearing, I am quite certain that, no matter how hungry it was, it would in the end help her lament her pain,

---

119. Compare Genesis 2:24: "and [a man and his wife] shall be one flesh."

and would make clear that she was to be pitied. Against her will she remained alive.

[5870] When she realized that she was not going to die, she really began to lament and almost killed herself. One never saw greater misery. She said, "My dear lord, since I must lose you, I renounce here forevermore all men except for the one whom I truly love in my heart with all my being. I have suddenly fallen in love with him. If, regarding him, I were deserving of his liking me, I would always be a loyal wife to him. Dear Death, it is you I mean. Out of my love for you it happens that I, a woman, reverse the custom and court you, a man. I need your love so much. Accept me, most perfect Death. Alas, how well it suits me, poor woman, to be in your arms! You are a very good match for me. Why do you not take me at once? Since you will of course have to take me sometime, I advise you to do it now. I suit you well as a wife. I still have both beauty and youth, and have noble qualities. You cannot come quickly enough for me. What good am I to you later when both age and grief have robbed me of my beauty and youth? What will I be to you then? Now I still suit a noble man."

[5908] When she had spoken at length and was unable to convince Death with her pleading, and could not get her way and have him take her in his power, she scolded him in typical womanly fashion, as her will ordered. She said, "Alas to you, most evil Death! May you be cursed! What a clear picture you give of your stupidity! The world speaks truthfully of you when it says that you are full of treachery. You make every effort to harm many who should never suffer grief. I have witnessed this often regarding you. You have very bad advisers, for you suddenly take the life of such a capable man, whose loss the world cannot get over, and let go the one whose death the world has long desired, and you let him grow old. You exercise your power stupidly. You have brought down here a gallant man and have tried to bind me to him in a way you should not have, if you wanted to deserve that I always speak well of you. Now I do not know where I, poor woman, should turn. I was born to misfortune, for now I have lost both body and soul, as a woman deserves for such a great wrongdoing of having betrayed her husband as I did mine.

[5947] "He would have been spared death here if I had not brought him to it. He would never have thought about this fateful journey if I had refrained from the lamenting sigh I uttered so deeply when I thought he was asleep that day on which I lay next to him. Cursed be the day when I mentioned the matter, for I destroyed my good fortune, great honor, and comfort. Alas, how badly I have acted! Why did I, foolish woman, want to speak of that? Indeed, God had given me the life my heart desired, where things for me were as I wished. Unwisely I acted as fools do who begrudge themselves honor and wealth and cannot bear it when things go well for them, and on the advice of the devil do things that destroy their good fortune, for he is glad when they do without their honor.

[5974] "Alas, dear mother and good father! My great affliction is still completely unknown to you at this time. You both supposed that my lot had greatly improved, and that was certainly to be expected, since you gave me as wife to a mighty king. This expectation has turned into loss for me. He is mistaken who thinks he can divert from being completed what God has ordained. No trick will be of any use. His will must be done. This must also happen to me. I must suffer misfortune. That has become apparent to me from the bitter hardships I have suffered up to now. He has condemned my very existence. That has been made clear to me. What He is planning to do with my soul I cannot know. I shall not complain about whatever now happens to my body if my soul is saved. What I have often heard is now clear to me: no matter what one does for an unfortunate person, his luck will never improve.

[6008] "Whoever might take a linden tree from being miserably cared for at the side of a road and plant it in his garden, compensating it with a gardener's care for its earlier miserable existence in arid soil, and whoever might do that with the thought of caring for it in his orchard so that it might become a good fruit tree, could not be more greatly deceived by a dream, for no matter how diligent one might be, it could not be grown to produce better fruit than earlier, as was its nature, before it was dug up from poor soil at the side of the road where it seemed to be badly cared for. However beautiful and noble a tree it is, a lot of digging and manure can be wasted on it. One can gain an example of this from poor, God-forsaken me, and the world might take pity on my very great fall. And if the entire world crowned me queen of all women, God has still destined my existence to misfortune, so that I must suffer affliction as long as I live, unless God puts an end to my life.

[6042] "Since things have turned out for me such that God has taken from me the dearest man a woman ever had, and since Death does not want me, then let him bear the consequences. The loyalty between us will not end like this. I shall surely find some shrewd way for him to make me, against his will, part of his retinue. Why should I be so eager to fall at his feet, since he will not concern himself with me? I can surely give myself here on the spot what I so urgently implored of him. I shall not wait any longer. It will be done. Truly, I have made a good decision."

[6062] She slid her hand to the ground where she grasped her husband's sword and drew it from its sheath as though she wanted to stab herself out of grief and childishly take revenge on herself for her husband's death, but God forbade her to

t her alive with a merciful trick, so that she began at once to curse
on as she saw it. It was a miracle that her heart did not break from
fury of her misery her voice broke right in two, into tones high and
echoed frighteningly what she cried out. Often it resounded, "Alas,
alas!" Crying out very loudly in a lamenting voice, she said when she looked at the
sword, "Alas, cursed be the hour when you were forged! You have killed my hus-
band. It is your fault that he has lost his life. Indeed, neither here nor elsewhere
would he have fought terrible battles had he not had assurance of your help. In
this way you have robbed me of him. Risking his life, he undertook many a jour-
ney that he would have forgone had they not been undertaken because my dear
lord trusted in you so completely. He said very often that you were splendid. You
have not watched over him well. I do not know if you are sorry. You have betrayed
your loyalty to him. Revenge will be taken against you. You will not get off so eas-
ily. You must commit one more murder."

[6110] She kept her word completely and turned the point against her breast,
eager for death, as though she wanted to fall on it. Then a man came riding up,
whom God had sent, and prevented her from doing so. This was a noble lord, a
count, whose residence was not very far away. The powerful man was called
Oringles, from the race of Limors. God had chosen him to save her life. [He came
from his castle,] riding through the forest, to her good fortune. Why, I have not
been told, but I feel in my heart that it was a blessing for her that he had ridden
out on this day. He had with him a number of knights. By chance he was led into
the forest by the same road where the knight Erec lay in such great affliction, being
cared for by Lady Enite.

[6138] When the lord was still quite far from them, he heard the woman tor-
menting herself with her wailing. And when he heard her voice he came up out
of curiosity in order to see what strange things were happening there and came
right at the moment when she had set the sword against her noble breast to kill
herself. Now he came riding up to the spot, and when he saw her gesticulations,
how she thrust the sword against her body, he jumped quickly from his horse, for
he could have easily come too late, and the thrust would have been carried out.
He quickly grabbed hold of her and warded off the thrust. He tore the sword from
her hand, threw it down, and said, "Tell me, strange woman, why did you want to
take your own life, thereby destroying the most beautiful creature, tame or wild,
that a man ever laid eyes on?" Lady Enite could hardly speak, "See for yourself,
my dear lord, what troubles me." "Did you want to kill yourself?" "My lord, I had
no other choice." "Was he your beloved or your husband?" "Both, my lord." "Now

tell me, who killed him?" Now Lady Enite began to tell in detail the story of what had happened to him.

[6178] The count grew attentive and considered that in all his days he had never seen, near or far, a more beautiful woman. His knights told him the same. He let the lady go and went to have a short talk with his knights. He said to his companions, "One thing is apparent, as you can tell from looking at this lady. Wherever the knight may have found her or however she came here, she is truly a noble woman. Her magnificent person is proof of this. Now tell me, what is your advice? You know well how matters stand with me, that I have no wife. My heart strongly advises me to take her as my wife. It seems to me that she would be well suited as lady over my lands. I saw right away by looking at her that she is of sufficiently high birth for me. My heart's advice as well is to choose her as my wife. Now I ask for your consent with no objection—I shall gladly be in your debt as long as I live— that this might please all of you the same way, with no dissent." They all gave him their consent.

[6212] The count was pleased at this advice. He consoled Lady Enite in an attentive and kind way, as one should a friend who has suffered. He said, "Lovely woman, why do you torment yourself so fiercely? Lady, for God's sake, and also for mine, comport yourself a little better than you have been doing. I must admit that you are behaving like a woman, and in my heart it seems right that you lament your husband, for that shows your loyalty. However, you have done enough of that, for it cannot help you. The smartest action helpful against loss, in my opinion, is to console oneself soon enough, for a long period of regret yields nothing but a miserable life. Think about this, beautiful woman. If you could give him back his life by crying, we would all help you lament and bear your pain equally. Unfortunately, that cannot happen. Moreover, as I can see, if I am not mistaken, your husband was neither so noble nor so wealthy, nor so powerful, nor so handsome and esteemed that your pain cannot be fully compensated. He will be replaced if you follow me. I believe that God has sent me to you at a propitious time. You will be helped greatly.

[6253] "What a person often considers as great misfortune turns quite easily into something more pleasant than what your thoughts have imagined here today, dear lady. They will turn into great honor. Your poverty will now change into great wealth. I am a count and also lord over a powerful land. You shall be the lady over it. See, now it will be apparent to you that your husband's death is to your benefit and works to your good fortune, for only now will you be well off. I do not have a wife. I want to take you as my wife. This life will suit you better than riding unprotected across the land with a man, which is not at all right for you. Knights and squires, ladies, powerful vassals—no count ever had more of them—I shall make them all subject to you, if you will just stop your crying."

[6282] Now the good lady was unable to answer him because of her great distress and her heartfelt misery. She spoke as her heart compelled her, "Enough, my lord, of your long speech. My lord, enough of your derision of me, for God's sake. If you are wealthy, that is fortunate for you. Know, my lord, what I am thinking. I shall tell you in a few words: it can never happen that I become your wife, or anyone's in the world, now or later, unless it were to happen against my will, or unless God gave me back my husband. The first husband I ever had shall also be the last. Believe me, my lord, this is how it will be."

[6302] The count then said to the knights, "Women will talk like that. One should not chide her for that. She will surely get over her distress. I shall bring things to a happy conclusion." He was very pleased with the lady. He ordered all the knights there to cut wood to make a horse-drawn stretcher. This was ready very quickly. Erec was laid upon it as a dead man. They then took him to Limors, and the count had a wake held for him by all he could muster and ordered candles be brought that were to burn over him until he was buried. Lady Enite had reason for her bitter sadness, for she thought Erec was dead.

[6324] When the lord of the castle had fully observed her beauty, she had the effect on him that he could not wait until her husband had been buried, but wanted to have her elevated to the lady of the land that night. Although all his vassals thought it was a disgrace, he sent his messengers throughout the land so that the lords whose office it is to consider God's law would come immediately so that she could be given to him as wife, for he thought he could no longer live without her. So great is the power of love. He truly wanted to be married that night.

[6342] Bishops and abbots came there, and all the priests one was able to reach in the space of a day. However repugnant and painful it was to the lady, she was married to him against her will. Her resistance did her no good. He was going to have her as his wife. He had the intentions, but God had the power.

[6352] Now it was time to eat. The lord of the castle had nothing against this, for he was looking forward to the night. He thought he was going to spend a very pleasurable night with her, which certainly did not happen. I don't care if his hopes deceived him. The lord went to eat, and when he had sat down he sent two chaplains and three of his vassals to the lady, who was caring for her husband as he lay on the bier, to ask her to come to the dinner table. But I think this was for nought, for she did not look at them when the one spoke to her. They reported this to the lord of the castle. Once again he sent for her, this time with many more lords. He did that to honor her, so that she would come more willingly when she heard that food had been set on the table. Because of the pain in her heart she paid no heed at all to the messengers. The lord of the castle said, "I must go to her myself."

[6378] When he came to her, he took her by the hand and asked her to go with him to dinner. The lady asked to be excused. She said, "If I were to eat now and so quickly forget the very dearest man a woman ever had, that would be a meal against womanly decorum. Alas, how would that befit me?"

[6388] He replied, "What are you saying? You are lamenting so much for no reason. You have lost a man whose place I shall take in very good fashion, God willing. I shall very gladly compensate you with my life and my wealth. My mind is set on this, but you are hindering me with conduct that does not become you, such that no one has been able to console you the entire day. It is silly defiance you are engaged in. Your loss is not so great. I am surely more than his equal, or at least as noble. My lady, come here then. I shall place in your hands myself and my land and such great wealth that you can forget your poverty and your grief. So come now and eat dinner with me."

[6412] She replied, "God would not want me to abandon my companion." She swore very solemnly, "I would prefer to be committed to the earth with him. For ever more I shall do without a husband, since God has taken him from me."

[6420] He replied, "Enough of this talk, for my sake. Now come with me to dinner, for truly do I insist upon it."

[6424] No matter how much he beseeched her, she did not want to budge from the spot until he forced her. He dragged her away against her will, for she could not fight him. He did not seat her at his side. A folding chair was set up for her opposite him, as he requested, so that he could gaze upon the lady even better. Repeatedly he asked her to eat, but she could not forget her dear companion. Tears began to fall. The end of the table where she sat became wet from her eyes. She wrung her hands in misery, the very miserable woman, and lamented unceasingly. No matter how much the lord of the castle beseeched her to control herself, she could not stop.

[6446] Then he spoke to her again, "Lady, in your stubbornness you are making things miserable for you and me and my dear guests, who have come here to enjoy themselves. And if you would not act like a child, you would cease your lamenting, and if you could only rightly understand how things have improved for you so magnificently in such a short time, then there would be little that troubled you. I have never seen anything so strange as this: that you cannot be silent and do not want to accept that things are now very good for you and have changed for the better. Whoever has been as fortunate as you will be here would do better to

sing than to weep and lament. I must tell you honestly that your misery is too stead-
fast. If you compare today with yesterday, there is no similarity between how things
are for you. You were poor before; now you are wealthy. No one esteemed you
before; now God has granted you honor. You were completely unknown before;
now you rule over a land. In poor circumstances before; now a lady of means. Not
respected before; now a powerful countess. You traveled about aimlessly before,
until your good fortune chose me. You were bereft of all comforts before; now you
have full honor. You suffered many hardships before, but God has led you away
from that. You led a miserable life before; now God has given you everything you
could wish for. Many things troubled you before; now praise our Lord that He has
delivered you from them, and quit your silly lamenting. You lived without honor
before; now you have more than any other woman in your land. You castigate your-
self, if you wish to know, for no reason. Your poor husband has died on you, but I
have compensated you for this. You should always be happy to make such an
exchange. I would advise it to all women, for it should not trouble them to have a
wealthy husband in place of such a man. I forbid this foolishness of yours. Now
do as I say and eat!"

[6507] Then the noble queen replied, "My lord, you have said enough to me,
and it would have been better left unsaid. I shall answer you very briefly. Your long
speech is in vain. On my oath believe me: food will never cross my lips unless my
dead husband eats first."

[6515] Now the count could no longer control himself and showed his ignoble
side. His anger led him to great foolishness [and great uncouthness] so that he
struck her with his hand such that the good lady bled profusely. He said, "Eat, you
stupid cow!" All present, in a similar fashion, both in their thoughts and in their
words, found this to be very uncouth. Several reproached the count severely to his
face. The others said secretly that it was a foolish thing to have done and that he
should not have done it. He was berated greatly for it. They reproached him to the
point that the wicked man flew into a rage. Their reproach vexed him. He said
very coarsely, "You lords, you amaze me that you reprimand me for what I do to
my wife. It's nobody's business to say anything good or bad about what a man does
to his wife. She belongs to me and I to her. How do you want to prevent me from
doing to her what I want?" These words silenced them all.

[6550] We shall not conceal from you the lady's conduct upon being struck: she
was pleased, and more so than at any time that day, by the blow. Where did her
joy come from? You might like to hear this, for blows seldom make anyone happy.
Her joy came about in the following way: she would have preferred a thousand

times over to be dead than alive, and when she received the blow—which was delivered with a man's strength—she had the hope and solace of being delivered from this life, and that he would punish with blows anything further she said until he had beaten her to death. Therefore her lamenting became vehement, and she cried out against all propriety, hoping thereby to earn her death. She stepped far away from him and said, "Believe me, my lord, I shall pay no attention to your blows, and whatever else you do to me. Even if you take my life, I shall never become your wife. Of this you can rest assured." She continued speaking so long until he once again struck her severely on the mouth. She did not duck his blow, but rather moved toward him to get more. She thought she would get what she wanted. She said, "Alas for me, poor woman! If my companion were alive, these blows would not be tolerated."

[6587] When she began to lament so loudly, Erec fil de roi Lac [was still lying unconscious], seemingly dead, yet not actually dead. He had recovered somewhat, but had not improved greatly. He lay dazed and was startled by the noise like one who awakens frightened by a bad dream. He started up from the bier with a bewildered look and glanced around. He wondered what had happened to him and did not know how he had gotten there. He heard her a second time, for she cried out quite often, "Alas, dear lord, alas! It is in vain that I desire your help, for you are unfortunately dead." When she called him thus, he recognized her immediately and heard clearly that she was in some difficulty, but he did not know how or where. He did not remain lying there. When he recognized her voice, he jumped up furiously and stormed in among them.

[6617] Nearby a number of swords were hanging on a wall. He took one in his hand. He was full of rage. On the first charge he struck the lord of the castle and two others who sat on either side of him. The others took flight. No one stood on ceremony. One saw no one step back and say, "My lord, after you," for anyone having a clear path got out of there—this is how matters stood for them—the laity before the clergy. No matter how highly placed the tonsure was, little distinction was made even if it was an abbot or bishop. The entire court fled. At the doors it had become very narrow because of the great throng. The squire shoved his way ahead of his lord. The way to the doors seemed to them all too long. I never attended such a wedding. A step seemed like a mile to them.

[6643] They quickly began to flee and scatter. Many a splendid squire lay under a bench, contrary to knightly etiquette. One thing often happens that does not surprise me: whoever fears for his life often flees for safety from the tumult from the valley below up to the castle, but these fled from the castle and crawled into holes like mice. The wide castle gate was inside and out too small and too narrow for them, so that they fell over the walls in droves, like a hailstorm, driven by terrible fear. Limors was depopulated. They had good reason to flee, for they feared death. Their flight was not a disgrace. Anyone who might think they were dishonorable would be speaking too hastily. Tell me yourselves: if a dead man with bloody wounds, laid out on a bier, with head and hands covered, and feet in bandages,[120] should suddenly charge with a bare sword at a group without warning, yelling a battle cry, then anyone who valued his life would flee. And if I had been there, I would have fled as well, as brave as I am otherwise. No one dared wait for him except for lady Enite. She was happy to see the dead man. Her distress all turned to happiness, and her joy grew.

[6688] He took her by the hand and urgently went searching until he found his armor, and also his shield and lance, and armed himself as before, as though he had never been injured. He did not find his horses. "Alas, what fate! Do we have to go on foot now? Never before have we done that." May God send Erec and Enite, strangers in this land, horses to ride.

[6702] When he could not find the horses anywhere, he acted as the situation warranted: he took his shield and his lance in his left hand, and leading Lady Enite at his right side he hurried out the castle gate. In front of the gate his steed was brought to him, which he expected just as little as the person did who was riding it. But in this way his good fortune became very apparent. One of the count's pages had led it to water. He was sitting on the steed singing a rotrouenge,[121] unconcerned about anything, for he knew nothing of what had happened. He was now riding up the road to the castle. Erec recognized his steed as soon as he saw it at a distance. This made him very happy. God's will had brought it about. Erec stood very still until his horse came so close that he could take it by the bridle and have it again in his care. He set out on his way. In front of him he seated the queen, Lady Enite—it was the best he could do—and thought he would ride straight through the land, but he did not know the way. His journey was also hindered by the fact that the night was dark. He also feared that he might suffer harm and disgrace in the land at the hands of the local people once they learned what he had done. With Lady Enite's help—for she showed him the way—he turned back to the road on which he had come on the bier. He did this for safety's sake.

---

120. See John 11:44: "The dead man [that is, Lazarus] came out, his hands and feet bound with bandages, and his face wrapped with a cloth."

121. This apparently connotes a certain singing style or type of song in the medieval music of the French troubadours and trouvères, but a further definition remains elusive.

[6750] These three lands bordered each other and were quite close together: the one where he had killed the count, the one belonging to the little man from whom he had suffered the wound, and that of King Arthur. These three were separated only by the forest through which he was riding after this last ordeal.

[6760] When they had come into the forest, out of harm's way, back on to the familiar road, King Erec then asked Lady Enite how he had fallen into the hands of the count about whose slaying I have told you. She now told him the entire story, her eyes distressed and weeping the whole time. Immediately the distressing, strange matter came to an end, as well as the peculiar pretense with which he had treated her up to that day without cause, in that he had avoided speaking to her ever since they had ridden from home. The reason this strange matter had been undertaken became clear to Erec, and he knew it completely without a doubt. It had been done to test her, to see whether she were a good wife for him. Now he had tested her fully, as one has to refine gold in the furnace, so that he was now certain that he could consider her loyal and faithful, and that she was a trustworthy woman.

[6792] He pressed her to his breast, kissed her any number of times very lovingly, and asked the virtuous lady to forgive him for the irksome life and the many hardships she had suffered on the journey. He promised her a better life, which he truly kept. She forgave him on the spot, since he had asked her in a loving way. She said, "Dear lord, no other misfortune, of which there were innumerably many, troubled me so much. They were all small in comparison to the one whereby I had to avoid you. Had I had to suffer that any longer, I would have quickly died from it."

[6814] While this miracle was happening at Limors, just look! A page escaped. He ran away through the forest in order to tell the brave little king, as soon as he could, what had happened. I have already told you about him: he was called Guivreiz, the same one who with his own hands inflicted the wound on Erec. The page knew the way well enough and hurried quickly. Moreover, it was nearby. Only the forest separated the two territories. He pounded on the castle gate. He did not have to wait long, but was let in very quickly. He went before the king and told him how Count Oringles had been killed, and that a dead man had done it. From the story Guivreiz then at last realized that it was Erec. He had not yet gone to bed and very loudly he cried out, "To arms! What a misfortune it would be if the best knight living were to lose his life! May God protect him! If the local people find out, they will murder him at once. Alas, if I could only stand in front of him, I would do that for my friend. In any case I shall try, God willing."

[6852] He quickly armed himself and all his knights. All in all there were thirty knights. Their horses were brought out. Anxious and grieving, the king hurriedly turned toward the forest so that he could help the stranger get out of the land.

[6862] They both happened upon the same road, on this side Erec and he on the other, the one riding in this direction, the other in that, so that they could not help encountering each other. Thus fate would have it. Neither of them knew of the other's journey. Therefore Erec came into great danger. When they were still far away from each other, the lord who was a stranger in the land became well aware of the armed troop, for the clatter and noise of the shields was great. He said to Lady Enite, "My lady, I hear a great army riding toward us. I do not want to avoid them without a fight, like a coward. I have very little strength, but I shall give them knightly combat in sufficient quantity. Dismount on the road now until you see how things turn out." I think the lady had few sufferings this great before, for she saw how weak he was.

[6892] Erec stopped on the road. Meanwhile the others came riding up. The moon, which had appeared from behind the clouds, offered them a clear night. Now the king noticed Erec, for he was at the head of his troop. He saw him stop on the road. Erec in the meantime readied himself for battle. May God now protect him! What do you want the king to do? He readied himself too, for he had to joust if he did not want to be a coward. I can most certainly say about him that he was not a coward. He showed that there and also often elsewhere.

[6910] They lowered their lances and showed their strength. They charged at each other. It was a magnificent joust. The two splendid knights hit their marks exactly. Only the strength of the better-rested man helped him gain victory and do so well. He thrust Erec a spear's length behind his horse. Then he dismounted over him. Lady Enite was dismayed at this.

[6926] This had never happened to Erec, and no one could claim, without lying, that any man had ever thrust him to the ground. Furthermore, the worthy knight would have overcome it immediately had he been healthy. His strength had left him such that he had to suffer the king's superiority. The king untied Erec's helmet and was about to kill him. Lady Enite could not stand for this. She did not remain a moment where she stood hiding in great anxiety. She sprang from the hedge and threw herself over her companion, saying, "No, brave knight, if you have ever had knightly spirit do not kill my husband! Consider that he is severely wounded. Therefore you will have no honor if you do anything further to him, for you would be committing a sin. King Guivreiz, if I remember his name, wounded him in the side."

[6957] Guivreiz recognized Lady Enite by her voice. Moreover, it helped that she said his name. He stepped back very quickly, saying, "Lady, tell me who this knight is, and tell me as well how you know me. I am the one whom you named. I think I have done something bad. Lady, you should tell me how things stand with you. Is this knight Erec, and are you Lady Enite? I do not want to remain here too long, for I have come because of him, and shall tell you how I heard the troubling news about him, that he was in danger here in the vicinity at Limors. According to what I have been told, I fear that he will be killed if in the meantime I do not immediately show that my companions and I intend to help him. I am delaying too long in the forest. I must go to him quickly. It will be terrible if he is killed."

[6985] Enite told him everything again and gave him proof. Because of this Erec kept his life. She undid his coif. The king recognized Erec without a doubt. He was very glad to see him and said in a friendly way, "Welcome, my lord, and tell me if something troubles you, and what the story is here." Erec answered, "Nothing troubles me. Except for where you wounded me I am uninjured."

[6998] This pleased Guivreiz greatly. He then removed his helmet. Out of joy the two men ran to each other and kissed each other sincerely. Guivreiz was pained by the distress Erec had suffered in the joust because of him. When he started to lament this, Erec said, "You need not speak of this or think about it. You did not treat me wrongly. If a man acts foolishly and gets his reward, that is good. Since I, fool that I was, could from my foolishness ever be so arrogant to want to take control of a stranger's road by myself and hold off so many brave knights, you treated me justly. My punishment was too small, since I, all by myself, wanted to have the honor of all of you. I should have been punished more severely." When they had finished talking, Guivreiz bowed before Lady Enite and bade her welcome. The queen thanked him for this. Now that they were assured that Erec's life was not in danger, they were all pleased.

[7031] They then mounted their horses and rode a short distance. Lord Guivreiz led them away from the road to a meadow, caring for them in a joyful fashion. For Lord Erec's sake they stayed there the night so that he could rest up from his exhaustion. As circumstances permitted they were provided with a very good fire. This was not a problem at all. There was plenty of wood there that only needed to be carried to the fire.

[7046] As they sat by the fire and forgot all about their grievous hardships, and when Erec had told of the afflictions he had suffered since he had ridden away from Guivreiz, after both had simultaneously wounded the other—this I have not kept from you, but have told you as much as I know—Guivreiz and his retinue greatly deplored these dear guests' situation and thanked God heartily that Erec was still alive, for his life had so often hung in the balance, like a shipwrecked man on the ocean's waves who swims to shore on a board. Erec had often led an anxious life similar to this one. Now God and his own bravery had led him from the waves' troubles to the sands of grace, so that he now had overcome all his grief and now sat there very happy. May God continue to help him. Without a doubt he has been successful up to now.

[7079] Now it was time to go to bed. The squires all went to look which place would be the most suitable to set up a bed for Erec. As they were searching, they saw three beech trees standing on one side of the fire, thick and well-formed, of equal height, with rich foliage and branches spread wide apart. Under one tree, separate from the rest, they prepared a bed for the dear guests, Erec and Lady Enite, who for some time had not lain next to each other or shared each other's company while sleeping or eating. The senseless animosity had come to an end, and they chose a better life. For the lord of the land they prepared a bed under the next beech tree, which stood in the middle, and for the knights a bed under the third. "Now tell me, what was their bedding?" Truly, what the forest gave: beautiful foliage and fresh grass, the best in the forest. Why all these questions when after all they were sleeping?

[7112] The night ended pleasantly. When day came they rode on. The tiny man, Guivreiz, their host, led them to better comfort nearby, at one of his castles, where he knew they would be safe and very comfortable. This castle was replete with good things, exactly as I shall tell you.

[7124] It stood in the middle of a lake that provided it with enough, and more than enough, of the best fish, of whatever kind that was, ever brought to a king's dinner table. In addition, there was the best hunting there that we have ever heard of. Around the lake the king had enclosed two miles or more of the forest and encircled it with a wall. There was no other gate than the one that led to the lake. This very circle, as I can tell you, was divided by walls into three equal parts. One of these parts contained a lot of red deer. Another part had wild boar. Are you asking what is in the third part? Only small game was segregated in the third part: fox, hare, and the like.

[7149] This preserve was fully stocked such that no one who liked to hunt could ever complain that he could find no game. In addition, the host had provided the hunting lodge with dogs that followed commands. Whenever he looked out from where he sat on the battlements at anyone running with them, those men who were running could not see any better than he. Who could blame him for wanting to watch from the castle with the ladies as the dogs ran? For whenever the red deer were flushed, their first run was toward the water at the lake, and they were never caught anywhere else but beneath the castle. And whoever felt like hunting boar or bear, he found for this purpose many strong, stout spears. And if he wanted to hunt hare, as you have heard before, he could find whatever he wanted in a harrier. Just hunt anything you want. Here are dogs and game and whatever one needs for hunting, nets and good bows, and whatever else your heart desires. The entertainment here was good.

[7188] Penefrec was the name of this castle where nothing could be found wanting, just a rich abundance of fish and roast game, bread and wine. Whatever else there should be, nothing was wanting. For this reason the host had brought the worthy guest there to rest, for he had in mind that Erec, along with his wife, could regain his health there. There was also an ample supply of rich bed linens. As a reward for his bravery he was greatly honored and well received there. He and the queen were taken care of in magnificent fashion. Who will be the doctor to heal his wounds? For this the host had found two very distinguished ladies, noble and beautiful, who were sisters of the king. They were very glad to do this and happy in their hearts that he had come to them thus, in need of their services. Such doctors suited him well. They healed his wounds, for they well knew how. In addition, the good lady Enite tended him with loving care. Because of this his side healed completely and well. The two ladies had in their possession part of the bandage I told you about that Morgain le Fay had made with her own hands. Lady Guinevere had sent them part of it as a gift. That helped cure this man.

[7232] King Erec stayed at Penefrec Castle until he had completely recovered and his wound had healed: exactly fourteen days. When his physical strength had been fully restored, he again thought of his journey. However comfortable he was there, he was still very distressed. The gallant warrior truly desired to leave there soon, just as he would were he in a forest, without shelter, alone with no comfort, where the honest warrior would be very severely troubled by wind and rain both. This came from his thinking that nothing in the world was more pleasant than knightly endeavors in which he had to use his own hands. This was the life he had chosen. He liked it. It was his sleep and his food. The fourteen days, it is true, seemed to him like many years. He did not want to stay there any longer and would have left earlier had he been able.

[7264] Alas, Lady Enite! What shall she ride, the beautiful, good, well-born lady? For she had lost her palfrey, as you heard earlier, when Count Oringles was killed at Limors, and when Erec just barely escaped with her from there. That she has lost it—she shall find help for that. She will be well compensated, for it will be replaced—such that she will never have to complain—with one, as I shall now tell you about: never indeed has one owned or seen one more beautiful. The ladies, the king's two sisters, gave it to her, and were very pleased that she deigned to accept it from them. Moreover, it suited her very well.

[7286] Is anyone asking if it were more beautiful than the one she had ridden up to now? They cannot be compared at all. It was adorned thus: it was of very different colors. The left side was a gleaming white that could not be whiter, and so splendid that the luster dazzled one's eyes. No one could look at it very long. This is what I heard the master say.[122] The other side had made every effort to compete with this. As completely white as it was on the left side—which I have just read aloud to you—this side was just as black wherever the white ended. It was actually black and white. This varied contrast was beautifully differentiated. Between the two colors ran a streak about half a finger in width. The streak was green and shiny like grass. It began at its mouth and ran like a brushstroke between its ears right over the mane down the backbone to the croup, down to where the horse ends, then likewise down the chest, as is certainly fitting. This was a wondrous thing. Around each eye went a ring of the same color, that is true. Its mane was soft and curly, the part gathered where it hung down, just the right thickness and not too long. It did not quite reach down to its knees. The forelock on front of its head was long, half black, half white, and divided by the green color. Its tail was the same.

[7336] Since I have told you a bit about the kind of horse it was, I shall now tell you about the rest of its appearance: it was as one would wish, neither too squat nor too high, neither too short nor too long, neither too strong nor too weak. It carried its narrow head just at the right height, its ears pricked up, not long, the one black, the other white. A white ring encircled the black one, a black ring the white one. Its neck, strong and extended, curved just right, and slender where it joined the head, shaped here and there in a way that would please you. It was strong and broad in the chest, with slim legs, neither too long nor too short. They were flat and straight like a deer's. It had, since I am praising it, short hocks and high hooves. These, too, were just right, all the same tone of black. And even if a groom never curried it, it would still be beautiful and smooth.

[7366] With regard to its perfection, its build was such that a wise man, who knows the ways of all things in the world, could think of nothing better if he turned his thoughts to it for eight years and forgot about everything except how his mind

---

122. Here and further (lines 7462, 7893, 8201), a reference to Chrétien (see note 2), who spends *only* fifty lines describing the horse's decoration, whereas Hartmann takes nearly five hundred.

might conceive of a beautiful and perfect horse. Thus was its make-up. And if he then had the power that this idea, as he had imagined the horse to be, could be fulfilled, and if he could bring about placing the horse in front of him, and if he had the power to remove from it what did not fit, it was still so perfect that he would not have removed even a hair. If anyone says, "He's not telling the truth," I shall explain things to him better so that he will realize that these things are not a lie. The horse was not bred in this land.

[7394] I shall tell you how it came there: the lord of the castle himself had taken it away from a savage dwarf in front of a mountain cave when he had ridden out seeking adventure in the forest, as he was wont to do. The dwarf had tied it very securely to a branch and had then left. Thus the lord found it. He untied it from the branch. When the dwarf returned and did not find the horse at the tree where he had tied it, he was greatly distressed. And when he saw the horse in a stranger's possession, he cried out loudly and wept bitterly and made it known how good the horse was. His outrage was very great. He offered the lord three thousand marks in gold to leave him his horse. The lord rejected what he offered him. He had no need of the money. He thus led the horse away. The little man raised such a great outcry in his misery that the mountain echoed back to him.

[7426] Regarding the little saddle on it, if one were to pay its weight in gold, one would not pay the right price for it. So that the story does not get too long, I shall not tell you any more about this except that the horse was too small for a grown man. And when the lord had brought it from the woods to Penefrec, he gave it to the ones for whom he had intended it: his two sisters. This showed that he loved them, for the horse carried a rider gently and quickly, and I shall tell you exactly how. Whenever it set a hoof on the ground, it stepped so gently that no one, no matter how sensitive, would at any time be able to hear the step. Whoever sat on it—this I tell you truly—felt as if he were floating. If it were not unjustified, and also a bit unfitting, to talk so much about a horse—which I shall not do—then I could tell wondrous things about it. But I shall refrain from any further praise. People can say what they will, tell stories, and speak their minds, but never has a man possessed such a magnificent horse. What more should I tell you?

[7462] As the master has told us, a lady's saddle had been placed on the horse. It displayed much masterly work and artistic skill. The most skillful man in saddlemaking had to work many days on it: a master by the name of Umbriz, who truly devoted all his hard work to it for nearly three and a half years in order to complete it as he had imagined it. If I wanted to tell you exactly how this saddle was made, that would be too difficult for such a simple fellow like me. Even if I could tell you exactly, it would take too long for one mouth to say. Besides, the fact that I have not seen the saddle weakens my observations. As briefly as I can, I shall let you know something of how it was made, as I was told by the person from whom I have the story, as I read in his book.

[7493] "Now keep quiet, dear Hartmann, and see if I can guess."[123] "I shall, but speak quickly." "I have to think about it first." "Then very quickly. I'm in a hurry." "Do you think I'm a smart man?" "Certainly, but tell me now, for God's sake." "I want to tell you a story." "You can refrain from speaking about the rest." "It was made of good ironwood." "Right, what else then?" "Brightly gilded." "Who could have told you that detail?" "With very strong bindings." "You have guessed correctly." "With a bright red woolen cloth." "That makes me laugh." "See, I can guess correctly." "Right, you're a good weather prophet." "You speak as though you were ridiculing me." "Oh, God, no." "But your mouth has a ridiculing look." "I always like to laugh." "So I did guess then?" "Yes, you hit it right on the head." "Have I perhaps forgotten something?" "Right now you don't know what you're saying." "So I'm not right?" "Not by a mile." "Did I lie then?" "No, your childish fancy betrayed you. You should let me tell you."

[7526] See how big a grain of sand is. There was not even that much wood in it. It was made of ivory and precious stones and also from the best gold ever purified in a fire. It was free of any adulteration. With great skill the master's artistry had fashioned this saddle out of these three materials. He set the ivory and the precious stones in a pleasing arrangement, as skill dictated. Between them he inlaid gold to hold them together.

[7545] The long Song of Troy[124] was engraved in this saddle. At the very front was how it all began, how Troy was conquered and then destroyed. That was the one part. On the other side was engraved how Lord Aeneas, the very wise man, sailed away over the sea, how he came to Carthage, and how the powerful Lady Dido took him into her favor, how he then abandoned her very meanly and did not carry out what he had promised. Thus the lady was deceived. At the back of the cantle was engraved the story of her great sorrow, and how she sent messengers to him, and how she could not change his mind at all. Here one could clearly see what deeds he did: all the noteworthy things up to the day when he conquered

123. As in *The Lament* (lines 1167ff.), Hartmann is here employing stichomythia, this time in order to inject humor (perhaps directed against a know-it-all critic, a heckler in the audience) and break up a long descriptive passage.

124. The story of Troy was very popular in the Middle Ages. Heinrich von Veldeke's *Eneid*, based on the Old French *Le Roman d'Enéas*, appeared shortly before *Erec*.

Laurentum. It would take too long to tell how he took control of the city. On the other side was depicted how he took Lady Lavinia as his wife, and how Lord Aeneas ruled the land without misfortune until the end of his life.

[7582] The saddle was covered with a fine cloth of silk and gold, the best there could be. The cloth was appropriately long, almost brushing the ground. Separately there to see were all the wonders of the world and whatever the heavens enclose. If you do not mind, I shall tell you about some of them, but refrain from telling about many more.

[7594] The four elements were clearly represented there, each in its own color,[125] and with each all that was subject to it. This was all created with exceptional skill. Of the four, the earth was depicted with its beasts—all of which no single man can imagine—in the forests and fields, tame and wild. The human creature was depicted there with such skill as though it wanted to speak and go beyond the proper nature of a picture.

[7610] Next to it undulated the oceans, and in it, as though alive, fish along with all the wonders of the sea and whatever else lives on the ocean floor. If any-one could inform me of their names, I would like to learn them and be able to name them. Therefore look for someone who can name them for you, but if you can find no one—which is quite possible—then take my advice and set out quickly and go yourselves to the ocean. You will find a great many creatures in it. Go and stand on the shore and ask them to come out to you on the sand. Then you will learn what they are. If that does not work—which is also quite possible—then look at the seafloor yourselves. There you will find out about them with great loss and little gain. Thus I advise some of my friends to suppress their curiosity and stay home. Whatever one always has to pay for dearly, without ever gaining any bene-fit from it, that, my friends, will be bothersome.

[7642] The third element was also depicted. Do you ask what that might be? Air with all its characteristics: birds of many kinds hovered in it, woven with such artistry as though they were alive and flying up to the sky. One also saw swarming about on the cloth fire with its dragons and with other things that live in fire. The edges were trimmed with a braid that hung down to the ground. It was the width of a hand and set with precious stones. The coverlet, on which Jupiter and the god-dess Juno sat on their bridal throne in their lofty realm, was indeed magnificent enough, but, I assure you, could be compared with this saddle cloth as could the

---

125. Since the ancient Greeks, the four elements were air, earth, fire, and water. The colors variously associated with these were usually white, black, yellow, and red.

moon with the sun. You should admit that I am telling the truth. The stirrups were both good and beautiful, wide gold rings in the shape of two dragons. The goldsmith, whose hand took great care with it, knew well how to make them. The tails arched around to their mouths, their wings were spread as though flying, their eyes were jewels, four small hyacinths.

[7680] Concerning the girth and also the stirrup straps: what was each of these made of? You would have to examine the work carefully before you would know to say whether they were trimmed in gold or lined with silk. From looking at the images it would not be apparent to you that they were made of braiding. Unless you took it in your hand you would never know. The buckles, strong and artistically beautiful, were silver, so that one saw a white gleam against the gold.

[7694] The saddle cloth was truly superb, not of calfskin, like many I have seen. No one could glimpse a fingernail's width of leather there. It was good and beautiful as suited the saddle and was appropriate, and magnificently padded, soft as cotton, so that it did not chafe the horse. What one saw of it peering out from the saddle was thickly quilted. Represented on it, in order to give it a pleasing appearance, was how Thisbe and Pyramus, compelled by love and robbed of their senses, came to a sad end when they arrived at the fountain.[126] Where the fringe was supposed to be was a golden netting, woven with golden thread, strong and sturdy, spread over the croup. Set around it at every seam, where the stitches were tied and crossed, were many precious jewels. At every knot there was a ruby in an azure setting. The stones sparkled uniformly from this side with a bright luster.

[7730] The breastplate strap was good and fitting, strong and very beautiful, a braided cord two fingers in width, exactly like the reins by which the horse was led. With great imagination eleven precious stones had been woven onto it. The twelfth had been set alone at the front of the bridle in a broad disk that lay below the forelock and hung in front of the head. The bright carbuncle fulfilled its task there, for brightness is such a part of its makeup that one—if one is riding at night—can see by its light. The eleven stones were set into the breastplate strap, spaced apart. Between them hung beautiful gold bells that one could hear ringing from afar. With such things the saddle had been finished, and better than I could have imagined. In fact, it seems to me right and fitting that it was—from the description—much more beautiful than any other saddle, for it was truly given to the most beautiful woman alive at that time: noble Lady Enite.

[7767] Now it is time for Erec and Enite to ride, for their horses have been

---

126. See Ovid's *Metamorphoses* 4.55ff.

brought up. Did they take their leave from the courtly retinue? Yes, from all the young knights and from the king's sisters. One never saw, either before or since, a firmer resolve in any other ladies to do a variety of good deeds. Good upbringing was in their care. These ladies had the achievement of being rightly included among the finest, wherever noble women are singled out. Whatever a woman can do to gain the deserved favor of God and the world, my ladies Filledamur and her sister Genteflur[127] did this without any gall.

[7788] They now rode off, Enite and these two men: the host himself and Erec. The palfrey carried Lady Enite so gently over the road that even someone floating on the ocean with a favorable wind, whose ship sails along without danger, at no time ever experienced anything more gentle. They intended to ride immediately to Britanje, to the land of King Arthur. At the moment they did not know at which of his castles they might actually find him. King Guivreiz spoke as they rode along, "We shall find him at Karidol or surely at Tintajol."

[7808] They thus rode with this in mind, and yet without any certainty, until midday. Hoof tracks guided them to a crossroad on a beautiful meadow. They did not know which way led to Britanje. The road to the right they did not take, but chose the one better maintained. And after riding about five miles they saw a castle in front of them, large and beautifully constructed. And when Guivreiz saw it, he became very troubled and regretted greatly that they had come there. "Now tell me, why?" I know well and shall tell you when I ought to. Now is not yet the time. How impatient you are! Who would want to get ahead of his story? I shall not keep from you how the castle looked. Listen now to the story.

[7834] The site was excellent. As the source of the story bears witness, it was twelve hides[128] across. It was a round rock without any bulges, smooth as though turned on a lathe, and formed as one would wish, high enough up from the ground to be out of the range of catapults. A high thick wall enclosed the hill. The castle inside was knightly in appearance. Above the battlements rose towers of ashlar whose joints were not held together by sandy mortar. They were bound more securely with iron brackets and lead and set closely together in groups of three. Between the towers there was no lack of structures. There the castle dwellers lived in great splendor. Thus the castle lay spread out with its towers. Their number was thirty in all. Otherwise the castle was laid out in a square. The towers were adorned on top with knobs of reddish gold. Each of them sparkled far out over the land.

---

127. "Speaking names" in Old French: "girl (young woman) of love," and "noble flower."
128. A "hide" was an ancient measurement of various sizes. Here it would mean a large site.

This showed the way to strangers who came riding that way, for they could see the reflection from far away and could not miss the castle when riding by day. A river flowed under the castle. Its falling waters caused a great roar, for it ran through a chasm. This very gorge was so deep that whoever sat on the battlements and let his gaze fall below thought that looking down into the chasm was like looking into hell. Dizziness would draw him down into it such that he fled back inside. On the other side, where one could enter, there stood a very prosperous settlement with numerous buildings that on the one side went down to the water. On the opposite side lay a beautiful, wide park. A more beautiful one has never been seen, either before or since. This is what I heard the master say about it.

[7894] When Erec saw the castle, he asked his companion if he knew of the fortification, and asked him to tell him its name. The lord answered him thus, "I do know of it. We have ridden far from our road. May God damn it! Every time I have ridden this way things have gone badly for me. I have made a bad mistake and have led us to the left."[129] He went on, "The land of Britanje lies far away in that direction. Let us turn around in time. I shall bring you back to the road."

[7911] Then King Erec said, "Would that be the right thing, my noble friend, if we rode off thus? Since we have come so close, come on then, for my sake, so that I can see the castle. Indeed, this is how it must be. This castle is so magnificent and beautiful that I can see very well from the outside that on the inside it is full of things well worth seeing. It will not be lacking in ladies. I want to see the castle. This you should not begrudge me."

[7926] "I am sorry to have to begrudge you this. Alas that you should learn about it!" "What do you mean, King Guivreiz?" "I mean nothing more than what I know." "For God's sake, tell me, what?" "Turn back. That will be better for us." "I can only wonder what you mean." "You will find out well enough if you do not turn back." "Indeed, I must see it. It cannot be worse than death." "Then you will surely run into such danger that your friends will not be able to lament enough." "Will you tell me now, for God's sake, what it is? I can only wonder what it might be." "Turn around then, for my sake. I shall forever be beholden to you." "That would not suit me, for you might think that I forsook this very journey out of fear. Besides, there is no danger you cannot tell me about. And if it were such that I should turn back, I would do so."

[7952] "My lord and king," replied Guivreiz, "I shall tell you exactly what I know: the danger is not slight, and in the hope that you will forsake this journey,

---

129. Since Roman times, left (*sinister*) was considered unlucky. Perhaps Hartmann implies here "into misfortune."

as you have said, I shall tell you. The castle is called Brandigan, and many brave knights have boldly come here in search of adventure, and have all, the best in all the lands, come to harm and disgrace. This has been going on for a long time, and none of them was ever successful, for the same befell all alike: they were all killed in pitiable fashion. What more can I tell you? For I shall, and must, fall down at your feet so that you take my advice and turn back. The adventure here is at such a price that in my heart I fear very greatly that things will turn out the same for you as they have for all the others who have ever come here."

[7982] Erec replied thus, "Then I would be a cowardly man and would be acting disgracefully. I would not know the end of the story if I turned back now. Can you not let me know what the adventure is and what it is called? I would always be ashamed if I were to fear what I do not know. Why are you doing this, keeping it from me so long and not telling me the whole story? For whatever may happen to me, I certainly shall not turn back until I know more of the story."

[7997] Then King Guivreiz said, "Now I shall tell you what the adventure is and exactly what it is all about, since you will not take my advice. It is called Joie de la curt. This phrase is not known among the German peoples, so I shall translate it: it means "the joy of the court." And he told him more, saying, "Take a look. Do you see the park lying below the castle? For some time a knight has been residing there. The adventure has a price, as I shall tell you exactly. Whoever wants to pursue the adventure here has the task of winning it by conquering him in combat. The lord of the castle is his uncle. As far as strength and manly courage are concerned it has always been apparent that nowhere in the realm lives his equal. He has killed whatever knight rode against him pursuing this adventure. No one can withstand him. Turn back, for my sake."

[8028] King Erec then sprang back on the road, laughing loudly and saying, "Noble knight, on then! If it is only a man against whom the adventure is to be won, things will turn out well. Why are you making such a big deal out of it? Is he either a mountain or anything like it that one should fear him so? I thought the castle would be full of dragons or wild beasts that would immediately kill us as soon as we arrived, without our being able to defend ourselves. But I still expect to stay alive. He will not be spared, God willing, another challenge. If he kills me, then I shall be dead. That is of little consequence for the world."

[8048] Guivreiz, the noble king, recognized that Erec was indeed determined to ride there and that he would not avoid it for anyone. This had distressed him from the moment he had first seen the castle. No contrary argument helped. Erec wanted to ride on.

[8056] They now set off on their way, and as King Erec, at the risk of his life, now rode toward Brandigan with his beautiful wife, the town he saw lying below the castle was filled with joy, dancing, and all kinds of entertainment that well befits young people. And when he came riding up, and the townspeople saw beautiful Enite riding in front, and after her the two men, they gazed at the lady, and all said that they had never before seen any lady so beautiful and majestic with regard to her figure and clothing, and her horse and its outfitting. At that very moment they all, man and woman alike, instantly lost their joy because of the intense sorrow that troubled their hearts, and they began to lament miserably for the lovely woman, and that such a brave man should have to lose his life, for they did not doubt that at all.

[8086] They said, "Lord, almighty God, why was it Your will to create such a perfect man? It would have been a sign of Your mercy if You had kept him from this fateful journey, so that he would not have come at all, for here he will lose his life. Alas, you poor woman! How you would torture yourself if you knew what is to happen to you here! How misery will cause your bright eyes to deny that they are now so beaming and know no care, and will change your very red lips that now make people smile at you! And how you will have to give up your cheerful spirit for sorrow when you lose your husband!" They all lamented her. This was not done loudly but in a murmur so that Erec would not notice it.

[8112] They spoke at length about this. Many a woman beat her breast; others wept grievously. Gallant Erec knew what they meant by this, but acted as though he knew nothing about it. Undaunted Erec considered matters in a happy and good way, as a brave man should who cannot easily be disheartened by words. He did not harbor any superstitious thoughts. He wished neither to punish nor make any use of the women's prattle. He paid no attention to what he dreamt.[130] He did not go in for prophesying the weather. He viewed as an old wives' tale whether an owl or a falcon flew across his path in the morning. He also never had a fire made from dry twigs to have his fortune told. He heeded no strange arts. He was a man who was indifferent whether the lines in his hand were wide or narrow, and he paid no attention to whatever superstitions there were. He was such a resolute man that however much the people disheartened him he was not in the least shaken in his manly resolve, and he took it all as a joke. He thought: as long as God keeps me under His protection, nothing bad can happen to me, and if He does not want to put it off, then I might just as well die right now, since we must all die sometime.

130. Compare *Iwein*, lines 3505–48.

[8154] He was free of heartfelt worries. Now he rode up and greeted them with a smile and began at once to sing a very joyful song. But the peopled again murmured, "It seems you do not know what will happen to you here. Unfortunately it will not be long before your joyful song comes to a very sad end. That will happen before this time tomorrow. If you and your wife knew that you were to have this joyful life such a short time, then you would stop your singing."

[8170] The very brave man then rode away from them to the castle of Brandigan. There he was treated as befitted his station and was received magnificently. The lord of the castle came to meet him far in front of the castle gate. He and the residents of the castle greeted him there. As his guest, Erec caused him both joy and pain, for the lord greatly feared that he would lose his life there. Otherwise he was welcome. The lord displayed this clearly to the two men and the queen, for she was treated as befitted her station. It was still midday.

[8188] When these worthy guests were seated in the castle, the host and the residents of the castle entertained them as best they could with many a story so that they would not get bored. After a while he asked whether they wanted to join the ladies. The question pleased them, so he led them, the lady and the two men, to a stairway and, if the master is not lying, into such a beautiful palace that would have suited the rank of the goddess Pallas[131] when she ruled on earth, had she been provided with such a chamber.

[8208] It was very beautifully decorated, round, not square, fine and beautiful, of the most expensive stone ever won from marble, pleasing to the eye, and as one could only wish: yellow, green, brown, red, black, white, and blue. This multicolored appearance was so smooth and so polished that it glowed like a mirror crafted with beauty.

[8221] They saw sitting in here the embodiment of woman. Who could even describe them to you and praise them justly? One had never seen the likes of such a lovely group. There were eighty women, all dressed alike. They had put on splendid dresses that were, however, mournful, and very costly. Thereby they clearly showed that their hearts were in some pain, for one also seldom saw them smile. Their dresses and their outer garments were of black samite. Neither the sleeves nor the sides were laced up. As was pointed out to me, they were loath at this time to display any haughtiness or pride. Their heads were wrapped, in the best manner, with fillets that were white. Regarding them, there was no other intention but simplicity and restraint, without gold embellishment.

---

131. Pallas Athena, the Greek goddess of wisdom.

[8250] When the guests arrived, these ladies received them in a better manner than they were disposed to, as wise people do who never have others suffer their grief when they can keep it from them. The host sat down next to them. Then the guests sat down: Erec with Lady Enite and Guivreiz at their side. He let his eyes roam. Now he thought the one lady was lovely, but the one next to her even lovelier, and the third made them ugly by comparison. The fourth beat her in loveliness of figure. He awarded the prize to the fifth, until he saw the sixth. The seventh made her pale in comparison, until he noticed the eighth. The ninth seemed to him to take the crown, but the tenth was even more beautiful, formed with God's care. The eleventh was so formed as to put to shame the tenth, if the twelfth had not surpassed her. The thirteenth would have been perfect if the fourteenth had not stolen it from her. The fifteenth was all one could wish for, yet her beauty was nothing when compared with the sixteenth. He preferred still to look at the seventeenth, who sat there. But the eighteenth pleased him more than any of these ladies, until the nineteenth appeared, but he liked the twentieth most of all. Who could describe them all? The least of these women would adorn a realm with her beauty.

[8292] When he had gazed at the lovely group at length, he thought to himself: almighty, merciful God, I can see from this that You are rightly called the most miraculous God, and that Your power and Your will have gathered in such a small space so many women who, as You Yourself know, would so splendidly adorn many a vast land that You, through their presence here, are robbing of joy. With this thought he grew silent. The host was in the middle of telling the ladies the story of why the guest had come there with his wife. When the ladies had heard this, they were immediately reminded of the heartfelt sorrow they had all experienced. They now absolutely put to the lie that one had earlier seen them with a joyful appearance. The blood drained from their cheeks. Their noses and cheeks grew pale. Their tears caused this.

[8321] Heroic Erec did not know what this all meant until Guivreiz explained it to him. He said, "Can you see how these noble ladies torment themselves with misery? They were the wives of the knights who were slain here. Why was I not able to convince you to forgo this journey? Beautiful Lady Enite must now remain here if you are unsuccessful in this battle."

[8334] The ladies' pain touched Erec's heart very deeply, since they had been created as a cause for joy and had now relinquished their youth and lives to so much worry, for because of their fidelity their misery was as fresh as when it began. Now and then they looked at the stranger with grief-stricken eyes, lamented his pleasing figure, and were moved to pity that his wife would have to remain there with them. Of this they were certain beyond doubt.

[8350] Erec, who was a stranger there, thought: may God prevent something like that happening to me, that I should fail, thereby adding my wife to this joyless group. The two guests had here a very painful sight, for the ladies' sorrow pained them.

[8359] Now it is time for them to go. The lord led them to dinner. Nothing was forgotten. They had an abundance of everything that is called hospitality. They had finished eating and remained seated and talked about all sorts of things. The king of the land asked them whether they had any news from along their way. The guests then told him what each knew that was worthy of telling. Erec said to his host, "Dear lord and host, near and far people have told me many wondrous things about the splendor of this castle. Now I shall not ask any more about it, for I have seen it myself and must agree with good cause that they have indeed told the truth. I was told further that there is an adventure here, for high stakes, against a brave knight. Now I would like to know exactly what the situation is. Tell me about it, my lord and host."

[8390] The king remained silent for a while. His head sank, and he sat in deep sorrow. This was due to his honest sympathy, and especially because of his goodness the guest's question pained him, for he had already heard earlier that he had come there seeking adventure's prize. This troubled him, and he thought of various ways he might avert that, and how he might help him so that he did not lose his life, and how he might change his mind in a way that befitted them both. Finally, he looked at him and said, hesitantly, "My lord, I shall give you some good advice, as I should to my guest, who is the dearest I have ever had, and for whom I therefore want only good things. Forget your question and ignore this adventure. Last year, and this, and now for the past twelve years, great harm has come from this, as I can tell you truly. Besides, we have both seen so many other things that can help us pass the time. Let us talk of other matters."

[8424] Erec answered him as a brave man whose heart was very constant and harder than diamond, of whose strength it is said that if it were placed between two steel mountains — what greater wonder could there be? — it would grind them to pieces before one could see any effect on the stone. Nevertheless, this man was more constant in bravery, since a certain kind of blood can soften this stone.[132] But except for a deadly blow nothing could vanquish his heart or make it cowardly. He

---

132. Goat's blood was believed to soften a diamond.

laughed at these words and said, "Whatever matter I dare not ask about must be horrible indeed. That I asked about it was not done because I thought I could gain from it greater fame than all the others who have ever come here, but it would bother me if everyone asked me about it and I could not tell them anything, even though I have for a fact been here. They would think I were dishonest."

[8458] Now the host believed he meant what he said. Therefore he explained the matter to him, as I told you earlier: exactly as his companion had told him on the way there. And in case he had kept something from Erec, the lord now told him everything and explained it better. He said the park was strongly fortified, and although it was not enclosed, no one dared enter it if his life and honor still meant something to him.

[8474] He continued, "Living in the park with his lady friend is a knight so manly that with his own strength he has slain all those who, driven by their foolish hearts, could not be dissuaded from seeking adventure. I tell you, any brave knight who comes here with this in mind needs only to go to the gate. At his first word it will open. He can ride inside or walk. The others have to remain outside. Then the gate will close. The matter must then be decided between the two, for whatever happens to either, they will not have any mediator. I do not know how things proceed then. For half a year or longer no one has come to him, ever since he took the lives of these knights I can name. Indeed, he slew three knights here who were recognized as the best in any land. The one was called Venegus, who never missed an opportunity to show his manly courage; Opinaus, who never fled; Libaut was the third man, who earlier had won much honor; he was from the land of the Wends.[133] Even if these knights have lost their lives, you need not risk yours, and if you deign to listen, I shall give you the best advice, and that is that you forgo the battle, for the powerful man is wont to cut off the head of anyone he defeats. If you do not believe this and want to see for yourself, then the same thing will happen to you."

[8520] Then King Erec replied, "I knew well that the Road to Salvation[134] passed somewhere in the world, but I did not know exactly where, so in great uncertainty I rode out seeking until I found it here. God has treated me well by directing me here, where I may find, according to my heart's desire, the ideal game in which with one throw I can wager a little to win a lot. Until today I have been seeking it.

133. Historically, a Slavic people, descendants of the Sorbs, centered in eastern Germany. However, at this time the term was generic, applying to any Slavs living between the Elbe and Oder rivers.

134. *Sælden* is a scholarly emendation of *selbig*, "the same," which does not make sense in this context. See *Gregorius*, line 63, for a similar construction.

Praise God, now I have found it, where I can wager a penny against a thousand pounds. It is a fortunate thing to find such a game here. I shall explain to you better what I mean. I have heard from you that this lord is perfect in heroic manly courage. Therefore his renown is widespread and is greatly praised throughout these lands, for he has done wondrous things. I, in comparison, have unfortunately achieved nothing of the sort. My honor carries little weight. My hand has acquired for me as yet very little of that which distinguishes a knight. Up until today I have done nothing to gain fame. Thus I would gladly risk the little honor I have to increase it here so that I achieve great fame, or lose it entirely. If God grants me the honor of defeating this man, then I shall be rich with honor. And notice how unequal the stakes are in this game. He has more than twelve times as much to lose as I have. He is putting his gold up against counterfeit goods. With regard to honor, he will not gain much if he is accorded the victory over me, for he has often had greater success. Besides, people will quickly get over lamenting me. I assure you, he will not be let off the hook. I shall fight against him."

[8576] The host replied, "Tell me, my lord, why should you mean more to me than you do to yourself? Let us go to bed now; it is time. If we live to see tomorrow, I shall take you to him, if I can. But I advise you in all sincerity to think better of this matter. This seems reasonable to me, for if you do indeed go there, then I shall be very sorry for you, for then we shall never see each other again. You can rest assured of that."

[8591] "My lord, as God will," replied Erec the knight. Therewith they went off to their room to sleep. It was well furnished with costly bedding and with other fittings: it was beautifully covered with splendid wall hangings, richly painted with gold. In addition, the stone floor was covered with splendid rugs, as the host's wealth could well provide, and as befitted his honor, for he was lord of the land and was King Ivreins by name. He ordered the chamber servants to be diligent in their care of them, as one should be for mighty kings. Thus these three guests were honored in splendid and great fashion. Guivreiz, the king, lay nearby in a chamber where he was well cared for as befitted his standing.

[8614] Erec and Lady Enite had a pleasant time as they lay together and cherished a wonderful love until morning came. His heart was not completely free of manly worries, for it is said that he who knows no fear is not a perfect man, but is counted among the fools.[135] Never was there such a courageous heart that was not

135. Compare a similar sentiment about Guillaume d'Orange in the Old French *The Coronation of Louis* (c. 1150, trans. Joan M. Ferrante. New York: Columbia University Press, 1991): "William climbed the

well served by justified fear. No matter how readily one fears that which puts his life in danger, let him be free of such fear that is cowardly. Erec's heart was free of such fear.

[8632] Since he was to fight that day, he did as wise men do, for there was reason to be afraid. He got up very early. With Lady Enite he went to hear a mass in honor of the Holy Spirit, and he begged God fervently that He preserve his life. His wife pleaded for the same. He zealously took communion as a knight should who is to go and fight a skilled man. After mass he left. A meal was made ready, a large affair, which he avoided. He did not partake of a large meal. He took three bites from some chicken; that seemed enough to him. A drink was brought to him, and he drank a toast to St. John.[136] The hero immediately donned his armor and prepared himself as he should, as though he wanted to ride directly to the park. Now Lady Enite's worries had never been so great. Tears flowed like rain from her eyes.

[8660] The city was now full of the news. All the people knew, as you heard earlier, that a knight had come there who declared his readiness to fight the knight in the park. King Ivreins von Brandigan wanted to watch. The castle residents did not want to be left behind. The castle was deserted of people save for the sad group of ladies that stayed up there, for they had suffered so much grief that they did not want to see anything that would trouble them more. Of all their heartfelt misery, their greatest distress was that death paid them no heed.[137]

[8680] The streets in the town and the roofs were now all crowded with people who waited for Erec to come riding by. He came riding down the middle of the castle road that led him to the park. He now heard many discomfiting things and furtive murmuring. The people prophesied for him nothing better and no less misfortune than that he was assured of dying. They spoke so much about it that if he had wanted to be cowardly because of prophecies of evil or serious threats, he would have been so there. He did not take this seriously and paid no attention to it.

[8698] If our source book is not lying, the nature of this very park was such that it might amaze us all, smart and dumb alike. I am telling you that neither a wall nor a moat went around it, nor was it enclosed by a fence, water, hedge, or anything tangible. A level path went around it, and yet no one could walk or ride into it, except on one side, at a very secret place, where there was a narrow trail. Not many people knew of it. Whoever entered there by chance found there whatever

---

hill, there he remained with fine weapons and armor well arrayed, and watched as the furious pagan came. It is not to his shame that he was afraid" (lines 682–85).

136. St. John was toasted and asked for protection against poisoning and other dangers.

137. That is, their desire to die went unheeded.

he desired of beautiful things: many kinds of trees that bore fruit on one side and had beautiful blossoms on the other. In addition, the sweet sound of birds gladdened his heart. Also, there was not a hand's width of ground there that was bare. It was covered with flowers of various colors that emitted a sweet odor.

[8730] Magnificent was the fragrance of the fruit and the blossoms, and the ongoing competition among the birds, and the view was such that whoever might come there heavily afflicted with heartfelt sorrow would have to forget about it. One could eat however much fruit and wherever one wanted. The rest one was supposed to, and had to, leave there. It was such that no one could carry it out. Would you not like to hear what enclosed the park so securely? I know that not many people nowadays are familiar with the sorcery that brought this about. One could see a cloud going around it through which no one could pass, except as you have heard.

[8754] Now the host himself rode ahead of them toward the park in order to direct Erec, as he requested, to the hidden entrance and to the knight. All the people remained outside, except Lady Enite. Lord Guivreiz had to ride along. Their number was no more than these four. Now they came very soon to where they could see what they rightly had to say was a strange thing: a large circle of oak poles had been set up. That amazed Erec. Each of the poles was covered such that a man's head was stuck on it. But one of them was empty. Why would that be? A large horn hung from it.

[8777] Erec asked what all of this meant. "You would be better off leaving this," the host said to his guest, "and you may greatly regret having come here. Your eagerness has misled you. Now see for yourself the proof that I did not lie. If you still do not believe, look, those are the heads the knight cut off. I shall tell you more: the pole standing there empty has been waiting for you. Your head shall be on it. If, however, you or any other man were spared this by defeating this knight, which, however, cannot happen—it has been a long time in coming—he is to blow this horn—that is why it is there—very loudly three times to announce that he is victorious. His honor would be everlasting, and he would be acclaimed in every land above all men. Why all this talk? It won't happen. I think the man is not yet born whose lot it will be to blow this horn. All living knights are nothing compared to this knight. Since you will not forgo this, noble knight, may God be your shield and take care of your soul. No one can keep you from losing your life."

[8817] When the beautiful woman then saw this horrible sight and heard these disheartening words as well, her heart was completely bereft of happiness and joy, if she had even brought any along. Her strength faded along with her color, and she grew deathly pale and fell unconscious out of grief. Bright day turned to night for her, for she neither heard nor saw anything. However often she had suffered grief, as her bearing betrayed, never in her life had her heart's distress been greater. The host and her husband revived her and commiserated with her.

[8836] When she looked up and regained her senses, Erec very bravely said, "Lady, my sweet Enite, put an end to your distress. This is no time to weep. What reason do you have for such lamenting? Am I sick or dead? Indeed, I am standing here before you completely healthy. You could at least wait until you see me covered with blood or my shield hacked to pieces or my helmet split in two and me dead beneath it. Then you would have plenty of time. To be sure, a battle is now going to take place between us knights. We cannot have any certainty who will be adjudged the victor. I have been assured that God is as benevolent as He ever was. Oh, how often has the one been saved toward whom He wanted to be merciful! If He so wants, I trust I shall survive. Your weeping troubles me, and if you knew how I felt, you would not lament so bitterly, for I shall tell you truthfully: if I did not have as much as a hair's breadth of manly courage save that which I have from you, things could never go badly for me. Whenever I think of you, my hand is victorious, for your true love strengthens me so that nothing can happen to me the whole day long."

[8874] Here he had to part company from both of his companions and ride on alone. This troubled them greatly, Enite and the noble king, and they were concerned about Lord Erec. The host himself, with his hand, directed Erec to a path he found there in front of the poles. It was narrow and covered with grass. They all stayed behind. Erec alone rode on. I do not know what happened to him, but never was there a knight more worried than he was. He was traveling down a fearful path. This saddened his companions. May God's power keep him and save his life. Help his wife, all of you, pray to God that he be victorious.

[8896] King Erec rode alone along the grassy path, about three times the length of a horse's charge,[138] through flowers and the singing of birds, on into that park. Then he saw standing before him a tent, splendid and beautiful, both tall and wide, made of two kinds of samite, with black and white stripes, and carefully painted. Both men and women were portrayed on it, and birds as though in flight, which was, however, an illusion, and wild and tame animals, each with its name above it; the pictures were of gold. Where the knob on top was supposed to be, there was a beautifully fashioned eagle, entirely inlaid with gold. Set up on the grass, this

---

138. Sixteen *rosseloufe* (charges of a horse) made up the length of a medieval mile.

tent was fashioned with honor and splendor. The tent ropes were entirely of silk and not of one color, but red, green, white, yellow, and brown, all twisted together.

[8926] Beneath the tent he saw a woman sitting, about whom his heart told him that in all his life he had never seen any more beautiful, except for Lady Enite. For one had to concede to the latter that her beautiful figure had to be praised above all women who ever lived, either then or now. Enite was the child of Perfection, which had forgotten nothing on her behalf. The lady who was now sitting here was dressed most splendidly. She had put on a long ermine mantle. She had wrapped herself in it. Her outer garmet was of rich samite, that looked like brown glass, with sable cuffs. A headband held her hair together. What was her dress like? Ask her chamber servants about that. God knows I never saw it, for I never got close to her. Erec could not see it either. That was because the mantle in which she was wrapped was all around it. The bed on which she sat was beautifully made: the frame was large and of silver. The entire appearance was one of good workmanship.

[8958] When Erec saw her sitting there, he, the stranger, dismounted out of propriety and courtesy. He tied his steed to a branch, leaned both his shield and lance against the tree trunk, untied his helmet, and turned it over and set it on top of his shield. He then removed his coif, for he was very courtly. Thus he stepped up to her. She would have preferred that it had not happened, for she feared trouble would come to her because of it. Nevertheless, she greeted the lord, for custom compelled her to. She received him with these words, "My lord, I would be glad to greet you, but no one should offer anyone an insincere greeting. If it were not that harm and misfortune will befall you here, I would have been glad to see you. Whose advice brought you here? Or did you think of it yourself for your heart's pleasure? If so, you are carrying in your breast a disloyal adviser, for he has betrayed your life. My lord, for God's sake, go away. It will cost you your life if my lord sees you. He is not far from us."

[8990] Before she had finished speaking and had warned him, he heard a voice, loud and fierce, that sounded like a horn blasting, for the one who emitted the sound had a large throat. This was her husband. In armor that lacked nothing, just like that of the stranger, he had ridden away from her through the garden, going out for a ride and waiting to see if he could find something to do. He now at once caught sight of this stranger standing in front of the lady. To him this seemed to be an act of foolishness and dishonorable to him. He turned around and rode quickly toward the stranger. Erec saw him riding up from a distance. The lord of the park was tall and big, almost like a giant. He yelled loud threats. His steed was big and long-legged, bright red as tinder. His shield was the same color, as was his

tabard, and he himself was, as I have read, in red armor that suited his tempera-
ment. I think his heart bled when he found no opportunity to fight, so bloodthirsty
was his hand.

[9024] Now he rode up to the stranger and, like an ill-natured man, greeted him
very brusquely. He said, "Impostor, tell me, who told you to get so close to the
lady?" "What have I done wrong in doing so?" "It is very foolish." "My lord, why
are you insulting me?" "I think you are being insolent to the lady." "My lord, you
are speaking harshly." "Tell me, who brought you here?" "Good friends." "Then
tell me, who?" "My heart and my own intentions." "They have advised you badly."
"Before this they have directed me well." "That will end here." "It will not." "Why
do I see you armed?" "My lord, that is my armor." "Do you want to fight me?" "If
you want to, so do I." "What can you be thinking of, stupid fool?" "You will soon
find out." "It will turn out badly for you." "You do not mention: 'God willing.'"
"Why are you so disdainful of my words?" "I pay no heed to your threats and com-
pare them to two large mountains. They swore after some reasoning that they
wanted to produce together a handsome child, a huge one, too, like them. Then
God ordained that it was to be the laughing-stock of all the people, and they gave
birth to a field mouse. Big houses have been burned down by small fires. Those
who act so fiercely are lacking in courage. That will turn out to be the case here.
Before we part company today, one or both of us will cease boasting." "Indeed, I
shall see to that," said the red knight. With these words Erec then left.

[9070] Very quickly he returned to where he had left his steed standing. He
strapped on his helmet and immediately prepared himself. He mounted his steed
quickly. The other did not delay either; he prepared himself likewise. Each of them
took up his shield and held it glued[139] securely against his body. The lord of the
park and the stranger pressed their thighs against their horses. Truly they displayed
fierce anger. They spurred their horses on and charged at each other with great
boldness and all their strength. The ashen lance shafts were lowered and shown
the way to the four nails on the handgrip of the other's shield. Their aim was
directed very well, for they both hit the mark. The path of the lances passed through
both shields, and went in as far as their hands, stopping short of their bodies. The
strong shafts remained whole, however forcefully they had been driven in. They
pulled out their lances again with manly eagerness and then rode away from each
other, the two men, with the same intention: to joust again.

---

139. *Gelîmet*, literally "limed." Bird-lime was spread on branches to catch birds. The word often appears
in an image or metaphor in medieval literature. See *Gregorius*, line 373.

[9103] Once again the horses were spurred on strongly and forcefully and again sent against each other. Here arose heartfelt love that was after a great prize. They made love without a bed. The prize of their love was that whoever lay down was allotted death. With a lance through the shield to the breast they kissed each other with such passion that the ashen shafts splintered right down to the hand so that the chips flew like dust. With the weight of the knights the horses crashed together so hard that the heads of the combatants were greatly stunned and that both horses sat back on the ground. The reins were let loose, and they dismounted. Lord God, deign to take care of King Erec, for he is fighting a warrior who is courageous and strong. This is why I am anxious about him.

[9134] Now they both drew their swords from their sheaths and swung them rapidly. When they stepped up to each other, blows rained over the top of the shields. They struck furious blows. They extended their shields. These were completely hacked down to the boss, so that they could no longer hold them against their arms, and they offered no protection. They threw them aside. Now their armor repeatedly protected them from the closeness of death. Their weapons produced hot, fiery sparks wherever they struck each other. So many furious blows were struck here that the world may well be astonished that their helmets and swords withstood them. Quite often it happened that the very large man quickly drove the smaller man far away from him. But Erec then drove him back the same way. They went back and forth so much that they trampled down both the flowers and grass, so that there was no more greenery than in the middle of winter. This battle thus lasted from morning until midday.

[9169] "Friend Hartmann, tell now how they withstood that." Their wives gave them the strength. The one sitting there affected her husband thus: if he started to despair, her beauty gave him renewed energy, whenever he looked at her, so that he regained his strength without losing heart and fought like a rested man. In this way he was incapable of losing heart. I shall tell you the same about Erec: whenever Erec thought of Lady Enite, her love strengthened his heart and mind, so that he too fought with renewed force and manly excellence.

[9188] When they had carried on long enough and both of them were uninjured, the large man thought: it angers me that this little man has held out so long against me. With fury he seized hold of his sword and intended to strike down his opponent. He swung his sword around. The huge devil knew no mercy. His heart gave his arms mighty strength. With great determination he struck a blow. He hit Erec on the helmet, right in the middle of the head, and struck so mightily that from the blow a broad, fiery flame sparkled like glass, such that a bundle of straw could have been set on fire. May God reward the one who believes this, for I cannot swear to it.

[9211] This furious blow resounded in Erec's head such that he barely kept from falling. His ears and eyes began to fail him, so that he could neither hear nor see. If the sword had not broken in two, it would have been the end of him. Very quickly the stranger regained his strength, so that he could see and think and hear as before. The misfortune and shame, that any man had ever gained the upper hand against him, pained him. He took revenge for having been so greatly weakened by the other's superiority. The thought of his beautiful wife strengthened him. He avenged his misfortune, and fiercely took in both hands his sword, and struck for blood against the hard steel armor.

[9237] Even though the knight seemed liked a mountain compared to Erec, since he had lost his weapon he had to retreat against Erec's blows. He did this without disgrace, for I know for certain, and better than anything else, that he would not have suffered blows in vain without defending himself if his sword had stayed in one piece. Thus he was driven back forcefully by the stranger. Erec quickly avenged the mighty blow. He struck not as he usually had. His blows were furious and not timorous. He struck blow after blow, so that blow after blow hit the mark. He hit the knight's armor until the sword was glowing in his hand from the blows and the quality of the blade's edge was almost wrecked. Its brown color[140] turned pale, and it broke as the other had before. Now what do you want him to do? The piece that was left in his hand he threw so hard against the chest of the knight he was pushing back in front of him that the knight almost stumbled and fell on the grass from the jolt of it.

[9270] Nevertheless, the devil remained standing and saw that Erec's hand was empty and that his sword was broken. Now I shall be avenged, thought the man in red. In a fury he ran at Erec and tried in great haste to seize him, lift him up, and throw him down with his great strength in order to crush him. It is said that Erec, in his childhood in England, had learned, to his advantage, to wrestle well, along with other athletic endeavors. It also helped that it is difficult to hold onto a man in armor. Thus he was able to slip away from him such that the other could not carry out his will. Erec grabbed him in front by the belt and twisted down away from him. The other man wanted to pull him against himself, but this did not happen.

---

140. Compare verse 1953 in the Old French *La Chanson de Roland* (c. 1100), "[Olivier] Tient Halteclere dunt li acer fut bruns" [Olivier held (his sword) Hauteclaire, whose blade was brown (burnished)].

[9296] Erec showed his strength. When the other man bent over, Erec pressed his shoulder against the man's chest so that he could not get at him. He forcefully thrust him away and then pulled him back so quickly that the huge man started to fall. Because of his weight he could not keep his balance and fell to the ground. The worthy knight jumped on him. The amazing Erec brought upon him as much distress as he did joy upon himself. He kneeled down on his chest and struck him so many blows that the man lying under him grew weary of living and gave up all resistance.

[9316] When the man in red started to despair, he asked the smaller man for a truce. He said, "Knight, let me live a while longer and then take my life." "Will you concede me the victory?" "That cannot yet be." "What do you want then?" "Noble knight, stop and tell me who you are." Thus answered the knight lying on top, "You have never witnessed that before, and will not now in regard to me, for it would be strange if the man on top had to surrender to the one on the bottom. If you want to stay alive a while, then follow my good advice and tell me very quickly where you are from and who you are, and whatever else I desire."

[9338] The knight in red answered him thus, "You are fooling yourself; that is out of the question. Although you have defeated me and are forcibly lying on top of me, I would rather be killed than not be told who you are or where you are from. Indeed, this disgrace may have been inflicted on me by a man who has never been victorious, in which case I would prefer to be killed. If a man of low birth has done this, in no way would I want to live. But if God has granted me that you are by birth worthy of this victory, then deign to end this battle, for I shall give you my pledge that I shall gladly submit to all of your demands. I beseech you further, for God's sake, to be truthful and to know that if that is not the case, my life will end here, for otherwise I shall be disgraced. I am convinced that it would bother me less to die with honor than to have none."

[9366] The excellent man answered him with a smile, "Very gladly shall I let myself be entreated in this matter. Even though it goes against custom, I shall tell you: my father is a mighty king over the land of Destrigales; my mother is of equal birth. My name is Erec." "Can I be sure of this?" "Indeed." "Then let me live and take my pledge. You see, I am prepared to fulfill it. Thus you can have my services, which you would have to do without if you were to kill me. I shall tell you my name: I am Mabonagrin." Erec had mercy and let him live.

[9387] When Erec had accepted his pledge, he helped him up by the hand. Each of them untied the other's straps to his armor, for no one else could help them, and they took off their helmets. Animosity vanished from them, and they wished each other honor and good fortune, as friends should. They sat down together on the grass, for they were both quite exhausted from the battle.

[9401] Now for a time they talked at length and about various matters, about their circumstances, and about what had happened to them both. King Erec then said, "Regarding your affairs, I have heard that the king of Brandigan, the lord here, is your uncle. There is not one of your affairs I have not heard something about, and I have not failed to understand how things stand with you. There is one matter that remains unclear: all the time that you have been inside here, tell me, how did you spend your time if there were not more people with you? No matter how beautiful it is in here, and no matter that nothing good soothes the heart as much as when love lies next to love, as is the case with you and your wife, one should surely withdraw from women from time to time. I have heard it from their own mouths, in private, that coming and going can happen without raising their ire. Although they do not want to admit it openly, they want one to seem new to them and not be around all the time.[141] Besides, it would suit this lady better, who has been sitting in here all these years, to be together with other women. It amazes me that you, such a handsome man, could stay here, for it is so good to be among people. Does your decision to remain in here come from someone's command? Or do you want to be rewarded by God for it? Or are you to remain in here forever?"

[9443] Mabonagrin answered him thus, "I shall explain it to you in detail. I have not chosen this life of my own free will, since no one was ever born who liked to see people more. Hear now under what strange circumstances I have chosen this very life. If I did not want to be unfaithful, I had to keep on here, even if I was to grow old in here, if God had not helped me, as He has done in His mercy. It is coming to an end today, with some misfortune, which I can easily get over. My lord, I shall tell you to whom I gave my word for this life. It happened that I rode out from here in my youth into another land where I found this lady, a child of eleven years and from a noble family, in her mother's custody. I had never seen greater beauty in a child, male or female, as my senses told me then. And when my eyes caught sight of her, so noble and so beautiful, my heart gathered her in, for we were both equally young in years. Immediately I courted her. This courtship was successful, for she ran away with me. When I brought her home to this castle, my uncle did not want to wait any longer to knight me.

[9486] "I was knighted in here. When my lady friend and I were sitting at the table, halfway through the meal, she obtained an oath from me accordingly. She

141. For similar thoughts, see *Iwein*, lines 2845–78.

said: 'Bear in mind, my dear lord, what I have done for you,' and she requested that she should have some benefit from that. I was strongly exhorted, and she had me give her my hand upon it, to carry out whatever she requested. I promised her that faithfully, as love compelled me to do. Besides, I had no idea that she would request something of me I would not gladly do. Yet I would have granted her whatever she would have desired, whatever I could accomplish and would be appropriate for me to do, and I am still doing what she desires of me. I am assured of the same on her part. Whatever she wants, I too want, and whatever I want, she grants me. How could a partnership between man and woman have any strong love if they appeared to be friends in body only while their minds are so divided that the one more or less desires what the other does not want? Such impropriety can not be found between us. For a hundred years, starting with today, I would never waver a hair's breadth from believing that her will is my greatest fortune, for that is the greatest part of true joy that I have: to carry out things, wherever I can, such that her will is done. She does the same for me. Therefore, if I did not gladly do whatever she requested, I would harm myself much more than her.

[9532] "And when the pledge had been given, she embraced me joyfully. She said: 'How lucky I am to experience such a magnificent gift that God has granted me. Everything my heart desires I hold in my arms. Things have turned out well for me. And I shall be so bold as to say that we have here a second paradise. This very place I praise above all parks. As you yourself can see, there is in here a great splendor of all kinds of birds and many-colored flowers. In here would be a good place to live.' She added: 'In here I shall eagerly rejoice in your love. This is the gift I request of you. Thereby I am assured that I can remain yours without fear of other women: that you stay in here with me, just the two of us, until the time that one man, all by himself, defeats you, before my eyes, so that I see the truth of the matter myself.'

[9562] "Now why did she do this? I shall explain this to you in more detail. She never imagined that it could ever happen, or that one could ever find someone who would conquer me. So magnificent did she consider me to be. Indeed, I have been unconquered until this very day, which I can easily prove if you do not believe me. Do you see then these heads? I cut them all off. And I shall tell you more: the post standing there empty with no head on it, on which that horn is hanging, has been waiting for a new man. I was to decorate it with you and set your head on it. God has preserved us both from that. I think I have gained today disgrace without harm, since your hand has freed me from this bond. God has sent you here. Today is the end of my affliction. I shall now leave and go wherever I want.

[9590] "And I can assure you that you have come as a great good fortune to this court, for because of me it was robbed of all its joy, and was indeed devoid of all great happiness. Since those at court no longer had me present, there was indeed no kind of entertainment here, because for them my youth and my noble birth had been buried alive; thus indeed did Joie de la curt vanish completely. Those at court shall now cherish it again, for they now have their defender back. Your brave hand has freed this very sad land from great sorrow and has returned happiness to it. For this you will always be honored. My lord, you should now stand up and go joyfully and blow that very horn, for it has been designated that the one who conquers me is immediately to blow the horn three times to announce it to the people. It has hung there unblown many a day—much too long for me—as long as this has been my home." He then took it down from the pole and asked Erec to blow it. He immediately put it to his mouth. The blast of the horn was very great, for it was long and large.

[9628] When those who were waiting outside the garden to see who was victorious heard the blast of the horn all over, they all looked at each other, for no one there would ever have imagined that things would have turned out thus: that the knight Mabonagrin would be conquered. The residents thought it was a trick until Erec announced it to them a second time with the horn, and then a third time. Now, without delay, they acted against past custom. King Ivreins von Brandigan took Lady Enite and led her at his side into the park. No one there besides him knew how to get inside if he did not lead. Now they all hurried with shouts of joy to where they saw the lords. The two, Erec and Mabonagrin, were greeted joyfully by the entire crowd, and the day was celebrated with happy battle songs.

[9661] While their hearts had been saddened repeatedly, and had been for so long, happiness was now forthcoming, and Erec was greatly honored, his renown increased. With one voice they all then cried out, "Sir knight, may you be honored! May you always live with good fortune! God has sent you and directed you to this land to aid us. Be of good joy and be honored, you, the flower of all knighthood! Indeed, for ever more God and your brave hand have given you the crown over all lands. May you have good fortune as you grow old!" Joy took on many forms here.

[9680] Lady Enite, too, had not experienced any heartfelt grief at this time. I can swear and do maintain that the moods of these two ladies, the one who sat under the tent and the one who had gained more success from the battle, were different: their mouths did not speak; the one's heart sang out. The one wore the crown of joy; the other had grief enough, laden with heartfelt misery, because she, and her beloved Mabonagrin, could no longer remain in the park. In addition, she wrung her hands because of the misfortune that had befallen her husband there.

[9699] When Lady Enite saw her sitting there weeping, she displayed clearly her womanly heart. Her very great goodness moved the sweet lady to greet her, despite the other's grief. They then exchanged many a story of joy and also of grief, and thereby became friends as women do. They asked about their lands and their families, and by talking became intimate and told whatever they knew. They figured out immediately that they were close relatives. How could the relationship have been closer? Because Duke Imain, the lord of Tulmein, Lady Enite's uncle, was also this lady's uncle on her father's side.[142]

[9723] In addition, they were both, as I have read, born in the town of Lut. Look, they no longer paid sorrow any heed. They then embraced each other and were happy for each other. They showed this by weeping for joy. They quickly stopped weeping, and laughed, which suited them better. The ladies took each other by the hand and went to where they found their lords. Out of joy they could no longer keep it quiet and had to tell everyone that they were cousins. Upon these latest tidings everyone said that God had brought them together in a miraculous way in a land so foreign to them both.

[9744] Everyone then left the park. The heads that had been cut off in the park, as you have heard, were then taken from the poles—may God reward Erec for this—and messengers were sent out into the country for priests so that the heads would have an honorable burial. Only now did the joy at Brandigan intensify. This happened for a good reason, for as soon as the news spread throughout the land that the joy at court, which they had lost, had been restored, the king's family and vassals all came to court with the ladies of the land to see the new good fortune.

[9766] The most noble people gathered here. The host and his guests, whom he was able to bring, invite, and compel to come there, held festivities whose feasting lasted four weeks. The sorrowful conditions the host had suffered because of his nephew were put to an end through joy. He was compensated and well reimbursed with a wealth of joy.

[9779] Erec and his companions participated in the festivities. The king did not allow them to ride away. But Erec stayed there without joy, because he could not free his heart of sorrowful affliction. Whenever he thought about it, his heart was

142. The Middle High German *veter* is related to *vater*, father. The adjective *veterlich*, "like a father," is a variant of *vaterlich*, "fatherly." In Chrétien the two women are indeed related through their fathers; here they are cousins. *Veter* may thus be a scribal misreading of *vater*. Regarding Enite's origins, see lines 435–36.

moved as it will a compassionate man whose eyes often fill with tears, both openly and in private, whenever he sees something that moves him to compassion. The situation here was worthy of compassion. No man has such a wealth of happiness that he should be without compassion. I know for sure that if he had seen this distress, he would have wept.

[9798] Erec's compassion was stirred by the miserable company of eighty ladies here who were robbed of joy, as was quite sorrowfully apparent from their demeanor. The red knight Mabonagrin had killed each one's beloved. Both mourning and lamentation were their daily occupation. Just as the hunted hare shuns its own pasture, out of grief they fled any place where they might find joy. For as long as they lived they especially did not voluntarily want to see the man who had caused their grief.

[9816] Erec now helped them mourn. That was quite apparent from the fact that at no time did he and Lady Enite voluntarily leave them. With consoling words he took away some of their heartfelt grief. What can be better for a person than to be tenderly consoled after sorrow? That's what one friend owes another.

[9826] Erec advised them—which they gladly accepted—to remain there no longer but to make their lives better by taking leave and coming with him to the court of King Arthur, for in this castle here they would never be happy.

[9835] They then requested leave. This did not make the lord sad, for he, to be sure, had been told that they had said they had experienced such sorrow there that they could never find happiness at Brandigan castle. Thus he gladly gave them leave if they could turn their lives around for the better, but if they could have found happiness under his authority, he would be unhappy to see them spend their years anywhere else but in his care. He very gladly prepared things for their journey; he respected their wishes by clothing them in mourning as befitted their current spirit, and also by preparing horses such that the color of both, the horses and the clothing, were the same and went well together, everything in black mourning.

[9858] The festivities came to an end. The foreigner now left there with these ladies. It was courtly of him to take them from where the life did not suit them. The lord of Brandigan now mounted a beautiful Castilian, and his knights their fast horses, the best they had, and accompanied the guests a good distance from the castle. Lord Erec then asked them to stay behind with his best wishes, and he rode on with the women and brought them to King Arthur at his castle.

[9876] There he was greeted most heartily, and people clearly observed that the ladies were dressed the same and had like mounts, and people said with good reason that they had never seen a stranger company, with so many ladies in one color.

And those who did not know the situation kept asking the guests what their story was, until Erec told them. Erec, free of falsehood, received from the entire retinue as a reward for his hardships the crown of honor, such that it was said to his praise that no one in the world was his equal in exceptional manly courage, nor as noble or as amicable, for no man in all the lands had accomplished such a great thing, so rich in adventure. If Lady Fortune had not supported his nursemaid who cared for him when he lay in the cradle, it never could have happened. When they saw the ladies, it seemed strange to them. The noble queen now led them to their chambers. Bless her soul, for without being asked she acted very virtuously.

[9910] King Arthur was pleased to have the guests at his castle. And when he had waited long enough until it seemed to him time to go visit them, Erec and Walwan and also Guivreiz, these three, and the rest of the retinue, were all very glad. The king then said to them, "You lords, we should go see our newly arrived ladies and comfort them after their grief." They both stood up, King Arthur and Erec. Hand in hand they made their way to the ladies' chamber. This was furnished more magnificently with ladies than ever before. The host went and sat down next to them, and the others also immediately sat down, the one here, the other there.

[9932] And when the king saw them suffering in their distress, with the same lamentation, the same sadness, the same constancy, the same loyalty, the same beauty, the same youth, the same courtliness, the same virtue, the same dress, the same goodness, the same station, the same bearing, this seemed to him to be womanly and good, and it moved his heart and pleased him well. He said before them all, "Erec, my dear nephew, with good reason you should always be praised and honored, for you have increased the joy of our court. May whoever does not wish you well never be happy again." "Amen," they all said then, for they wished him well. The women in deep mourning were persuaded to turn their hearts and their lives to joy, and honored the king by letting him take the clothes that did not befit joy and dress them in such clothing best suitable for joy: of silk and gold.

[9962] Erec, favored by Honor, and Guivreiz le pitiz were honored and attended with great care and taken care of as befitted their standing, until Erec received the news that his father was dead. Now it was necessary for his land that he forgo such wandering and return home. That was a benefit to his land and his people. He took leave of King Arthur in order to travel home.

[9980] When he parted from the court, he aided the needy people who could make use of his wealth—even though they did not seek it—each according to need, as best he could afford it, so that they in all sincerity said a common blessing over the hero that God might protect his honor and preserve his soul. The little man,

King Guivreiz, also parted with him then, toward his realm. They were both con-
ducted with dignity to the crossroads. Now they parted from each other, I am sure,
as two friends never did better, without hostile sentiments, Guivreiz toward Ireland,
Erec toward Karnant.

[10002] Erec's people now knew exactly both the day and the hour when he
was to arrive in the land. Six thousand or more of them, recognized as the noblest
in the land, were immediately selected. To honor their lord, for they were happy
to see him, they hurried a good three days in his direction to receive him.[143] Unless
one lies, one cannot maintain ever to have seen a friendlier reception. Compelled
by their debt of loyalty, they all received him with courtly jubilation and with
caparisoned horses, and those who could afford it and were called knights also held
in their hands magnificent banners matching the caparisons, expensively inter-
mixed with colors, with artistry from foreign parts.

[10028] The field here was colored red, white, yellow, and green as grass from
their silk clothing, the best the world has. As befits a powerful king, the people of
Karnant, from the land of Destrigales, thus received their returning lord back to
his kingdom. In many a land he had succeeded with good fortune in attaining—
as our source tells us about him—that no one's fame for manly deeds, among the
living, stood as high as his. It was a sign of his fame that he was called Erec the
Doer of Wondrous Deeds. Things were such that his being and aura spread over
all the lands. Do you ask how that might be? It was thus: when his body appeared
in one place, his fame was elsewhere; thus the world was filled with him. No one
was spoken of so well.

[10054] When God had sent him home to the joy of his land, he ordered that
festivities be arranged such that neither before nor since in that very land was there
ever one so joyful and organized by such great lords. Many of his friends came,
whom I would gladly name for you if I knew their names. Here he received with
praise the crown of the realm that his father, King Lac, had worn with honor until
then, for he had done many virtuous deeds. In addition, never was an honorable
father better replaced by his son. Who would be better suited in his place? May
God bless his realm. He rules it by rights. We must not begrudge it to him, for he
has started out well by bringing joy and being hospitable. For six weeks one could
indeed see there a great number of knights and ladies. Whatever one desired there
regarding amusement, one could find it in abundance, however long the festivi-
ties lasted. He organized his land such that it was at peace. He did as wise men do

---

143. For similar homecomings, see *Gregorius*, lines 3754ff. and note 117, and *Poor Heinrich*, line 1391.

who thank God for whatever honors they attain, wanting to h
Many a man is thus deceived by an idea that truly cheats him
happen to him, he acquires a wealth of arrogance that he has
things solely because of his own abilities, and he does not thar
How easily this can end![144] But the king did not do this. Since (
honor on him, it too was at all times returned to Him in praise
enced the magnificence his heart desired, for his honor continued unharmed until
his death, as the Lord in Heaven commanded.

[10107] In foreign lands Lady Enite had suffered hard times. She turned this
around, for they ended here and changed into comfort and honor and great joy.
Her mother and her father spent a happy old age, for God had sent them back to
their own land, to their joy. The king himself fulfilled her will wherever he could,
and yet as was proper for him, and not as he did earlier, when he, on her account,
spent all his time in bed, for he now lived for honor's sake, such that God, with
fatherly grace, bestowed on him and his wife, after the worldly crown, eternal life.
For God's sake, let us all pray that the same reward might fall to us that makes us
favorable in God's eyes—that is worth more than gold—after our time in exile. My
song ends here.[145]

144. Similar sentiments are found in *Gregorius*, lines 1–170, and in *Poor Heinrich*, lines 75–119.
145. Compare the end of *Gregorius*, lines 3989ff.

GREGORIUS

Introduction

Like the Arthurian epics *Erec* and *Iwein*, and possibly also *Poor Heinrich*, *Gregorius* is modeled after a French prototype. But whereas the literary ancestry of the Arthurian epics is fairly, though not indisputably, clear—Chrétien de Troyes's *Erec* and *Yvain ou Chevalier au Lion*—*Gregorius* can be likened to a child whose resemblance to its parents is clear, but where because of dissimilarities one suspects that it bears a closer likeness to a vanished generation.

The Old French archetype *La Vie du Pape Saint Grégoire*—if we judge from its numerous versions and rich manuscript tradition—obviously enjoyed great popularity. While Hartmann's *Gregorius* shares the basic plot of the French work, no single version can be shown to have served as the direct model. In fact, *Gregorius* shows similarities with varying versions, leading to the conjecture that an *Ur-Gregorius* existed at some point. Bearing in mind the popularity of the tale, however, one cannot dismiss the possibility that Hartmann based his story on an oral version, one narrated in either Old French or Middle High German. But considering Hartmann's apparent ability to read or understand Old French, the likelihood exists that he came into contact with a French source, probably at court.

Whatever the exemplar of *Gregorius*, we can rest assured that Hartmann's use of it, as with *Erec* and *Iwein*, amounts more to a reworking or adaptation than to a strict translation. Compared to the extant Old French versions, *Gregorius* is between one-third and one-half again as long, showing once more that for Hartmann the French original served only as a foundation on which he could use his poetic skill to erect a vastly different structure.

Regarding the genre of *Gregorius*, perhaps one can best define it as neither fish nor fowl. Although the title of the French version, *La Vie du Pape Saint Grégoire*, reads like a typical medieval *vita* that details the exemplary life of a holy man or woman, the saint's life thus depicted is fictitious—there was no such Saint

Gregory—and most of the usual hagiographic trappings are missing, even though the typically edifying, didactic tone rings through quite clearly. Some contemporaries obviously viewed *Gregorius* as a religious legend, hence its fairly quick translation into Latin and its inclusion into collections of saints' lives. Coming from a secular author, however, and hardly intended originally for an ecclesiastical or monastic audience, and with its depiction of the knightly life, *Gregorius* can scarcely be claimed as a typical *legenda*. Perhaps we have in *Gregorius* a further step on the road to the prose tale.

While the dating and chronology of Hartmann's work are not without controversy, one can fairly securely posit that *Gregorius* follows the *Lament* and *Erec*, perhaps toward the end of the 1180s, and this positioning of the work has led to one aspect of its interpretation, that *Gregorius* is "anti-*Erec*," or anti-chivalry, a rejection by a maturer author of his earlier work, namely *Erec*, but also, by implication, a repudiation of some ideas expressed in *The Lament* and his early lyric poetry. Older literary criticism of *Gregorius* dealt frequently with Gregorius's guilt or lack thereof. More recent investigations have generally left this question aside, focusing instead on other aspects of the work, although the matter of guilt does resurface and in the end cannot go unanswered.

The thread of individual self-realization, a kind of *rite de passage*, ties Hartmann's major works together. Gregorius, moving as he does from infancy through boyhood to manhood and finally to a precocious "middle age" of insight and wisdom, comes closest among Hartmann's characters to the *Bildungsfigur* of Wolfram von Eschenbach's Parzival.

Perhaps the interpretive focus should not rest so heavily on the incest of Gregorius's parents or on his own incest with his mother—for these acts, given their mitigating circumstances, seem "pardonable" to both medieval and modern thinking—or even on his own *superbia* at leaving the monastic world, but rather on the journey that Gregorius undertakes, both physically and spiritually, on the path that is mentioned both in the prologue and toward the end of the tale, when Gregorius seeks to do penance in the "wilderness." This path may be seen as the path we all take in life, or *can* and *should* take.

Of primary importance to an understanding of *Gregorius* is the "prologue," a "homily" of 50 or 170 lines (depending on interpretation), whose meaning, and even authenticity, is disputed. This "prologue" appears in only two manuscripts, and because of stylistic differences and its straightforwardness some have questioned whether Hartmann wrote it. Hartmann names himself early in *Poor Heinrich* and *Iwein*. Whether he would have mentioned himself in *Erec* will remain an open question, since the beginning is missing. If one limits this "prologue" to 50 lines,

Hartmann's name appears in line 121, which would still be quite a bit later than in the other works. If one regards the first 170 lines as spurious, the "opening" lines seem too abrupt to be the beginning of a work.

What speaks more for the authenticity of the "prologue" are several key words or phrases that are repeated later, in important situations. The narrator Hartmann's "naïve years" (line 5) are paralleled in Gregorius's criticism of his "youthful blind spirit" (line 1484), which harkens back to the "youthful naïveté" (line 327) of his father; when Gregorius's mother laments that she has turned from the soul "to the body and toward this world" (lines 2672–73), she repeats the narrator's criticism of his heart turning to "worldly reward" (line 4); the thought of "eternal life" (line 32) that the unrepentant will not gain is used by the abbot to try to convince Gregorius that he should stay (line 1797); "God's grace" (line 154), which is bestowed if one turns back to God, is something Gregorius fears he has lost when he learns of his past (lines 1777–84); and when Gregorius admonishes his mother not to "despair of God" (line 2698), he underscores the narrator's statement that "despair is a deadly gall that leads to an eternal fall" (lines 167–168). Similar echoes at the end of the tale speak not only to the authenticity of the "prologue" but also to Hartmann's skill in the repeated use of key words or images.

While the knightly Gregorius leads an exemplary life, much like Erec early on— thus putting in doubt the conjecture that *Gregorius* is an anti-chivalric work—he falls, as Erec does, but differently, and like Erec he must come to an understanding of what has happened to him. He takes the initiative, he directs his mother's actions, and he sets out to do penance, for, after all, as the prologue and ending state, no one is so stricken with sin that he cannot rise again, cleansed, and attain grace.

Gregorius, as a son of Adam, is Everyman. The fact that we are all tainted because of original sin is not as important as how we deal with this sin. That Gregorius ascends the seat of Saint Peter and rises as high as one can in this life can be seen as a metaphor, for from this lofty elevation he can look back clearly upon his previous life, upon his mistakes, travails, and achievements, and see that he has indeed risen above himself.

Text

My heart has often compelled my tongue to speak much of things that seek worldly reward. My naïve years advised it thus. Now this I know to be true indeed: who-ever in his youth trusts the scheming of hell's jailer, and, trusting in his youth, sins and says to himself: you are still a young man; there is still plenty of help for all your wrongdoings; you can certainly do penance for them in your old age—such a person thinks other than he should. These thoughts will easily vanish when the common fate of us all hinders his will to repent, in that bitter death takes vengeance on this earlier way of thinking, cutting short his life with a sudden end. Bereft of grace, he has then chosen the worse course. And even if he were born of Adam, at the time of Abel, and were to preserve his soul unmarred by sin until Judgment Day, he still would not have done enough to gain eternal life that has no beginning and will also never pass.

[35] For this reason I am ready and willing to speak the truth, what God's will is, and thus lessen a bit the great weight of the sinful burden that I, through frivolous pursuits, have loaded on myself through my words. For of this I have no doubt: as God has shown us and proved through the example of one man,[1] never was a man's wrongdoing in this world so great that he cannot be free and rid of it, provided he repents it in his heart and nevermore repeats it.

[51] I shall now speak of one whose guilt was great and manifold; it is strong stuff to hear, but for the following reasons one dare not hush it up: of all the sinful people whom the devil has led astray onto the path to hell one of them might, through it, consider whether he wants to increase the number of God's children and himself return to the path of salvation,[2] abandoning despair that sinks so many.

[66] However, if a person reflects upon the capital sins,[3] having perhaps committed many of them, and if he then despairs of God, thinking that He will not look with favor upon him if he seeks mercy, and that he has no hope in rising again,[4] then such a person acts against the commandment, and despair has robbed him of the fruits of penitence. This is the true trust he should have in God: do penance after confessing.

[79] Yet sweetness that is very bitter forces his feet onto the more comfortable path.[5] It has neither stones nor defiles, marsh, mountains, nor forest; it is neither too hot nor too cold. One travels it without bodily distress. But it leads to eternal

1. That is, Gregorius.
2. Latin *via salutis*. See Acts 16:17: "These men are the servants of the most high God, which show unto us the way of salvation." See also *Erec*, lines 8520f.
3. The seven deadly sins (*capitalia vitia*) are *superbia* (pride), *invidia* (envy), *ira* (anger), *acedia* or *tristitia* (melancholy), *avaritia* (avarice), *gula* (gluttony), and *luxuria* (luxury).
4. "Rising again" continues the imagery of line 65 (sinking into despair).
5. A variant has "common path." See Matthew 7:13–14: "and broad is the way, that leadeth to destruction, and many there be which go in thereat . . . and narrow is the way, which leadeth unto life, and few there be that find it."

death. The path of salvation is to a great extent both uneven and narrow. Along the entire length of it one must wander and climb, wade and swim, until it leads out to where it widens pleasantly, out of this banishment[6] to a very sweet end.

[97] A certain man happened upon this very path.[7] Just in time he escaped the murderers' power. He had landed in their clutches. They struck him down and ruthlessly removed from him the clothing that was his whole spirit, and inflicted on him many martyr-like wounds. In that hour the poverty of his soul was very great. Thus they left him lying naked and half dead. But God did not refuse him His usual mercy and sent him these two garments: hope and fear—which God himself fashioned so that they were protection for him and all sinners—the fear that he might die,[8] and the hope that he might not be lost.

[119] Fear did not let him lie there. He would have collapsed again, however, except that hope made him strong enough to sit, though wavering. Spiritual trust, mixed with sorrow, strengthened him all the more. They did him much good and cleansed his bloody wounds, pouring over them both oil and wine.[9] The ointment is mild and yet hurts; the oil is mercy, the wine is the law, both of which the sinner must have. Then he recovers from his weakness. Thus God's mercy raised him by the hand, as it found him, onto its kind shoulders and carried him home to care for him.[10] There his dangerous wounds were bandaged so that he recovered without scars, and was thereafter a true champion alone, o'er all Christendom.

[144] I still have not told you what the wounds were, from which he recovered with such difficulty, how he got the wounds, and how he fared afterward, escaping eternal death. It is necessary that all hear and heed this who have fallen under mountains of guilt. If one in spite of it all hurries back to God's grace, God will receive him eagerly. For His mercy is so great that there is one thing He does not want in the least, and has even forbidden: that one dwell in despair of Him because of some wrongdoing. There is no sin, save despair alone, that one cannot through sorrow be free of and become new, beautiful, and pure. Despair is a deadly gall that leads to an eternal fall; no one may sweeten it[11] or do penance for it to God.

6. See line 10107 in *Erec* ("exile")

7. Compare the parable of the good Samaritan, especially Luke 10:30–37.

8. That is, die in the state of serious (mortal) sin.

9. Compare Luke 10:34: "And [a certain Samaritan] went to him, and bound up his wounds, pouring in oil and wine . . . and took care of him."

10. Compare Luke 15:5: "And when he hath found it [that is, the lost sheep], he layeth it on his shoulders, rejoicing."

11. Compare lines 108–9 in *Poor Heinrich*.

[171] The one who has fashioned this story into German poetry was Hartmann von Aue. Here begins from the start the wondrous tale of the good sinner.[12]

[177] There is a land called Aquitaine[13] where one speaks the Romance tongue, lying not far from the sea. The lord of that land got by his wife two children, who in appearance could not be more beautiful: a son and a little daughter. The mother of the children died after she had given them life. When the children had reached their tenth year, death seized the father as well. When death announced to him its coming by bringing him to the point where because of his illness he became aware of it, he did as wise men do: he immediately sent for the best of his vassals in the land, those he could trust and to whom he could commend his soul and also his children. When they had come before him—relatives, vassals, and ministerials[14]—he fixed his gaze upon his children. Both of them had turned out so fair in appearance that even a hard-bitten woman would have to smile if she were to look at them.

[209] This pained his heart very bitterly. The lord's grief grew so great that rain flowed from his eyes down onto the bedclothes. He said, "There's no avoiding it. I must take my leave of you. I should have now just begun to enjoy happiness with you and grow old joyfully. That happy thought has utterly faded; death has taken me captive." Taking them by the hand, he now entrusted them to the lords of the lands,[15] who had come at his request. One could hear there much weeping. Their lamentations as they swore loyalty caused much grief. All there conducted themselves as good liegemen do toward their lord.

[231] When the father saw the children crying, he said to his son, "Son, why are you crying? Truly, my lands and much honor now fall to you. Truly, it's for your beautiful sister that I have great fears. This is what is causing me the greater regret: I am now beginning to lament too late that in all my days I did not arrange her affairs better.[16] I did not do as a father should."

[243] He took them both by the hand and said, "Son, I admonish you to be true

---

12. "Good sinner," used on four other occasions to designate Gregorius (thus the subtitle of some English translations), is the same in the French version: *bon pecheor*. The expression has the overtone of "repentant" or "saintly," which is the case at the conclusion of the story.

13. In early medieval France, the late Roman province (Equitânjâ) between the Pyrenees and the Loire. By Hartmann's time, the duchy of Aquitaine north of the Garonne in southwestern France.

14. The Middle High German *mâge man und dienestman* would probably include all those subservient to the lord. Regarding "ministerial," see *Poor Heinrich*, line 5 and note 2.

15. That is, from hand to hand, according to Germanic tradition their legal safekeeping. Compare line 633.

16. That is, arrange a marriage for her.

to these final instructions your father gives you. Be loyal, be constant, be gener-
ous, be modest, be bold but kind. Keep your upbringing well in mind: be firm with
the lords, kind to the poor. You should honor your kin; turn strangers to your favor.
Share gladly the company of a wise man;[17] flee the fool wherever he may be. Above
all, love God; govern well through His commandment. I entrust to you my soul,
and this fair child, your sister, that you do your duty toward her well and treat her
as a brother should. Then you both will fare well. May God, Who will have mercy
on me, deign to care for the both of you." With this his speech and the strength of
his heart gave out, and the union that was his soul and his body was divided.
Everyone wept. His funeral was such as well befitted the lord of the land.

[273] Now that these noble children had lost both father and mother, the young
lord immediately assumed guardianship of his sister, taking care of her as best he
could, as suited his promises. He satisfied her wishes with his actions and posses-
sions. She never had to suffer on account of him. He took care of her in such a
way—I shall tell you how—that he denied her nothing she desired from him regard-
ing clothes and comforts. In all things they were together like friends; as good as
never did one of them spend time alone. At all times they remained side by side,
as suited them both quite well. They were inseparable at the dinner table and every-
where else. Their beds stood so close together that they could see each other. Of
him one can say simply that he took care of her as well as a loyal brother should
care for his dear sister. The great affection she had toward him was in return even
stronger; joy they had a plenty.

[303] When the enemy of the world, who for pride and envy lies locked away
in hell, beheld this joy and these comforts, the esteem that both of them enjoyed
vexed him, because it seemed to him too great, and he displayed his customary
behavior, because he has always hated and still hates it when good happens to
someone, and never allows it wherever he can avert it. And so he planned how to
rob them of their joy and their esteem, turning their joy into loss. The devil advised
him to go too far in his love of his sister, to the point that the young lord turned
his good devotion into a wrong way of thinking.

[323] Love was the first thing that seduced his senses; the second his sister's
beauty; the third the devil's contempt; the fourth was the lord's youthful naïveté
that, along with the devil, fought against him until the devil drove him to the point

---

17. The older, wise counselor is a common motif. See *Erec*, lines 270ff. In Wolfram von Eschenbach's
Parzival, Parzival's mother advises her son as he is about to set out into the world: "If a man grey with age
is willing to teach you behavior . . . you must follow him willingly" (*Parzival*, trans. Helen M. Mustard and
Charles E. Passage [New York: Vintage, 1961] 127, 11ff.).

of actually considering sleeping with his sister. To arms, Lord, to arms against the cunning of the hound of hell[18] who lies so menacingly in wait for us! Why does God allow him to bring such great disgrace over His creatures, whom He formed in His image?

[339] When through the scheming of the devil he decided to commit this great wrong, both day and night he acted with greater intimacy toward her than had been his custom before. Now the guileless child was blind to love of this kind, and the naïve, innocent girl, knowing nothing about what she should be on guard against, granted him everything he wanted. Now the devil did not let go of him until his will was carried out regarding her.[19]

[353] Now he put it off until one night when the maiden lay there, enveloped in sleep. Her brother was not asleep. The unsuspecting lad got up and crept ever so quietly to her bed, where he found her, and raised the top sheet with such care that she did not notice it at all until he came to her beneath it and took her in his arms. Alas! What did he want under there? He would have been better off lying apart! They were both free of clothing, except for the top sheet.[20] When she began to wake up, he had already embraced her. Her mouth and her cheeks she found so glued[21] to him, just as when the devil is about to triumph.

[375] Now he began to caress her more than had been his custom in the presence of others. By this she realized that things were meant in earnest. She asked, "What is this, brother? What are you trying to do? Do not let the devil deprive you of your senses. What is this tussling all about?" She thought: If I keep quiet, then the devil gets his way, and I shall become my brother's bride, but if I cry out, then we have forever lost our honor.

[391] This thought kept her from acting while he tussled with her. Because he was strong and she too weak, without the maiden willing it he brought the game to an end. This was certainly too much intimacy. Afterward there was not a sound. And so that very night she became pregnant by her brother. The lure[22] of devilish excitation began to drive them[23] on and on; they took pleasure in their sin. They kept it a secret until the moment when the woman perceived—as women very

18. Perhaps a conflation of the devil and Cerberus, the three-headed dog in mythology that guards the gate to Hades.

19. The "his" of "his will" has been variously interpreted as being the devil's or that of Gregorius's father.

20. At this time people slept naked.

21. *Gelîmet,* literally "limed." Bird-lime was spread on branches to catch birds. The word often appears in an image or metaphor in medieval literature. Compare *Erec,* line 9078.

22. In the language of falconry *luoder* (MHG) means "bait" or "lure."

23. *Si* is "her" or "them," and has been variously interpreted by other translators.

quickly do—that she was pregnant. Then her joy grew heavy because nothing helped her[24] hide it. She looked sad indeed.

[411] Ruin came upon them from great intimacy. If they had escaped that, they would not have been forsaken. Now let every single man heed this warning: not to be too intimate with his sister or any other close relative.[25] It incites one to licentiousness that one should certainly forswear.

[421] When the young man saw such a change in his sister, he took her aside and said, "Dearest sister, tell me, you are so sad. What is troubling you? I've noticed from looking at you that you seem very downcast. I've not been accustomed to that in you."

[430] From her heart she now began to sigh, and her eyes revealed anguished pain. She said, "There is no denying it. I have good reason to be sad. Brother, I am twice over dead, dead in soul and dead in body. Woe is me, poor woman. Why was I ever born? For on your account I have lost God and men's favor as well. The crime that we have hidden from the world till today can be concealed no longer. I am taking good care not to speak of it, but the child I am carrying here will certainly announce it to everyone." At once her brother helped her to grieve; his misery was even greater.

[451] In this sad matter Lady Love again showed her vexing habit: she always causes sorrow after love.[26] Just so does honey mixed with gall surge up. He began to weep bitterly, supporting his head with his hand, so sadly, as one with worries is wont to do. All his honor was at stake, yet he bemoaned more his sister's troubles than his own sorrows.

[465] Looking at her brother, the sister said, "Act like a man. Stop weeping like a woman[27]—that, unfortunately, cannot help us at all—and come up with something, so that, even if we must be without God's grace because of our wrongdoing, at least our child will not be lost with us, with all three of us being among the

---

24. *Si* here has also been interpreted as plural ("them"), referring to the two of them.

25. Church laws regarding consanguinity were much stricter in the Middle Ages than they are today, at times reaching the seventh degree of relationship.

26. Compare Proverbs 14:13: "Even in laughter the heart is sorrowful." The coexistence of happiness and sorrow is a sentiment often expressed at this time in literature. An anonymous poet writes, "Happiness cannot exist without suffering" [liep âne leit mac niht sîn]; in the penultimate strophe of *Das Nibelungenlied* one reads, "as joy always ultimately gives way to sorrow" [als ie diu liebe leide z'aller jungeste gît]; and Gottfried von Strassburg writes in *Tristan*, "Whoever never experienced suffering from love, he also never experienced joy from love. Suffering and joy, they have always been unseparated (when joined) to love" [swem nie von liebe leit geschach, dem geschach ouch liep von liebe nie. liep unde leit diu wâren ie an minnen ungescheiden] (lines 204–8). Compare further *The Lament*, line 792; the poem "These would be wonderful days," 3, 1; and *Erec*, line 2210.

27. Compare *Poor Heinrich*, line 1122.

fallen. We have often been told that a child never bears his father's guilt. Indeed, it shall not lose God's favor because of that, even if we were born for hell, because it shares no blame whatsoever in our wrongdoing."

[483] Now his heart began to waver among many thoughts. He sat silently a while, then said, "Sister, put on a happier face. I have come up with something that will certainly help us conceal our shame. I have in my lands a very wise vassal who can advise us well. My father assigned him to me and advised me to follow his counsel when he, as he lay dying, availed himself of his counsel.[28] Him we will take as an adviser—I know well that he will be loyal—and if we follow his counsel, then our honor will be preserved."

[501] The lady was happy about the plan. Her joy was such as befitted her at that moment; she did not know complete joy. What earlier might have caused her to grieve, when she was without sorrow, that was here her greatest joy—she ceased nothing save her weeping. The plan pleased her very well. She said, "Brother, send now for the one who is to advise us, because my day is not far off."

[513] He was quickly sent for. The messenger brought him immediately. He was received well. They went into a separate chamber where they asked him for his advice. The young man said, "I have not asked you here to court regarding a trifling matter. I don't know anyone who lives in my lands at this time whom I trust so well. Since God has so honored you, giving you loyalty and the skill of giving good advice, let us enjoy the benefit of that. We wish to reveal to you a secret matter that puts us in an uncomfortable position and jeopardizes our entire honor, unless your advice, with God's aid, saves us." And so both of them knelt down crying at his feet.

[536] He replied, "My lord, this greeting seems to me too great, even if I were your peer. Stand up, my lord, for God's sake. Let me hear your command, which I shall never break, and be more exact with your words. Tell me what troubles you. You are my legitimate lord. I shall advise you as best I can; never doubt that."

[547] Now they disclosed the matter to him. Immediately he helped them both to weep at their misfortune—he meant them both well—and did his best to console them, like one should a friend who experiences a calamity that no one can prevent. Then the youth said to the wise man, "My lord, come up with some plan that concerns us personally, since the time is now coming for my sister to lie in, where she might recover after the birth of the child, so that the birth might be kept

28. See line 254ff. where it is not specifically stated who the "wise man" is, but in line 554 the vassal is addressed as "the wise man."

secret. My thinking is: if I stay outside of the lands the entire time, away from my sister, our shame might better be kept secret."

[566] The wise man spoke, "I advise this then: you should summon to court both young and old who rule in your lands[29] as well as those who advised your father. You should reveal to them that you intend to go immediately, for God's sake, to the Holy Sepulcher.[30] Bid us swear allegiance to our lady—no one will refuse that— that she should reign o'er the lands as long as you remain away. Do penance there for your sin as God moves you. Your body has acted against God. Let it then do penance before Him. And if death takes hold of you there, then the force of the oath requires that she rule as our lady. In the presence of all the lords place her in my trust. That should please them well, since I am the oldest among them and also the most powerful. Then I shall take her home with me and arrange such comfort for her that she will give birth to the child, and no one will be the wiser of it.

[595] "May God send you back, my lord. I have great confidence in Him. If you die while away, you will have God's blessing. Truly, it is not my advice that she should flee the world or withdraw from the lands because of this misdeed.[31] If she remains in the lands, she may do penance even better for her sin and shame. She can greet the poor with goods[32] and with a generous disposition if she keeps her goods. If she lacks goods, she has nothing but her generous disposition. Now what use may her generous disposition be to someone if she has no goods? What use is a generous disposition without goods? Or goods without a generous disposition? A generous disposition is of some use without goods, but better are goods and a generous disposition. Therefore, it seems good to me if she retains goods and a generous disposition. Thus she may use her goods to satisfy her generous disposition. Let her thus do right by God with a generous disposition, with body,[33] and with goods. I also advise you to have the same generous disposition." The advice seemed good to them both, and so they followed without hesitation his good advice.

[627] When the lords across the lands were summoned to court, and when they came before him and heard from their lord, his request was obeyed immediately.

---

29. That is, those who hold a feudal benefice.

30. In Jerusalem. Jerusalem had been taken by the Christian forces during the First Crusade. Despite the failures of ensuing crusades, numerous pilgrims continued to make the arduous trek to the Holy Land. The Crusades and such pilgrimages feature prominently in medieval literature.

31. Implied is the customary withdrawal to a convent.

32. MHG *guot* normally implies property and possessions, by which wealth is measured, not by money. It also means "good(ness)," and Hartmann plays on this for a number of lines.

33. Compare lines 581–82.

He then entrusted the hand of his sister to the elder vassal.[34] Thus he thought to leave his lands. The treasure that their father had left them was divided with her at this time.

[637] And so they parted with great sorrow in their hearts. If they had not feared God, they would have preferred forever the scorn of the world to their parting. One could have seen great misery there on both faces. May such great woe never happen to me as happened to the lovers when they had to part. Truly, joy was as absent from them both as ice is in fire. A mutual exchange of fidelity took place when they had to part. His heart followed her from there; hers stayed with the man.[35] Parting perforce caused them pain. They never saw each other again.

[657] This wise man now led his young lady to his house, where she experienced much kindness and comfort. Now the mistress of the house was a woman who had given herself, body and mind, to God's service. No woman had need to live better. As befits a woman's kindness, she helped them secretly, without a breach of faith, conceal their lady's distress, so that when the lady's lying in ended no one was aware of it. It was a son she bore, the good sinner, about whom this tale only now takes its beginning. The child was a joy to behold. No one was present at the child's birth save these two women. The master of the house was called there, and when he saw the child, he swore along with the women that never had such a pleasing child been brought into the world.[36]

[683] Now they very quickly held counsel among themselves how it[37] might be concealed. They said it would be a shame if the fair little child were lost. Yet it was born with such very great sins that they would never know what the best plan was, if God did not make it known to them. They put the decision in God's hands that He might keep them from all wrongdoing in these matters. They had to succeed in this because things never go wrong for one who relies on God as he should.

[699] They fixed upon the idea that for them nothing would be as good as sending the child out to sea.[38] There was no putting it off. The master of the house stole away and acquired in secret a sturdy little casket, the best there was. Then, with abundant tears, the fair child was laid into it. Under and over it was spread expensive silk cloth, the best that could be had. There was also put in with the

---

34. As we have seen (line 223), this gesture had legal force.
35. A topos when lovers part. Compare line 1966, and *Erec*, lines 2358–67.
36. Compare further lines 1033–34 and lines 1264–84. External beauty, very important in medieval epics, was thought to reflect nobility and inner beauty.
37. The MHG also uses the pronoun *ez* (it) because of its neuter antecedent *kind* (child).
38. See the story of Moses in Exodus 2:3.

child, as I have been informed, twenty gold marks,[39] so that one could raise it if God were ever to send it ashore.

[719] A tablet was brought there to the lady who bore the child; it was made of very good ivory, embellished well, as I have read, with gold and precious stones. I never got one that good. Then the mother wrote on it as much as she could about the child's situation, because she hoped that God would deliver it into the hands of people who would recognize God's work in the child.[40]

[733] On it was written: the child was of noble birth, and she who bore it was its aunt; its father was its uncle. To conceal the crime it had been sent out to sea. On it she wrote still more: that one should baptize it and raise it with the gold, and if the finder were also a Christian, he should multiply the treasure, and teach it to read books.[41] One should keep the tablet for it and teach it writing so that if it ever became a man he[42] could read there this entire story and thus not become arrogant. And if he turned out to be of such goodness that he directed his thoughts to God, then he would at all times, following duty's counsel, do penance for his father's wrong, and also remember the one who brought him into the world. There was need of that for both of them to save them from eternal death. Neither his people nor land, ancestry nor home, was named; and it was good to conceal that from him.

[767] When the document had been prepared, the tablet was then laid next to him in the little casket. Then they closed it up with such care that no harm of any kind might come to the child, from rain or wind, or from the violence of the waves, during the trip of two or three days on the water. Thus by night they carried it to the sea. Because of daylight they could not do so earlier. There they found a skiff, empty and strong. Then with lamentations they laid the little seafarer in it. Thereupon, sweet Christ, whose mercy is more than mercy, sent him a very favorable, wished-for wind. They gave a push; the child floated away.

[789] Well do you know that a man who has experienced neither true joy nor great heartfelt sorrow does not have a mouth as ready to speak of these things as a man who has had the experience. Now I am between them, separated from them both, since something like that never happened to me: I never experienced joy or woe; I live neither badly nor well. Therefore I am unable to reveal as I should the sorrow of the lady or to narrate it in words, for a thousand hearts would be overwhelmed by the weight of her misfortune.

39. Twenty gold marks was a vast sum of money.
40. For a similar situation, see *Milon* (c. 1170), a *lai* by Marie de France, particularly lines 77–104.
41. Probably the (books of the) Bible and its commentary.
42. Here, because of the antecedent *man*, the masculine pronoun takes over.

[805] There were three kinds of sorrow that the lady at this time bore alone. Each of them by itself would be enough for the heart of many a woman. One pain she bore from the crime she committed with her brother, whom she had left. Her delicate health from giving birth to the child was another. The third was the anxiety caused by her misery over her dear child whom she had entrusted to the wild wind on the sea, not knowing how he fared, or whether he were well or were dead. She was born to great distress, and these three afflictions were not the end of it. Not many days had passed before bad news reached her, the greatest woe she ever experienced in her life: her brother was dead. Death came to him from the distress of longing.

[831] When she had parted from her brother, as the wise man had advised them both, he immediately grew ill—the bond of love caused that—and had to discontinue the journey he had agreed upon for God's sake. His misery because of his dear sister had grown even greater so that at no time could he find peace. And so his body wasted away. However much they claim that a woman loves more strongly than a man, that is not the case, as the following makes clear, because the heartfelt sorrow that came over him was small in comparison to his sister's. But such was not the case with the love that caused his death. She suffered from four kinds of sorrow and recovered. Longing for her so took hold of him that he lay dead from heartfelt woe. She was told of this news exactly three days before she was to go to church.[43] So she went there lamenting greatly and buried her brother and her husband.

[858] When she had assumed rule of the lands, and this news had resounded throughout the realm, many powerful lords, near and far, desired her for their wife. In nobility and in appearance, in wealth and in youth, in beauty and in virtue, in upbringing and in goodness, and in her entire being, she was worthy of a good man. However, they were all rejected.

[871] She had chosen for her love—God knows, a strong hero—the most worthy man who ever acquired the name of man. For him she adorned her body as a woman in love should for a worthy man whom she would like to please. However rigidly it is against custom that a woman ask something of a man, she nevertheless pressed Him, whenever she had the opportunity, at all times with her heart and also with words. I mean: our merciful God. Since the devil's scorn had robbed her of His grace, this had frightened her so much that she rejected joy and comfort to gain His grace, and preserved it day and night diligently in penitential acts against

---

43. Implied is her first visit to church after giving birth. Compare Leviticus 12:2–4, "If a woman have . . . born a man child: then she shall be unclean seven days. . . . And she shall then continue in the blood of her purifying three and thirty days; she shall . . . [not] come into the sanctuary, until the days of her purifying be fulfilled."

her body. Both with vigils and with prayers, with alms and with fasting, she never let her body rest. She had true contrition that frees one of all sins present.

[899] Now there was a lord who resided not far from her, whose social standing was much like hers, and was both noble and powerful. He made every effort to bring it about that she might take him as her husband. And when he had done with messengers and with personal requests what was right and proper for him to undertake, and she still did not want him, he thought he might win her through war and threats. He attacked her and laid waste to her lands. He wrested from her the best towns and castles until he forced her to retreat to the point that nothing remained to her any longer save one of her more important towns. This too was surrounded and guarded day and night. She must lose it as well unless our gracious God in His mercy wishes to prevent it.

[923] Now let us leave this tale here and tell how this lady's child fares, whom the wild winds were tossing wherever God commanded them, toward life or death. Our dear Lord God took him into His keeping, by whose mercy Jonah too was saved on the sea, who for three days and three nights in the billowing water was sheltered in the belly of a fish. God was the child's nurse until He sent him ashore, safe and sound.

[940] In two nights and one day the child came from the pounding of the waves to an island, where God had sent it. On the shore stood a monastery; a pious abbot had charge of it. He had ordered two fishermen to be sure to go fishing on the sea before break of day. There the weather was causing them great trouble. The wind raised such a din that they could catch neither small nor large fish. They hurried back. On the way, they found the child's skiff floating on the turbulent waves. Now they were very surprised how it had come there without anyone in it. They drew up so close to it that they saw the little casket lying in it. They lifted it out and laid it in their boat. The skiff darted off, empty.

[965] The windstorm became so severe that they were sorely tried on the sea. Conditions did not allow them to see what was in the casket. But they did not care about that, because they thought that when they had brought it home, they could inspect at their leisure what they had found. They threw their cloaks over it and pulled hard toward land.

[977] In the meantime, they noticed day dawning. The abbot who was in charge of the monastery went down to the sea for a stroll—all alone, and nobody else— and watched for the fishermen to see what luck they had had. In the meantime, they were approaching. That struck the abbot as too early. He asked, "How did it go? Did you catch anything?"

[987] They replied, "Beloved lord, we had sailed way too far out onto the wild sea. Never have we suffered so much from the weather. Death nearly overtook us; we just barely escaped with our lives."

[994] He said, "Well, no matter about the fish. Thank God you came away alive and have returned to shore." The abbot then asked them to tell him what it might be. He meant the little casket that had their cloaks spread over it. The question irked them both. They asked what kind of lord would thus inquire so exactly into poor people's affairs, to the irritation of them both. Then he reached over with his staff, pulling off the cloaks, and saw the little casket. He asked, "Where did you get that?" Now they thought of many lies and how they might deceive the abbot by withholding it from him, and they probably would have succeeded, except that he saw through them by the love of our Lord God.

[1015] When he was about to drop the questioning and go back to his monastery, the child began to cry very loudly, announcing to God's friend that it was there. Then the good man said, "There is a child in this casket. Tell me for the love of God, where did you get it? How did it happen to come to you? I want to know, *crede*⁴⁴ me." They thought it over and told him what I told you earlier, how they had found it on the sea. Now he directed them to lift it onto the sand and to undo the bands. There he saw lying a wondrous find: a child, about whom his heart declared that he had never seen one so fair.

[1035] The homeless orphan smiled at the abbot with a sweet mouth, since it did not know how to fear any danger. The learned man read on the tablet how the child was born [and that one should baptize it and raise it with the gold].⁴⁵ He knew well how to keep a secret. He bowed his head to God, raised secretly to himself his hands and eyes toward heaven, and praised God that the child had been found in good health.

[1051] They discovered the child wrapped in silk woven in Alexandria.⁴⁶ Now these three knew about it; the news was not spread any further. Our source⁴⁷ also tells us about the fishermen that they were brothers. With assurances and with oaths of fidelity they both had to affirm that they would never say anything further about it.

44. Latin: believe.

45. These two lines appear in only one manuscript. They are kept to preserve the traditional line numbering.

46. In Egypt. At this time in the Middle Ages, after two crusades to the Holy Land, there was vigorous trade to the south and the east in precious items unavailable in the West. In medieval epics, the more exotic the item, the more praiseworthy it was. Its availabilty was generally limited to the nobility.

47. Compare *Erec*, line 10039 and note 5.

[1063] The brothers were not equal; the one was poor, the other wealthy. The poor one lived near the monastery, the rich one quite a bit farther away, well over a mile.[48] The poor one had many children; the rich one never had any children, save for a daughter who was married.[49] Now the abbot reached a good agreement with the two: that the poorer man would take the child and raise it nearby. He would thus lie if anyone should ask how he had acquired the child, saying it had come to him from his brother's daughter—he could not devise any other clever plan so appropriate—and that they were keeping it until they had eaten, after mass,[50] and that the abbot would be asked to be so good as to baptize the child himself and thereby acquire God's grace and their devotion. The proposal was appropriate and good.

[1093] Now the abbot took what the child had been provided with, the gold and the silk material, and on the spot gave the poor man who had taken charge of the child two gold marks, so that he might raise it, and to the rich man one mark, so that he would guard the secret well. The remainder he took away with him, the very blessed man. He put it away very safely for the child. Indeed, he did even better by investing it and increasing it for him.[51]

[1107] The poor fisherman did not delay; he did as his lord directed. When midday came, he took the child in his arms. As always according to peasant custom, his wife went with him to the monastery where he saw the abbot among his brothers. He said, "My lord, this child is sent to you by people who are beholden to you: my brother's daughter and her husband, and they believe strongly that if you baptize it, the child will have a blessed life. And deign to give him your name."

[1123] The request was mocked by the monks. They said, "God help us, just look at how this peasant can speak." The abbot received the speech well, as befits a humble man. When he beheld the child up close, he said to his brothers, "It is such a fair child. Since they belong to God's house,[52] we should certainly not refuse them." He directed that the child be carried to the baptismal font. He himself raised it[53] and called it by his own name: Gregorius.[54]

---

48. A mile (*mîle*) at this time was more than the modern mile, but of various lengths.

49. A troublesome, perhaps corrupt, couplet. In the French source the rich fisherman has a married daughter, but the lack of other children is not indicated.

50. Christenings usually took place in the afternoon, mass in the morning. See lines 1927–28.

51. Given the strict religious prohibition against profit from interest, the abbot is probably involved in some form of investment and profit sharing, not loans.

52. That is, as servants of the monastery.

53. That is, raised it out of the baptismal water.

54. In the Middle Ages Gregorius was a name limited to men of the church.

[1137] When the child had received baptism, the abbot said, "Since I now have become his spiritual father,[55] I shall always be happy, for the gain of my salvation, to consider it in place of my own child—it is of such blessed nature." With loving words he asked his fisherman to take good care of the child. He said, "Now raise it well for me, so that I may reward you always." The two marks helped the child greatly, so that he was cared for even better. In addition, the abbot allowed hardly a day to pass without seeing for himself how the child was being cared for.

[1155] When the fisherman and his wife had so diligently taken care of the sweet child for six years, the abbot took it from them into the monastery and dressed it in such an outfit that befitted a cleric, and had him instructed to read books, which taught him to be loyal, honorable, and good; how seldom did he flee from that! How gladly he did his teacher's will when requested; he needed no beating! He did not let himself get bored. He, the blessed child, was eager to ask about all things that are good to know.

[1173] Because of his abilities he caught up so quickly with children who had begun instruction three years earlier that the teacher himself swore that he had never seen a youth so sharp in talents of every kind. He was—I am not lying to you—in years a child, in intelligence a man.

[1181] By his eleventh year there was truly no better student of *grammaticus*[56] than the child Gregorius. Three years later his mind had improved so much that he had command of *divinitas*:[57] this knowledge is about the godhead. Whatever was presented to him that is useful to body and soul, he always grasped the essentials of it. Afterward he read in *legibus*,[58] and the child thus became in that very field of learning a fine jurist. This knowledge concerns the law. He would have learned even more, except that he was prevented from it, as I can well tell you.

[1201] The fisherman had suffered great difficulties from poverty. His acreage was the sea. That made for a very hard life, since he supported himself thus and all the time protected his children from hunger only with his catch—before he had found the child. But then his life was immediately made much easier when he was given two gold marks. All matters of possessions and comfort improved greatly. Now his unreasonable wife never let him rest from her daily questioning.

---

55. According to canon law an abbot was not allowed to be a godfather. He is therefore the child's *pater spiritualis*.

56. Grammar (reading and writing skills in Latin) was part of the traditional trivium that also included rhetoric and logic.

57. Theology.

58. Probably Roman law, but maybe also canon law.

She set many a trap for him. She used her cunning, both early and late, so that she might discover where the gold came from. Many an oath she swore to him before she finally learned from him where the gold had come from, as you, indeed, learned earlier. When the woman had found out for certain that no one knew who Gregorius was, she told it no further. She kept it to herself, as is fitting, that is true, until his fifteenth year.

[1235] Now Lady Happiness had stamped him in every way with her distinctive mark: he was fair and strong; he was loyal and good, and had a patient disposition. He had enough of the social graces: a good upbringing and good manners. He had exchanged unreasonable anger for a gentle disposition. Every day he won friends and did not lose one among them. His joy and his sorrow he was able to bear in proper measure. He was receptive to instruction and generous with whatever he might have, daring when he should be, hesitant when he wanted to be. By all appearances a child, he walked the path of the wise. He never took back his word. He never did anything without prior reflection, as good sense commanded; therefore he never blushed at any of his actions. He sought mercy and counsel from God at all times and strictly observed His commandment.

[1264] God permitted Perfection to come over him so that it formed his body and mind according to its nature. Whatever praiseworthy quality any person on earth happened to have, it was not lacking in him either. Perfection had formed him in such a way that it was pleased with him as a child, because it had forgotten nothing. If it could have, it would have molded him even better. All the people who saw him said to the boy that no youth so blessed with good fortune had ever been born to a fisherman. It was a real shame that one could not praise him for his lineage, and they said over and over: if he were of noble birth, then a mighty land would certainly suit his capabilities.

[1285] Now it happened one day that the boy Gregorius came with his playmates to where they were wont to play. Now something unusual took place—it happened through no intention of his. He hurt, as he had never done before, the fisherman's son such that he began to cry. He ran off screaming. When his mother heard him come crying so, she ran to her child. She cried out gruffly, "See here, why are you crying like that?" "Gregorius hit me." "Why did he hit you?" "Mother, I have no idea." "See here, did you do something to him?" "Mother, God knows, no, I didn't." "Where is he now?" "Down by the sea."

[1306] She cried out, "Woe is me, poor woman, woe is me! That deceitful, foolish lout! Did I raise him to thrash my children, especially right here in front of their kin? It will not please your kin if I tolerate this insult from the kind of person who never had any kin here. It will always pain me that someone who just wandered in here dared thrash you. Unless one suffered it for the sake of God, one would not tolerate it long. After all, no one knows who he is. [And if it happens that I live on, I shall indeed tell all the world that he is a foundling—so help me holy Christ— no matter how high-placed he is now. He has completely forgotten that he was found in such a wretched state, tied in a casket, in a skiff on the sea. If he hurts my child, it won't be tolerated long. Indeed, no one here knows who he is.] Woe is me! What is he up to? The devil brought him here to torment me. Indeed, I know well where his road is leading, the miserable foundling. Why didn't he want his shameful lot to be kept secret? Then he would have had a pleasant life. A curse upon the fish that they did not eat him up when he was thrown out upon the sea. He chanced upon a blessed trip that brought him to the abbot. If the abbot, who is the boy's almoner,[59] had not taken him from your father, things would be quite different. He would be subject to us, Christ knows. He would have to drive our cattle and swine in and out. What was your father thinking when with a cold hand[60] he found him on the open sea,[61] and let the abbot keep him, and didn't order him to serve him, thus making him, as was his right, his subject and serf?"

[1359] Gregorius, when he had struck the child, felt very bad about it and ran home after him. He was in such a hurry because he feared greatly that the child would cause him to lose his foster mother's love. Now he heard her inside scolding unrestrainedly. Standing on the path, he heard about his disgrace and got to the bottom of things he had not known: that he was a stranger in the land,[62] as she often called him. His joy was clouded over by these new cares. Greatly troubled, he pondered whether these words that his foster mother had said were a lie or the truth, and he immediately hurried off to the monastery, where he found the abbot, and took the trustworthy man away from the other people.

[1386] He said, "My dear lord, by no means can I thank you enough as I would gladly do, if I could. Now I am resolved that till the day I die I shall ask Him who

---

59. That is, provider, but emphasizing the orphan's destitution. Although the wife appears to know about the origin of the gold, it is not certain that she (or her husband) knows about the large remaining amount.

60. Perhaps implying his labor under adverse (cold) conditions, since there was a storm, but it has been conjectured that it implies some kind of now unknown legal term.

61. "Open" (MHG *gemein*: common to all) implies that what is caught (found) there belongs to the finder.

62. Perhaps an extension of the earlier Moses imagery. Compare Exodus 2:22 (Vulgate), "quae peperit ei filium, quem vocavit Gersam, dicens: Advena fui in terra aliena." The New Revised Standard Version reads, "I have been an alien resident in a foreign land." King James Version has, "And [Zipporah] bare [Moses] a son, and he called his name Gershom: for he said, I have been a stranger in a strange land." Compare also *Erec*, line 1131 and note 34.

never leaves a good deed uncompensated to reward you with the heavenly crown—
I am certainly obligated to do that—for so lovingly raising me, a stranger, from a
foundling, favoring me more than those in your household. Unfortunately, I have
been deceived. I am not the one I thought I was. Now you should, my dear lord,
give me leave for God's sake. I shall and must give myself up to the hardship and
uncertainty of a stranger, as is right. My foster mother has admitted to me—it hap-
pened in a rage—that I was found. Dishonor will rob me of both body and soul if
I ever hear it again. God knows I shall never hear of it again, because I am not
staying here any longer. Indeed, somewhere I shall find a land where no one knows
where I came from. I have the intelligence and also the wit to recover quite well
from this, if God so wills. I fear derision so much that I would prefer to be where
no human being is rather than remain any longer here in this land. Indeed, dis-
grace is what is driving me away. Women are so indiscreet. As soon as they tell
somebody something, then very quickly three and four know about it, and then
everyone who is here."

[1432] The abbot replied, "Dear child, now listen. I shall advise you well, as I
should the dear one whom I have raised from a child. God has done very well by
you. Through His love He has given you much free choice regarding body and
soul, so that you yourself may direct your life and turn it to disgrace or to honor.
At this time, at your present age, you must, based on your own choices, now settle
this very dispute between these two things and decide what you want to gain: life
or death. You should begin thinking about the matter now. Son, be true to your-
self and follow my instruction—if you do, you will have chosen virtue and honor
over disgrace and scorn—so that, in your impetuous anger, you do not precipitately
do things you will regret later.

[1457] "You are a blessed young man; your affairs are as one could wish. You
have started out very well. The people in this land are favorably disposed toward
you. Now listen closely, dear child, to what I say: you are used to the life of a cleric.
Do not forsake that. You are becoming learned in books. I am gray in years; my
body will soon lie at rest. I want to pledge to you most assuredly that I shall bring
about for you at our gathering, among old and young alike, that they take you as
lord when I die. Now, how can the prattle of a foolish woman trouble you? I shall
also take care that this matter will henceforth never pass her lips."

[1479] Gregorius replied, "My lord, you have paid God great honor through
your care of the poor person that I am, and you have enhanced your salvation, and
have now proposed what is best. My youthful blind spirit has now so swelled in
anger that it will not let me follow you. Three things, to my vexation, are driving

me from this land: one is the disgrace that I have from the scolding. The second is such that it too chases me away. I know now that I am not the child of this fisherman. Now what if my relatives are of such lineage that I could be a knight if I had the will and the equipment?⁶³ God knows, it has always been my desire, that if I were of noble birth and had wealth, I would become a knight. Sweet honey is bitter to a man who cannot enjoy it. You have the sweetest life that God has given the world. Whoever has chosen it rightly has been born blessed. I could easily remain here if I had the will, which I unfortunately do not have.⁶⁴ My thoughts and wishes are fixed on knighthood."

[1515] "Son, your talk is not good. Redirect your thoughts for God's sake.⁶⁵ Whoever as priest⁶⁶ estranges himself from God and becomes a knight can lose his soul and his body from many wrongs. Any person who turns away from God thereby disgraces himself and will be delivered up to hell. Son, I had chosen you to be a child of God. If I find that yet in you, I shall always be happy."

[1530] Gregorius answered him, "Knighthood is a way of life; whoever knows how to pursue it with moderation⁶⁷ can't do better. One is better off being a knight of God⁶⁸ than a false monk."

[1536] "Son, I fear for you for the following reason: you are not capable of knightly skills. If one sees you riding clumsily, then you will forever have to suffer the derision of other knights. Turn back, dear son, while you can, for God's sake."

[1543] "My lord, I am a young man and shall learn what I can't now do. Whatever I put my mind to I shall learn very quickly."

[1547] "Son, many a person who knows something about knighthood has told me: he who remains in school until the age of twelve without learning to ride must always, to be sure, act like a priest. You are well suited to be a child of God and a member of the choir;⁶⁹ the cowl has never befitted a man better."

[1558] "My lord, try now and give me knightly clothing. For sure, if it does not suit me I shall not begrudge it another man and shall put the cowl back on. My lord, you have been told very correctly: whoever is to be a good knight needs a lot

---

63. It was very expensive to outfit a knight.

64. Perhaps the lack of will for the clerical life is the third "thing" (line 1487).

65. Compare line 755 ("that he directed his thoughts to God").

66. At this time in the Middle Ages the preponderance of monks were ordained as priests. It would thus be assumed that Gregorius would become a priest.

67. Moderation (*mâze*) is one of the key elements of the knightly ethos.

68. Since at least the First Crusade (1095), one finds the concept of *miles christianus*, the soldier (knight) in the service of God.

69. Implied is that Gregorius would become a "choir monk," an important member of the monastery.

of practice. But from childhood on I have learned it well here in my heart. It has never left my thoughts. I can tell you: from the moment I could distinguish between evil and good, my heart has taken aim at knighthood. Never in my thoughts was I a Bavarian or a Franconian knight. Whatever knight from Hennegau, from Brabant, and from Haspengau[70] rode his mount best, I could always do it better in my imagination. My lord, I shall never regret whatever ability I have in book learning; I would gladly know more. But as much as one forced me to the books up to now, my thoughts rode in tournaments.[71] As I was being introduced to books, how my heart yearned and my thoughts focused on a shield! The spear was always my desire and not the stylus, the sword and not the quill; that is what I always really wanted. My thoughts never had it better than when I sat mounted and held my shield up to my neck, tucked the lance properly under my arm, and the horse sprang away with me. Then I let my thighs fly. I could bow them in such a way that I struck the horse with my spurs, neither in the flanks nor in the shoulders, but toward the rear, a finger's width back, behind where the girth is laid. My legs flew up by the mane. If someone had seen me, I appeared in the saddle as though painted there. I carried myself so well that I rode without exerting myself. I took on the relaxed, appropriate conduct, as though it were a game, and when I rushed into the long approach with lowered lance, I could easily turn the horse to either side. If I jousted with any man, I never missed. My attention was well directed to the four studs over my opponent's hand.[72] Now help me, my dear lord, to turn my desire for knighthood into reality. Then you will have done me well."

[1625] "Son, you have told me much, have spoken many a German word that makes me very surprised at you, *crede* me,[73] and I don't know where it's all leading. I would understand Greek just as well.[74] You did not hear this from our teacher, who has overseen your lessons up to now. However it came to you, your disposi-

---

70. Bavaria, in the southeast of modern Germany, and Franconia, northwest of it, were important territories during the High Middle Ages. Knights from Hennegau (near Valenciennes in modern northeast France), Brabant (in modern Belgium), and Haspengau (Hesbaye, near Liège in eastern Belgium) were known for their prowess.

71. Gregorius is referring to the jousting tournaments that in the course of the Middle Ages took on more and more of a social function. They play an important role in many medieval epics.

72. The studs in the center of the shield that fastened the handhold. Much of the description here echoes *Erec*. See, for example, line 2795.

73. The abbot emphasizes German because Gregorius uses, in German and not in the Latin of the monastery, the new chivalric vocabulary in vogue at the time (though much of the terminology came from the French!). Whether or not the monk is feigning ignorance, for monastery scriptoria often served as distributors of secular manuscripts (one possible source for Gregorius about knighthood?), his conscious or unconscious reaction to this German may be the Latin *crede* ("believe"). See line 1025.

74. That is, not at all. Even for the educated in the Latin Middle Ages a knowledge of Greek was rare.

tion is not, as I can tell from all this, that of a monk. Now I shall no longer keep you from it. May God grant that things go well for you and give you through His might all the best for knighthood."

[1641] Now he arranged that someone cut for him clothing from the same silk material that he had once found with him. Never had better come into that land. He saw clearly that he was in a hurry and afterward made him, as quickly as he could, a knight, as befitted him.[75]

[1649] Although Gregorius had become a knight, the abbot had still not revealed anything about the tablet and the gold. He cared for him so much that he deliberately concealed it from him. He thought: since he is now a knight and has no possessions, perhaps he will listen to my advice and stay and lead a comfortable life. He tried again and said, "Dear son, do stay with me. I shall arrange for you such a favorable marriage that will fulfill all your wishes, and I shall give you every opportunity to lead a magnificent life. You have become a knight, but you must be ashamed of your poverty. Now what use is your knighthood if you do not have the power that wealth gives? You will not ride into any land where someone knows you. You will have neither friend nor considerable property. See, you will come to ruin there. Do change your mind yet and remain. That will be good for you."

[1676] Gregorius replied, "My lord, don't push matters any further. If I wanted comfort instead of honor, then I would follow your instructions and would lower my intentions, because my comfort here would be good. Indeed, harm comes to many a man who is overloaded with possessions. Because of comfort he just lies about,[76] which never happens to the poor man whose heart is right, because he makes every effort to gain wealth wherever he can. How could he turn things for the better? For if he can make himself esteemed, he will easily become a man blessed, and throughout all the lands will be favored over many a lord.

[1693] "That I am called a poor man—I am not to blame for that. Everything my father left me I carry here. Since it now is my lot that Lady Prosperity flees from me, and I can only earn her greeting through my ability—I can gain it, it is true[77]—unless she intends to refuse it to me more than she has refused it to anyone else who has pursued it in the right manner. This is the way one should run

---

75. The ritual of knighting by a priest or abbot alone is highly unusual. The little information the reader has regarding this monastery indicates that it is affluent, seemingly headed by a prince-abbot.

76. This same verb (*verligen*) is key in *Erec*. See there lines 2966–74. See here further line 1873 and *Iwein*, lines 2763–98.

77. For a similar sentiment about fleeting success and how one gains it, see *The Lament*, lines 781–85.

it down: gain prosperity through toil.[78] I have no doubts about this: if I become a very capable man in body and soul, I well deserve her love. But if I am a coward, I shall not live three days when I leave here. What should I do without honor? If I acquire wealth and honor through just effort, through intelligence and manliness, one will praise me more for that than the one whose father left him fabulous wealth that was wasted shamefully. What more do I need than I have? My horses are good and sturdy; my servants are capable and good and have a true heart. I am well equipped. Wherever wealth is to be gained, I trust I can succeed there. Let this be the end of our conversation. My lord, I bow before your kindness but respectfully refuse to remain here any longer."

[1732] "Son, then I shall no longer detain you beyond this moment—I see well that you are serious—however reluctantly I shall do without you. Dear son, now come with me, for I want to let you see what I still have of yours."

[1739] So the honest man, weeping profusely, then led him to a chamber that the young man found well furnished with silken material, and placed in his hand his tablet, on which he read how things really stood with him. He was sad and happy about it. His sadness came about as I shall make known to you here. He cried about the sin with which he was born. On the other hand, he felt great joy because of his high birth and great possessions, about which he had known nothing earlier.

[1756] Then the loyal, steadfast man who had been his lord said, "Son, now you have read everything that I kept secret from you until now. Your tablet has told you this clearly. Now I have managed your gold as I was supposed to, according to your mother's orders. With God's help I have increased it greatly. From seventeen gold marks we have acquired one hundred and fifty for you—however badly we understood what we were doing—from the time we first found you. I gave three marks and no more to those who brought you to me from the sea. This is the amount you have. You can live a good life from what you may still gain, if you but act with reason."

[1777] Gregorius, weeping profusely, answered, "Alas, dear lord, I have fallen far, and none of it my fault at all. How shall I gain God's grace after the misdeed that lies written here before me?"

[1785] "My dear son, I shall tell you. This is true, believe me. If you stay with knighthood, see, then the force of your wrongdoing increases daily, and there will never be help for you. So forsake your self-imposed folly and serve God here. Indeed, He has never overlooked service. Son, stand before Him as one accused

---

78. For a similar thought on the rewards of effort, see *The Lament*, lines 753–54.

and exchange your short days for eternal life. Son, this is my advice to you."

[1799] "Alas, beloved lord! My longing for the world is even greater than before. I shall never again rest and shall always be on the move, until God's mercy reveals to me where I come from or who I am."

[1806] "Son, may He who formed you in His image instruct you in this matter, since you reject my advice."

[1809] A ship was ready for him. Onto it was brought everything one could need: food, his gold, his clothing. And as he headed toward the ship, the abbot never left his side until he boarded. Thus Gregorius parted from the shore. No matter how much old age and youth differ, both of them indeed experienced a woeful parting. Neither could take his eyes from the other until they could no longer see each other because of the widening sea.

[1825] Now the stranger raised up heart and hands to heaven and beseeched Our Lord repeatedly to send him to some land where his journey would find an end. He ordered the sailors that all should be subject to the winds, to let the ship go wherever the winds instructed,[79] and not to turn otherwise. A strong wind blew. It remained steady, and in just a few days they were driven by a storm toward his mother's land. It had been sacked and burned, as I told you earlier, so that nothing was left her save for her most important city, which was also besieged by grief. And when he saw the city, he said to the sailors that they should turn the sails in that direction and land.

[1851] When the burghers saw the ship rushing up, they offered armed resistance. Now the stranger held up his hands to them in peace and asked the burghers what they were afraid of. They all were greatly surprised at how far the lord must have come, since he did not know of their situation. One of the nobles among them informed him completely about how they had fared, much as I told you earlier.

[1867] When he had heard about their plight, he said, "Well, I have come at the right moment. This is what I prayed to God for: that He would bring me to a place where I could act, so that I would not idly lie around, wasting the days of my youth while a war is going on. If my lady wishes it, I shall gladly be her warrior."

[1877] Now they saw that his figure and equipment were very praiseworthy. In a willing spirit he was offered lodging there. The lady was happy about the guest. However, she had not seen him yet. Now things went well for him. The man he had as host was very capable, one of the noblest in the city. Whatever he ordered and requested of him happened according to his wishes. He com-

---

79. See *Erec*, lines 5288–90, for a similar reliance on "fate."

pensated that generously with goods. His spending for food and drink was great, and yet so reasonable that he never wanted for anything. Because of that he was a valued guest.

[1895] When he heard the story that the lady was fair, young, and without a husband, and that the feud with her and her troubles arose because she had rebuffed the duke—and that she had vowed never to marry—he would gladly have seen her. The stranger asked how that might happen without being interpreted wrongly. She, on the other hand, was told about his refinement and his skills, so that she too would very much have liked to see him, which seldom happened to a guest, for this was her usual custom: she displayed her frightful sorrow—because joy was repugnant to her—whether the man were poor or wealthy, a stranger or a confidant; she never let him see her unless it might be in church, when she stood in prayer, as she did at all times, even if it robbed her of sleep and food.

[1922] Now the host advised the guest that he ask her steward[80] to bring him where he might see her. The steward arranged this. He took him early one day to mass, and led him by the hand[81] to where he found her at prayer, and let him observe her well. The steward said to the lady, "Lady, give this man your greetings, for he can serve you well." She received her child as a stranger. His heart, too, was blind to that, and he certainly was unaware that this same woman had carried him in her womb.

[1939] Now she scrutinized him carefully, and more than she had ever previously done any man. That was because of his clothes. When she examined them closely, she said to herself it was the silk garment that she with her own hands had put in with her child, and that this stranger's outfit was exactly like it in quality and color. It was in fact the same garment, or they were both made by the same hand.[82] That reminded her of her sorrow. Now the lady pleased him well, as a woman, in whom nothing is lacking, should please a man. The stranger pleased her too, better than a man ever had before. That was caused by the scheming of the one who also tempted Lady Eve when she parted from God's commandment.

[1963] Thus the good lady commended him to the steward's keeping, and thereupon they parted. His heart he left with her there[83] and strove even harder for fame and honor upon seeing her.[84] So good did he feel about this that he considered

---

80. Since at least the mid-tenth century one of the key positions at court. See *Erec*, note 37.
81. A man taking a man by the hand was customary in the Middle Ages. See *Erec*, note 38.
82. For a parallel situation regarding clothing and the revelation of identity, see the *lai* of Marie de France, *Le Frêne* (c. 1170).
83. See lines 651ff., note 35, and the poem "By rights I must ever hold dear the day," lines 9–10.
84. A major characteristic of *Minnesang*, medieval German poetry: the spiritual elevation of the man.

himself rich in joy. Daily one could see just outside the walls of the city examples of knighthood: on horseback and on foot,[85] whatever the man's heart could ask for. That became his occupation, and because of it he soon became well known. Whenever the burghers encountered the enemy, and no matter what casualties they took, rarely did he miss the chance to do something; because of this he was talked about and praised above all.

[1985] He carried on in this fashion until the time that with lance and with sword he could be the knight everyone desired. When he had gained great command of this skill by daily practice with his hands, and he knew in fact that he was the best, that he had courage and strength and all the skill for knighthood, only then did his boldness become great. How little did danger vex him! He was a hailstorm to the enemy, during the attack a head, in retreat a tail.[86]

[1999] Now the duke, a Roman,[87] who had sacked and burned their land, was known for his manliness and was much stronger than any other man. Furthermore, he had known such great success that with a common voice he was named the best knight in all the lands. Now it was his custom often to ride alone before the castle gate to joust.[88] There he acted in a knightly manner. When any good knight in knightly spirit came out to joust against him, he led him away a prisoner[89] in front of the burghers' eyes, in no way fearing them. He had done that so often that no one was left to fight against him; nevertheless he tried it very often.

[2023] Now Gregorius was ashamed that one man had thus struck down their great force without any kind of resistance. He often reflected on the matter: now I often see that when a man, who greatly loves games of chance, has gotten together the sum he wants to risk on the game, and then finds an opponent, he thinks he is very rich.[90] And even if the odds are very much against him, he risks it for a good throw. Now I have the chance to play; if I but have such courage that I risk my very meager wealth against such rich possessions, I shall henceforth always be honored and become powerful if the winnings fall to me. I am a man without fame, but have because of that never lost the courage to think every day how I might gain the bliss of having great renown. Now I do not know how that might come about.

---

85. That is, jousting on horseback and fighting on foot with a sword.
86. That is, the last to flee.
87. With Aquitaine (line 178) as the homeland of Gregorius, a "Roman" duke would be historically more accurate during the Early Middle Ages.
88. This is the area of the lists. See *Erec*, note 40.
89. That is, he did not kill those he defeated and forced to yield, a magnanimous, knightly act. See *Erec*, lines 1010ff.
90. Simply because he has the chance to win.

If I do not risk my life for it, one will always consider me a woman, and I shall be cheated out of honor. Can I now best this duke, hoping for God's favor? Now I know all too well that I have both strength and courage. I definitely do want to risk my poor wealth on this game. One will not bemoan my lot much if I lie dead because of him. But if I should happen to defeat him, then I shall be rich in honor forever and eternally. Let everyone know that. I prefer that my life have a fitting end than that I live in disgrace.

[2067] Gregorius determined that he would not put it off one day more. For God's sake and honor he would either lose his life or free the guiltless woman from the hand of the lord who had taken her land. This he told only to the One who could indeed advance his cause or hinder it: the Supreme Lord. He did not want to tell anyone else.

[2080] The next morning, when it began to dawn, he heard a mass early and prepared himself as one who was going to the jousting field. The host was brought in on the plan; he helped him out of the city. With great seriousness he asked his host that he take heed to let him back in when he returned, whether he won or lost.

[2091] And so the good man with the courageous heart came riding across the field in front of the duke's tent, where he knew the latter was. Now the imperturbable duke caught sight of him and armed himself immediately—no one else there did so. All the men he had there cried out that one should quickly get him his horse. He was afraid that Gregorius might get away.

[2103] When Gregorius saw him coming, a very sensible thought came to him. In a very clever way he began to retreat, going between him and his men before the gate. He waited for him in front, well-prepared, so that help from his army would be no use to him if Gregorius should get the advantage over him. Now the ramparts of the city wall were full of knights and ladies who wanted to observe which of the two would be successful.[91] Now the young man did not hesitate. Each of them eagerly undertook the long approach. Their desire was to get at each other. As soon as they slapped their lances under their arms, the horses carried them together. The lances were short and thick. They were of no use to either of them, because each of them struck that of the other such that it splintered, and yet they both remained in the saddle. How little they forgot the swords at their sides! Behold, they began to fight, two equally strong men, neither of whom had ever displayed a hair's breadth of unseemly cowardice—I tell you this truthfully—and, indeed, skill and good fortune would have to decide the battle between them.

91. This is a common motif in medieval manuscript illustrations.

[2139] When each of them had struck many a blow with his sword, able Gregorius brought the duke to such a pass that he was able to take his horse by the reins and lead him by force right up to the city gate that was still closed. He was not let in quickly. Now the duke's knights noticed this. With all their energy they rushed toward their lord. When the burghers saw that, they threw open the city gate. And so right there was staged the fiercest battle that before or since was ever fought by so many people. Yet Gregorius held fast his captive man here and took him off the field in a knightly fashion.[92] They closed the city gate. In front of it the enemy raised a fierce storm, but soon tired of it.

[2165] In this way blessed Gregorius gained for himself much honor that day, and with his bold hand had freed his mother's land from great suffering. Previously the praise of him had been so great that it did not trouble any valiant man to accord him his honor. But now he had more. In addition, the lady and her lands overcame through his helpful hand all of their distress. Whatever losses she had suffered were compensated completely, as she ordered and requested, and she received the lawful assurance that the duke would henceforth cause her no suffering. He held to that unswervingly.

[2185] When this oppressed land overcame its troubles and was at peace as before, the barons were pained by the daily fear caused them by the uncertainty that the same thing might happen again if any powerful lord wanted to attack them. They said that with a woman as leader the immense lands would be unprotected from unlawful arrogance,[93] "and that if we had a lord, nothing could harm us."

[2199] Now they quickly came up among them with the plan that they would put before the lady. They would earnestly request that she take a husband who would be appropriate as their lord. That would be good for them in all respects. They knew well that she had made her decision in God's name to forswear all men and wanted to continue to forswear them. It was wrong for her to do that. She would be living her life badly if she, by having no heirs, wanted to ruin such a powerful land intentionally. This was their advice: that she would do even better vis-à-vis the world and God—she would thus keep His commandment better—by taking a husband and having heirs. This was in fact the best advice, because lawful marriage is the best life of all that God has given the world.

[2225] When this very legitimate way of thinking was proposed to her, she followed their advice and their requests to take such actions in God, and she prom-

---

92. In capturing the still-mounted duke, Gregorius performs an unusual, extraordinary feat.
93. For similar thoughts about a woman as ruler, see *Iwein*, lines 1783ff.

ised to take a husband. And so they all saw their wishes fulfilled. Now they advised one and all that the choice would be left to her to take whomever she wanted. Since that was how it was going to be, the good woman then often turned over in her mind whom she could possibly take who would better suit her than the very man whom God had sent her to free her and her lands—she took up this idea enthusiastically—that was her son Gregorius. Thereupon he soon became his mother's husband. And so the devil's will came to pass.

[2247] When she told the lords who pleased her—no other man made them as happy—they then acknowledged him as their lord. There was never more bliss than that which the lady and the lord shared with each other, for they were endowed with passion and faithfulness. Behold, that ended in sorrow. He was a good regent, well-known for his generosity. He had what he could wish for: whatever a joyful life may give a man in this world. That took a fast fall.[94]

[2263] To his land and neighboring areas he brought such a secure peace[95] that he deprived of honor and property anyone wrongfully encroaching upon his lands. He had a firm disposition. Whatever bordered his lands would have fallen to him if he had not refused for God's sake to pursue such a course of action, but he wanted to cultivate moderation. For the honor of God he desired nothing more than what was supposed to serve Him. He wanted nothing further.

[2277] The tablet that was found with him he had constantly in his secret keeping, hidden in his fortress, where no one knew of it. On it he read daily about his sinful circumstances—this pained his eyes—about his birth, and about the sinful burden of his mother and his father. He beseeched Our Lord God to grant His favor to both of them, but did not know of the guilt that lay on his own back, that he increased night and day with his mother, by which he caused God grief.

[2295] Now there was at court a servant girl, so clever, one says, who noticed well his lament, as I shall tell you now, for she looked after the chamber in which the tablet lay. For his lamenting he had set aside a certain time of day that he never missed. Now the servant girl noticed that whenever she let him in the chamber, he went in cheerful, but departed from there a man with red eyes.

[2309] Now she took ever increasing pains, and very secretively, how she might find out for certain the cause of his lamenting. One day she crept after him, when, once again, according to his custom, he went to the chamber to lament. The servant girl was already there and hid until she closely observed his lamentable dis-

94. Compare *Poor Heinrich*, lines 29–96.
95. For a similar thought about the duty of a ruler to bring about peace, see *Erec*, lines 10083–84.

tress, and that he read the tablet as was his custom. When he had done that at length, while weeping and praying, he dried his eyes, thinking his secret was well kept from the world. Now the maiden had learned the following: she quickly saw where he laid the tablet.

[2329] When his lamentations had ended, the maiden went straight to her lady and asked, "Lady, what are the troubles that sadden my lord so but do not make you unhappy?"

[2335] The lady replied, "What do you mean? Indeed, just a moment ago he departed from us very happy. What news might he have heard, since he left me, that would make him sad? If such a thing had indeed been said to him, he would not have kept it secret from me. He is not given to weeping. You are certainly mistaken about what you saw."

[2345] "Lady, I'm sorry to say I am not mistaken. Truly, I saw him standing there today as he was seized by sorrow—that touched my heart."

[2349] "See, this has truly always been your way, and you have caused me much sorrow thereby; never have you brought good news. Better had you kept silent than to tell a lie that would bring harm to me."

[2356] "Lady, this is not a lie. I lament nothing so much as that I am telling you the truth."

[2359] "Come now, do you really mean this?"

[2360] "In truth, yes, he is unhappy. I thought you would know even more about it. Indeed, lady, what might it be that he has kept a complete secret from you, since except for this he has withheld nothing from you? Truly, lady, whatever it may be, great sorrow dwells within him. I have noticed it several times and now I have come to the conclusion that he bears a great sadness that he has revealed to no one. As long as he has lived here in these lands, he has never let one day pass without going early in the morning, alone and secretly, into the chamber, cheerful as can be. However joyfully he went in there, he eventually departed very troubled. Yet I had never noticed it so exactly as I did today. When I saw him go in there, I stole inside with him and hid there until I observed him and all his actions. I saw him performing woeful acts of unmanly lamentation, and saw that he had something in front of him with writing on it. When he looked at it and read, he beat his breast and fell to his knees and genuflected very often, repeatedly glancing upwards. I have never, to be sure, seen anyone weep so much. From this I could clearly tell that his heart is full of sorrow. Here I have no doubts concerning such a courageous man. Whatever makes him weep, as I saw him weep today, is not without deeply felt sorrow."

[2404] The lady replied sadly, "Alas for my dear lord! What might be troubling him then? I have no knowledge of any troubles, for he is young, healthy, and powerful in good measure. I always strive to do his will as I should. It is true, I am happy to do so because he knows well how to repay me. If any woman claims to have a dearer man, that certainly doesn't upset me, because such a man was, God knows, never born. Oh woe is me, wretched woman! Indeed, never has good of any kind been my lot, and it never will be, save that it alone comes from his virtuous being. Now what may have happened to him in his youth to cause such weeping as I just heard you talk about? Now give me some advice, since he has kept it a secret from me, how I might find out about his sorrow so that I might act for his good. I fear, if I ask him to tell me, I might lose him.[96] I know well that never will he keep secret from me whatever thing may have caused him sorrow or distress, if it can be told. Now I certainly do not desire to know anything against his will, except that I need to know for this reason: perhaps his difficulties are such that my help would be of use to him and would make them disappear. I have not been accustomed to his keeping any matter secret from me, whether it was a joyful matter or not, and I am very certain that he will not willingly tell me this."

[2448] "Now I do advise you," the servant girl replied, "to find out about it for certain and yet keep his favor. When I saw him standing there bemoaning his troubles, I noted very well the place, as I shall show you. When he had wept much and had beaten his breast, he quickly hid what he had in front of him in a hole in the wall above him. I noted the very place. If you can delay a while, lady—he wants to go hunting with the hounds—I shall then lead you there and show it to you. When you see what is written on it, then you will know. This is certain: something is written on it about the troubles he has hidden in this way."

[2471] When he had ridden out hunting in the woods, as was his custom, she quickly acted upon the advice of the servant girl and went where she found the tablet, and she saw at once that it was the same that she had laid next to her child— as you have earlier been told in the story. And when she had read it and realized that she had once again become engulfed by the deep waves of mortal sin, she thought she was damned for sure. She beat her breast and tore out her lovely hair.[97] She thought that she had indeed been born for hell, and that God had not heeded her heart's penitence she had carried out faithfully for her earlier misdeed—as you were told earlier—since He had once more allowed the devil's scheming to succeed, such that once again she had fallen into the abyss of sin.

96. In *Erec* (line 3012), Enite faces a similar dilemma.
97. For a similar reaction by a woman in distress, see *Erec*, lines 5755ff. and 8112f. See also lines 3313f. above.

[2499] Pitch black night covered up the sun of her joy. I think her heart would have broken from the sorrow, had a slight hope not eased her mind. Any comfort she had was completely tied up with it. She thought: what if this tablet were brought to my husband under other circumstances than I thought? What if God sent my son ashore healthy, and someone, who found him there, sold the tablet and the clothing to my lord? I shall live with that hope until I have found out the truth of the matter. A messenger was called, and she immediately sent for her lord in the forest.

[2519] The messenger hurried at once to where he found his lord. He spoke to him thus, "Duke Gregorius, if you ever want to see my lady alive, then go see her quickly or you will come too late. I left her grievously agitated." Now Gregorius was greatly disturbed and unhappy at this. He said, "Fellow, why are you talking like this? Indeed, I just left her extremely happy and very healthy." "Lord, I too affirm that. Indeed, it happened just now."

[2535] In the forest they tarried no longer. They rode straightaway homewards. On the way—I'll vouch for that—they did not dismount at all, until he arrived where his joy found an end, because, as he looked at his wife's face, he saw a sorry sight. Because of her sorrow the rose color had vanished from her cheeks; her beauty had paled completely. Thus he found her pale as a corpse. As a result, his joy too ebbed completely.

[2549] They suffered great heartfelt grief, because men's eyes have never seen two people more in love. The good sinner said, "Lady, why are you acting this way?"

[2556] She could hardly answer him at all because her sobbing choked off her words.[98] She said haltingly, "Lord, I have good reason to grieve."

[2559] "What troubles you, dear wife?"

[2560] "My lord, there is so much to bear that I shall complain to God that ever I came into this world. Fortune is angry with me. Cursed—by the mouth of our Lord—was the hour when I was born.[99] Misfortune has sworn to get me and is indeed keeping its oath regarding me, for a thousand heartfelt sorrows have befallen me for every moment of joy. Lord, you must tell me where you were born. Indeed, earlier would have been the time for the question I am now asking. I think I am asking too late."

[2575] "Lady, I know well why you are lamenting: someone told you that I am a man of low birth. If I knew who made you suffer because of that, my plotting

---

98. Compare *Erec*, line 5348, and *Poor Heinrich*, line 382.

99. Compare Job 3: 1–3, "After this opened Job his mouth, and cursed his day. And Job spake, and said, Let the day perish wherein I was born."

would not cease until he were dead. He had better hide well. He has reason to. Whoever he is, he lied. I was without a doubt born of ducal lineage. Don't be angry. You should agree to my wish that we end this conversation. I can tell you nothing more."

[2589] The lady answered him thus, "This is not what I'm talking about, my lord. Indeed, God knows I would never look in a friendly manner upon the man who told me things about you that you did not like. He would not get a good response from me. Indeed, I fear your birth is all too equal to mine." She brought forth the tablet and said, "Are you the man—keep nothing secret from me—about whom is written here? If so, then the devil's scheming has brought us to ruin in both body and soul. I am your mother and your wife."

[2605] Now tell me how the good sinner reacted then. He stood under the command of sorrow. His anger he directed toward God,[100] saying, "This is what I always asked for: that God might bring me to the place where I would be so fortunate as to gaze in joy upon my dear mother. Almighty, gracious God, You have granted that quite otherwise than I desired from You. In my thoughts I desired this reunion as something joyful and good. Now I have seen her in such a way that I shall never be happy, because I would have been better off completely without her than coming to know her this intimately."

[2623] I know well that Judas was not more sad when in despondency he hanged himself, than these two here now. David too did not mourn any more when tidings came to him that Saul and Jonathan had been slain, and Absalom, who was his son, the most beautiful man that woman ever bore.

[2635] Whoever might describe fully their grief and woe would have to be wiser than I. It would be, I think, impossible that some person alone could completely describe it to you. Death might almost have taken the measure of this distress. They would have received it with full hospitality, if it had come. They were united, both body and soul, in the same sorrow. Where did anyone ever hear of any kind of sorrow that was completely without some kind of consolation? Their souls were horrified at the thought of hell's fires. Their bodies were sorely troubled at the thought of their parting. God's power has created an antagonistic union that nevertheless stays together as soul and body. What pleases the body is not at all good for the soul. But whatever causes the soul to thrive must be the body's distress. Now they suffered distress on both sides; that was a twofold death.[101]

---

100. In *Erec* (line 5774), Enite also directs her anger against God.
101. Referring to the body and soul, not the two of them.

[2665] The lady spoke from great misery when she saw such misery up close. "Oh woe is me, a woman cursed! Indeed, if some afflict the body so that the soul might be happy, they are successful in that. But many a person turns away from the soul to the body and toward this world. Now I cannot and should not allow my body any good thing that might happen to it. If my soul is now lost, then God's burning wrath has fallen fully on me, as on all who are damned. I am surprised, after the wrong that my body has committed against me, that the earth deigns to bear me. My son and lord, can you tell me—for you have read much in books— if then, as I must certainly believe, there is no help against my residing in hell, could there be some kind of penance for such a wrong, some penance I can do to bring it about that things are somewhat gentler for me than they are for many who are delivered up to hell?"

[2695] "Mother," said Gregorius, "never again speak in this manner. It is against God's commandment. Do not despair of God. You shall be saved for sure. Indeed, I have read the consoling words that God accepts true sorrow as penance for every evil deed. Your soul is never that ill; if your eyes ever become wet from heartfelt sorrow, you will recover, believe that. Stay in your lands. You should be sparing in food and clothing for your body, and flee from comfort and joy. You should not keep these two things for the purpose of gaining any worldly honor. Rather, make amends to God all the more with your possessions. Indeed, it harms the spirit more when the person who has the choice of a good life lives not in this manner, than when a man does without things he never had a chance to have anyway.

[2721] "You are a guilty woman. Let your body atone for that with daily toil, so that it is refused what it desires most. Keep it thus, as long as it is allotted to you, in the bonds of sorrow. Share the income from your land with the poor; thus God will have mercy on you. Set up wealthy monasteries on your property,[102] as your counselors advise. Ease thus His wrath that we have so fully deserved. I shall also do penance to Him. Lady, my dear mother, these shall be the last words I ever address to you. We shall succeed in having God bring us together as equals in His kingdom. I shall never see you again. We should have parted earlier. Today I renounce these lands, my possessions, and worldly ways." He set aside his costly apparel and parted from the lands in shabby clothing.

[2751] All favors were denied the wealthy beggar, save that he bore all his troubles with a willing spirit. He desired deep down that gracious God would send him

---

102. A traditional means of expressing repentance. Compare *Poor Heinrich*, line 256.

into a wilderness[103] where he might do penance till his death. Cheerfully did he endure this distress. He shunned entirely people and roads and open fields. The wretched man directed his way unerringly toward the wilderness. He waded through water next to a footbridge. With tender, shoeless feet he trod through forests and bogs, tending his prayers and not eating until the third day.

[2771] Now a path—it was narrow—led down along a lake. The man, weary of life, took it and followed it until he caught sight of a little hut. The wretched man made his way there to rest. A fisherman dwelled there who thought that nowhere else would fishing be more to his advantage. The penitent asked him in God's name for lodging. He suffered more scorn from him than had been his wont. When the fisherman saw his fair body, he shook his head and said, "Indeed, you great charlatan! If it happened now that I were to commit the folly of putting you up, you glutton, then without batting an eye you, you fat peasant, would, while my wife and I were sleeping tonight, take both of our lives just to get our property. Alas, how badly the world acts: in that people tolerate such waste in their midst and many a worthless man who pillages people, and from whom God never gained any honor! What your arms need is a broad, cleared field to labor on. You would be better off with a hoe and a herdsman's staff than with your wandering. Bread that is much needed by others is wasted by you, you glutton—May the devil be the death of you!—Strong as you are, aren't you ashamed to be begging? Leave this hut at once."

[2812] Now it had grown very late. The sinner received this chiding unconcerned and with a cheerful spirit. Thus the good man answered the fisherman, "Sir, you have spoken the truth. Whoever provides securely for his own existence— that makes sense." He wished him good night and then parted, smiling. The helpless[104] man listened gladly to the scorn and praised God for it and for this undeserved treatment. He would willingly have undergone any kind of insult and injury directed at his person. If the lowly born man had rained down wrathful blows upon his back, he would gladly have endured it, if the weight of his sins might become even a little less.

[2835] The wife of the evil fisherman took pity on him. She thought he was not a charlatan. The chiding that her husband directed against him because of his modest requests filled her eyes with tears. She said, "He's a good man; that's no

103. From the time of the earliest Christian eremites, the place of isolation was often called "wilderness," even if it meant a woods or mountain top and not what is today often thought of as wilderness. See lines 3224–30.

104. In MHG *wîselôs*: without a guide, that is, lost and thus helpless. Compare line 2879.

lie. Truly, I can tell by looking at him. May God not make you pay for it. You have scolded him so severely that it affects your salvation. You know well that your hut is far removed from people. When our Lord, to warn you about your salvation, sends you His messenger, you should receive him better and consider the following very carefully: never has a needy man come to you since we began living here, save for this poor man, and he has not gained much from coming here. Whoever must feed himself every day from his catch as you have done, but must be always uncertain about that catch, should keep God before his eyes. Do this. That's my advice. May God help you and let me call him back. His journey is bitter. Indeed, if he does not leave soon, he'll have to spend the night in the woods. If the wolves don't eat him—which can happen very easily—then he must lie there, going hungry, forgoing all comfort. Let me have my way; let me help him here after all." With kindness she thus assuaged the fisherman's mood so that he allowed her to run immediately after the helpless man and call him back.

[2881] When she had gotten him back, the fisherman's dinner was then readied. His wife wanted to make the noble beggar forget the great abuse that the fisherman had heaped upon him without cause, and she put before him her choicest food. The wise man refused it, however much she entreated him. A crust of oat bread[105] was given him and a drink from a spring. He told the woman that his sinful body was hardly worthy of the food.

[2898] When the fisherman saw him eating the meager food, he chided him once again, saying, "Alas that I should see this! Indeed, I see through charlatans and all their devious ways. You have not lived from such meager food up to now. Your cheeks show they have borne the distress of neither thirst nor hunger. They are so chubby and so red. No one has ever seen a more splendid body. You have not gotten that just from bread and spring water. You have been fattened quite nicely. Your thighs are sleek, your feet well-arched, your toes close together and long, your nails clean and shiny. The feet of a pilgrim should be broad and cracked on the bottom. Now I observe on your thighs no evidence of a fall or blow. They have not been bare for long. How well they have been spared frost or wind touching them at all. Smooth and not disheveled is your hair, and your figure is like that of a fattened glutton. Your arms and your hands are without a blemish; they are so smooth and so white. You have given them a different kind of care in your secret chamber than you do here. I have no fear that tomorrow you will make up to your-

---

105. The daily bread of most people in the Middle Ages was a dark, coarse bread made from oats or barley. Normally only the rich had white wheat bread.

self for the want you suffer here. You can find better lodging where you will find everything for sale, and where you, God knows, can get over all your troubles. There your mouth would find repugnant this dry oat bread and this spring water."

[2945] The good man received these words with a smile and wanted to find before God some reward by suffering such great scorn from such a lowly knave. He gave him no answer until the fisherman asked him the story of his life. Gregorius replied, "Sir, I am a man who cannot calculate his sinful guilt, and who for God's grace seeks a place in this wilderness where I can constantly, till death, do severe penance by chastising my body. Today is the third day since I gave up having anything to do with the world and headed unerringly toward the wilderness. I did not expect here a building or people. Since my way today has brought me to you, I therefore seek favor and advice. If you know of a place anywhere hereabouts that would be suitable for me, a desolate crag or cave, tell me about it. You do well by that."

[2975] The fisherman answered him thus, "Since you desire that, friend, be happy. For sure, I shall bring you to your home. I know of a crag near us here, rising out a bit over the lake. There you will surely have misery enough. As soon as we manage to bring you there, then you may well bemoan your troubles through oppressive days. It will be wilderness enough for you. If ever you pictured your spirit prepared for repentance, then I shall be of great help. I have for some time kept some leg irons. I shall give them to you for support, so that you may make your life on that very crag secure. Lock them onto your foot. If you then regret this change in your life, you nevertheless, against your will, must stay on it. The crag is formed in such a way that even someone with unencumbered feet would have trouble getting off. If you are serious about it, go to sleep then and be up early. Bring your leg irons with you and sit next to me in my boat when I head out before daybreak to fish. For your sake I shall head out and help you onto the crag and bind your legs with the irons, so that you will grow old out there and without a doubt will never again bother me in this earthly kingdom. I truly have no fear of that." Although the fisher had said this in derision, the proposals were as Gregorius would wish, if wish he should.

[3019] Now the spiteful man was so pitiless that he begrudged him any comfort in his house, such as lodging. His wife could not, with all her ingenuity, persuade him to let the man stay inside. He was driven like a dog out into the yard before the entrance. He went joyfully.

[3031] That night he went to sleep, contrary to his usual practice, in such a wretched hut that it could not have been more wretched. It was dilapidated, without a roof. The ruler was provided the kind of comfort that his kitchen boy would find very repugnant. He found poor furnishings inside: neither straw nor bedding. The good woman brought in for him some bulrushes to place beneath him. He put aside his leg irons and next to it his tablet, so that he could find them in the morning.

[3047] How little did he lie there during the night! He tended his prayers until exhaustion overcame him. By the time he had fallen asleep, it was close to day-break. The fisherman was setting out for the catch. He was ready early, as was his custom. Now he called out to his guest who was sleeping so soundly—as happens from great exhaustion—that he did not hear him shouting. Then the fisherman called out again, saying, "I knew well that this charlatan's words weren't serious. I'll never call you again." Then he hurried to the lake.

[3065] When the good woman saw this, she woke him up and said, "If you want to go, good man, see, you are late. My husband is heading down to the lake." He tarried no longer. He feared greatly that he might be left behind. On the other hand, he was very happy that the fisherman was to lead him where he had prom-ised. Both joy and sorrow made him hurry so much that he forgot the tablet he carried at all times at his side. He seized the leg irons and hurried after the man.

[3085] He called out that he should wait for him, for God's sake. Thus the fish-erman, treating him badly, led him to the top of the desolate crag. Here he locked up his legs securely in the irons and said, "Here you must grow old. If the devil with his tricks doesn't lead you away from here, you'll never escape." He threw the key into the lake and said, "I know this for certain: if ever I find this key from out of the depths of the surging waters, then you are without sin and a holy man for sure." He left him there and then departed.

[3101] Wretched Gregorius thus remained on the desolate crag bereft of all comforts. He had no other abode; heaven alone was his roof. He had no other shield against frost or snow, against wind or rain, than God's blessing. Clothing he lacked, save for a hair shirt. His legs and arms were bare. He could not, as I tell you now in truth, have lived fourteen days, God knows, from the food that he had, had he not been given the consoling Spirit of Christ, which sustained his life and saved him from starvation. I shall tell you what kind of food he had. Water dripped slowly from the crag. Beneath it he dug a hole; that filled up with drink. The amount of water was so small that, according to my sources, the hole hardly filled up between night and day. The forsaken man drank that. Thus he lived for sev-enteen years. Many think this is not true, but I say they are wrong, because it is not impossible for God to do whatever He wishes. No miracle is too great for Him.

[3137] When Gregorius, bereft of comforts, had spent seventeen years on the desolate crag, and God had forgotten his enormous guilt, to the point of granting His favor, the pope in Rome died, as I read. As soon as he had died, every Roman tried to gain that very power for his kith and kin because of the magnificent benefice. Their dispute ranged so widely that they could not decide, out of both envy and ambition, on whom they should bestow the Holy See.

[3155] Now they all advised that they should leave the choice to our Lord God, that His mercy and His command would reveal who would be a good ruler over them. They provided for devotions to God that were accompanied by alms and prayers. God, who always responds to questions asked in good faith, acted with benevolence. One night He revealed His will to two wise Romans whose loyalty and truthfulness were so completely in evidence that their words were like an oath.

[3171] When each—in a different place—was lying in bed and saying his prayers, the voice of God told them that early the next day they should call together the Romans and announce to them what God's will was concerning their ruler: in Aquitaine a man had been living alone on a desolate crag a full seventeen years—no one in Rome knew him—in him the Holy See would be well served; his name was Gregorius. That He announced it to both of them meant that one man's voice cannot reveal what is supposed to have the force of great power.[106]

[3191] Now until they came together and heard it from each other, neither of them knew, regarding this matter, that the story had been revealed to both of them during the night. And when they had related what they had heard, the one telling his story and the other agreeing, the Romans believed this tale willingly. To God they showed their great joy. The elderly men were then both sent as legates to the land of Aquitaine to seek out the good man and bring him back.

[3209] One thing troubled them: the crag on which he lived had not been named. Full of uncertainty they traveled to the land. They inquired a great deal, wherever their way took them, but no one could tell them anything. With all their heart they lamented about that to the One who takes care of those who seek mercy from Him. Now God put this thought in their minds: if they were ever going to find him they should be looking in the wilderness. And so they hurried to where they saw mountains and a desolate area near the lake. They were greatly grieved because they doubted they could ever know where to find him.

[3229] In this wilderness their way led from fields into woods. They followed

---

106. See Matthew 18:16: "But if he will not hear thee, then take with thee one or two more, that . . . every word may be established."

no path, wandering about as their feelings advised them until the third day. Then they took a path free of hoofprints. They were very glad they had. The grassy, untrampled way carried them far, to a peninsula, where by the lake lived the fisherman who, as I told you earlier, had in such an unmannerly way received the blessed one in his need, and who was so malicious toward him that in his hate he put him on the barren, desolate crag—where he still was—and locked his legs in irons. When the two old men saw the hut, they affirmed it as their good fortune that they could rest up for the night from their exhaustion.

[3255] They had brought with them the food they needed—that was smart—both wine and bread, and also whatever else was necessary to bring along. Therefore the fisherman received the well-provisioned guests joyfully, without a grumble. He saw well and knew he might make use of them. He took great pains to provide them with ample comfort for he saw they were well-provisioned. He did that more because of their possessions than through any generous spirit on his part. He received them better than the guest who was lacking possessions: Gregorius, the pure man. The fisherman had thought he would gain nothing from him.

[3275] When they had been made very comfortable, the fisherman spoke to his guests, "I am very fortunate indeed, since I see here such noble men. Today I caught a very fine fish." It was laid on the table before the gentlemen. Now he had not spoken falsely, because it was long and big. He hoped to profit from that in copper pennies. They bargained briefly. They immediately ordered him to be paid for it.[107] Now they asked the host to gut it himself. As he was cleaning it, they all watched. The greedy man found in its stomach the key that you heard about earlier when in ill will he locked up Gregorius seventeen years ago and threw the key into the lake, saying that when he found it in the surging waters Gregorius would be without sin. When he found it in the fish, he immediately knew that he had acted out of rage, and quickly seized his hair with both hands. Truly I would have helped him, if I had been there with him, however enraged I am at him otherwise.

[3313] When he had torn at his hair for a while and had beat his breast, the gentlemen asked him what might be troubling him, since they saw him lamenting so bitterly. He told them in detail about his guest Gregorius, so that they would be privy to the whole story. I think it would be useless if I set forth a second time, word for word, the earlier part of the story; one story would turn into two.[108] The mes-

---

107. The two men apparently have servants with them.
108. The French version does indeed repeat the story, so this may be some literary criticism from Hartmann.

sengers were very glad because they learned from the story that he was the very one whom God Himself had recommended to them and had designated as their pope.

[3331] When he had openly made his confession before both of them, he fell at their feet, praying that they might give him some advice regarding his evil deed. When they saw the wretched man ruing his actions greatly, with devout sincerity, they took pity on him and promised him he might get off from his misdeed much better if in the morning he would direct them to the crag.

[3346] Now the graybeards saw his eyes overflow and hot tears fall down his hoary beard. He said, "What use to us is the trip? Of course I shall direct you there, but we are making the trip in vain. I know well he has been dead a long time. I left him with needs aplenty on the desolate crag, and even had he had only one of them, no living thing could have survived. You need have no hope that we'll find him alive, for if he had not been killed by cold winds or by freezing weather, hunger would have done him in." Now they recognized that the power of God was so great and manifold, that if He deigned to care for him, His blessing would preserve him very well from all danger. The fisherman was solemnly exhorted to make the short journey. He pledged to undertake it.

[3371] Very early the next morning they headed toward the crag. With difficulty they maneuvered the rudder and, coming up to the crag, observed where Gregorius was, the living martyr, a very handsome man on whom was hardly visible anywhere any trace from hunger or freezing weather, or any kind of want; with graceful jewelry on his body and his clothes so that no one could be said to have any better precious stones, or silk and gold, made well to order; who went with a cheerful air, with sparkling eyes, and received dear friends; with gold-colored hair, so that he was a joy for you to behold; with well-trimmed beard, well-groomed in every way as though he were going dancing; with such tight leggings that were the best in the world. In no way did they find this there. Maybe he was somewhere else.[109]

[3403] I shall tell you what they found. When they began to search on the desolate crag, the good and pure one soon noticed them. Now he wanted to run away from them because his shame was great; he was bare and naked. He could not run fast because he had shackles on each leg. He fell down on the crag; thus he wanted to hide himself. When he saw them coming toward him, he broke off a plant in shame.[110] Thus they found God's friend, a needy man on earth, greatly esteemed by God, repugnant to people, pleasing to heaven.

---

109. Hartmann also purposely misleads his audience in *Erec* (lines 366ff.).
110. Compare Genesis 2:25 and 3:7.

[3423] The wretched man was totally overgrown with hair, matted to his skin, on his head, and in his beard. Once it had been fashionably curled, now soot-colored from his troubles. Once his cheeks had been touched with red, mixed with white,[111] and filled out—color and plumpness vying with each other—now black and sunken, his face bleached. Once his eyes had been, alas, truly sparkling and clear, his mouth formed for joy, now pale and cold, his eyes deep-set, dull, and red, as privation had rendered them, with overhanging brows, coarse and long. His flesh, once filled out on all his limbs, was now wasted away down to the bone. He was so thin everywhere on his legs and arms that God might have felt pity.

[3449] Since he had had on leg irons both day and night, they had very severely eaten away the flesh above his feet down to the bone, so that the leg irons were ever covered with blood from the fresh wounds. That was a painful hardship for him even without the other troubles he suffered. I shall compare him thus: one could count through his skin all his bones, large and small, just as easily as when one spreads a bedsheet over thorns. However much the body of God's friend had changed from his difficulties, the Holy Spirit had been his support, so completely that his mind had not diminished at all. Throughout he had retained his previous knowledge of speaking and reading. When those who had come looking for him saw him in his pitiful condition, as I just told you now, they took pity on him, so much so that streams from their eyes, like rain, poured over their clothes. They implored him in the name of God and His commandment that he let them know if his name were Gregorius.

[3487] Since he was beseeched so solemnly, he let them know that he was Gregorius. Now they told him the story and why they had set out—as you heard earlier—when it was disclosed by God to both of them in the night that He had named him, chosen him Himself, acknowledged him, and had put him here on earth to rule in His stead.

[3499] When he heard the message, how intimately did it touch his heart! Then the man worthy of God bowed his head to the ground. With abundant tears he spoke, not looking at them, "If you are Christians, then honor God today and leave in all haste, since I am not worthy of the honor—accorded by heavenly grace—of looking with such sinful eyes at someone who is good. It is not hidden from God that my flesh is so impure that by rights I ought to remain alone until my death. I am paying on earth that my soul might overcome eternal suffering.

---

111. That is, his cheeks were ruddy and his complexion pale (which is very desirable), but we have translated literally as red and white to show the importance in medieval literature of contrasting colors.

[3519] "If I were among good men today, they would have to pay for my evil deeds. As great as my guilt is, trees and grass and whatever was green around me would wither from the fury of my impure voice and from the repugnance of my bare feet. That the greeting of sweet weather, on which the world thrives, and the familiar mildness of rain and wind are shared by me as though I were pure; that the shining of the bright sun deigns to be so humble by shining fully on me as on any person—my flesh would not be worthy of that favor. That you desire me as your master was thought up to mock me. Alas, I have earned from Our Lord God much more His angry hate than a bestowal of favor and honor that a pope should have. One can well do without me in Rome. You would not do well under me.

[3550] "Just take a look at my body! It is so unpleasing, repugnant to any honors. If I once was familiar with a lord's life, it is now forgotten. I am not used to humankind; by rights I have nothing to do with it. You, sirs, observe for yourself: a sound mind, body, and way of life that by rights belong to one who is supposed to wield great power, have been completely deformed in me. I am not well suited to be pope. Blessed men that you are, now let what has happened here today—the fact that you have seen me—be to my salvation, and deign to have pity on me, most wretched of men, and remember me in your prayers to God.

[3570] "We have His commandment: whoever prays for the sinner redeems himself as well.[112] Now it is time for us to part company. What use is all this to both of you? You are encouraging the devil's way of thinking in me. For me this excitement is far too good. I have been living here, it's true, for seventeen years without seeing a person. I fear that for the joy and comfort I have had talking with you here I must do penance before Him who never leaves any wrong unexpiated."

[3585] With this he stood up and was about to go. But the two men implored him so earnestly in the name of God, and His fearful commandment to seek him out, that he sat down quietly and continued listening to their words. With pledges and oaths they now both offered him such assurances regarding the message they brought him that he believed them more. He said, "I was a vat full of sinful shame when I was placed on this crag with these shackles that you see here around my legs. [I wear them here in grief. Then the key was hidden in such a way that I am thus securely locked up; it was thrown into the lake. The one who threw it said that only when he found it would I be without sin.][113] Now no one's sin is so great that His mercy, whose might burst open hell, cannot be greater. If Our Lord God,

---

112. For similar thoughts on the value of praying for others, see *Poor Heinrich*, lines 19–28.
113. Lines 3601–9 appear in only one manuscript.

in His kindness, has forgiven my many wrongs, and if I have become pure, He must give the three of us[114] a true sign, or else my life must end on this crag. He must send me the key with which I was thus locked up, or I shall never leave here."

[3624] Now the fisherman, with abundant tears, fell to his knees before him. He said, "My dear lord, I am that sinful man who has acted so wrongly in that matter. I, forlorn wretch, received you in anger. This was the hospitality I offered you: I gave you a chiding instead of bread; I eagerly poured you many a reproach. Thus did I lodge you one night with contempt and loud berating. I have grown old without repenting my sins. This remains for my soul: unless I reap the benefits of this trip taken in good faith, then I must do penance for what I have done. Afterward I did fulfill your request, except that I did it in derision. I brought you to this crag. Then I locked up your legs and threw the key into the lake, never giving you another thought, until my sinful hand found the key yesterday in a fish. These gentlemen clearly saw that, as I shall bear witness along with them."

[3653] He unlocked the leg irons. Then the aged men shared their priestly robes with him. And when they had been placed around him, they led this sinless man off the desolate crag. Now his poor body had little strength. Therefore they stayed the night with the fisherman. His anguish was great indeed. The fisherman sought penance and help for the great wrong he had earlier committed against him when he had received him so contemptuously. Now his great sincerity and his sorrow and the torrent from his eyes washed away the stain of his sin so that his soul was healed.

[3674] At the time Gregorius was still under sin's sway, as you were told earlier, and when he left his rulership, and the fisherman received him in his house in such a degrading manner and provided him at night with discomfort, he left the next day and forgot the tablet. All the while he sat on the crag, nothing troubled him more. Now he remembered it again and beseeched the fisherman that he would be acting as God would wish, if he had found it, to let him have it back so that the burden of his sin[115] would be even less.

[3694] Then the fisherman said, "Unfortunately, I never saw it. Now tell me, where did you leave it here, or how did you forget it?"

[3698] "I left it," Gregorius answered, "in the hut where I slept. When I was called in the morning, I feared greatly that I was too late. I started from my sleep and hurried after you, and was unfortunately in such a hurry that I forgot the tablet."

114. That is, the two legates and Gregorius.
115. "His sin" has been interpreted variously as the fisherman's or Gregorius's.

[3706] The fisherman replied, "How would it help us if we looked where it was? It rotted away a long time ago. Alas, my dear lord! For sure, that very hut did not remain standing twelve weeks after your stay before it crumbled. I burned it all, both roof[116] and walls. I was so ill-disposed toward you then that if the hut had been any good against wind or rain, you never would have lain down in there. Where the hut stood earlier, there now grows worthless grass, nettles, and weeds."

[3722] Then God's friend sighed and asked God to help him, since he would never leave this place if he did not find it. They went immediately with pitchforks and rakes and began to break up the weeds and the dung. Now the One who is merciful revealed in the person of good Gregorius a very great sign, because he found his tablet as new as it had come from the hand of the one who crafted it. Those who saw that felt joy and fear. Weeping, they swore that this was a holy man. And that was no lie.

[3741] When they started out the next day on their trip to Rome, they often saw on the way that God's blessing was manifest in this pure man, night and day. No danger at all did they encounter on their journey. Their food supply flourished all the way to Rome; their barrels were always full, however much they took out, until they arrived.

[3753] I shall cite you one example of God's favor: three days before his arrival there was a great din in Rome. Everywhere the bells began to ring by themselves and announced to the people that their sovereign was about to arrive. Everyone recognized thereby his sanctity. Immediately they rode in the direction of Aquitaine to meet him, a three-day trip.[117] Across the land came the godly procession: clad in wool and barefoot, they carried their relic. Gregorius heard their greetings of goodwill as he was received with praise and song. Countless sick people lay in the street. They came there to be consoled by him that they might be freed from their distress. His blessing healed a great many on the way. Wherever they led him, whomever he touched, whether by his good will or his hand, his word or his robe, was immediately cured of his trouble. Glorious Rome received her sovereign with a smile. That did the city much good, for never had a pope ruled in the city who was a better healer of the soul's wounds.

[3793] He knew well how to live rightly because moderation had been given him by the teachings of the Holy Spirit. He ruled justly. It is right that one pre-

---

116. But compare line 3035, where it is stated that the hut had no roof.

117. A customary show of respect. The greater the distance, the greater the homage. See *Erec*, lines 1508–11, and *Poor Heinrich*, line 1391.

serves humility in power—the poor are healed thereby—and one should arouse
fear through bold actions and subjugate rightfully those who are against justice.
But if a child of the devil fails to heed the priestly stole, then force should be used.
The two ways of ruling are good for this. They teach and strike down the arrogant,
but one should alleviate the sinner's penance through gentle penitence, so that his
sorrow is sweetened. True justice is therefore difficult. If one puts too heavy a bur-
den of penance on the sinner, his body cannot well endure that. If he wants to
seek mercy, and one suddenly gives him a heavy penance, this can easily make
him so lose his courage that he again renounces God and becomes the devil's ser-
vant. Mercy therefore takes precedence over justice. Thus Gregorius knew how to
practice moderation in the spiritual life, so that the sinner was healed and the good
man was constant. From his powerful teaching, God's honor thus grew very pow-
erfully throughout the Roman realm.

[3831] His mother, his aunt, and his wife—these three were one—when she
heard in Aquitaine about the pope that he was such a great consolation to sinners,
she sought help from him concerning her grievous sin so that she might be freed
of her burden of sin through him. And when she saw him and confessed before
him, the good woman knew nothing at all about the pope's person and that he was
her son. Since they had parted she had also taken upon herself sorrow and a life
of penance that caused her body's vigor and color to vanish completely, such that
he did not recognize her until she said her name and that of Aquitaine.

[3856] In confessing to him, she told him nothing other than the same story
that was known to him before. Then he recognized immediately that she was his
mother. The good and trustworthy man rejoiced to God that she had subjected
herself so extensively to His law, because he saw well that she cultivated sorrow
and true penance. With a kindly greeting he received his mother and was heartily
happy that he had the good fortune of seeing her before her end, and could keep
her there in her aged years and give her spiritual help for her soul and for her life.

[3877] At that time it was still unknown to her that she had ever seen him.
Skillfully he then said to her, "Lady, tell me for God's sake whether you have in
the meantime heard where your son went, and whether he is alive or dead."

[3884] She sighed, and she had reason to. She replied, "Lord, I have not. I do
know that he placed upon himself great distress because of his sorrow, and unless
I hear the truth to the contrary, I do not think he is still alive."

[3890] He replied, "If it could ever happen by the gift of God that you might
see him, would you trust yourself to recognize him?"

[3895] She replied, "If my senses did not betray me, I would indeed recognize him if only I could see him."

[3897] He said, "Now tell me what I ask you. Would you be pleased or not if you had the opportunity to see him?"

[3901] She answered, "You may note this well. I have indeed forsworn the body and possessions, joy and feelings, and have lived like a poor woman. No other joy could happen to me in this life save this: that I might see him."

[3909] He said, "Be of good cheer, because I am about to tell you something joyful. It was not long ago that I saw him and that he swore to me before God that he had no friend dearer than you so constant and true."

[3916] "Please, my lord," the woman said, "is he still alive?"

"Yes, he is."

"Well, how?"

"He is well and is here."

"May I see him, my lord?"

"Yes, indeed. He is not far from here."

"My lord, so let me see him."

[3922] "My lady, that can easily be done. Since you want to see him, there is no need for you to delay. Dearest mother, look at me. I am your son and your husband. However great and however heavy the burden of my sins was, God has now forgiven that, and I have now taken possession of this powerful office from God. It came from His command that I was chosen to come here. And so I have offered up to Him both body and soul."

[3936] The forsaken woman was compensated for the sorrow she had known. God had miraculously sent her there for the joy of them both. Thus they were together until death, our common lot. Gregorius, departing from her lands, had bid and urged her to do penance, with a patient spirit, in body and with what she possessed. All this she had done so that nothing of this troubled her. Whatever years they spent thereafter together in Rome were thus so directed to God that now they are forever two chosen children of God. Gregorius also brought about that his father[118] occupied with him the see,[119] whose joy never subsides. Happy is he who has occupied it.

[3959] Regarding these good tales of these sinners—how they acquired God's grace after great guilt—no sinful man should take them as an example in an evil

118. Some see this father as his biological father, others as his "spiritual father" (line 1139), the abbot who helped raise him.

119. Since the father cannot literally occupy the Holy See with Gregorius, heaven may be implied. "See" in this sense appears elsewhere in Middle High German literature.

way such that he, if he is estranged from God, might think thus: be daring and happy. Why should you be damned? Since these two were saved after their great crime, then there is good help for you. And if things are such that I might be healed, then I shall be healed. Whomever the devil drives to the point that he sins trusting in this, the devil has overcome him and bound him in his power. And even if his sin is slight, the same thought accompanies crimes a thousandfold, and there is no further help for him. From this tale the sinful man should take a blessed example—however much he has sinned—that he will get good help when he has true sorrow and does the right penance.

[3989] Hartmann, who has put his efforts into this song[120] out of love for God and you, hopes to gain from it that you bestow on him a reward from all those who hear or read it: that they pray that he might attain blessedness and might yet see you in heaven. Let all of you alike send this good sinner as a messenger of our troubles, so that we take from this grievous exile an ending just as healing as the one they took! To this end may God direct us. Amen.

---

120. Medieval epics and tales were usually recited or sung. Compare the conclusions of *Poor Heinrich, Erec,* and *Iwein.*

POOR HEINRICH

Introduction

"Greater love has no man than this, that a man lay down his life for his friends" (John 15:13). Nothing could seem more heroic or more in line with Christian ideals than this. Yet if we apply these words of Jesus spoken to his disciples at the Last Supper to *Poor Heinrich*, we find that being a Christian martyr may not be so simple and straightforward. Briefly, the situation of the protagonist is this: though he is the embodiment of knightly virtues, Heinrich is stricken with leprosy. He is told that his only chance for a cure would be to obtain the heart's blood of a virgin. Dejected by this news he takes refuge in the household of one of his farmers. A young daughter in the family boldly proclaims that she is willing to give her life so that Heinrich may be cured. The strong-willed girl's arguments for her proposed sacrifice, her parents' predictable shock at the thought, and the evolution in Heinrich's attitude offer the reader a variety of perspectives from which to ponder the matter. Though the material could be the stuff of tragedy, the ensuing actions of Heinrich and the girl lead to a fairy-tale conclusion, and the narrator's occasional comments on the characters and their actions often complicate rather than clarify the reader's wish to understand the significance of the tale as it progresses toward a happy resolution.

Poor Heinrich has much in common with Hartmann's other narratives. The structure, though abbreviated, is similar. Instead of watching the hero struggle to attain a goal that proves illusory and then struggle again to attain his true goal, we here find the hero already in possession of his illusory goal when the catastrophe in the form of leprosy occurs. As in the other narratives, the essential turning point here is the hero's moment of insight rather than a physical event. Here also, the hero rides forth twice to seek his fortune.

Commentators usually consider *Poor Heinrich* to have been composed after *Erec* and *Gregorius* and before *Iwein*, though their reasons for doing so have often had more to do with their conjectures about the evolution of Hartmann's thought than with solid evidence. Juxtaposing it to its non-Arthurian counterpart *Gregorius*, we can note a pervasive lightheartedness in the narrative despite the temporarily wretched fate of its hero. In contrast, *Gregorius* is somber, and no real reconciliation with the world is possible. One is left with the impression that Gregorius, deeply scarred by his experiences, is forever incapable of laughter. Despite its religious theme, in *Poor Heinrich* we leave the dreary landscape inhabited by the penitential saint of legend and enter the land of fairy tales, where dire events have no lasting effects and living happily ever after is never in serious doubt. In at least one respect, however, Hartmann has seen fit to raise his story above the level of fairy tale, where cause-effect relationships are magical, where a kiss awakens the fair maiden or turns a frog back into a prince. In Hartmann's story it is not simply the blood from the heart of a virgin that Heinrich must find. The blood must flow from the heart of a virgin who sacrifices herself knowingly and willingly. In other words, it must be a fully human act.

Finally, it should be mentioned that the poet's discussion of the social status of the peasant family has left many commentators puzzled. The father is called both *vrîer bûman* and *meier*. The first term, "free peasant," indicates that, though a member of the peasant class, he is not an unfree serf. Therefore, though obviously holding the farm in dependence on Heinrich, he possesses the rights of a freeman or a freeborn person. *Meier*, which comes from the Latin *major* (a greater man), also indicates a farmer but frequently refers to someone of greater stature, such as the steward of an estate. This peasant farmer probably should be thought of in this way because when there is talk of the family's possibly losing much through Heinrich's death, they fear losing not just *lant* but *liute* (people; i.e., workers) as well. In any case, the poet takes several opportunities to point out this family's high standing. At least two possible reasons for his doing so have been adduced. First, the poet might be defending a questionable marriage in the past which casts its shadow on the von Aue family he serves, for the climax of this theme occurs when Heinrich, in vowing to marry the girl or to marry no one, proclaims her to be as free as he is. Second, Hartmann might be indicating his opposition to the late-twelfth-century trend toward greater and stricter stratification, as the distinctions between free and unfree, and between higher and lower nobility, became of greater social and legal significance.

Text

There was once a knight so well educated that he was able to read whatever he found written in books.[1] Hartmann was his name and he served the House of Aue.[2] He undertook a careful search among many kinds of books, trying to find something with which he could make oppressive hours more pleasant, the kinds of things that would be fitting to God's honor and through which he could ingratiate himself to people.

[16] He now begins to relate to you a story he found in a written source. He has mentioned his name so that the efforts he has invested in it may not go unrewarded, and so that whoever might hear it recited or might read it after his death might pray to God for the salvation of his soul.[3] One says that whoever prays to lessen the guilt of another is his own intercessor and thereby redeems himself.

[29] He read this same tale—how there was a lord situated in Swabia[4] in whom no quality had been forgotten that a knight in his prime should have to win full esteem. In all the lands one spoke of no one so highly. He had readily at hand noble birth and abundant means. He possessed a wide range of abilities as well. But no matter how ample his possessions or how flawless his ancestry—easily comparable to princes—he was still not nearly so endowed in birth and possessions as he was in reputation and noble attitude. His name was well known. It was Lord Heinrich and he was born of the House of Aue. His heart had foresworn duplicity and all ill-mannered conduct, and he held fast to this oath with constancy till death. His lineage and his conduct were free of defect. All the worldly honors that one might wish for had been given him, and he well knew how to increase them by sterling qualities of all kinds. He was a blossom of youth, a mirror of worldly joy, a diamond of constant loyalty,[5] a flawless crown of good breeding. He was a refuge to those in need, a shield of protection for his kin, an evenly balanced scale of generosity: he was neither prodigal nor niggardly. He bore well upon his back the weari-

---

1. Since most books were written in Latin, Hartmann seems to be claiming for himself knowledge of that language. To have such knowledge as a member of the knightly class is unusual enough to be worth mentioning.

2. Hartmann refers to himself as a *dienestman* (Latin: *ministerialis*). *Ministeriales* were lower nobles, often without property of their own, who served more powerful lords. They sometimes rose to great prominence and power. They usually came from the ranks of the unfree serfs, and their own status (free or unfree) was sometimes in doubt.

3. In *Gregorius* (lines 3989ff.), Hartmann similarly gives a spiritual reason for having composed the story.

4. A large area in southern Germany to the west of Bavaria.

5. The diamond's most valued quality for people then was its hardness and imperviousness to change.

some burden of honors. He was a bridge of help and could sing quite well of love.[6] Thus did he succeed in winning the world's praise and esteem. He was courtly and had good sense born of experience.[7]

[75] As Lord Heinrich was thus intently pursuing honors, possessions, good humor, and worldly happiness—he was praised and honored above all his kin—his exhilarating existence was transformed into a life of utter dejection. As in the case of Absalom,[8] so with him it was revealed that the empty crown of worldly sweetness falls underfoot from its lofty prominence, as scripture has told us. In one passage it says: *media vita in morte sumus.* This means: just when we think we are enjoying life at its best, we are hovering in the midst of death.

[97] The stability of this world, its constancy, its perfection, and its great power—no one can control them. We can see a clear picture of this in what happens to a candle. As it gives forth light it is, at the same time, turning to ashes. We are made of fragile stuff. Just look how our laughter is snuffed out by weeping, our sweetness mixed with bitter gall.[9] Our blossom must fall just when it seems to be its greenest. In the case of Lord Heinrich it was made evident that he who lives in highest esteem on this earth is despised before God. By His command Heinrich fell from his lofty position of esteem into despicable misery: leprosy took hold of him.

[120] When people noticed on his body God's severe punishment, he became repulsive to man and woman. Just look how appealing he had been to the world before. And now he was of so little consequence that no one cared to look at him. This is just what happened to the noble and rich Job, whose wretched lot became the dung heap in the midst of a prosperous life.

[133] As soon as poor Heinrich realized that he was repulsive to the world—as all those like him are—his bitterness at his suffering set him apart from Job's patience. When suffering was visited upon good Job, he endured the disease and weakness he got from the world with a patient spirit for his soul's benefit. He praised God for it and rejoiced. Alas, poor Heinrich did nothing of the sort. He was sad and gloomy. His soaring heart plummeted, his buoyant joyfulness drowned. His bright spirits had to fall, his honey turned to gall. A sudden dark thunderclap shat-

---

6. That is, Heinrich was quite adept at composing the songs of courtly love.

7. The translation "good sense born of experience" is an attempt to render *wîs*, which is related to the English "wise." In Middle High German it denotes being intelligent, sensible, reasonable, circumspect, prudent—qualities gained through experience. Rendering it simply as "wise" would be misleading because wisdom seems to be a virtue of a higher order and, as we shall see through Heinrich's subsequent actions, not a quality he possesses at this point in his life.

8. See 2 Samuel, chaps. 13–19, for the fortunes of King David's son Absalom.

9. See *Gregorius*, lines 167–69, for a similar image.

tered his noontime; a gloomy thick cloud covered the radiance of his sun. He sighed deeply and often that he had to forsake so many honors, very often cursing and damning the day of his birth.[10]

[163] He still had one bit of consolation to gladden him. He had often been told that this disease took on various forms, and some of them could be cured. And so he entertained all sorts of thoughts and hopes. He fancied he might very well be curable and set out immediately for Montpellier to seek the advice of doctors. There he very soon found nothing but the depressing news that he could never be freed of the disease. Not liking what he heard, he journeyed to Salerno[11] and, in hopes of a cure, sought the skills of the learned doctors there.

[183] The most expert physician he found gave him straightway puzzling information: that he was curable and yet would remain forever uncured. Heinrich said, "How can that be? What you are saying is quite impossible. If I am curable, I'll recover. And whatever the cost in wealth or whatever the difficulties of the cure might be, I'm confident that I'll accomplish it."

[193] "Let go of such hopes," replied the doctor. "The nature of your disease is such that—but what good will it do for me to be telling you this?—a certain medicine is required. And so, in that regard, you would be curable. But no one is so wealthy or has the strength of purpose to be able to attain it. And so you will never get well—unless God wants to be your physician."

[205] Poor Heinrich then said, "Why are you discouraging me? I certainly have the power of wealth. Unless you are intent on refusing me your skills and neglecting your duty—not to mention rejecting both my silver and my gold—I shall make you so favorably disposed toward me that you will be quite happy to cure me."

[214] "It's not a question of my not wanting to," replied the doctor. "And if the medicine were such that one found it for sale or that one could procure it by any means at all, I would not let you waste away. Unfortunately, however, nothing can be done. And so my help must be denied you throughout all your trials. You would have to have a virgin of clearly marriageable age willing to suffer death for your sake. Now it's not the usual behavior of people to do this eagerly. Nothing else is required for a cure than the blood from the heart of a virgin. That would be the cure for your disease."

---

10. The comparison of Heinrich's reaction to his fate with that of Job presents us with a puzzle. On the one hand, the poet presents us with the proverbial image of Job as a model of patience and contrasts Heinrich's behavior with this image. On the other, Heinrich curses the day of his birth. In this they are similar; for Job, too, curses the day of his birth (Job 1:3). The poet, however, does not seem to wish us to see them in any way as similar.

11. Montpellier, in southern France, and Salerno, near Naples, were renowned in medieval times for their schools of medicine.

[233] Then poor Heinrich acknowledged that it would be impossible for anyone to find a person who would willingly die for him. And so the hope that had made him come there was taken from him, and from then on he had no more hopes for his recovery. The suffering in his heart became so strong and great that what distressed him most of all was that he had to go on living. He journeyed home and began to distribute his inheritable property as well as his personal effects in the manner that his own disposition and prudent counsel advised him would do the most good. He began judiciously to bestow wealth on his poor friends and relatives, giving away his resources to poor people unknown to him as well, so that God might deign mercifully to grant his soul salvation. The rest was distributed to monasteries.

[257] Thus did he divest himself of all his major possessions except for one farm on cleared land. There he fled to avoid people. It was not just he who bemoaned this wretched state of things. In all the lands where he was known, and even in foreign lands where people had only heard tell of him, there was much grief.

[267] The man who had been working the farm, and was still working it, was a free peasant[12] who never suffered any of the misfortunes that indeed happened to other peasants who had worse lords, ones who did not spare them from taxes and other demands. This peasant's lord was satisfied with whatever he did of his own accord. In addition, Heinrich protected him from having to toil for other powerful men. As a result, no one in the country was as well off as he. It was to the house of this peasant that poor Heinrich withdrew. How well was he now looked after and how richly did he now reap the benefits of having spared the peasant in the past! He was not in the least annoyed by whatever fell to him to do for Heinrich's welfare. Being loyal and thoughtful, he endured very willingly the trouble and the work that thus fell to his lot, and he provided Heinrich with great comfort. God had given the farmer, according to his station, a good life. He had a very industrious wife and a body capable of hard work. In addition, he had handsome children, who are indeed a man's joy. And among them, it is said, he had a young girl, a child eight years old who knew how to behave very kindly. She never wanted to budge one foot from her lord. To receive his greeting and his favor she served him constantly with her kind attention. Also, she was so charming that in her loveliness she could easily have been the emperor's daughter.

[315] The others were adept at knowing how to keep their distance from him, but she fled *to* him and nowhere else at every opportunity. She was his whole enter-

---

12. That is, though belonging to the farming class and, as we shall see, dependent on Lord Heinrich, this peasant was not a serf, the property of some feudal lord. Rather, he was a freeman.

tainment. With the pure goodness of a child she had directed her affections to her lord, so that one always found her at his feet. She was ever bustling sweetly about her lord. For his part, he delighted her in any way he could and gave her much that was suitable for a girl in her innocent play. It was also a great help to him that children are so easily won over. He got her whatever he found for sale—a mirror, hair ribbons, belts, and rings—whatever a child might like. With such service he brought things to the point that she became so close to him that he called her his bride. The dear child seldom let him be alone, thinking of him as completely healthy. However strongly the gifts for her to play with moved her, it was most of all the sweet spirit given her by God that made her delight in this behavior. Her service was kind indeed.

[350] When Heinrich had spent three years there and God had tormented his body with great affliction, the farmer, his wife, and their daughter—the girl I've been telling you about—were one day sitting together with him as they worked, and they were lamenting the suffering of their lord. They had good reason to lament. They feared that his death would bring them great harm and sever them completely from honors and possessions, and that some other lord would be more hard-hearted. They went on thinking like this until the farmer asked a question. He said, "My dear lord, if it might be with your favor, I would very much like to ask: there are so many masters of medicine in Salerno. How is it that the skills of none of them can provide help for your sickness? That, lord, is what puzzles me."

[378] Then poor Heinrich sighed from the depths of his heart in bitter pain. He spoke with such sadness that his sighs fragmented his words, "I fully deserve this shameful humiliation at God's hands. For you could well see how formerly my gate stood wide open to worldly pleasure, and how no one among his kinsmen had his will more than I did. That was indeed impossible, because I had my way completely. I then ignored utterly the One who had given me this same ideal life through His favor. My heart was then disposed as it is for all total fools whose heart tells them that they can have honors and possessions independently of God. Thus did my foolish thinking also deceive me. For little did I look to Him from whose favor I had many honors and possessions. When this arrogance angered the exalted Gatekeeper, He shut the gates of happiness in my face. Alas, I'll never get in. My foolishness ruined that for me. As vengeance, God has inflicted on me a sickness from which no one can free me. Now I'm contemptible to common people. Good people take no notice of me. No matter how lowly a person is who looks at me, I am lowlier still. He shows me his contempt by casting his glance away from me.

[418] "Now the loyal devotion you have is really evident. Despite my disease, you let me stay with you and you do not in the least flee from me. But even though you do not shun me, even though no one likes me except you, and even though your welfare depends on me, still you would endure my death well enough. Whose worthlessness and whose distress was ever greater in the whole wide world? Formerly I was your lord, and now I am your indigent. My dear friend, you, my bride, and your wife are buying yourselves eternal life because you are letting me remain with you, diseased though I be.

[435] "I'll gladly tell you what you were asking me about. At Salerno I was unable to find a doctor who was willing or dared to take me into his care. For in order to be cured of my disease, I would have to procure a kind of thing that no one in the world has the means or ability to obtain. I was told simply that I would have to have a virgin of clearly marriageable age who would be willing to suffer death for my sake. One would cut through to her heart. Nothing else would help me but blood from her heart. Now it is impossible enough that any one of them would willingly suffer death for my sake. And so I must bear shameful distress till my death. May God send it to me soon!"

[459] The innocent girl heard and understood what he was saying to her father, for the delightful thing had her dear lord's feet resting in her lap. One might rightfully compare her childlike heart to the goodness of the angels. She took note of what he said, marking every bit of it. It never left her heart, remaining there till she went to bed that night, lying, as usual, at the feet of her father and mother. While they were falling off to sleep, she pressed many a deep sigh from her heart. Her sadness because of the suffering of her lord was so intense that the rain from her eyes wet the feet of her sleeping parents. Thus did the sweet girl wake them.

[481] When they felt the tears, they awoke and started asking her what was wrong and what kind of trouble was able to make her fret so quietly. She wanted to make no mention of it to them; but when her father then pleaded with her and threatened, saying that she had to tell them, she said, "You might well lament along with me. What can upset us more about our lord than that we shall lose him and, in doing so, shall be deprived of honor and possessions. Never again shall we have a lord as good as him, one who treats us like he does."

[499] They replied, "Daughter, what you say is true, but our sadness and complaints don't do us the least bit of good. Dear child, no more of this. We are as sorry about it as you are. Unfortunately we can be of no help to him. God has taken him from us. If anyone else had done it, he would have our curse." Thus did they reduce her to silence.

[510] That night she remained sad and the whole following day as well. No matter what someone else was doing, this did not leave her heart for a minute. Then, as usual, they all went to bed the following night. When she had lain down on her usual sleeping place, she again prepared a bath with her weeping eyes. For hidden close by in her heart she bore the greatest goodness that I have ever heard of in a child. What child has ever done something like this? She was utterly resolved to do this one thing: if she were to live to the next day, she would actually give her life for her lord.

[529] At this thought she became light-hearted and cheerful, and she had not a single care left except for one fear that caused her pain: that, when she told her plan to her lord, he might be cowardly about it; and that, when she had told all three of them about it, she would not find in them the firm resolve to let her go through with it. She was so upset at this thought that her mother and father were awakened again by this, as in the previous night. They sat up facing her and said, "Look, what is troubling you? You are very silly for taking upon yourself so much misery from this sad business that no one can put an end to. Why won't you let us sleep?"

[550] Thus did they rebuke her. What good did her lamenting do her about something that no one could prevent or compensate for? And so they imagined for a second time that they had silenced the sweet thing, but they did not know the strength of her will. This is how the girl responded, "As my lord told us, one can heal him very well. And truly, unless you shall stop me, I am the right medicine. I am a virgin and have the resolve. Rather than see him go to ruin, I shall die for him."

[565] Her words made both father and mother sad and downcast. The father told his daughter to quit talking like this, promising her lord something she could not follow through on. Such an idea was not at all right for her, "Daughter, you are just a child and your devotion is just too much in these matters. You can't accomplish what you have just now claimed. You have never seen death. When the time comes for you and there is no way out for you and you have to die, you would still prefer to live if you could make that happen. You have never fallen into a more deplorable pit. So be quiet, and if you ever again mention this matter, you'll get what's coming to you." With this he imagined that through both his entreaties and his threats he had silenced her. But he could not.

[592] His daughter answered him as follows, "Father mine, no matter how young and inexperienced I am, I do have the wits to know well from what people say that this misery, the death of the body, is violent and severe. And yet someone who lives a long life of toil doesn't have it easy either. For when he has struggled here and, having endured much distress, has lived to old age, he still has to suffer death any-

way. If he then has lost his soul, it would have been better for him not to have been born. I have been presented with the opportunity—something I shall always praise God for—of giving up my young life in exchange for eternal life. Now you should not ruin it for me. I want to do something very good for both you and me. I am the only one who can preserve us from harm and suffering, as I shall now explain to you. We have honor and possessions as a result of my lord's good will, for he has never imposed suffering on us or ever taken away possessions. As long as he lives, things will go well for us; but if we let him die, we will go to ruin, too. I want to preserve his life for our sake through this excellent idea so that we all benefit from it. So let me do it because it has to be."

[629] When the mother saw the earnestness of her daughter, she said tearfully, "Daughter, dear child, remember how great the hardships are that I have suffered for your sake, and let me receive a better reward than what I hear you saying. You're going to break my heart. For my sake soften a bit what you are saying. In doing this to us you will offend God and totally forfeit your salvation. Don't you remember his commandment? He certainly commanded and bid that one offer love and honor to father and mother, and he promised as a reward the soul's salvation and a long life on earth. You say you want to sacrifice your life for the happiness of us both, and yet you are willing to ruin our lives completely. It is because of you that your father and I are glad to be alive. What meaning do life, possessions, and property in the world have for us if we lose you? You should not make things hard for us. Really, my dear daughter, you are supposed to be the joy of us both, our pleasure unmixed with pain, the radiant delight of our eyes, the bliss of our life, a blossom among your kin, a staff for our old age. But if through your own fault you should make us stand at your grave, you will be cut off from God's favor forever. That's what you will gain from your efforts on our behalf. Daughter, by our Lord's grace, if you want to do well by us, you should quit talking and thinking as I've been hearing you do."

[663] "Mother, I confidently expect from you and my father all the favors that a father and mother should provide for their child, as I well experience it from you day after day. From your favor I have my soul and a fair body. All who see me—men and women—praise me, saying I'm the most beautiful child they've seen in their lives. Whom, after God, do I have to thank for this except the two of you? Because of this I shall ever stand ready for your command. How right it is for me to do so! Mother, blessed woman, because I have soul and body from your good graces, let it be with your favor that I then preserve them both from the devil and may offer myself to God. Truly, the life of this world is nothing other than the loss

of the soul. Also, till now worldly desires that lead to hell have not touched me. Now I thank God that in my young days he has given me the good sense to scorn this fragile life completely. I intend to surrender myself into God's power, pure as I am now. I fear that if I get old, the sweetness of the world will draw me underfoot, as it has drawn very many whom its sweetness has duped. Then I might well be denied to God. To Him one should complain that I shall live till tomorrow. I am not at all comfortable in the world. Its pleasure is much hardship, its greatest delight is a heart of pain, its sweet reward is bitter want, its long life a sudden death. Nothing is more certain for us than that well-being today means suffering tomorrow, and always at the end—death. It's a misery that makes you weep. Birth and wealth are no protection, nor are beauty, strength, or a joyous spirit. Virtue and honor do you no more good in the face of death than low birth and vice. Our life and our youth are mist and dust. Our stability trembles like a leaf. He is surely a misguided fool who likes to fill himself with smoke—be it woman or man—who cannot grasp this and who pursues the world; for a silk cloth is spread over the foul dung before us. He whom the splendor seduces is born for hell and has lost nothing less than both soul and body. Just remember, dear woman, the loyalty you owe me as my mother and soften the sorrow you have because of me.

[740] "Father, too, should reconsider the matter. I know quite well that he wants me to be saved. He is a man of such good sense that he knows very well that you can have your joy with me only for a short time, even if I go on living. If I were to remain with you here unmarried two or three years, my lord will probably be dead and we might easily come into such dire straits because of poverty that you would not be able to give me a dowry to get a husband. Then I would live in such want that you would rather see me dead.

[756] "But let's put aside for a moment that sad fate, as though it could not befall us, and assume that my dear lord goes on living long enough for me to be given to a prosperous and respected man. Then what has happened is just what you wanted, and you imagine that things have turned out well for me. But my heart has told me otherwise. If I love him, that is a misfortune. If I don't care for him, that is death. And so suffering will always be my lot and, toiling all the while, I shall be excluded from comfort in all kinds of ways that trouble women and lead them astray as to joys. Now give me that full abundance that never runs out. A free Yeoman desires me, and I give myself to Him eagerly. Truly you should give me to Him. Then my life is well taken care of. His plow glides along smoothly;[13] His

13. That is, in heaven's rich soil there are no rocks or boulders.

household is filled with supplies. There neither horse nor cattle die. There crying children are not a bother. There it is never too hot or too cold. There one never grows old in years. The old become young. Neither frost not hunger exist there, nor any kind of suffering. There one finds full joy and an absence of hardship. It is there I want to go, fleeing the farm that rain and hail beat down on and floods wash away, though one struggle against them time and again. One can work a whole year long to achieve something and lose it completely in half a day. This is the farm I shall leave behind. I curse this farm!

[798] "You love me. That is as it should be. I would now like to see that your love not turn into its opposite. If you know how to apply your good sense to my situation and if you wish me to have wealth and honor, then let me turn to our Lord, Jesus Christ, whose favor is so constant that it is never exhausted. Even for a poor maid like me He has as much love as He does for a queen. God willing, I shall never fall from your favor through any fault of mine. It is certainly His commandment that I be subject to you, for I have my life from you. I submit to this without regrets, but I should not violate my duties to myself either. I have always heard it said that if you make someone happy but thereby become unhappy yourself, or if you treat someone like a king and despise yourself—well, that's just too much devotion to others. How eager I am to be obedient and true to you! But most of all I shall be true to myself. If you want to interfere with my salvation, then I would rather let you cry a bit for me than not let happen what I owe myself. I have always wanted to reach the place where I shall find complete joy. You have other children. Let them be your joy and let them comfort you for the loss of me. Truly, no one can stop me from saving my lord and myself.

[844] "Mother, I heard you complaining and saying just now that you would suffer in your heart if you were to stand at my grave. You will certainly be spared this. You won't stand at my grave because no one's going to let you see where I die. It's going to happen in Salerno. There death shall release all four of us from all kinds of misery. We shall all be made well by death, I much more so than you."

[855] When they saw the child thus rushing toward death, speaking so wisely, and violating merely human norms, they began to consider that no tongue in the mouth of a child could ever show such wisdom and such insight. They avowed that the Holy Spirit was the cause of this way of talking, who was at work in Saint Nicholas as he lay in the cradle,[14] teaching him wisdom, so that he turned his childlike goodness toward God. In their hearts they considered that they did not

14. Legendary for his great wisdom and asceticism, even as an infant.

in the least want to stop her from accomplishing what she had taken upon herself;
nor should they. The idea must have come to her from God. They tortured them-
selves with grief.

[876] The peasant and his wife sat there on the bed, forgetting their tongues
and their senses for the love of their child. Neither of them could utter a single
word. Cramps from weeping began to plague the mother in her suffering. They
both just sat there sad and dejected until they realized what little good their griev-
ing did them, since nothing could take away her intention and her resolve. Thus
the best thing for them to do would be to give in to her; for, after all, they could
not lose her in a better way. If they showed hostility toward the plan, it could get
them into a lot of trouble with their lord; and that is all they would accomplish.
And so with a great show of approval they both asserted that they were happy with
the plan.

[903] This made the innocent girl happy. Barely had it dawned when she went
to where her lord was sleeping. His bride called to him and said, "Lord, are you
sleeping?"

"No, I am not, my bride. Tell me, why are you up so early this morning?"

"Lord, grief at your sickness weighs on me."

He said, "My bride, you make it very apparent that you feel sorry for me, and
God shall repay you for it; but nothing can be done about it."

"Truly, my dear lord, you can be helped a great deal. Since your situation is
such that one can help you, I shall not delay one more day. Lord, you told us, after
all, that if you had a virgin who would freely suffer death for your sake, you would
thereby be healed. I myself shall be this virgin, so help me God. Your life is of
more use than mine."

[927] The lord thanked her very much for her good intentions, and, unnoticed,
his eyes filled up from grief. He said, "My bride, death is not at all a pleasant affair,
as you perhaps have imagined. You have certainly made it clear to me that if you
could, you would help me. That is enough for me. I know your sweet affection.
Your will is pure and good. I can demand nothing more of you. You obviously can-
not grant me what you have just said. God shall repay you for your devotion to me.
I would be the laughingstock of the people all around, given what up till now I
have tried in the way of medicines, if this did me no good and my sickness just
kept getting worse. My bride, you act like children who act on impulse. What
comes into their head, be it bad or good, they are all quick to do it, but they are
sorry for it afterward. My bride, you are acting this way, too. You are enthusiastic
about this plan now. But if someone were to take you up on it and it should then

be carried out, then you would very likely regret it." He asked her to think a bit more about the matter. He added, "Your mother and your father cannot well do without you. And, for my part, I should not demand suffering from those who have always been good to me. Dear bride, do whatever they both advise you." Saying this, he smiled, for little did he realize what had happened there in the meantime. This was how the noble man spoke to her.

[969] Her father and her mother said, "Dear lord, you have made things very pleasant for us and have shown us honor. That would not be well returned if we did not pay you back in kind. Our daughter has the desire to suffer death for your sake. We are quite ready to let her do this, so completely has she convinced us. She has not just considered the matter for a short time. Today is the third day that she has been at us all the time to allow her to do it. She has now convinced us. So may God let you recover through her. We are willing to give her up for your sake."

[987] As his bride was offering him her death in exchange for his disease, and one saw her seriousness, there was much joylessness and display of sorrow. Concerns of various kinds arose among them, between the child and the other three. Her father and mother began to weep profusely. They had great need of weeping for the death of their very dear child. Then the lord also began to reflect further on the devotion of the child, and sadness gripped him, too, so that he began to weep much; and he had very serious doubts whether it were better done or left undone. The girl was weeping, too—out of fear. She imagined he had turned coward. Thus they were all gloomy and saw no way out.

[1011] Finally their lord, poor Heinrich, made his decision and began to express great thanks to all three of them for their loyalty and generosity. The girl was over-joyed that he was willing to follow her plan, and Heinrich prepared himself for Salerno as quickly as he could. What was suitable for the girl was very quickly pre-pared—beautiful palfreys and costly clothes, the kind that she had never worn pre-viously: ermine, velvet, and the best sable to be found. That was the girl's attire.

[1027] Now who could fully express the deep sorrow, the lamenting, her mother's bitter suffering, and the misery of her father as well? It would have been for them both a parting full of grief, as they sent their dear child away to her death so healthy, never to see her again, if the pure goodness of God, from which, after all, the deci-sion came to the child to accept death willingly, had not eased their distress. It had come about without any doing of theirs. Hence all self-incrimination and sadness was taken from them; for otherwise, it would have been a miracle that their hearts did not break. Their sadness turned to joy, so that henceforth they suffered no mis-ery because of the child's death.

[1049] And so, cheerfully and willingly, the girl rode off toward Salerno with her lord. What could trouble her now, except that the way there was so long and that she remained healthy for so long a time? And when finally, as he had intended, he had brought her to where he found his physician, he, the physician, was quickly told with great joy that he, Heinrich, had brought the kind of a girl he had told him to get. Then he let him see her. This seemed incredible to the physician. He asked, "Child, did you reach this decision on your own, or did you become convinced of this plan by the entreaties or threats of your lord?"

[1068] The girl replied that these very same plans came from her heart. He was greatly surprised at this and took her aside and pleaded with her very seriously to tell him whether her lord had at all urged this plan on her by means of threats. He said, "Child, there is need for you to consider the matter further, and I'll tell you exactly why. If you suffer death and do not do so willingly, then your youthful body is dead and it helps us, alas, not one single bit. Now keep nothing back from me concerning your intention. I shall tell you what will happen to you. I shall undress you and you will stand there naked. Your shame will be very great, and rightly so, when you stand naked before me. I'll bind your legs and arms. If you have any pity for your body, then consider this pain: I'll cut into your heart and tear it out of you still beating. Miss, now tell me, how do you feel about this? Never did a child feel such pain as I'll inflict upon you. That I have to cause it and see it makes me fearful. Look at what it will do to your body. If you regret it the least little bit, then I will have done my work and you will have lost your life in vain."

[1104] Very dearly she was again entreated that she should refrain from doing this if she were unsure that she was steadfast. Well realizing that on this day death would help her leave worldly cares, the girl said, laughing, "May God reward you, dear sir, that you told me the truth in such detail. Indeed, I am a little hesitant. I do have misgivings. I shall tell you exactly what these misgivings are which I have developed. I fear that our efforts might be entirely lost because of your cowardice. Your words would be more fitting for a woman. You are the equal of a rabbit. Your anxiety about my dying is too great. The fact is, you are not handling this affair well despite your great skill. I am a woman and have the strength. If you dare to cut me open, I certainly dare to suffer it. As for the gruesome business you have just explained to me, I heard about it well enough apart from you. Indeed, I would not have come here if I did not know myself to be steadfast enough in my resolve that I can endure it for certain. There is no paleness about me, if you please, and an even firmer resolve has arisen, so that I am standing here as fearful as if I were about to go to a dance. For it would seem to me that no distress of the body that can take place within one day is so great that this one day would be too much to pay for eternal life, which never passes away. As my mind now stands, nothing about me should make you uneasy. If you are confident that you can give my lord his health back and give me eternal life, then, for God's sake, do it now! Let's see what kind of a physician you are. He in whose name it shall take place is urging me on to do it. I well know for whose sake I do it. He recognizes service very well and leaves none of it unrewarded. I know well that He Himself says that the person who performs the greatest service shall also receive the greatest reward. And so I consider this death no more than a sweet affliction for so certain a reward. If I were to abandon this heavenly crown, I would have a foolish mind, for I am, after all, of humble origin."

[1171] He now understood that she was sufficiently unshakable, and he led her back again to the infirm man and said to her lord, "Nothing can stop us. Your girl is fully suitable. So be of good cheer. I shall quickly make you healthy." Again he led her back into his private room where her lord would see none of it. He closed the door in his face and threw the bolt, not wanting to let him see what her death would be like.

[1187] In a room he found well supplied with good medicines he immediately commanded the girl to take off her clothes. She was cheerful and happy to do so. She tore the clothes at the seams. In no time at all she stood there without clothes and was naked and bare, but she was not the least bit ashamed.

[1197] When the doctor looked at her, he swore in his heart that a more beautiful creature was rare indeed in all the world. So utterly did he feel pity for her that in his heart and mind he very nearly lost his courage because of it. Then the dear girl saw a high table standing there. He told her to get up on it. He tied her upon it very tightly and took in his hand a sharp knife that was lying there that he used for such purposes. It was long and broad, but it did not at all cut as well as he would have wished. Since she was not to survive, her sad condition caused him to feel pity, and he wanted to soften death for her.

[1217] Now there lay next to him a very fine whetstone. He began to stroke the knife on it very carefully, thereby sharpening it. Poor Heinrich, who was soon to disturb her joy, heard this as he stood outside in front of the door, and it saddened him very much that he was never again to see her alive. Now he began searching and looking about until he found a hole going through the wall, and through the crack he caught a glimpse of her naked and bound. Her body was quite lovely. He looked at her and then at himself, and a new way of thinking took hold of him.

What he had thought before did not seem good to him, and he suddenly changed his old way of thinking into a new goodness.

[1241] Seeing that she was so beautiful, he said to himself, "You are harboring a foolish thought, that you desire to live even one day in opposition to the will of Him against whom no one can do anything. Since you must die anyway, you really don't know what you are doing, that you do not bear very willingly this wretched existence God has given you. And besides, you do not even know whether the death of the child will cure you. Whatever God has assigned for you, let it all be done. I will not see the death of the child."

[1257] He made up his mind immediately and began pounding on the wall, commanding that he be let in. The doctor said, "I don't have the time now to open up for you."

"No, doctor, talk to me."

"Sir, I cannot. Wait until this is over and done with."

"No, doctor, talk to me before that."

"Well then, tell me through the wall."

"It's not that kind of thing."

[1269] Immediately he let him in. Then poor Heinrich went to where he saw the girl tied. To the physician he said, "This child is so lovely. I simply cannot watch her die. May God's will with regard to me be done! We shall let her up again. I'll give you the silver, as I have agreed with you. You must let the girl live."

[1280] The doctor of Salerno was glad to hear this and obeyed him immediately, untying the girl. When the girl realized for certain that she was not going to die, she was disappointed. She broke with her usual good manners. She was sad indeed. She beat her breast, tore and pulled at herself. Her carrying on became so pitiful that no one could have seen her without bursting into tears. Very bitterly she shrieked, "Alas, woe is poor me! What is going to become of me now? Have I then lost the splendid heavenly crown? It would have been given to me as a reward for this ordeal. Now I am really dead. Alas, powerful Christ, what honors have been taken from us, my lord and me! Now he and I shall do without the honors that were preordained for us. If this had been done, then his body would have been healed and I would have been blessed forever."

[1305] Thus did she well enough beg for death. No matter how much she felt in need of it, she did not get her request. Since no one did anything she wanted, she began to scold. She said, "I have to pay for my lord's cowardice. People didn't tell me the truth. That I have seen for myself. I always heard people say you were honorable and good, and had the firm character of a man. So help me God, they lied. The world was always deceived in you. All your days you were and still are a great big coward. I know this because, although I dare to suffer, you do not dare to allow it. Sir, what caused you to become afraid when I was being tied? There was, after all, a thick wall between you and me. My lord, don't you have the courage to endure someone else's death? I shall promise you and declare that no one will do anything to you, and that it is useful and good for you. If you left it undone out of thoughtfulness for me, that is a very poor idea for which God shall not reward you; for that is too much thoughtfulness."

[1333] No matter how much she begged, pleaded, and even scolded, it did her no good. She still had to go on living. No matter how much she scolded, poor Heinrich accepted it well and with good grace, as an able knight should in whom no quality of fine breeding was lacking. When the luckless visitor had dressed the girl again and had paid the doctor as he had agreed, he rode straight back home again to his country, even though he well knew that he would find there at home in everybody's mouth nothing but ridicule and scorn. This he left completely in God's hands.

[1353] In the meantime the dear girl had lamented and cried herself very nearly to death. Then the *Cordis Speculator*,[15] before whom no heart's gate is closed, saw her devotion and her distress. Since He in His sweet providence had seen fit to try them both, just as thoroughly as He had the prosperous Job, holy Christ showed how dear to Him loyalty and compassion are. He freed them both from all their suffering and made him then and there clean and completely healthy. Good lord Heinrich recovered so well that on the homeward journey under our Lord God's treatment he was so wonderfully restored to health that he became as he had been at the age of twenty. When they had thus been made happy, he had it proclaimed in his home country to those who, he knew, given their goodness and kindness, would be happy at his good fortune. Rightfully they would have to be joyful because of the favors that God had worked on him.

[1387] His closest friends, who knew of his arrival, rode out or went on foot to meet him for a good three days.[16] They did not believe what people were saying, but only their own eyes. They recognized the mysterious workings of God on his fair body. As for the peasant and his wife, one can certainly believe it of them, unless one wants to rob them of their due, that they did not remain at

---

15. Latin: Scrutinizer of the heart
16. A customary show of respect. The greater the distance, the greater the homage. See *Gregorius*, lines 3763–65, and *Erec*, lines 1510ff.

home. The joy they experienced has never been put down in writing, for God had provided them with a dear feast for their eyes. This both their daughter and their lord gave them. Never was there joy greater than what they then experienced when they saw that they were both hale and hearty. They didn't know how to act. Their manner of greeting was interrupted by strange behavior. The joy in their hearts was so intense that the rain of their eyes poured down on their laughter. It cannot be denied: they kissed their daughter's mouth a bit more than three times.

[1419] The Swabians received him with a praiseworthy gift: that is, their eager greeting. God knows, an honest man who has seen them at home has to admit that there was never better will than that which the Swabians showed as they received him on his journey home. What happened afterward? What more can I say? He became much richer than before both in honor and possessions. He referred it all to God steadfastly and observed His commandment better than he had formerly.[17]

Because of this his honor stands firm.

[1437] The peasant and his wife richly deserved honor and possessions because of their caring for him. Since he was incapable of dishonesty, it would hardly turn out otherwise for them. He gave them straightway as their own the extensive farm, both the land and the people, where he had been lying while sick. His bride he provided with goods, comfort, and those kinds of things fitting for a noblewoman or better. Justice required this of him.

[1451] At this time wise counselors began to advise him and praise the state of marriage. Their advice went in various directions. Then he told them what his disposition was. He intended, if it seemed good to them, to send for his closest friends and relatives and bring matters to a conclusion according to how they advised him. He ordered invitations and summonses to be sent out as far as his word reached. When he had gotten them all there, both relatives and vassals, he put the matter before them. They all agreed that it was time to marry and was the right thing to do. Then a vigorous dispute arose among them as they gave their advice. Their counsels varied greatly. The one advised this, the other that—as people always do when they are supposed to give advice.

[1474] Finally Lord Heinrich said, "It is well known to all of you that a short time ago I was very repugnant and repulsive to people. Now neither men nor women shun me. By our Lord's command I have been given a sound body. Now,

---

17. In *Erec* (lines 10,085–106), Hartmann also expresses the necessity of receiving all good things as coming from God's hands.

for God's sake, tell me, all of you, how can I repay the person through whom I received this favor that God has worked on me?"

[1487] They answered, "Resolve that your life and possessions shall ever be at the service of this person."

[1490] His bride was standing nearby and he looked at her lovingly. Embracing her, he said, "Certainly, you have all been told that I have my health again through this kind young girl standing next to me. She is just as freeborn as I am. Now my every thought counsels me to take her as my wife. May God grant that this seem fitting to you. Then I shall take her as my wife. But if that cannot be, then truly, I shall die without a wife. For I have my honor and my life because of her. By our Lord's favor, I now want to bid all of you to be happy about it."

[1509] Then all of them, poor and rich alike, said it was indeed very fitting. There were clergymen enough present there who gave her to him in marriage. After a long and happy life, together they came into the possession of the eternal kingdom. May this ultimately be the lot of us all! May God help us attain the reward that they received. Amen.

IWEIN

Introduction

Hartmann's *Iwein*, like his *Erec*, is a translation of a French Arthurian romance, in this case *Yvain* (about 1177) by Chrétien de Troyes. Hartmann completed his *Iwein*, apparently the last of his longer works, sometime before 1203. Whether his translation was commissioned by a patron or written on his own initiative we do not know.

Again like *Erec*, *Iwein* is more an adaptation than a translation in the strict sense. It is twenty percent longer than *Yvain*: Chrétien's epic totals 6,818 lines; Hartmann's, 8,166. Hartmann's intercalations consist largely of conversation and often didactic elaboration and reflection. *Iwein* finds Hartmann at the peak of his creative and adaptive powers—which does not exclude a penchant for preachiness.

Whether *Iwein* was commissioned or not, Hartmann was writing for a court, and his concern was with the noble class that comprised or was attached to a court, and with how the members of that class acted and interacted—or, above all, should act and interact. The court is that of King Arthur, transposed as in Chrétien from sixth-century Celtic antiquity into the contemporaneous twelfth century of knighthood and courtly society. Arthur himself plays a consequential though not a principal role, as do several knights of the Round Table.

The full title of Chrétien's prototype romance was *Yvain: Le Chevalier au lion*, and the lion, introduced after the knight Iwein's mental breakdown and recovery, is no less his companion and frequent savior, as Iwein undertakes a series of conceivably redemptive, sometimes overlapping, knightly "adventures." The adventures are in fact quests involving adventure, missions of rescue and of righting wrongs. For example, Iwein heroically defeats the minions of an oppressor, thus freeing three hundred ladies who had been bound to a sweatshop as wage-slaves. (Predictably, they are all noble ladies, not a commoner among them.) Iwein's friendship for the lion should also be seen in conjunction with his friendship with

Gawein, that most perfect of knights. The narrator Hartmann states unequivocally that Gawein "turned out to be [Iwein's] downfall," for it is Gawein who first lures Iwein away from his wife Laudine, and who then seems purposefully to keep Iwein from returning home within the time limit. The lion becomes a better companion for Iwein, and the two often save each other from death. Finally, the joust between Iwein and Gawein seems to end in a draw, but Gawein—with a guilty conscience?—insists that Iwein is the victor. The fact that Gawein precipitately took up the unjust cause of the older sister while Iwein defended the magnanimous younger sister, who ultimately gains her inheritance, shows that Iwein overcomes Gawein, and, correspondingly, what Gawein represents: a lack of moderation and forethought.

But Hartmann presents much more than a string of perilous adventures undertaken by Iwein and his lion. For participation in these knightly missions of righting wrong brings Iwein into conflict with his obligations and vows as a husband. The theme thus becomes the necessary reconciliation of individual, personal love with chivalric adventure or generalized love. As with many American Western novels, we seem to have in *Iwein* an initiation story. Early on, the hero, oblivious to his true needs (and those of his wife) goes to ruin—his wilderness period—then recovers; in the course of his knightly feats he undergoes a character development or perhaps a transformation and comes to see the light. That light, in his knightly world, is moderation, balance. And while the ending of *Iwein* is not closed, the hero does seem to be headed for happiness.

It is fair to add that recent criticism casts doubts on Iwein's presumed development or transformation, preferring to see a merely static character. Still other criticism points to the importance of Hartmann's irony. King Arthur's court, as well as the king and queen themselves, are perceived, chiefly by Sir Kei, as flawed emblems of perfection, as creatures of ritual rather than of effective human sympathy, and unworthy of emulation. But Hartmann's goal of ethical perfectibility remains implicit.

Other factors suggest that *Iwein* is a Christian allegory. It is God, for example, not man, who bestows on Iwein the capacity for *triuwe*, or faithfulness in fulfilling one's duty to others. And the lion, a symbol of Christ, allegorizes compassion, self-sacrifice, and generosity. As a further example, the various castles where Iwein overnights or bases himself for his combats with various adversaries may be thought of as stations on his spiritual—or spiritualized—journey through life. That journey through life, as Iwein lives it, parallels, and so may exemplify, the Christian story of man's sin, fall, and redemption.

Hartmann does not in general meld the features of put: and Iwein's martial feats into a flowing whole; they remain crete. If we prefer to find no moral development, perhaps formation of Iwein, then the case for an interpretation as severely compromised. For a work that two or three genera regarded as relatively shallow, *Iwein*, with its self-reflexiven and its range of allusion, emerges today as tantalizingly complex.

Text

He who turns his mind to true goodness will be attended by happiness and honor. Good King Arthur, who knew how to fight laudably and chivalrously, gives clear proof of this. He lived in such a beautiful way that he wore the crown of honor in his time, and his name does so still. That is why his countrymen are right when they say that he still lives today. He has attained such fame that even though he has died, his name will live forever. Even now, whoever acts as Arthur did is completely protected from shame and dishonor.

[21] There was an educated knight who read books, and when he had nothing better to do with his time he also wrote poetry. He devoted his best energies to everything that people like to hear. This knight was called Hartmann, and he came from Aue.[1] It is he who wrote this story.

[31] On a certain Whitsuntide[2] King Arthur in his usual generous way had arranged a magnificent festival at his castle in Karidol. It was such a splendid festival that the like has not been seen before or since.[3] Indeed, an ordinary man counted for nothing there — never before had so many good knights assembled anywhere else on earth. And in every way the happiest possible life was offered to them there at court. Many a girl, many a woman, the fairest in the country, made the court and the life there pleasant for the knights. It really bothers me — and if it would do any good I would complain about it — that in our present day there can never be joy equal to what was to be found in those days. Still, we have advantages now too. I wouldn't want to have lived then and not now, since we can enjoy the

1. Hartmann similarly introduces himself in *Poor Heinrich*, lines 1–6.
2. Pentecost. See *Erec*, note 65.
3. See *Erec*, line 2165 and note 76.

ry of what those knights did. But they thrived in doing the actual deeds.

[59] Arthur and the queen both outdid themselves to meet everyone's expectations. On Whitsuntide, after everyone had finished eating, each person did what appealed to him most. Some conversed with the women, some took walks, some danced, others sang. Some ran races, while others leaped. Some listened to string music, some shot at a target. Some spoke of the woes of love, while others told tales of great valor.[4] Gawein saw to his weapons, while Kei,[5] who looked to his own comfort more than to honor, lay down to sleep among the people in the hall.

[76] The king and queen had taken each other by the hand and gone to an adjacent private room where—more to share companionship than to rest—they had gone to bed. They soon fell fast asleep. Four knights had sat down outside by the wattlewall: Dodines and Gawein, Segremors and Iwein. The ill-bred Kei was also lying nearby. A sixth knight, Kalogrenant, began telling them a story of a great tribulation of his that hardly testified to his knightly prowess. When he had told just a little bit, the queen woke up and heard him speaking. Leaving her husband the king lying there, she departed from him secretly, gliding quietly over to the group of knights until she was very near them, practically in their midst—so quietly that none of them was aware of it, except Kalogrenant. He quickly jumped to his feet, bowed to her, and greeted her.

[108] Kei, however, followed his usual habit. Distressed that Kalogrenant had had the honor, he berated the latter insultingly. He said, "Sir Kalogrenant, we already knew that none among us was so courtly and honorable as you imagine yourself to be. We therefore concede that you are more deserving than your companions, whether we like to or not. So it seems to you that we should give in to you. My lady, the queen, has to concede as much too, so as not to do you an injustice. Your good breeding is so extreme, and you imagine yourself to be so perfect— surely today you have undertaken more than you realize. None of us was so careless but what—had he but seen the queen—he would have acted in the same well-bred way as you alone did. Inasmuch as none of us saw her—or however we overlooked the fact and were sitting there inattentively—you could have just sat there too."

[136] To that the queen replied, "Kei, that is just like you. You harm no one more than yourself when you always feel obliged to be jealous of someone who is

---

4. Compare *Erec*, lines 2142–65.
5. Sir Kei, uncourtly in every way, is a contrast figure at King Arthur's court. Boastfulness is just one aspect of this contrast. A comic figure by virtue of his incongruity, he is given to making a fool of himself. But if he fails to see his own self-righteousness, he may well see that of the court all too clearly. Compare *Erec*, lines 4629⁵–859.

being honored in one way or another. From your malice you exempt neither household nor guests. To you, the most worthless man is the best, and the best is the most worthless. In only one respect can I console you: people always put up with you. That is because you are in the habit of excusing the worthless and abusing only the honorable. In the opinion of all who are wise, being reviled by you amounts to being praised. If you had not spoken as you just did, you would have actually burst—which, God knows, would be a very good thing. Because you are full of bitter venom in which your heart floats, striving against your honor."

[159] Unable to contain his rage at the queen's outburst, Kei said, "Lady, that is enough. In fact you have said too much. It would well befit your station if you had said less. I willingly accept, as I should, your dominion and your discipline. But you are going way too far, speaking to knights about their honor. We are not used to that from you, and it demeans you. You reprimand me as if I were a boy. Tact is better than justice. Since I have done nothing to you, you could afford to let me be. If my guilt were the least bit greater, my life would be forfeit. Lady, have mercy on me and forgo such anger, because your anger is too harsh. Do not compromise your courtliness because of me. If you will say no more, I will bear my humiliation. If I was wrong I am ready to submit to Kalogrenant's pardon. Invite him now, for your sake, to tell the rest of the story that he started earlier, because one is more than willing to remain silent in your presence."

[189] Kalogrenant replied, "Since you are who you are, no one should pay any attention to your criticizing. One thing I know: no one's mouth speaks other than as his heart advises, for whomever your tongue dishonors, your heart is responsible. Many men in this world are false and fickle who would like to be upright, but their hearts will not let them. No matter who tries to teach you, it is wasted effort, because you will not change your habits for anyone. The bumblebee is destined to sting, and it is proper that manure, wherever it is, should stink. The hornet has to buzz. I wouldn't enjoy praise from you, nor your friendship, because your words mean nothing, and I will not be harmed, no matter how you revile me. Why should you spare me? You have reviled better men. But at this moment and from now on, whenever you are around, I am not about to tell a story. My lady will grant me the favor of being excused."

[222] Sir Kei then said, "These lords should not have to suffer for my offenses, for they did nothing to you. My lady should not excuse you from telling your story, because it wouldn't be right for all of them to be punished along with me." "Sir Kalogrenant," said the good queen, "You know very well—you have grown up with him—that his bad manners have often disgraced him and that no one pays any

attention to his derision. It is my request and my command that you tell your story, for it would make him happy if he should succeed in depriving us of it."

[242] Kalogrenant answered, "Whatever you command will be done. Since you will not excuse me, then reward me by listening politely. I will be happier to tell it to you if you listen attentively. A lot of storytelling is wasted when people don't keep quiet and don't pay attention. Many listeners lend their ears, but if they don't pay attention with their hearts, then nothing registers but the sound. It is a great loss, because both parties are wasting their efforts, the listener as well as the narrator. Because I am not going to tell you any lies, you can all the more readily give me silence.

[259] "It happened to me and it is therefore true. About ten years ago I rode off into the forest of Breziljan,[6] armed as usual, in search of adventure.[7] There were several ways to go. I turned to the right, onto a path I found there, which was very narrow and overgrown. I rode all day through thorns and underbrush, so that I can truly say I had never suffered such great distress from hard going. When it was getting on toward evening, I took a path that led me out of the wilderness and into open country. I followed the path for a while, less than five miles,[8] until I saw a castle, where I turned in to rest. I rode up to the castle gate, before which a knight was standing. The man I saw standing there—it was the lord of the castle—had a fledgling hawk on his hand. And when he saw me riding toward him from a distance, he did not allow me the leisure of responding fully to his greeting before he took hold of my reins and stirrup.[9] When he had thus taken hold of me, he welcomed me in a very friendly way. May God forever reward him for this!

[297] "Before the gate a metal plate was hanging on two chains. He struck this so that it rang out and resounded in the castle. Shortly afterward, the host's retinue rushed forth, fair and young, squires and servants, attired according to their rank, bidding me welcome. My horse and I were well taken care of. When I entered the castle, I saw a girl approaching very quickly to welcome me. I still say, as I said then, that I had never seen a more beautiful girl. She helped me out of my armor. I have just one regret—let no one be surprised about it—namely, there being precious few straps on one's armor, that it didn't take her longer to fuss over me. Too

---

6. In Chrétien this is the vast, ancient forest Brocéliande, now called Paimpont Forest, in eastern Brittany, France. In legend the home of Merlin and the fairy Viviane, even today one can see there such things as "Merlin's tomb."

7. See introduction and *Erec*, note 6.

8. In the text, *eine mîle*, which is more than a modern mile, but of varying lengths.

9. A sign of the host's gracious hospitality.

quickly it was all over with—I wouldn't have minded if it had taken forever! She put a fine red wool cloak on me. Oh, unhappy man, that I had ever seen her, when the time came for parting!

[331] "We two remained alone. The lovely girl was well aware that I liked being with her. She led me to the finest lawn the world has ever produced, a little away from the other people. God knows I was glad to let it happen. In her I found wisdom together with youth, great beauty, total perfection. She was kind enough to sit next to me, listening to whatever I was saying, and answering amiably. Never before had a girl or a woman so completely captured my heart and troubled my spirit—and it will most likely never happen again. Alas and ever alas, what then robbed me of my joy: a messenger's arrival from my host! Since he bade us both go to eat, I had to leave my conversation and my joy behind.

[353] "When I went with her to the table, the host greeted me again. Never did a host offer his guest greater honor. Again and again he blessed kindly the paths and the byways that had led me there. He completely surpassed himself in goodness by not separating me from the girl, kindly allowing me to eat with her. He left nothing undone, seeing to it that we had an abundance of everything that is called hospitality. We were provided with both good food and an obliging spirit.

[369] "After we had eaten an enjoyable meal and, sitting around afterward, I had told the host that I was riding out on an adventure, he was greatly surprised. He said he had never before had a guest who claimed to be seeking an adventure. He asked me not to avoid him on my return trip. Having no quarrel with that, I gave him my promise, which I afterward kept.

[383] "When it was time to go to bed, I began to think about my journey. Since I by no means wanted to stay, nor should I have, I gave my thanks to the noble girl for her kind hospitality. The sweet young thing smiled and nodded. Look, I had to leave her! Commending the household to God, I offered myself repeatedly to my host's service. I departed very early in the morning, riding from the open country back into the forest. Heading for the wilderness, sometime after mid-morning I came upon a broad clearing hidden in the forest and empty of people. There, to my distress, I saw a terrible sight. All the kinds of beasts I had ever heard of were fighting and struggling in the most horrible way. Bison and aurochs[10] were fighting ferociously, emitting terrifying roars. I stopped short, regretting that I had come here. If they had caught sight of me, I would have had no confidence in my ability to defend myself, other than to ask God to save me. I very much wanted to get

---

10. Aurochs, now extinct, are believed to have been the forerunners of domestic cattle.

away from there. Then I saw a man sitting in their very midst, which reassured me. When I came closer, though, and got a good look at him, I grew just as frightened of him as of the beasts—perhaps even more. He was human in form but otherwise very wild looking. Like a Moor, he was huge and horrible beyond belief. His head, in fact, was larger than that of an aurochs. This crude fellow's soot-colored hair was standing on end. Both the hair on his head and that of his beard was matted to his skin. His face, furrowed with deep wrinkles, was more than a yard wide. And his ears were like those of a goblin, as wide as a tub and covered with hair several inches long. The beard and brows of this uncouth man were long, shaggy, and gray. His nose was as big as an aurochs's snout, but short, broad, and nowhere without hair. His face was flat and emaciated. Oh, how horrible he looked! His eyes were red with anger. On both sides, his mouth extended the full width of his cheeks. He was powerfully tusked, like a boar, not a man. From the door of his mouth his tusks protruded up and out, long, sharp, big, and wide. His head was placed in such a way that his bristly chin seemed to be grown onto his chest. His back was drawn up, hunched, and bent outward. He was wearing weird clothing. He had put on two skins that he had recently stripped from two beasts. He carried such a huge club that I felt daunted there near him.

[471] "When I had approached him so closely that he had to take note of me, I saw him stand up suddenly and come over to me. Whether his attitude toward me was unfriendly or well disposed—I had no idea, but in any case I was ready to defend myself. Neither he nor I said anything. Because he remained silent, I got the notion that he was a mute and I asked him to speak out to me. I said, 'Are you friend or foe?' He replied, 'He who never bothers me shall also have me for a friend.' 'Can you tell me what kind of creature you are?' 'A man, as you can well see.' 'Tell me, what is your job?' 'I take care of these beasts.' 'Tell me, do they do anything to you?' 'They feel lucky when I don't do anything to them.' 'Are they really afraid of you?' 'I take care of them, and they fear me as their lord and master.' 'Tell me, how can your mastery and surveillance stop them from running off at their whim to the woods and fields? For I can see they are wild and recognize neither man nor his command. I don't think it would be possible for anyone, except for God, to wield the power to constrain them without lock and fetters.' He answered, 'My voice and my hand, my command and my threats have brought them to the point where they stand trembling before me and act—or desist from acting—in accordance with my wish. If anyone else were to be among them as I am, he would quickly be lost.' 'Sir, if they fear your wrath, then bid them leave me in peace.' He replied, 'Don't be afraid. With me here they will do you no harm. Now that I have

told you everything you have seen fit to ask, it shouldn't be too much trouble for you to tell me what you are after. If you want anything of me, it is as good as done.' I said, 'I'll tell you: I am on a quest.'[11] The monster replied, 'Quest? What is that?' 'I'll explain it to you more clearly. See how I am armed. I am called a knight, and my intention is to ride out looking for a man armed like me, who will engage in combat with me. If he kills me, he gains fame. But if I conquer him, I am considered a brave man and am thought more worthy than I actually am. If you know anything about such a potential challenge here or nearby, do not keep it from me, but show me the way there, for I am proceeding for no other reason.'

[543] "He answered me as follows, 'Since your attitude is that of looking for trouble and not enjoying a comfortable life—never in all my life have I heard tell what a quest might be—I'll tell you something: if you want to risk your life, you need ask no further. Near here is a spring, a dozen short miles or more distant. If you go there and give it its full and proper due, and if you then make the return trip from there without great dishonor to yourself, then I do not doubt you are a capable man. What is the point of telling you more? If you are not a coward, you will shortly see for yourself what it is all about.

[565] 'But let me tell you what the spring is like. There is a chapel nearby, beautiful but small. The spring water itself is cold and very pure. It is touched by neither rain nor sun, nor do the winds disturb its surface. It is protected from such by a linden tree—more beautiful than has ever been seen—which is its shade and its roof. The tree is widespread, tall, and so dense that neither rain nor sun's ray ever penetrates it. Winter neither harms nor improves its beauty the least bit, but instead it is leafy all year long. Above the spring stands a very ornate stone, supported by four marble animals. The stone is extensively perforated. Hanging down from a branch is a basin made of gold. I certainly doubt that anyone possesses better gold than this. The chain by which the basin hangs is hammered out of silver. If you are not a coward, then do just this to the basin: with it pour some of the spring water onto the stone that stands there. Truly, good fortune is yours if you depart from there with honor.'

[598] "The man of the woods showed me a path on the left. I rode off in that direction and discovered the truth of the matter, as he had told me, and I found great honor there. No matter how long the world lasts, one will never hear such

---

11. The Middle High German original has *aventiure*. In Arthurian material, *aventiure* entailed a knightly obligation to seek and carry out adventure for the sake of love or at least for the sake of goodness. The crass and superficial explanation given to the rustic "monster" may indicate Hartmann's criticism of a standard knightly practice (at least as it was depicted in literature).

delightful bird song as I heard in the linden tree when I came riding up to it. Whoever may have been utterly weary of life—his heart would have rejoiced there. The tree was filled with birds, so that I lost sight of the branches and perceived very little of the foliage. No two birds were alike. Their song was quite varied, pitched both high and low. The forest gave their voices back again with the same sound. How song echoed song! I saw the spring beneath the tree and everything that the man of the woods had told me. The stone was an emerald. From its every corner shone such a sparkling ruby that the morning star could not be more beautiful when it rises, ascending above the haze in the air.

[629] "When I found the basin hanging there, I immediately thought—since I had after all ridden out on a quest—that it would be cowardice on my part if I should forbear from learning what it was all about. And my foolhardiness, which very often causes me trouble, counseled me to pour water on the stone. Whereupon the sun, which had been ablaze, disappeared, and the bird song faded away, checked by a violent storm. At the same moment, clouds built up from all four directions. The bright day turned into one on which I could scarcely see the linden tree. A great tumult occurred there. Very soon I saw, around me in every direction, a good thousand lightning flashes. Afterward and just as often, such a mighty thunderclap resounded that I fell to the ground. A rain- and hailstorm arose. Had not God's blessing spared me from the storm's affliction, I would have been very quickly dead. The storm grew so violent that it leveled the forest. If there was anywhere a tree so big that it remained standing, it was bare, as stripped of foliage as if it had gone up in flames. Whatever dwelt in the forest perished immediately if it did not make a quick escape. Because of the violence of the storm I had given myself up for lost and had no hope for my life. Doubtless I would have died, except that in a little while the hailstorm and the danger abated and the day began to brighten.

[673] "After the danger was passed and the weather had improved, believe me, I could have spent ten years by the spring without pouring water on it again. I would have been better off if I had refrained in the first place. The birds came back, the linden tree was again covered with their feathers. Again they raised their sweet cry, singing even better than before. Depressed as I had been earlier, that was all forgotten now. It was as though I were in paradise itself. I praise this joy above all joys I have ever known. Yes, I imagined that from then on I would enjoy unalloyed happiness with no hint of fear. Look—my expectations deceived me.

[693] "Dishonor and distress were approaching me. Look, here came a knight riding up, galloping so hard and fiercely that I thought it was an army. Even so, I prepared to defend myself. His horse was powerful, he himself was big—all of

which gave me scant pleasure. His voice resounded like a horn, and I could see he was angry at me. When I saw he was alone, though, my concern and fear subsided, and thinking I might survive after all, I cinched up my horse's girth. By the time I had remounted, he was close enough to see me. He called out loudly from a distance, saying, 'Treacherous knight, you have broken the peace. Without having declared a feud against me, you in your arrogance have grievously dishonored me. Just look at my forest! You have destroyed it, killing my animals and driving away my birds. I declare you my enemy. You shall give me satisfaction, or I will die in the pursuit of it. A child who has been struck must certainly cry and level accusations. Similarly, I am justified in accusing you. I have never knowingly caused you harm. Unjustly I have suffered a great loss. Peace no longer prevails here. If you want to survive, defend yourself.'

[731] "Since he was bigger than I, I claimed I was innocent and sought his mercy. But he said only that I'd better put up a defense if I wanted to save myself. I did what I could, but it didn't do me much good. I jousted with him, which led to his taking my horse from me.[12] The best thing that happened to me was that I broke my lance. Very dexterously he lifted me onto the ground behind my horse, so that I quite forgot I had ever sat on a horse. He took my horse and left me lying there, out of luck. What irritated me most, though, was that he didn't even do me the honor of looking at me. When he had won the honors, he acted as if this happened to him ten times daily. The prize was his, the shame was mine. But whatever shame I gained there, I was at least partly blameless because I had the best of intentions—I just couldn't bring them to bear on him. Owing to this, I was bound to fail.

[763] "Since my horse was gone, and I couldn't lie there forever, it seemed like a good idea to walk away as a dishonored man, and I sat down again at the spring. As eager for novelty as I am otherwise, you should not attribute to me this breach of good manners: if I were to sit forever by the spring, I would never again pour water on it, because I had paid so dearly earlier.

[773] "I sat there for quite a while pondering what to do, because my armor was too heavy to walk in. What more can I tell you? I took it off and walked away. I, unhappy man, considered where I could turn, until my heart advised me to return to my host, whom I had left that morning. Though I arrived on foot, I was received no differently than the previous evening when I was mounted: such was my host's courtesy. Had I returned in honor, rather than being revealed in disgrace, his treat-

---

12. To the victor belong the spoils. Compare *Erec*, note 86.

ment of me would have been appropriate. Thus did he and the girl console me. May God forever bless them for that!

[795] "I have acted like a fool, not being able to keep quiet about this disgraceful matter. I have never before had the urge to tell it. If something better had befallen me, you would also hear me tell that. If something better has happened to any one of you, tell it now if you want to."

[803] Sir Iwein, counting on the kinship between them, said, "Cousin Kalogrenant, my hand shall by rights avenge whatever dishonor has befallen you. I, too, want to go and see the spring and whatever wonders are associated with it." But then Kei said something that was just his kind of thing, because he couldn't let things be, when someone else excelled—it got under his skin. "God knows," he said, "it seems that this is after-dinner talk. You didn't abstain, that I can tell. One cup of wine, I tell you, produces more eloquence and valor than forty-four of water or beer. When the cat has eaten its fill, it immediately becomes playful, just as you do, Sir Iwein. If my advice is good, take it. Your words are too rash, sleep on it a little. And if you have a bad dream, you can restrain yourself. But if not, go your way with good fortune. You don't need to go halves with me on either the honors or the misfortunes that come your way."

[837] "Sir Kei," said the queen, "Shame on your tongue, which is silent about everything good and says only the very worst things you can think up. But I suppose I do your tongue an injustice because it is impelled by your heart, to which no act of malice seems too great. The tongue speaks what the heart commands. I can't separate them, so I condemn them both. I tell you for sure, if you had killed a man's father, he would spare no more effort to strip you of all honors than does your tongue. If you alone suffer because of that, you deserve to."

[855] Sir Iwein laughed and said, "Lady, I'm not bothered by what Sir Kei tells me. I know he is punishing me for being so stupid. My uncouthness bothers him, and he is not about to overlook it. He knows how to reprove me with his customary tact, which can offend no one. My lord Kei is so wise, so honorable and praiseworthy, that he is entitled to an audience—you know I'm speaking the truth. So I will always be a coward for putting up with what he says. The man who strikes first does not necessarily start a quarrel. As long as the other man endures it, the quarrel is averted. I don't want to be like the dog that is ready to snarl back whenever another dog snarls."

[879] A great deal of such mockery followed. Meanwhile the king had gotten plenty of sleep. When he awoke, he arose and promptly went out to where he found them all sitting together. They jumped to their feet, which angered him because

of the camaraderie he felt for them. God knows, he was much more a comrade than their master. After he had sat down with them, the queen told him of Kalogrenant's misfortune—and the whole story.

[893] The king's habit was never to swear an oath by his father's soul—Utpandragon was his name—without fully and literally carrying it out. So at that instant he swore by him—and ordered it to be proclaimed everywhere—that in two weeks' time, right on St. John's Eve,[13] he would go to the spring with all his armed force. When the knights heard that, they were all in favor of going there; it seemed to them knightly and good. In spite of the general happiness, Sir Iwein was uneasy, having already undertaken to go there alone. He thought, "If the king himself goes, I'll lose my chance for knightly deeds, because I can't prevent Sir Gawein from getting ahead of me. Without doubt, as soon as he asks for the contest, it will be granted to him rather than to me. But in fact things shall proceed differently. I can very easily prevent anyone who waits two weeks from fighting before I do. For within three days I will secretly set out and search the forest of Breziljan until I find the narrow, overgrown path that Kalogrenant found. Afterward I will see the beautiful girl, the child of the esteemed host—both of whom are so courtly. After I depart, I'll get to see the uncouth man who takes care of the beasts. And very soon after that I'll see the stone and the spring. They will have to allow me to pour water on it by myself, whether I suffer for it, or obtain pleasure. No one will notice anything until after I have done it. If they find out afterward, it will be all right."

[945] So he stole away, and like a man who knew how to gain and preserve honor by being clever, he went to where the squires were. He quickly picked the best one, from whom he concealed nothing. Very quietly he told him to saddle his horse. And he, Iwein, would ride out and wait at some distance for the squire to bring him his armor. He said, "Hurry now, and see to it that you keep quiet about it. For sure, if you tell anyone, our friendship is over forever."

[963] So he rode off, leaving the squire behind. Very soon the squire brought him his armor and his battle steed. Speedily arming himself, he mounted his steed and rode on randomly. With great difficulty he reconnoitered a large wilderness, both field and forest, until he discovered the narrow path on which his cousin Kalogrenant had barely been able to force his way. Iwein, too, encountered great difficulty before he got out into open country, where he found the fine lodging. No host had ever put him up for the night in such comfort. In the morning he departed and came upon the terrifying man in a field, standing beside his wild

---

13. This is perhaps a reference to John the Baptist, whose feast day is June 24.

beasts. At the sight of him he crossed himself repeatedly, amazed that it had ever pleased God to create so horrible a creature. That creature directed him to what he was looking for.

[989] Sir Iwein soon spotted the tree, the spring, and the stone, and he heard the bird song. Without hesitating, he poured water on the stone. There was such a rushing and roaring, and such a storm came up, that he thought he had been too quick about pouring the water and he was convinced he wouldn't survive.

[999] When the storm was over, he heard the lord of the forest himself come riding up. From a distance the latter addressed Iwein as his enemy. Iwein understood that he had better defend himself, if he didn't want to incur dishonor and distress. Dominated by great bitterness and anger, each man was prepared to defeat the other. In their desire to get at each other, they spurred their horses on. Each stuck his lance through his opponent's shield and up against his chain mail, so that the lances shattered in a hundred pieces. Both then drew their swords.[14] Such a battle now began, that God himself would have looked on respectfully, had the battle been unfolding before him. Targeted were the shields that each held in front of himself for protection. This went on until the shields were chopped to pieces by the sword blows and became useless to their owners.

[1029] With my description I could make a big thing of the battle, but I will not do so, as I will here explain to you. They were alone there; no one else was there to confirm my words. Since no one saw it, I could describe how this one hit and that one stabbed. One of them was killed there, and he couldn't tell of it. The victor, though, was such a courtly man that he would not have wanted to say much about his own valor. Therefore I could well limit the scope of their thrusts and blows and tell you just this one thing: neither of them was a coward, and many blows were exchanged before the stranger gave the host a blow that penetrated and shattered his helmet and went clear down to his life-center. When the host felt his mortal wound, it was more the fear of death than cowardice that made him turn and flee. In an unchivalrous manner Sir Iwein pursued him to his castle. The half-dead man was determined to flee, and his horse was so fast that he almost escaped. Sir Iwein thought that if he didn't kill or capture him, it would turn out as predicted by Sir Kei, who spared no one his mockery. Because no one else was there, what good would his efforts do him when he had no witness to confirm what he had done? And Kei would deny him his honors. So he hastened after his adversary—their hoofbeats were in rhythm—until the castle came into view.

14. This is the usual progress of knightly combat. Compare *Erec*, lines 755ff.

[1075] The road to the castle was not wide enough for two, so they had to ride to the great hall close upon one another. In front of the hall hung a portcullis, which one had to pass through, watching very carefully so as not to get killed by it. If either horse or man stepped in the wrong place, it would release the mechanism that held the heavy portcullis suspended aloft. It would fall so quickly that no one could escape it; thus many a man had been left dead. The lord of the castle rode in first, who had the wit and the skill to avoid a bad outcome there, for he, after all, had had the device built. It was so heavy and so sharp that it could cut through iron and bone. Sir Iwein, unaware that he should watch out for it, caused the portcullis to fall. At the same moment, he struck and wounded the lord of the castle and did not get killed himself, as I will relate. In order to strike the blow, he had leaned forward, which saved his life. When the portcullis fell, it missed him. I heard that it cut his horse in two at the saddle. It cut away his sword sheath and cut both spurs from his heels, but he himself emerged whole.

[1119] Since his horse lay dead, he could not keep up the pursuit. He had, however, mortally wounded the lord of the castle, who fled on through a second portcullis and let it fall behind him. So Sir Iwein could go neither forward nor back. He was caught, trapped between the two gates. However badly things had turned out for him—what with being imprisoned—still his chief regret was that his opponent had gotten away from him alive.

[1135] I'll tell you about the building in which he was trapped. As he himself later declared, it was more beautiful than any building he had ever seen, before or since. It was tall, expansive, and strongly built, all painted with gold. It would have seemed a delightful place to anyone who had been in it without having to bear the burden of fear. Sir Iwein looked all around but discovered no window or door by which he could escape. He began to consider what to do. While he was worrying about this, a little door near him quickly opened, and a girl walked through it in his direction. She would have been beautiful, had she not been so caught up in grief. At first she said only, "Alas, knight, alas, it is your doom that you have come here, for you have killed my lord. So deep is the grief, so ferocious the anger both of my lady and the court, that you will have to die. Only their grieving for my lord has delayed them from killing you, but they will kill you soon."

[1169] Iwein said, "I won't lose my life like a woman. They won't find me defenseless." To that she replied, "May God save you. If He alone does not protect you, you will die. Still, no one in great peril has ever conducted himself better than you. You are very brave and you should be rewarded for it. However much you have harmed me, I don't hate you. I'll tell you why:

[1181] "My lady once sent me to Britanje,[15] where I gave the king a message from her. Believe me, sir, I left there without anyone having spoken to me. I know this was owing to my uncourtly behavior, because, judged by local custom, I had acted in such a way as not to be worthy of their greetings. As I well know, I have paid for it. You greeted me then, sir, but no one else did. You showed respect then, for which I shall reward you now. Sir, I know you well. Your father, whom I also knew, was King Urien. You will be safe from harm, Sir Iwein, if you take this ring. The stone is such that whoever holds it in his bare hand cannot be seen or located as long as he keeps it in his bare hand. You will be hidden like wood under bark and you need worry no more."

[1211] With that, she gave him the ring. There was a couch nearby, adorned as splendidly as a couch can be—no king had ever had a better one. She told him to sit down, and when he had done so, she asked, "Would you like something to eat?" "I would be grateful," he replied. She left, to return shortly, carrying a nice, plentiful quick lunch, for which he thanked her. After he had finished eating and drinking, the courtiers at both gates raised a great hue and cry, declaring they would not put up with the man who had killed their lord.

[1229] "Sir Iwein," she said, "do you hear? They are looking for you. Follow my instructions: don't leave the couch. Nothing less than your life is at stake. Enclose in your hand the stone I gave you. Let my soul be your guarantee that you will suffer no harm, because it is a fact that no one will see you. How could there be a better situation for you than to see all your enemies standing near you and walking around you issuing threats, while yet so blinded that they can't find you, even though you are in their very midst? My lord's dear friends will carry my lord on a bier in front of you on the way to bury him. They will search for you everywhere, but you won't need to be concerned. Do as I say, and you will be all right. I don't dare stay with you any longer, because if they found me here it would be too bad for us."

[1257] So saying, she left. The people who had come to the outer portcullis saw in front of it the chopped-off half of a dead horse. Who could have challenged their conviction that if the gate were opened, they would find the rider inside? They quickly pushed both gates open. They found no one there, however, just half a horse, from the middle of the saddle forward. They raged in anger, praising neither God nor the devil. "Where did the man go?" they asked. "Who has robbed us of our sight and our senses? He has to be in here. With seeing eyes we are blind.

15. See *Erec*, note 35.

Everyone here has good eyes. As long as this castle was closed, no living creature could get out, unless it was as small as a mouse. How did this man get away from us? Although he may find temporary respite with his magic tricks, we'll find him this very day. Look in the corners and under the benches, good people. He can't successfully hide from such a search. He will have to show up." Blocking the entrances, they walked around swinging their swords like blind men. If they were ever going to find him, this would have been the time. The couch was not spared from the search, and they even looked underneath it. From Iwein's escape I conclude that as long as a man is not destined to die, he can be saved by a very small ruse.

[1301] While Iwein was sitting there apprehensively, everything that his friend, the kindly girl, had foretold actually happened to him. He saw the lord whom he had killed being carried toward him on a bier. And walking behind the bier was the most beautiful woman he had ever seen. In her grief she was tearing at her hair and clothing.[16] No woman in the world could have been more deeply marked by sorrow, for she was obliged to look at the dead body of one of the dearest men a woman ever loved. No woman could have ever imposed on herself such a burden of lamentation in mock-seriousness. Her demeanor as well as her voice revealed the sorrow in her heart. In her untrammeled grief she fainted so often that the bright day turned into night for her. When she opened her eyes again, she couldn't hear or speak, but her hands were tearing at her hair and her headdress. Sir Iwein caught sight of her bare figure.[17] Her hair and her body were so lovely that love confused his senses, and he forgot himself completely, unable to ignore her tearing her hair and striking herself. He could not stand it and wanted to go up to her and restrain her hands, so she wouldn't strike herself anymore. So worried was he about the lovely woman, that he would rather have borne the pain himself. He lamented to God his responsibility for any of her distress. Her misery affected him so deeply that he would have preferred his own death to seeing her injure her finger.

[1355] One thing has often been told to us as true: if a slain man is borne past his murderer, no matter how long ago his wounds were incurred, he will start bleeding again. Now look! The lord's wounds were bleeding again as he was being carried into the hall—because he was near the man who had killed him. Upon seeing this, the lady cried aloud, "The killer is in here and he has cast a spell on our senses." Those who had given up the search began searching again. They slashed

---

16. In *Erec* (lines 5755ff.), this is also how Enite displays her grief.
17. For the effect on a knight of seeing the bare skin of a woman, see also *Erec*, lines 323ff.

often at the couch, and many slashes and stabs penetrated its covering, so that Iwein often had to dodge. The searchers' swords sought him in corners and under benches. Livid with rage, they desired his death just like a wolf desires to kill sheep.

[1381] The lady, addressing her anger to God, declared, "God, I have lost my husband in the strangest way, and You alone are to blame.[18] You gave him such strength and courage that he could never fail against natural forces. So the only way it could have happened is that some invisible spirit took his life. Lord God, You know well that against anyone but a sorcerer he could have easily defended himself. This death was foreordained for him. His murderer is among us, listening. Come and see how brave the murderer is. Since he killed my lord, how can he be afraid of letting a woman see him? What could she do to him?"

[1403] After they had searched a while, during which Iwein's magic stone prevented anything bad from happening to him—because he was invisible to them—they quit looking around and carried the dead man to the cathedral, where the rites were performed with prayer and the giving of alms. He was then borne to his grave. There arose a piteous outcry of profound grief. The girl stole away from the retinue to check on Iwein, still hidden, and to console him, as is proper for a courtly maid. He proved undaunted. As is often the case, love had given him courage, and death held no terror for him. Still, he did not reveal to the girl that he was so in love with his enemy.

[1425] He thought, "How can I get to see her?" The place where the lord had been laid to rest was so near that Iwein could readily hear their lamenting, just as if he were among them. He said slyly, "Alas, these people are very sad, and their grief goes to my heart more than I can say. If there is an opportunity, I would very much like to witness the grief of those whom I hear at the graveside."

[1439] But he didn't mean what he said, because he would not have cared a straw if similar destruction had been visited on them all, and they had all been lying on their biers—only excepting the lady. He was quite perturbed that he could hear her but could not see her. Responding to his plea, the girl relieved his distress by opening a window above his head, so that he could see the lady. He saw that she was suffering deep grief. She was saying, "My dear companion, with you has died the most worthy man ever to win the name of knight for his valor and generosity. Never was a shield carried by such a perfect knight. Alas, I don't know why or how you were taken from me. Death should compensate me for all the wrongs he has done me by granting me a single wish: to let me go with you. What shall I

---

18. In *Erec* (lines 5774ff.), Enite expresses similar anger.

do without you? Of what use are goods and life? What shall I do, unhappy woman that I am? Why was I ever born! Alas, how did I lose you? Alas, heart's companion, may God keep you from hell and by his power give you the company of angels, for you were always the best." She was so shattered by grief that she was tearing her hair and maiming herself. When Sir Iwein saw this, he ran to the door, wanting to go to her and stay her hands.

[1483] On seeing this, the girl pulled him back, saying, "Where are you headed? Where did you get such an idea? A great crowd is at the gate, and they're all very angry at you. If you don't listen to me, you're going to die for sure." Her anger deterred him. "What in the world were you thinking of?" she continued, "If you had followed through with your notion, you would have gotten into deep trouble. I can't hope to save your life unless you cooperate. For God's sake, sit still. He is a wise man who can reject stupid thinking in favor of sensible deeds. Whereas he whose mind-set is such that he wants to take action on every wild idea he gets is usually a loser. If some silly idea or other occurs to you, just put it out of your mind. If you have a good idea, though, it is smart to carry it out. Sir, I have to leave you alone now and get back to the courtiers immediately. I'm afraid they will discover that I have joined you. If they miss me, they'll soon grow suspicious." And she departed, leaving him there.

[1519] Although the power of love had seriously overburdened his mind, he still was mindful of one disadvantage he was laboring under: namely, that he could not overcome the mockery he would find at court when he couldn't produce any plausible proof of his success. What good then were all his efforts? And knowing that Kei would never stop mocking him and harming him, he feared being the victim of a trick. These two worries weighed equally on him. Soon, though, one of them prevailed. Lady Love gained the upper hand, seizing and binding him, besetting him irresistibly, and her dominion forced him to ardently love his mortal enemy. The lady had been avenged on him better than she knew, for he was mortally wounded, and Love's hand had inflicted the wounds. Such wounds are supposedly more painful than those inflicted by a sword or a lance. Because someone who is wounded by a weapon recovers quickly if his doctor is handy. But people suppose this wound of love, because of the presence of its doctor, the loved one, results in ever-increasing distress and death.

[1558] Earlier, Love had been spreading uninvited over many a poor place, with scant gain. But now she turned there with full force, so that her dominion would be more complete. One thing is to be regretted: although Love is so mighty that she controls whomever she wishes and constrains every reigning king more easily than she does a child, she is still of such a common nature that she was always humble enough to concern herself with the disreputable and to seek out such ordinary places that are, properly speaking, too petty and distasteful for her. Charming as she is, she has often fallen under the feet of Shame, like someone pouring sweet honey onto bile, even while allowing balsam—for which there is surely a better use—to flow from his hand into the ashes. But Love did nothing wrong in this case, and we shall leave her unscathed. Here she chose a host who will never demean or dishonor her. She comes to the right place and she can stay here with honor. She should always stop at such places.

[1593] After the lord had been buried, the mourners departed, laymen and ecclesiastics returning to their own occupations. The lady remained at the grave, all alone with her sorrow. When Sir Iwein saw her alone, so intensely agitated, so profoundly discomfited, saw her enduring goodness, her wifely loyalty, and her yearning sadness, he loved her all the more. He longed for her so deeply that Lady Love had never exercised greater influence on any man. He reflected, Who, Good God, is so powerfully enabling me to passionately love a woman who is my mortal enemy? How can it happen that she be kind to me, even after the grave offense for which I alone am responsible? I'm certain that I can never gain her favor, for after all, I did kill her husband.

[1621] I can be daunted only by my great despair. I have just one hope to cling to. If Lady Love should become her mistress as she has become mine, I'll bet that in a short time she will make an impropriety seem quite proper. It's not at all impossible, if Lady Love controls her as she did me and guides her to me, no matter how completely I lack her favor now—and even if I had harmed her more than I did—that she would have to give up all her anger and take me into her heart. Lady Love must incline her toward me, because strictly on my own merits I would never be able to lessen her grief. If she knew what forced me to kill her husband, and if she knew how I feel—namely, that in exchange for him I want to give myself and my life—well, then things would be better for me.

[1647] Since Love has taken charge of me, it is highly proper for her to do one of two things: either incline the lady toward me or remove her from my thoughts. Otherwise I am lost. Choosing my mortal enemy to be my beloved was not my idea but rather the command of Love. So it would be improper for Love to desert me. Oh, if she would just act in accordance with her goodness! Happiness and good spirits would suit my lady better than self-hatred. The pain and distress she inflicts on herself should rather be my burden. Alas, what have her beautiful face and body—the equal of which I have never seen—done to her? I certainly don't know what she is avenging on her golden hair and on her body that she should be maiming herself? For she herself is innocent. Sadly, it is I who killed her husband. This punishment and this revenge might better be inflicted on me, and it would be better for her to induce God to leave their marks on my own body. Oh, that good woman, even in such distress, is so truly attractive! If she were liberated from her grief, who could possibly equal her? Surely, God applied all His skill and power, His industry and His talent to this praiseworthy woman—she is an angel, not a woman.

[1691] Thus in joy and sorrow Sir Iwein sat hidden. The window through which he was looking made him happy, because he enjoyed seeing her. Yet on the other hand he feared he might die. So it was that he experienced both joy and pain. He sat there watching her until she went back through the hall. When he saw her walking by, he was barely able to keep from speaking to her! Fear, however, obliged him to exercise restraint. After she had gone through, the gates were closed. Because Iwein's exit was closed off again, he was a prisoner again. That was fine with him, though, because even if both gates had been opened wide and he had been wholly cleared of guilt, so that he would be permitted to go where he wanted, he still would have had no other wish than to stay where he was. And if he had been some-place else, he would have wanted to be back here. His heart was never anywhere but where he knew her to be. For him that was the best place.

[1723] Thus Sir Iwein was sorely pressed by these two afflictions. However well the matter had turned out for him, he would still be dishonored if he should return to court without proof of his story, for it simply would not be believed. On the other hand, he was disturbed by the feeling that he would in no way value all the honor that might otherwise come his way unless he could see the lady who was holding him prisoner. The worthy girl who was protecting him quickly returned and said, "You must be having an unpleasant day and a miserable time in here." "On the contrary," he answered, "I never have had a happier day." "A happier day? Tell me, sir, how does that figure? All around you here you see those who would like to kill you. Can a man who is a captive awaiting death have a good day and a comfort-able time, unless he is actually happy at the prospect of death?" He replied, "I surely have no wish to die. And yet I rejoice in my oppression—and have done so today and even have hope of further happiness."

[1757] Before he had halfway finished speaking, the clever girl realized that he meant her lady, as she afterward gave him to understand. "You may well be happy," she said, "for I will secretly arrange matters in one way or another so that either today or tomorrow I will secretly get you out of here." "If I get out of here secretly and on foot," he said, "I would only gain dishonor and infamy. When I leave here, the whole country will know it." Taking him by the hand, she replied, "I am certainly not telling you to go anywhere. I want to protect you as best I can. Come now, Sir Iwein, to where you will be safer." She took him to a place close by, where all kinds of good things were done for him. She provided him with every bodily comfort that he needed. She took such good care of him that he recovered completely.

[1783] When he was completely at ease, she left him, doing so with the best intentions, for she was striving intently toward his becoming master there. Then she went to her lady with whom she was on such confidential terms that her lady fully shared her secrets with her and was her closest and best friend. The lady followed the girl's advice and guidance more than that of all her other confidants. The girl said, "Now at last people shall see your excellence in the correct and proper way in which you bear your sorrow. It is womanly of you to lament, and you may even lament too much. Our worthy lord has been slain; now may God give you an equally worthy lord." "Do you really think so?" "Yes, lady." "Where would he be?" "Somewhere or other." "You are mad, or else you are joking. Even if our Lord God had devoted all His effort to it, He never would have created a better man. So whether God wills it or not, right up to my death my yearning and mourning will never end. May God give me death, so that I can follow my lord. You will lose my friendship if you ever praise another man as his equal—because you are talking nonsense."

[1819] The girl replied, "Let me say one thing to you that you ought to consider, whether you take it amiss or favorably. Your situation is not what you assume. If you don't want to lose your spring, your land, and the respect of others, you must choose someone who can defend your spring and save it for you. Unless there is someone to defend it, many a brave knight will come to take it from you by force.[19] And one thing you don't know: a messenger just came to my lord. When he found him dead, though, and you in such distress he said nothing to you but instead asked me to tell you that in twelve days, perhaps sooner, King Arthur will arrive at the spring with his knights. Unless there is someone to defend it, your honor is lost. But if you have chosen someone from your retinue to defend it, then you are quite deceived. For if all the courage of your retinue were concentrated in one of its members, he would still not be a very courageous man. Whoever claims to be the best of them never would dare to come to the defense of the spring, because King Arthur is bringing a war party selected from the most courageous men ever born.

---

19. For the similar plight of a woman ruler, see *Gregorius*, lines 2199ff.

Therefore, lady, be warned: if you do not want to lose both the spring and the country without a fight, forsake your melancholy mood and prepare a defense before it's too late. Only with the best of intentions do I advise you thus."

[1863] However accurately the truth had been expounded to her, and however clearly she understood, still she did what women do: by nature they contradict what they often regard as good. Quite a few people reproach them for doing what they have vowed not to do. Yet this impresses me as a good idea, and whoever says that this is a result of their inconstancy is mistaken. I have a better idea of why they are often seen as being of a wavering nature. It comes from their goodness. Such a wrong state of mind can certainly be changed to goodness, and yet goodness can't convert to a wrong state of mind. Such changeability is good; and none of them behaves otherwise. Whoever then accuses women of inconstancy—of him I am no follower. I impute nothing but good to women. May everything good befall them!

[1889] In her grief the lady said, "I lament my misery to God that I cannot die right now. I am not happy that I should ever have to live a single day longer than my lord. And if I could find a knife or sword and exchange my life for death, without mortal sin, I would instantly do so. If I can't escape having to exchange my husband for another man, the world will not understand it in the way that God does. He knows very well that I wouldn't do it if my land could be guaranteed peace under me alone. Advise me, Love, what to do, if any advice can help. Since I cannot secure peace for my country without a champion, I will gladly get one— and no one else—whom I would know to be so brave that he would secure peace for my land, but without being my husband."

[1917] The girl replied, "I beg to differ. Who would ever undertake such an effort for you, unless he were your husband? You are talking just like a woman. Even if you were to give him your possessions and your person, you could count it an unexpected boon if he did his part with enthusiasm. You have youth and beauty, noble birth, wealth, and respect. So you can easily win a worthy man, God willing. Now weep no more and remember your honor; certainly, lady, that is essential. My lord is dead, but only he. Do you think the whole world's courage has gone to the grave with him? That is not at all the case. There are still a hundred knights, all of whom are better than him with the sword, the shield, and the lance." "You have spoken falsely." "Lady, I have spoken the truth." "Then show me one of them." "If you would stop crying, I would quite easily find him for you." "I don't know what to do with you—because the idea seems impossible to me. God help you if you are lying to me and trying to dupe me." "Lady, if I have lied to you, then I have duped myself because I have always been with you and my fate is tied to yours. If I were to delude you, what would become of me? You shall be my judge. Decide this for me (you are a woman too): when two knights are locked in mortal combat, which is better: the one who wins or the one who lies vanquished?" "The one who wins, I suppose." "Lady, it is not a matter of supposition. It is simply the truth. As I've told you: a certain man has properly defeated our lord. I assert that in opposition to you, for you have buried him. I want to make it amply evident: the knight who chased him down and killed him has proved the more worthy. Our lord is dead and the other knight is alive."

[1971] The assertion that someone else was superior to her lord pained the lady's heart. She spoke rudely to the girl, telling her to get out immediately, because she never wanted to see her again. The girl said, "I may suffer for my devotion but I do so gladly and do not regret it. I much prefer to be driven off because of my loyalty than to remain and be faithless. I'm leaving you now, lady, and once I am sent away, then for God's sake reflect on what is needful and good for you. Only with the best of intentions have I given you my advice. In case I never see you again, may God bring you honor and good fortune."

[1993] Arising, she went off to the hidden knight and brought him the bad news: that her lady's mind was not about to be changed, that she could in no way persuade her lady to do what was best, and that she had received only anger and threats. This made Sir Iwein unhappy. The girl and Iwein considered how they might better seek with kindness to change the lady's hatred to a milder attitude.

[2009] After the lady had driven the girl away and she found herself alone, she very much regretted having so badly repaid the girl's deep loyalty, the girl's deep devotion to her—for she had cursed and scolded her. "What have I done?" she thought. "I ought to have rewarded her for serving me so well. I know quite well that she advised me as she did only out of devotion. Whenever I have taken her advice, it hasn't harmed me. And this time, too, she told me the truth. I've known her for a long time, and she is faithful and good. I made a mistake in sending her away. I could curse my angry behavior, because all that one gains from that is shame and hurt. It would most likely be better for me to invite her back. I was angry with her without good reason. My lord was brave enough, but the knight who killed him would have to be even braver; otherwise he would not have been able to chase him back here. She spoke the truth about that.

[2039] "I have plenty of reason to be hostile toward whoever it was who killed him. Yet when you look at the matter correctly, that knight was also innocent, because he did what he did while he was defending himself. After all, my husband tried to kill him. Had the stranger indulged my husband for my sake and spared him, I would have cost him too dearly, for then he would be dead himself. He was forced to slay him." In this way she prepared her mind to be kind and conciliatory and absolved him of doing her any wrong. Mighty Lady Love was ready at hand, a true conciliator between men and women. The lady thought, "By myself I cannot defend the spring. A brave man has to protect me, or I am truly lost. God knows, I'll leave off my anger and, if it is possible, desire none other than the man who killed my husband. If he passes muster in other ways, I shall marry him, and then he must faithfully atone for my grief. And because he has done me harm he must treat me all the better."

[2073] She was so uneasy about having berated the girl that she regretted it deeply. Early next morning, when the girl returned, she was received more graciously than she had been dismissed. The lady's gracious reception relieved her own distress. They had not been sitting together very long before the lady started to question her, saying, "For God's sake, who is this man whose praises you were singing to me yesterday and who killed my husband? (I don't believe you were out of your mind after all, because he is certainly not a coward.) If he is of noble birth and not too old and has other good qualities, so that he would be suitable to be my husband; if, when people hear about it, they can't reproach me for having taken a husband who has killed my former lord; if you can declare to me that my shameful misfortune will be compensated by his many excellent qualities; and, finally, if you advise me to, I will take him as a husband."

[2101] "That seems like a good idea to me," said the girl. "I am glad to see you have changed your mind so sensibly. It does you honor to be united with him; you will never need to be ashamed of it." "Tell me his name," said the lady, "My lady, his name is Sir Iwein." They were in immediate agreement. The lady said, "I have known of him for a long time. He is the son of King Urien. At last I really understand everything. If he will be mine, I'm in luck. But do you really know, my friend, if he will have me?" "He wishes it had already happened." "Tell me, when can I see him?" "Within four days, my lady." "Alas, what in God's name are you saying? You are making me wait too long. Arrange for me to see him today or tomorrow." "How do you expect that to happen, my lady? I cannot guarantee you that. No one is fast enough to go there and return in so short a time — not unless he has wings. You surely know how far it is." "Then follow my advice. My page is a fast runner. In one day he can go as far on foot as someone can ride in two days. He will be helped by the moonlight, which turns night into day. Also, the days now are unusually long. Tell him I will be forever grateful to him and that if he is back by tomorrow it will redound to his benefit for a long time. Tell him to run swiftly and turn four days into two. Have him hurry now, and afterward he can rest for as long as he wants. Urge him to do it, dear friend."

[2147] "I will do so," replied the girl. "There is one other thing you should do: send for your people today and tomorrow. Without their consent you really cannot marry anyone. A person who follows good advice rarely fails, but if a person does something on his own, and it turns out poorly, then he has lost in two ways: he must endure the injury as well as his friends' anger." "Oh, dear friend," said the lady, "I'm afraid things won't work out well for me: my people may withhold their consent." "Do not fret about it, my lady. You won't find a champion anywhere who wouldn't let you marry whomever you want in preference to defending the spring himself. Your plan will find ready acceptance. Your people will be only too happy not to have anything to do with defending the country. When they hear your plan, they'll be falling at your feet and pleading with you to marry him." "Send the page on his way now," the lady answered. "Meanwhile I will also send my messengers to my people, so that we can carry out our plan."

[2177] The girl quickly summoned Iwein, and in an instant he was there. The page did as she instructed, concealing himself, for he was game for any kind of clever deception. He knew how to help her lie and dupe in a good cause. When the lady got the idea that the page was under way—which wasn't at all the case— the girl got the knight ready. May God reward her. She first gave him a fine bath. Then there were three kinds of clothing ready: gray fur, multicolored fur, and ermine. For the slain lord had always been a courtly man who knew how to dress and had the finery to do so. She picked out the best clothing for Iwein and dressed him in it. The next evening she went to where she found her lady alone, and she quickly made her blanch and blush for joy. She said, "Give me the messenger's reward. Your page has returned." "What news have you heard?" "Good news." "Tell me!" "My lord Iwein is here too." "How did he get here so soon?" "Love impelled him." "Tell me, for God's sake, who else knows about it?" "No one knows it yet, my lady. Just we two and the page." "Why not bring him here to me? Go. I'll wait for him here." When the girl went to fetch him, out of pure mischievousness she acted as if she had been sent to him with bad news. On catching sight of him, she hung her head and said sadly, "I don't know what to do. My lady knows you are here and she is very angry at me. I have lost her favor by keeping you here. She commands me to bring you to her." "I'd rather die than miss the chance to see her." "How could a woman capture you then?" "Well, she has a big army of peo-

ple." "You won't have to defend yourself. I have her word that she will in no way
harm you. She just wants to see you privately. You must surrender to her; other
than that she'll leave you unharmed." "She is a perfect woman," he said. "I am
glad that my body will always be her prisoner—and my heart too!"

[2245] He rose and went to her joyously, as if blessed by fate. But he was still
received in an unfriendly way. For as he approached, she said nothing and did not
bow. Her continued silence troubled him greatly, and he didn't know what to do
other than sit down at a distance and look at her shyly.

[2255] Since neither of them said anything, the girl spoke up, "Sir Iwein, how
is it you are so daunted? Are you alive, do you have a mouth? You were talking just
recently. When did you become a mute? Tell me, for God's sake, why are you flee-
ing from such a beautiful woman? May God damn the person who reluctantly
brings to a beautiful woman a man who can talk nicely but who then crassly avoids
her. You might better sit a little closer. I promise you, my lady won't bite you.
Whoever has done such wrong to another person, as you have done, has to be more
obliging if he wants to be forgiven. You have killed King Ascalon, her dearly beloved
husband. Who is going to forgive you for that? You bear a heavy burden of guilt—
seek her mercy now. And let us both ask her to please forget her distress." At that,
he sat no longer. Quickly falling to his knees before her, he acknowledged his guilt
and sought her mercy and her recognition. He said, "I cannot offer you more by
way of atonement and homage than that you yourself judge me. Whatever you
wish, that I too wish."

[2291] "You will comply with whatever I wish?" "Yes, that seems to be by no
means too much." "Then I'll perhaps take your life." "As you command, lovely
woman." "What is the point, then, of making a long speech? Since you have vol-
untarily put yourself in my power, it would be most unladylike of me if I should
then take your life. Sir Iwein, don't think I am being inconstant when I pardon
you so quickly. You have done me such harm that I would not and should not be
in such haste to pardon you, if I had my status and my property, as other ladies do.
Now I am compelled to hurry because I am in such a situation that today or tomor-
row I can easily lose my country. Before then I must provide my country with a
husband who will defend it for me. Since the killing of the king there is no one
in my army to do that. So within a very few days I must choose a husband or else
lose my land. I ask you not to say anything more about it. Since you have killed
my husband, you must be such a thoroughly brave man that if God gives you to
me, I will be well protected against all foreign arrogance. Believe me, rather than
give you up I would rather give up woman's customary prerogative—for it is hardly

the usual thing for a woman to ask a man to marry her.[20] But I ask you to marry me. I will not put on any more airs: I will marry you gladly; do you want me?" "Lady, if I said no, I would be an ill-starred man. This is the happiest day I have ever known. May God preserve my good fortune: that we shall be man and wife."

[2340] "Oh my lord Iwein," said the queen. "Who has brought about this love between us? I can't imagine who in the world gave you the notion that, after all the pain you have caused me, I would ever become your wife." "No one advised me but my own self." "Yes, but who, for God's sake, advised your own self?" "It was the command of my heart." "Yes, but who told your heart?" "My eyes." "Who advised your eyes then?" "An adviser you can be happy about: your beauty and nothing else." "Since each of us declares he is in love with the other one," the queen said, "who is going to keep us from resolving the matter? None of us three will manage that. Let's go to my people. Yesterday I summoned the best from all over my country: we shall hide nothing from them. I have thoroughly briefed them as to my desire. Let us consult with them—it will certainly be best that way." And they did so.

[2371] Walking hand in hand, they entered the hall. When the people saw Sir Iwein, they declared they had never seen such a splendid man, and they were not lying. For their part, never had a knight been better received than Iwein was then. The people looked at him as if he were a marvel, asking each other, "Who brought this knight here? God willing, it is he whom my lady should marry." Never had a knight pleased them so well. They led him in through the midst of the throng, and he and the lady sat down together. The lady asked her seneschal to speak for her, to tell them that she requested them all to give their approval to her choice of this husband. They said that that was fine with them and that nothing had ever pleased them more. A horse that wants to run runs even better if someone spurs it. It wasn't hard for them to persuade her to do what was already her will and her joy. I believe they did the right thing, because even if it had seemed a mistake to them, she would still have married him.

[2403] After the seneschal had given out his lady's statement, as she requested, and after they had also heard that within two weeks King Arthur was coming there with his army, as he had sworn, and that if he found the spring undefended, it would certainly be lost, and after they had been accurately informed of Iwein's lineage and prowess (they had already seen how splendid he looked), they fittingly declared the marriage to be a good thing that did them honor. What is the point of more dis-

20. Compare *Erec*, lines 5886ff.

cussion? Everything was perfectly set up, there were plenty of priests at hand who promptly married them,[21] giving over to Iwein both the lady and the land.

[2421] Lady Laudine was his wife's name. Her qualities were such that she was able to make life sweet for him: she had noble birth, youth, beauty, and wealth. He to whom God has given loyalty and other manifestations of a noble spirit, total excellence as well, as He had to Sir Iwein, and the merit of a good wife, who wants only what her husband wants—to him God has given great happiness, if the two live long with love. In their case there was every reason to expect this. The wedding festivities soon began, and the dead man was forgotten. The latter's land and power were taken over by the survivor—everything was turned over to the survivor. Neither before nor since did the country know a bigger wedding. There was delight and honor, pleasure and knightly deeds, an abundance of everything a man would desire. The knightly games lasted until King Arthur entered the country, as he had vowed to do, and with his army proceeded to the spring. The spring then needed a good defense. A coward would not be suitable as its master, because never at one time had so many good knights come there.

[2454] Sir Kei was happy at having found an opportunity for mockery. He said, "Sir Kalogrenant, where is your cousin, Sir Iwein? Things still look like they did earlier, and I believe they will always look this way. He spoke after drinking wine, when he avenged you here with words. Oh my! How he struck and stabbed! If one more drink had been brought to him, he would have killed twelve giants! Such is his valor. If he intends to avenge you, then he's late getting here, and your avenger— that's going to be me! Again I must confront hardship, as I have often done when I stood up for my friend. Those who talk a lot about their own accomplishments when no one believes them—I don't know why they do it or what they are punishing themselves for. It is easy to fight when no one retaliates. Now, to his own disgrace, he has eluded us. He was afraid to come here because he imagined he would have to face danger, although I surely would have excused him.

[2485] "Many worthless men debase the virtuous on any occasion they can. Performing no brave deeds themselves, it is a source of grief to them if honor accrues to someone else. But look! I don't do that; for I am happy to grant honor to every man, I praise him when he does things right and I keep quiet when he runs into misfortune—that is only right. It is also right that I should be successful, because no one speaks of his own deeds less than I do. Still, the worthless man gets ahead by praising himself, for no one likes to make a fool of himself by praising another's

---

21. A similar (ironic?) statement can be found in *Poor Heinrich*, line 1512.

incompetence. Sir Iwein is not wise. If he were, he would be able to keep silent, as I do."

[2504] This speech seemed ridiculous to the others—that he seemed so good in his own eyes—for never did any knight have such a malicious nature. Sir Gawein said, "Wait a minute now, Sir Kei, you are claiming you are free of malicious talk? But how does it look? It looks like you are showing a deep hatred of this good warrior. You do him an injustice. He has never thought other than well of you, as one knight should of another. And as to the fact that he hasn't showed up here: perhaps on this occasion some important deed has occupied him so that it was impossible for him to get here. So for God's sake, shut your mouth." "I will do so," said Sir Kei. "I thought I was addressing the matter properly. One might as well do evil as good, since no one is going to talk about it. I'll say no more—the honor is yours."

[2529] King Arthur took the basin he found hanging there, filled it from the spring, and, wanting to find out if the celebrated story was true or false—that was the reason he had come there—he drenched the stone. The weather then turned so violent that it struck fear into all who had come there, and they almost despaired of being spared. Then Sir Iwein quickly rode from the castle in full armor, because he knew quite well that if he failed to protect his spring, it would be taken from him.

[2557] Sir Kei, also armed, was ready. He wanted the first joust, and the king had already granted it to him. Sir Iwein rode rapidly out of the forest, galloping onto the field, decked out like an angel. He was aided by his steed as well as his own courage, both of which were first-rate. His heart was delighted when he saw waiting there the knight who turned everything good into bad. He was delighted, too, that God so honored him as to let him repay Kei for the latter's crude abuse and incessant mockery. For this opportunity he praised God. I'll tell you something else: however malicious Kei was, he was still very brave. If his tongue hadn't ruined him, the court would never have had a worthier hero. You can tell this, if you wish, by the position he held. Had he been different, that is, a coward, King Arthur would not for a moment have kept him in his castle as a seneschal.

[2575] Both knights shared the same wish. Each was thinking of the other's fame, but their success was unequal. It was a good and well-fought joust. Sir Kei, however worthless you may think him, shattered his lance clear up to his hand. At the same moment, though, he was lifted out of his saddle like a sack, so that when he landed he didn't know where he was lying.[22] That done, Iwein was reluctant to dishonor him further other than to say mockingly, when he saw him lying there before

22. Kei suffers a similar fate at the hands of Erec. Compare *Erec*, lines 4704–34.

him, "Why in God's name are you lying there? You always taunted those who failed through no fault of their own. Did you fall unintentionally? Unless I'm mistaken, you wanted to fall, for it couldn't have happened otherwise. You just wanted to see what falling was like. Well, it's degrading."

[2601] After he had gotten Kei's horse and taken it to the king, he said, "Sir, I have won this horse.[23] Have someone in your retinue come and take charge of it. I don't want any possession of yours unless I get it in a different way." Thanking him cordially, the king asked, "Who are you, sir?" "I am Iwein." "Well, for God's sake!" "I'm not joking, sir," said Iwein. "I am he." He then told the king how he had become lord of the land. Everybody was pleased at his winning and at Kei's disgrace, but no one was as pleased as Sir Gawein, for between them there had always been a true friendship, and their mutual fame was now all the greater. Sir Kei, having taken a very hard fall, was still lying there, to everyone's amusement. If such disgrace had been visited—as it often had on Kei—on a proper man, with any real sense of shame, that man would have fled people forever. Kei's body hurt, but everything else was nothing to him, for the weight of disgrace had already burdened his back. But because he was used to disgrace, he wasn't the least bit unhappy about his plight.

[2643] So the conflict ended with his misfortune, and loud laughter at his disgrace. The others could not begrudge Iwein his land or the spring or his honor. He had so gained their admiration that they had no other idea but that of spreading his fame.

[2653] At Iwein's request King Arthur rode back with him to the castle. There no imaginable insufficiency or intention could keep the hospitality from being so good that the king had never enjoyed himself so much beyond the boundaries of his own country. However, nothing could equal the joy and festivities in Arthur's own country, and it is inconceivable that anything on earth could ever equal it.

[2663] The queen, pleased with the guest, said to Sir Iwein, "Companion and lord, I thank you deeply for bringing our esteemed guest here. I will always be obliged to you." She had good reason to be happy, because until this moment she wasn't certain that she had married well. Now there was no doubt about it, and for the first time she was truly fond of her husband. When, thanks to him, she had the honor of meeting the king, she rightly perceived that she had been lucky and that her husband had won the spring with courage and defended it heroically. "I have chosen well," she thought.

23. Compare *Erec*, note 86.

[2682] If a guest is not a complete fool, he quickly senses what his host thinks of him; because, if he is unwelcome, some evidence of distress will be manifest to him. If a man is put up by a well-disposed host, he enjoys the entertainment and the food all the more. Yet without good will there is not good hospitality. In this castle King Arthur found both the will to please and the actual pleasure. And Sir Gawein, who was nothing if not courtly and good, showed his loyalty to his friend, Sir Iwein. As wise men like to put it, there is no greater force than when a friendship between two unrelated people turns out well. They will be loyal to each other even when brothers would part. Such was the relationship between the host and Sir Gawein. They loved each other so much that each of them shared the joy and the sorrow of the other. In this respect the sensible Sir Gawein showed his courtliness, and I'll tell you how.

[2717] Lunete was the name of the girl who had acted with such good sense, saving Sir Iwein from great distress by using her wits. Gawein sat down by her and thanked her warmly for having brought such honor to his friend, Sir Iwein, because it was owing to her that he had survived various dangers unharmed and had become lord of the land. For that reason he was grateful for her loyalty. When someone is happy to give help, it is surely a good thing to offer him thanks, so that he doesn't grow weary of it—because it does take effort. And the person who fails to offer thanks, so that one gets angry at him—he can perhaps draw a lesson from it.

[2739] "Lady Lunete," said Sir Gawein, "your help and intercession have made me very happy for the best friend I have. He told me everything about how your sensitive intervention brought him this honor, with which he is well satisfied. Thanks to you he has a beautiful wife, a rich land, his very life, and whatever one desires in this world. If I were so highly regarded and so worthy that a woman might be honored through me, I would have no greater happiness than to devote my life to you in exchange for my friend's crown, which he wears thanks to you." With this, an enduring friendship was formed between the two. In their castle Lady Laudine and Sir Iwein offered King Arthur such honors that nobody could possibly be displeased.

[2763] After the guests had been there for seven nights it was time for them to leave. While they were getting ready to ride off, the faithful Sir Gawein took Sir Iwein aside, saying, "It's no wonder that a lucky man, endowed with courage, and knowing how to strive for excellence, is accorded great honor. But many strive every day as best they can and do not gain honor. Luck is not with them. But your endeavors have been blessed with fortune. Your efforts have won you a beautiful wife as well as lands. Now, since fortune has smiled on you, watch out that your wife's beauty does not expose you to scorn. Beware, friend, that you do not soon repeat the mistake of those who, because of their wives, are reproached for losing their honor owing to sloth. Do not turn wholly to a comfortable life, as Sir Erec did, who, because of Lady Enite, idled about for a long while. If he had not recovered later and done what a knight should, his honor would have been forfeit. He loved too much.[24]

[2799] "You have all you need to be satisfied. Meanwhile I'm going to instruct you how to preserve your honor: you ought to leave with us, and we'll take part in knightly contests as before. Because if your knightliness vanishes, I'll forever regret having known you. Many a man excuses himself, saying that when one is married, it is then part of householding to avoid, for a while, practicing knighthood as well as giving parties. He claims he needs to attend to household matters. He gives up social pleasures as well as clothes styled and tailored according to knightly fashion. Whatever he puts on to keep warm, he calls it the household fashion. Going around unkempt, barelegged, and barefooted, he takes to complaining about life. The second thing he always tells a visitor is this: 'since I've become a landowner—nobody believes this—I've never gone more than half a year without having to buy grain. This year I am ruined. Sorry I have to bother you about it, but the hail has ruined the best field I have. I'm afraid I'll have to give up my castle. One way or another I could get by but I still have to worry about my wife. I have no idea what I'll do with her. Whoever has a household inevitably has a lot of grief, and no one has a clue as to what it costs. If I could manage the household problem, then all my other worldly problems would evaporate.'

[2845] "So he commences lamenting and whining and telling his guest so many sad stories that the latter wishes he had never come there. The host is right, but not completely so. A household has to cost a rather large sum, and whoever really wants it to contribute to his fame must stay at home all the more often. But occasionally he also has to give some indication that he still has some knightly spirit, and that is done by attending those tournaments that he ought to attend. I know what I am talking about. For whose sake could a good man be better esteemed than for that of his good wife? If he has renounced honor and desires to idle away his time in her company, and then, like a man of no breeding, asserts that he's doing it all for her sake—she should never accept that. For his worthlessness and idleness will drive her to exasperation. However fond of him she is, if he is around too much, it will vex her. Many wives, out of fear of their husbands, pretend that

24. A central issue in *Erec*. Compare *Erec*, lines 2966ff. and note 99.

they're not bothered by this, but such enjoyment as he may get from idling around at home with her—nobody's going to envy him that.[25]

[2879] "You have acquired a queen and a land, but if this becomes your ruination, then I'll bet a worthy man without land would be richer. Think about this, Sir Iwein, and leave with us. With affection get the queen's consent to a leave of suitable length, commending people and land to her care. A wife in whom one has seen such steadfastness requires no more in the way of overseers than her own honor. Overseers are appropriate for faithless women and for girls who are so foolish that even the advice of an old woman can induce them to do wrong.

[2899] "I wouldn't want you to change the way you have lived up till now, seeking honors as a proper knight. So now, more than ever, you have the right to see that your fame spreads and grows. If sometimes you have been bothered by having much less wealth than good intentions, now your riches complement your good intentions. Be happy and valiant. Thanks to us two, the tournaments in many lands will be enriched. So take my advice, Sir Iwein."

[2913] Iwein immediately sought and found his wife. When he presented his request, she did not have the slightest notion that he would ask for anything she wouldn't gladly grant. She quickly regretted her assent, though, when he asked permission to participate in tournaments. "I should have been on watch against that," she said, but she could not prevail, and he took leave for a whole year. She swore that if he stayed away any longer, she would never forgive him. He swore too, compelled by love, that even a year seemed too long, he would not be away any longer than that, and he would, if he could, return sooner, unless prevented by such valid hindrances as sickness, prison, or death.

[2935] "You know quite well," she said, "that our honor and our country are very much hanging in the balance, and that if you don't come back in time, we may suffer great damage. Today is the eighth day after the solstice, and that is when your year will be up. So be back then or earlier—I won't wait for you any longer. Let this ring bear witness to our agreement. I have never loved a man enough to lend or give him this gold ring. So life must be all the kinder to him who wears it and contemplates it. Do not lose it, Sir Iwein. Its stone has the power to give good fortune and happiness. Lucky is he who wears it."

[2956] King Arthur was now ready and, taking leave, rode off. Lady Laudine rode with her husband fifteen miles or more. The parting saddened her greatly, and that was reflected in the way she acted. As best he could, Sir Iwein masked his

---

25. Compare *Erec*, lines 9417–42.

longing for her with a smile, but his eyes were misty. To tell the truth, he would have wept openly, were it not for his pride. King Arthur rode to his own land, and the lady rode back home.

[2971] Lady Love then put a question to me that I was not clever enough to answer. "Tell me, Hartmann," she said, "do you claim that King Arthur took Sir Iwein to his castle and let his wife ride back home?" I could only defend myself by saying it was true, for it was told me as fact. Looking at me askance, she said, "You have it wrong, Hartmann." "Lady, I have it right." "No," she replied, and our dispute continued for quite a while before she got me onto the right track, so that I could agree with her. Arthur had led both the man and wife away, and yet neither of them followed him, as I will now explain to you. They exchanged hearts between them, the lady and Sir Iwein. Her heart in Iwein's breast followed the king, while Iwein's heart in her body remained behind.[26]

[2995] At that I said, "My dear Lady Love, to my mind it seems that Sir Iwein is lost, if he has taken leave of his heart, because that is what has given him strength and boldness. How can he be up to doing knightly deeds now? He will be as hesitant as a woman because he has a woman's heart, while she has a man's. She will perform manly deeds and might well participate in tournaments, while he stays home and takes care of the castle. I am really very sorry that both their natures have been altered by the exchange of hearts, for neither has been helped by it."

[3011] Lady Love accused me of being not quite right in the head. "Shut your mouth," she said. "You know nothing of how best to live, because you were never touched by my power. I am Love and I often enable men and women to lose their hearts and be all the stronger because of it." I didn't dare inquire further because I had never seen such a wonder as men and women living without hearts. In this case, though, it happened as she said. All I know about their exchange of hearts is what the story tells us: Sir Iwein was surely a great hero before this time and a better one afterward.

[3029] His friend Sir Gawein turned out to be his downfall. I am obliged to tell you how, because it is in general unusual for a person to lose by choosing a good comrade. In fact this had never happened before. But it happened to Sir Iwein, and I'll tell you how. Sir Gawein was the most courtly man who ever attained the name of knight. If he caused Iwein any grief, he was sorry for it, and he devoted all his efforts to serving Iwein by increasing his fame. Whenever they took part in a tournament—which was often—there occurred such deeds of knighthood that God him-

26. For a similar image, compare *Erec*, lines 2358–67, and *Gregorius*, lines 651–54.

self might be honored to witness. He helped Iwein in every way, even arranging matters so that the prize went to Iwein more often than anyone else until, however, too many days had elapsed. Iwein passed the time happily. It is said that Sir Gawein detained him and pressed good times on him, causing him to forget his deadline and to overlook his vow until well along in August, as the next year began.

[3059] They had just come, full of happiness, from a tournament at which Sir Iwein had won the praise of both sides. Their lord, King Arthur, was now hosting a festival at his castle at Karidol. They pitched their tent on the field in front of the castle and were resting comfortably there, until the king together with his highest nobles saw them and cried out in joy, for they had heard reports of their success. The king thanked them repeatedly for having performed so well and so consistently. It is a good idea to compliment him who likes to act honorably: it makes him feel better about his effort. Wherever people sat talking, the conversation was only about Iwein and Gawein. Then Sir Iwein began to reflect longingly, and it occurred to him that he had been away from his wife for too long, that he had disregarded both her command and her request. His heart was heavy with devotion and yearning, and he was overcome by such deep regret that he forgot everything else and just sat there quietly, like a fool, not hearing, not seeing what people were saying and doing. Bad news was coming, of which he had a premonition. That has happened with me, too: when I am happy, I sigh at my coming misfortune. Thus his grief, too, was approaching. Look! Someone's riding up. It is Lady Lunete, his wife's emissary, through whose good offices he had been selected in the first place. Racing across the field, she dismounted in front of the tents.

[3109] The instant she saw the king, she approached him and said, "King Arthur, my lady has dispatched me to your land. She told me to greet you on her behalf, and all your companions as well, except one, who is excluded and should be repugnant to you as a traitor. That is Sir Iwein. When I first knew him, he didn't seem to be the type who would be disloyal and cause pain to the person to whom he had pledged to be faithful. His words are noble, his character is anything but. My lady is a woman, and so it is true, Christ knows, that she can't avenge herself. If he had feared retaliation, he would surely have avoided doing her wrong like this. To him, it didn't seem sufficient harm to have killed her husband; he had to abuse her even more by depriving her of her honor and her existence.

[3137] "Sir Iwein, since my lady's youth, beauty, wealth, and virtue had no effect on you, why didn't you at least remember what I've done for you, and allow her to benefit from my coming to your aid when I saved your life? You would have been doomed if I hadn't intervened. I will always regret intervening and not just letting you die. It's all my fault, even though I acted out of loyalty. On my advice she ignored the pain and distress you had caused her. I said too much to her about your excellent qualities, until she voluntarily gave you herself and her country, which you were supposed to protect. When you treat a woman the way you treated her, no woman can defend herself against it. True, we reacted to you too impetuously, but we deserved a better reward than what we received from you. It was not what you had promised.

[3167] "Although what you have done is disgraceful and unjust, my lady will get along fine. She is too noble and too powerful for you to treat like a concubine, even if it were now to dawn on you what knightly faithfulness is. Loyalty is a matter of indifference to you, but you should reap all the more scorn from all those who love loyalty and honor and who realize that no one can be noble who is without loyalty.

[3181] "I will now proclaim to these lords that from this moment on they should regard you as a traitor. (And when you became one, I became a disloyal perjurer as well.) As much as the king esteems loyalty and honor, if he keeps you here any longer in the role of knight, he will always have reason to be ashamed. From now on you are to stay away from my lady. She wants to go on living even without you. And give her ring back. It is no longer to be worn on a faithless hand. That is why she sent me to retrieve it." In his deep sorrow, Iwein just sat there and let her take the ring off his hand. Bowing to the king, she left.

[3201] The disdain with which Lady Lunete had treated Sir Iwein, her abrupt departure, the blow to his honor from the way she left him, uncomforted and unhelped, the insult that she should question his loyalty, the belated regret, the underlying constancy of his heart, the loss of his country, and the grieving for his wife—all this robbed him utterly of his reason and happiness. In his despair he yearned only to be somewhere unknown to both men and women, who also would not have heard the news of where he had gone.

[3221] Unable to put the blame on anyone else, he lost his self-respect. He had in effect been killed by his own sword. He was concerned with neither man nor woman, only with himself. Without anyone's seeing him, he quietly stole away until he was out of sight of the tents and in the open field. His remorse grew so great that anger and rage assaulted his brain. Breaking with custom and good breeding, he tore off his clothing until he was as bare as one's hand, and he ran naked across the fields toward the wilderness.[27]

27. Compare *Gregorius*, lines 2721–78 and note 103.

[3239] After the girl had ridden off, the king, deeply troubled by Sir Iwein's misfortune, asked where he was. He asked that someone go after him because he wanted to be of assistance. When Iwein was not found, they called out, but without success, for he was running to the woods. He was a proven warrior, a fearless hero. But as heroic as he was, and as steadfast in body and mind, still Lady Love enabled a frail woman to transform both his body and mind. For he who had been a real jewel of knightly virtue was now, in no time at all, running about in the forest, a fool.

[3261] Beneficent God, Who had still not wholly withdrawn His protection, now allowed a page to meet up with him. The page had a good bow, which Iwein took from him, together with many arrows. When he was hungry, he did as fools do, who, even if they know nothing else, still know how to feed their mouths. He was a splendid shot, and the woods were full of game. He shot a goodly amount of what he aimed at. Lacking hounds, he had to chase down the game himself. And since he had neither kettle nor lard, neither salt nor pepper, his sauce was the pangs of hunger, which broiled and stewed the game, making it a delicious meal that satisfied his hunger.

[3283] After he had been doing this for a long time, one day about noon he came to a recent clearing. There he discovered a lone man, who could easily see that he wasn't in his right mind. For safety the man fled into the hut nearby. Still not feeling safe, he bolted the door fast, before which stood the madman, who seemed to him all too huge. He thought, "If he gives a push, the door will come off its hinges and I'll be done for. Poor me! How can I save myself?" Finally he reflected, "If I give him some of my bread, maybe he will let me live." Extending his hand through a window in the wall, he placed a loaf of bread on the window sill.

[3306] The pangs of hunger, God knows, made it taste good to the madman, who had never before bitten into anything quite so wretched. What do you expect a madman to do? He ate the bread, drank some water he found in a bucket by the wall, and promptly left. The hermit, watching him go, prayed fervently to God to spare him such guests forever. After all, he had no idea what the story was concerning his guest. The madman wasted no time in demonstrating that fools and children adapt easily. For he was smart enough to return for more food in two days, carrying on his back a deer, which he threw down by the door. That made the hermit more willing to offer him bread and water. No longer afraid, he was friendlier than before and thereafter always had bread and water ready. The game repaid his efforts. It was roasted over the fire without any added ingredients, because the hermit had no salt, pepper, or vinegar. Finally he got into the habit of selling the skins and buying for the two of them what they needed most: salt and better bread.

[3345] So the demented man stayed in the forest and lived on this food until the noble fool's whole body resembled that of a Moor. In no way did he resemble the man who was so well regarded by a high-born lady, who had broken a hundred lances, who had struck fire from a helmet, who had bravely won praise and honor, who had been courtly and wise, noble and rich. For now he ran around bereft of his clothing and his senses, until one noon when three ladies found him lying asleep beside the highway on which they were riding. As soon as one of the ladies caught sight of him, she bent over him and looked carefully. Everyone had been talking of his disappearance, which was a well-circulated tale throughout the land. It was partly owing to this report that she recognized him—but only partly. For she also noticed one of his scars that had been well known for a long time. She quickly spoke his name and, looking back toward the other two ladies, said, "My lady, if Sir Iwein is alive, then there is no doubt that this is he lying here, or else I've never seen him." Her graciousness and kindness made her feel so depressed that, moved by her deep sorrow and her pure sympathy, she began to weep bitterly that such a disgrace should befall so worthy a man and that he should be seen in such a shameful state.

[3395] She then said to the lady who was mistress of the two others, "Lady, you can see very well that he has lost his mind. Never was a knight born of better breeding than Sir Iwein, whom I see here in such an ignoble condition. Either he has eaten something poisonous, or else love is responsible for his losing his mind. And, my lady, I am as sure of this as I am of my own death: if we heal him, you will be relieved of all the hardship that Count Aliers in his arrogance has imposed upon you and still intends to impose upon you. Sir Iwein's bravery is well known to me. If his life is saved, he will quickly take care of the count. If you are to be saved from the count, it must be with Sir Iwein's help."

[3419] Happy at this assurance, the lady replied, "If Sir Iwein's sickness comes from his brain, I can easily help him, because I have still a salve that the fairy Morgan le Fay[28] made with her own hands. It is so constituted that anyone suffering madness will swiftly regain his well-being and his health, upon being treated with it." They all three agreed and rode off quickly to get the salve, for their castle was nearby, hardly five miles away. Within an hour the young lady was sent back, to find him still asleep.

Magic Healing

Lady wants Iwein to free her from a count.

28. In Celtic folklore the fairy sister of King Arthur. Compare *Erec*, lines 5153–242.

[3439] When her mistress had given her the box with the salve, she had given a strict injunction not to spread it all over him, but only where he felt pain. When it was applied there, the sickness would leave, and he would speedily recover. The young lady was to apply just enough and bring the rest back, because there was enough to heal many people. Her mistress also sent fresh clothing by her: one fine scarlet, woolen garment, another of fine linen, shoes, and fine woolen trousers.

[3457] So she rode swiftly to where she found him, still sleeping in the forest. She also led a very gentle horse—with a splendid bridle, and a saddle trimmed with gold—which he was to ride, if God granted that she might heal him.

[3467] On seeing him lying there as before, she delayed no longer. Having tied both horses to a branch, she approached him so quietly that he was unaware of her. Saying not a word, she applied the precious ointment all over him, smearing it everywhere from head to foot. So great was her pity, that she kept doing it until no salve was left in the box. This wasn't necessary at all. What's more, it had been forbidden, but her good will would not have thought it enough, had there been six times as much, so eager was she to see him recover. After applying it all, she quickly withdrew, for she was well aware that the shame of nakedness is painful to a virtuous man. She courteously hid in such a way that she could observe him but he couldn't see her. "If he comes to his senses," she thought, "and realizes that I saw him naked, it will go badly for me, because he'll be so ashamed that he'll never want to look me in the face." So she didn't show herself until the salve had taken effect, and he came to his senses.

[3505] When he sat up, observed himself, and saw how terrifying he looked, he addressed himself, saying, "Is it you, Iwein, or somebody else? Have I been sleeping till now? Help, Lord, help! Let me sleep forever! My dream presented me with a very splendid life. Oh, what fame I had while I lay sleeping! I dreamed of great accomplishments. I was young and of noble birth, I was handsome and rich—nothing like this—I was courtly and clever and, if my dream did not deceive me, I had gained many a hard-won prize with knightly deeds. I got whatever I wanted with lance and sword. On my own I won a wife and a rich land. But, so I dreamed, I spent only a short time with her before King Arthur led me away from her to his castle. It seemed in my dream that my companion was Sir Gawein. She gave me leave to be gone a year (none of this is really true). I stayed away longer, without having to, until she withdrew her favor. That undid me. In the midst of this fantasy I was awakened. My dream had made me a powerful lord. Well, what could trouble me even if I died while enjoying these honors? But my dream needlessly mocked me. Whoever turns his attention to dreams is dishonored.[29]

[3549] "Dream, how strange you are! In a flash you confer wealth and power on an insignificant man, who never dared to strive for honors. Whenever he wakes up, though, you make him a fool like me. Yet I get the notion, as crude a peasant as I am, that if I were present at knightly games, armed and mounted, I could acquit myself as well as those who have always been knights."

[3563] So he was a stranger to himself, confused, and it seemed to him that he had dreamed of being a knight and going on all his journeys. He said, "My dream taught me something: I will win honors if I can get a suit of armor. The dream estranged me from the marks of my class. But however completely I may be a peasant, my mind is full of jousting.[30] My heart is incommensurable with my body: my body is poor, my heart is rich. Did I dream my life? Or, if not, then who has made me look so ugly? Probably, though, I should give up this knightly attitude, because I lack both the appearance and the wealth for it." When he saw the fresh clothing lying at his side, he was surprised, saying, "These are clothes like those I often wore in my dream. Since I don't see anyone here to whom they belong, and since I need them, let them be mine. I wonder if they will become me. Before, in my dream, rich clothing looked very good on me." He quickly put the clothes on. As soon as he had covered his black body, he looked just like a knight.

[3597] When the young lady saw him sitting there, irreproachably dressed, she discreetly mounted her horse and rode toward him, leading the second horse. Acting as if she were just riding by, she neither spoke nor looked his way. When he saw her riding by, he would have jumped up, except that sickness kept him from getting up as readily as he wanted. So he called after her. She pretended she was in a hurry and unaware of his presence, until he called out a second time. At that, she quickly turned and replied, "Who's calling me? Who's there?" "Lady," he said, "come over this way." "I shall do so, sir," she replied, riding up to him. "I'm at your service," she said. "Your wish is my command." She asked how he had gotten there.

[3625] Sir Iwein replied—and his looks were proof enough—"I just found myself here, sick. I can't tell you what momentous happening brought me here, but I certainly have no wish to stay. Please take me with you. If you'll do that for me, I'll forever do my best to repay you." "I'll do it, knight," she said. "For your sake I'll give up the journey that my lady, ruler of this land, sent me on. I'll take you to her. I advise you to rest after your ordeal." So he mounted and rode the horse.

29. Compare *Erec*, line 8126.

30. A frequently expressed thought in medieval literature was that one's nature (and nobility) would of necessity manifest itself. Compare *Gregorius*, lines 1496–503.

[3645] She took him to her lady, who had never been so happy to see a person. He was well taken care of—clothes, food, bath—until he showed no more signs of his misfortune. Sir Iwein found good treatment here and he recovered from his affliction.

[3655] The lady did not forget to ask the girl what had happened to her salve. But the girl fibbed her way out of the difficulty, saying, "I am sorry to tell you, lady, what happened to me and the box. The knight saw it happen: I came close to drowning, and it's a miracle that I escaped. I got into severe difficulty riding over the river on the nearby high bridge. The darn horse! It stumbled and fell clear to its knees, so that I lost the rein and could barely stay on. I forgot about the box; it fell from my grasp into the water. Believe me, no loss ever distressed me so much. What good does it do to be careful? What you are not destined to keep is easily lost."

[3679] As convincing as this fib was, her mistress was still a little peeved. "We've had good luck and bad," she observed. "I can say that for sure. We'll have to lament the loss and be thankful to God for what we've gained. Within a short time I've lost my magic salve and found a knight. Given the net gain, the loss can be forgotten. One should not yearn for lost property that can't be recouped." With this, her anger was gone.

[3695] So Sir Iwein remained here until his wild look disappeared and he became a handsome man again. They immediately got him the best armor obtainable and the best-looking horse in all the land. The guest was outfitted so that he lacked nothing.

[3703] One morning, they saw Count Aliers riding up with his army.[31] The knights of the land and their squires set up a defense, and Sir Iwein was out in front. Formerly, having been literally overridden and completely hemmed in, they had given up defending the land and had virtually lost their courage. They took heart now, seeing their guest charge the enemy so courageously. Those who had earlier been cowards all looked up to him now and took courage. From the fortification Sir Iwein let the lady see that the time often comes when a favor done a good man is repaid. She regretted nothing she had done for him, because his courage alone made the faithless enemy retreat to a ford. There they regrouped. Here a blow, there a thrust! Who could count all the lances that Sir Iwein broke there? He and all his men hit and thrust so relentlessly that the enemy, with many losses, had to retreat in confusion from the ford, conceding the victory. Of those who neglected to flee, most were quickly killed, and the rest were taken captive.

---

31. Compare the similar situation in *Gregorius*, lines 2023ff.

Battle with Aliers

Thus the battle had redounded to Sir Iwein's honor. Everybody praised him, saying he was brave, courtly, and wise, and that nothing could stop them, if they had him or someone like him for their lord. So they fervently wished that the two would find it suitable for their lady to marry him.

[3759] And so it was that the members of Count Aliers's army were swiftly and resolutely killed or captured. Still, he and a small force chose to fight on, performing valiant deeds that nobody could belittle. When that no longer was effective, he, too, was obliged to retreat, and fighting as he went, he fled to one of his nearby strongholds. In flight to his mountaintop castle, he found the road so steep and so long that in spite of his exertions he was overtaken at the gate by Sir Iwein. Iwein captured him and accepted his oath that he would ride back as a prisoner and would put himself in the power of the lady who had so often suffered because of him and whose land he had laid waste. He gave her hostages as well as his oath that he would compensate her for the damage he had done, until she was completely satisfied. Iwein captures Aliers, makes him Lady's vassel

[3785] Never was a knight accorded greater honor than Sir Iwein, when his troops saw him riding up with his prisoner beside him. When the countess received him and went to him with all her ladies, you could see her very affectionate glances. Again and again she looked at him, and had he wanted a reward, she would have granted it, withholding neither her property nor herself. But that was not at all what he was thinking: he wanted no reward at all. Now that his helping hand had freed the lady of Narison from her oppression, he wanted to take leave. She would not accede to that, for she was in love with him and thought he would be a fine lord for her land. If it had not seemed shameful to her, she would have asked for his hand. If I'm not mistaken, it would have been smarter for her—although no lady would do such a thing—to woo some man who would not cause her harm than to let herself be courted by a man who would surely be the ruin of her. Her gestures spoke clearly enough, but he ignored it. Both gestures and words, aimed at keeping him there, were in vain.

[3823] He said good-bye and rode off, quickly taking the first road he happened on. Following the road, he heard an exceedingly loud voice, plaintive yet fearsome. Sir Iwein didn't know from which of the two creatures it came, a dragon or a wild animal. He quickly found out, though, for the same voice guided him through a great tangle of fallen trees to a clearing where he saw a terrible battle in progress. A dragon and a lion were locked in fierce combat. The dragon was big and strong, and fire was shooting from its mouth. This heat and the stench made the lion bellow so loudly. Sir Iwein was assaulted by doubt as to which animal he should help,

Dragon + lion

Iwein helps Lion

Lion—Iweins servant

but he decided to help the noble lion. However, he was afraid that as soon as the dragon was killed, his intervention would not keep the lion from promptly attacking him. For that is how it works, among people, too: after you have served a stranger as best you can, you had better watch out, lest you then be betrayed. The situation here was similar. He was a brave man, though, and he took the chance. Dismounting, he charged the dragon, very quickly striking it dead. Thus did he help the lion in its need.

[3865] Still, after killing the dragon, he was apprehensive about the lion's possibly attacking him. He soon learned differently. The lion stretched out at his feet and by gesture and voice gave him a wordless greeting. It stopped its raging and showed its affection as best it knew how and as well as a beast could. It acknowledged its dependence on him and it consistently served him from then on, following him wherever he went and standing by him in every danger, until death parted them.

[3883] The lion and its master hadn't gone very far before the lion scented prey. Its instinct, embracing both its inner nature and its hunger, made it want to hunt down the animal as soon as it was aware of it. It could express that desire to Sir Iwein only by stopping, looking at him, and pointing with its muzzle—that is how it informed him. Iwein sicced it like a hound and followed it off the road, perhaps a stone's throw. The lion found a deer standing there, seized it suddenly, and sucked its warm blood. Since this did its master no good, Iwein skinned it where he knew the meat to be the fattest and best and cut out a tender piece. Since night was then falling, he started a fire and roasted his meat. He ate his meal unsalted, without bread or wine. Nothing could have been finer. The lion ate the remainder, right down to the bones.

[3911] Sir Iwein lay down, and as he slept, the lion stayed awake, pacing watchfully around him and his horse. At all times, both then and later, it had the noble intention of guarding him. For the next fourteen days their joint endeavors consisted in Iwein's seeking knightly adventure and the wild lion's hunting down and providing food for the man.

once again: Iwein provided with food

[3923] Although it was not Iwein's intention, fate led him right to his lady's land, where he found the same spring that, as I told you earlier, had brought him great happiness and severe distress. When he saw the linden tree above the spring and when the chapel and the stone appeared before him, his heart was reminded of how he had lost his honor, his land, and his wife. He grew so full of regret and so stricken by grief, that, as before, he almost lost his mind. His heart so failed him that, pale as death, he fell from his horse, bending forward so far that his sword shot out of its scabbard. The blade was so sharp that it cut through his chain mail,

Iwein wounds himself at the spring

giving him a big wound that bled heavily. This deeply grieved the lion, which thought its master dead, and it longed to die too. The lion leaned the sword against a bush and was about to stab itself through the belly, when Iwein began to show signs of life. When he sat up, this kept the lion from stabbing itself to death. Sir Iwein, bemoaning his misfortune, said, "Unhappy man, what now! You are the unluckiest person ever born. How could you lose your lady's favor! If anyone else in the world were guilty of this, it would be the end of him.

[3969] "A happy man who never won honor is better off than a man who gains honor but is not smart enough to retain it. I lament to God that I had so much of both honor and happiness and that it was not destined to last. If I hadn't enjoyed a great deal of love and happiness, I wouldn't have known what it was like; I would have lived on as before, without the pangs of yearning. But yearning hurts me now. It has come to the point where I have to look at my loss and my shame in my lady's land. This is her honor and her land, which was once in my hand, so that I was lacking nothing—to all that I have become a stranger. I have good reason to bemoan the loss of my lovely wife. Why, then, do I spare my own life? It would be what I deserve if my own sword avenged me on myself and ran me through. Since I have done this to myself, since my own misdeed and no fault of my lady caused me quite needlessly to lose her affection and to trade laughter for tears, I should be punished for it. This wild lion, which wanted to kill itself out of compassion for me, has shown me a compelling instance of true loyalty."

[4011] This bitter lament was witnessed by a girl suffering greater misery out of fear than any woman before her, for she lay imprisoned and awaiting death in the chapel. While Iwein was lamenting, she was peering through a crack in the door. "Who is lamenting there?" she asked. "Who is there?" He in turn asked, "Who is asking?" "Sir," she replied, "the person lamenting in here is such a miserable girl, more miserable than any girl alive, no matter her circumstances, no matter how great her distress." Iwein asked, "Who could possibly cause you affliction equal to mine? You could well stop lamenting, for I am the one who is really accursed." "It's impossible," she replied, "that your affliction could ever be the equal of mine. I see that you can stand and ride and walk wherever you want; while I, a prisoner, have been sentenced to be incinerated or hanged tomorrow, for there is no one to save me from being killed."

[4044] "Lady," said Iwein, "how did that come about?" She replied, "May I never gain God's grace if I am the least bit guilty; but I am imprisoned here as a traitor. My countrymen have accused me of such a serious crime that I would deserve severe punishment if I were in fact culpable. Last year the mistress of the land mar-

Girl who helped Iwein about to be hung, no one to help

she made a challange with the 3 knights.

ried a man. The marriage unfortunately failed, and she blamed me for it. My God, what did I have to do with her making a mistake? True, I had advised her to marry, but I did so just to preserve her honor, and I am more and more surprised that such a good man could act so badly. He was really the best man I've ever known. My plight, though, is in no way his fault; it's just my misfortune. That is why I'm struggling with despair. They have given me till tomorrow; then they'll take my life, because I am, alas, a woman. I can't defend myself by combat, and there is also no one to save me."

[4075] "I grant," said Sir Iwein, "that you are in a more frightening situation than I am, because you will die if you have no way to defend yourself." "Who could save me?" she asked. "Even if someone wanted to, who would have the strength to cope with overwhelming power? For three strong men are accusing me. I know just two men that strong, who are so virtuous and valiant and who would undertake such a great effort for a poor creature like me. There are two such men, each of whom, even unarmed, could kill an army of people like these. As sure as death, I know that if either of them knew of my jeopardy, he would come and fight for me. But I can't reach either of them in time and I must forfeit my life because I can't expect anyone else."

[4102] Sir Iwein replied, "Give me the names of the three who are challenging you, also the names of the two knights, either one of whom is brave enough to fight one against three." "I'll tell you who they all are," she said. "First, the three who have me in their power: the seneschal and his brothers. They always hated and envied me, because my lady favored me more than they liked; and now they have so won her over that she overlooks the predicament I'm in. After my lady married her husband, who supposedly was suitable to her, yet afterward left her, the seneschal and his brothers never let up in making trouble for me every day. They never ceased accusing me of disloyalty, saying that it was solely my cunning that made things go so badly for her. Whatever happens to me from all this, I won't deny that my advice and suggestions led her to marry him. For I was well convinced that, happen what may, she would derive benefit and honor from the match. Now they are telling lies about me, saying I betrayed her. After they had started treating me unjustly and violently, I suffered great distress and, miserable and alone, I was too quick to get angry. It is the ruination of good fortune when you can't control your anger and you speak rashly. That, unfortunately, is what I did; I brought about my own destruction. Because I was angry, I said that if the three most powerful men at court presumed to bring charges against me, I would within forty days find a knight who would fight all three at once. They accepted my challenge, which

had been too rashly spoken, and refused to let me change it. I also had to take a proper oath that I was prepared to carry out my offer just the way I had spoken it, that in six weeks I would redeem myself by combat.

[4162] "I rode off to look for the two knights in whom I had put my hopes, but found neither. I then went looking for King Arthur but found no one in his castle who would take up my cause, and I left still without a champion. Because of this I was subjected to so much mockery here that it almost broke my heart. Then they threw me in this prison, and I am waiting for my life to end, for those who would help me are now quite inaccessible. If they knew about my misery, either of the two would come and rescue me, either Sir Gawein or Sir Iwein."

[4179] "Which Iwein do you mean?"[32] asked the knight. "Sir," she said, "the one who is responsible for my imprisonment. His father is King Urien. That Iwein is responsible for my distress. I was too nice and too eager for his favor and strove to make him lord here—which, unfortunately, happened. I was too impetuous in becoming his partisan, for whoever wants to know somebody really needs quite a long time for it. It's too bad I started singing his praises way too soon, thinking he would reward me better than he did. It was on my advice that my lady gave herself over to him—both her person and her realm. Now he has deceived and hurt both us and himself. It is his misfortune, because—I'll swear an oath to it—my lady is such a noble woman that he will never in the world make a better marriage. She is so beautiful and rich that, even if she were only his social equal, he ought to be happy that she would accept him."

[4210] At this the knight asked, "Are you Lunete?" "Yes," she replied, "I am." "Then learn who I am," he said. "I am Iwein the wretched. May God have pity on me that I was ever born! How could I have lost my lady's affection! Since the fault is no one's but mine, the damage as well should be borne only by me: I don't know to whom else to give it by now. Nothing burdens me more than the fact I'm alive, but I'll soon be lying dead. I am quite sure I can defeat all three of the knights who have imprisoned you here. And when I have freed you, I'll kill myself. My lady can't miss witnessing the combat, because it is going to take place before her eyes. I don't know what more I can do than to condemn myself before her tomorrow morning and die for her sake, before her own eyes. My pain and yearning will find their end with my death. All of this is to happen without her knowing who I am until I die—as well as the three knights on whom I shall avenge you. When my

They figure out who they are

---

32. Other Iweins (Iwans) are mentioned as members of the Round Table, so unless the father's name were mentioned, there could be confusion. See *Erec*, lines 1630ff.

lady finds out who I am, she will know that I lost my life and my mind because of grief. Her vengeance will take place before her very eyes.

[4247] "It is right that I repay you for the noble crown that I wore, thanks to you. I had many honors. What good did it do me to find gold? A fool is not benefited a bit by finding gold, because he promptly throws it away. Whatever I have done to myself, though, you may be certain I will not desert you, for when I would have been killed, you rescued me. I will do the same for you tomorrow." He then took his helmet off, confirming that it was indeed he, Sir Iwein. Distressed no longer, she cried for joy and said what was in her mind: "Now that I have seen my lord alive, nothing can harm me. It was my fantasy and my fear that you had been killed. I heard no news at court about where you might be."

[4275] "Lady Lunete," Iwein replied, "where was the knight who always did what was desired by the ladies who sought his aid, my good friend, Sir Gawein, who always strove, and still does, to please the ladies? If you had told him what was on your mind, he would have done everything you asked of him." "If I had found him," she replied, "I would have quickly overcome my worries. That I didn't find him was owing to a strange event. The queen had been kidnapped from court by a knight whom everyone was eager to put to shame.[33] Sir Gawein had ridden off in pursuit at the very time when I arrived to lodge my complaint. Indeed, I left them all lamenting both the lady and Gawein's giving chase. For they feared they had lost the lady and he had lost his life, because he would not return before he found out where she had been taken."

[4303] The story left Sir Iwein worrying about his friend. "May God protect him," he said. "I must leave, lady, and get ready. Expect me tomorrow morning. I'll come in plenty of time for combat. And, courtly as you are, tell no one who I am. I will help you in your distress and kill all three of your adversaries or I'll die for your sake." She replied, "Dear sir, it would be going too far to risk such a distinguished life for such a poor woman. That would be too much to ask. I want you to know that I'll accept the intention in place of the deed. I'll release you from your promise. Your life is more valuable than mine. If it could be an equal fight, I would venture to ask your help, but it is completely contrary to custom for one man to fight three. People even claim that two are the master of one, so that with three it's simply no contest. If you were to lose your life for my sake, I'd be the most unhappy poor woman who ever lived—and they'd still kill me, too. It's better that I perish than that we both die."

33. This adventure is related in Chrétien de Troyes's *Lancelot*.

[4337] "It will turn out better than that," he answered. "For we'll both survive. I want to protect you from harm and I shall make it come true. You have done so much for me that if I have any sense of loyalty, I cannot see any harm come to you, if I can prevent it. But enough of talking. Either they let you go or I'll kill all three of them."

[4349] Her sense of decency caused her to regret that her own honor and advantage were to be thus defended. She wanted to be rescued, but not if it were going to cost him his life. But since he had chosen combat of his own free will, she agreed to it; in fact could not have stopped it. He chose to stay no longer, rode on, his lion following him as usual. He saw a castle, home of a good knight. Strongly fortified, it was well protected in every way against assaults and catapults by a high thick wall that enclosed the hill on which it stood. Still, the lord of the castle had an unpleasant view, because the town buildings had been burned down, clear to the castle wall.

[4370] Sir Iwein rode along, following the road, then turning toward the castle. After the drawbridge had been lowered, he saw six handsome squires riding toward him. Both as to their figures and their clothing, the way they all looked would befit an emperor. They gave him a friendly reception. Soon their lord, a courteous man, walked up, greeted him, and led him to a fine hall in the castle, where he saw a group of dignified knights and ladies. He observed their manners and behavior, which he found impeccable.

[4389] He who has experienced severe troubles is much more appreciative of someone else's travail than is one who lacks such experience. The host had fought as a knight himself and had often risked his life, which made it all the easier for him to sympathize with his guest. He sat beside Iwein while the latter's armor was being removed. Both men and women were forthcoming with their good will. They paid their respects and honored him beyond what courtesy demanded. For their guest's sake they were very intent on pretending to be happy, although their hearts weren't at all in it. A profound sorrow, of which Sir Iwein and other guests knew nothing, daily dispersed their joy. Their happiness and joviality lacked any sort of appropriate expression. Feigned happiness, projected by artifice, lacks substance; while the mouth is smiling, the heart is breaking from grief and worry. Moreover, such artifice is transparent. Anyone with his wits about him will recognize artificial happiness, which does not come from the heart. The deception of the courtiers helped them only temporarily. Their fears and their concern about the next day dissolved everybody's happiness. Sorrow won the contest. In less time than it takes to tell about it, the joy that they had been proclaiming turned into weeping and lamentation.

Giant is tormenting the castle

Giant = Herpin

Giant

[4432] When Sir Iwein saw that, he asked his host what had happened, "For God's sake, sir, tell us what the trouble is and what this transformation means. Why have you and your people, so recently happy, changed so?" The lord of the castle replied, "It would be better if you didn't know what sort of evil afflicts us. But since you insist on it, I'll tell you our problem. If it saddens you, I apologize. It would be better for you not to hear it, so you can be happy amongst those who are happy. I am Misfortune's child and must grieve with those who are unhappy, because that is where I belong." His guest kept pressing, until the moment came when his host told him all his woe. "My life," he said, "is forever repugnant to me, because I am getting old without honor. I'd be better off dead, for I am suffering shame and distress from such a powerful man, that I'll never be able to avenge myself. A giant has made a wasteland of my estate and robbed me of everything I rightfully own, except for this castle. Let me tell you how little I'm to blame for all this.

[4470] "I have a child, a daughter, a beautiful girl. Because I refused to give her to him, he plunders me. To be sure, I'd rather lose my property and risk my life than have her become his wife. I also have six sons, all knights. He captured them and hanged two of them before my own eyes. Who ever suffered more grievously? He still has four of them, and I'll soon lose them, too. Tomorrow he's going to bring them right up in front of the castle and he threatens to kill them in my presence, thereby compelling me to give him their sister. May God let me die tonight, so I may be spared this. My greatest distress is that when he steals my daughter in this evil way, he might have second thoughts about taking her as his wife and will give her to the meanest of his grooms. Won't my life be misery then? His name, by the way, is Harpin. If I have ever done anything to deserve such scorn from God, I wish He would punish only me and not punish my innocent children, who are upright and good."

[4507] When Sir Iwein heard and saw the lord's grief, it went straight to his heart. "Why have you neglected such help where it can be found?" he asked. "Namely, in King Arthur's land. There was no reason for you to suffer this outrage for so long. You ought to have ridden to his court. Among his companions you would have found someone who would have rid you of the giant."

[4520] The lord answered, "He who would have helped me the most and would have come if he had known, or if I had found him, is at present out of the country. The king is also suffering an outrage that he would gladly do without. If you want to listen, I'll tell you a strange story. A week ago a knight arrived there, very well aware that at that very hour he could see the members of the Round Table sitting with the king. Dismounting in front of them, he said, 'I have come with a request. Lord, I have heard of your generosity and courage and I hope the boon that I ask of you, and for which I came here, will not be denied.' King Arthur replied, 'Whatever you request here will be granted, if you ask properly.'

[4547] "The guest responded, 'You should leave that to me. From what I have heard of you, it would compromise your fame for you to make any stipulations. Whatever I may ask, honor me by leaving me free to formulate my request. Otherwise I shall forgo it.' When King Arthur declined, the knight left the castle in a towering rage, declaring, 'A lot of people have been deceived about this king, and the whole world has lied about him. They say of his generosity that no knight was ever refused what he had asked for. Whoever likes him is of dubious respectability.'

[4566] "His loud shouting was heard by all the knights of the Round Table, who spoke to the king with one voice: 'Sir, you would be making a mistake if you allow the knight to leave like this. Whom have you ever refused anything? Rely on his courtliness. He looks like a man who would be making reasonable requests. If he departs in such a rage, he will never again speak of your good name.'

[4579] "After thinking about it, the king had someone bring the knight back, to whom he gave a firm promise to do whatever he asked. Because King Arthur's word was his bond, no further guarantees were necessary. The fellow then arrogantly asked to be allowed to take away the queen, King Arthur's wife. The king, beside himself, exclaimed, 'I've been tricked! Those who advised me have betrayed me.'

[4593] "Upon seeing how angry the king was, the knight reassured him, saying, 'Sir, remember your manners. I'm only asking for her under the condition that I can get her out of the country. You have an army made up of the best knights there are. I stipulate further that I'll defeat everyone who pursues me to rescue her. I won't hurry—just my usual pace. Whoever chases me may be sure that I won't on his account ride the slightest bit faster and that I will await his approach.' The king had to keep his promise, and the knight took off with the queen. On departing, she looked woefully at all the knights, acting like a woman much worried about her honor and imploring them as best she could, with words and gestures, to free her quickly. Never had the court been so troubled, but those who saw her leave were undaunted.

[4624] "There was a great rush, and from all sides the cry resounded, 'Get my horse and armor here.' As soon as each knight was readied, he set out in pursuit. They said, 'Success will attend us; he could not have put this task in more capable hands. Unless God is with the knight and against us, he won't get far with her.' Sir Kei then said, 'If neither God nor the devil protects him who has insulted us by abducting my lady, the queen, he'll forfeit his honor. I'm the seneschal here and I owe it to King Arthur to free my lady, his wife. For sure it will cost that knight his life. Against my will he won't take her a field's length away. By God, had he known I was here, he would never have come to court with a request like that. I'll soon get her away from him. You ought to be ashamed, chasing after him all together. Why this vulgar uproar? And why is the whole court riding out after just one man? I'm sure I can beat him, for I alone will seem to him like an army. He'll never bother defending himself when he sees that it's me. What good would it do him? You can all just stay here. Since I have taken on the task, I'll spare you the exertion.'

[4664] "By now he was ready, and he was the first to approach the knight. And, to his shame, he was the first to be defeated. They were in a forest when he told the knight to turn around. The latter suddenly did so and with great force thrust Kei up out of his saddle so that his helmet got caught on a branch, while he himself was left hanging by his neck. He would have died then and there, except that his friend, the devil, saved him. He did suffer a lot, though, hanging there. Although he was later unfortunately freed, he hung there long enough for all to see him in his misery and distress.

[4683] "The next after him was Kalogrenant, who found him hanging there like a common thief. Kalogrenant, who enjoyed seeing Kei hanging up there, did not release him. He, too, rushed at the stranger and came very close to suffering the same fate as Kei when he, too, was unhorsed. Haste, ill will, and Kei's rascally nature caused each of those who later saw him hanging there to ride on. The fierce Dodines caught up with the stranger in a clearing and broke his lance on him. After that he, too, was thrown to the turf a good lance's length behind his horse.

[4701] "Segremors was the next to ride him down, and the same thing happened to him. Then Henete caught up with him and suffered the same fate. Pliopleherin and Millemargot, to their chagrin, encountered similar misfortune, as did their friend Iders.[34] I may as well desist from naming all those knights there whom I know, because everyone who pursued the stranger was strewn along the way, one after the other. No one was to be found there who could liberate the lady.

[4716] "Sir Gawein, always the paragon of knighthood, would have come to her aid but unfortunately he was nowhere around. He arrived early the next day, though. And, because of the king's grievance, he hurried after the stranger, determined to get the queen back for Arthur or to die in the attempt. That same day I came looking for him, and, as I lament to God, I didn't find him there. The way things stand

34. Perhaps the same knight Erec defeated. See *Erec*, lines 1–1283.

between us, because my wife is his sister, he would have come to my aid if I were in trouble. I just got back yesterday and, having returned without him, I have no hope at all. Do I not have good cause to grieve? For tomorrow I shall lose all of my honor."

[4740] The knight with the lion, feeling very sorry for him said, "Tomorrow noon I'm supposed to be at a certain place in response to the plea of a lady who has done me great service and who will lose her life if I don't arrive on time. But if you are sure that the giant will come to us early enough for me to do my duty—conquer him or succumb to him—and still by noon get to the place where I have promised to be, then I shall fight him for you and for your noble wife. For her brother is as dear to me as my own self." At this moment the lord's wife and daughter approached. Sir Iwein had never seen a prettier girl—if only she had not been consumed by weeping. They both greeted him cordially, as one does a dear guest.

[4767] "It would be well," said the host, "for you to pay your dutiful respects to our guest. He has taken such a keen interest in our problem that if it pleases God, he will help us prevail. He says he will fight our enemy. When I told him my problem, he promised, without my asking, that he would either die in the attempt or he would vanquish the giant who has made me endure so much. My request and my command is that you fall at his feet in gratitude. "God forbid," said Sir Iwein, "that I should ever commit the impropriety of having Sir Gawein's sister kneel before me. Even for King Arthur that would be, as Christ is my witness, too much. I should be and will be eternally grateful for her excusing me from accepting so great an honor. On the contrary, moderation satisfies me. As I promised you earlier, I'll tell you under what conditions I will fight him. If he shows up early enough so that after the fight I can at noon come to the aid of her to whom I've already promised it, then I will fight him for your sake, for my lady's favor, and because you are innocent."

[4803] Happy to be reassured, they arranged pleasant diversions for him, outdoing themselves in showing the esteem they thought was his due. Because he seemed to them good, honorable, and in every way courtly, they loudly sang his praises. They observed, too, that the lion lay by him and acted just like a sheep. Iwein had a good meal here, as well as restful sleep. Awakening at daybreak, he heard early mass and prepared to fight the giant who was supposed to come.

[4825] When he saw no one approaching, he grew troubled, saying, "Lord, I am ready and perfectly willing to serve you. But where is he who is supposed to be here? I don't feel right remaining here and I've been waiting too long. Passing the time here entails risking my honor. It's high time for me to go." The threat of his leaving troubled his hosts, who grew as sad as before. One thing troubled them before all else: they didn't know what effort on their part would do him the greatest honor and thus help change his mind. When the lord offered him his estate, Iwein answered, "It is not my intention to risk my life to offer myself for sale."

[4845] And he absolutely refused. Then the host, the lady, the girl, and the whole company turned pale in their anxiety. In their supplications the wife and daughter often mentioned Sir Gawein, invoking his name in their behalf. They also reminded Iwein that our Lord God gives happiness and honor to him who is merciful, and that God would reward him for having mercy on them. Good and kind as he was, that touched his heart. It is said that their worthy pleas coerced him, when he rightly perceived their need and heard them mention God and Sir Gawein so often, for he would have been more than happy to serve either of them.

[4869] So he was of two minds. He thought: I really need wisdom to decide which is better, because the game I'm playing suddenly presents two options, and my very honor is at stake—neither more nor less. I really need some good advice. Whichever course I choose, I know I'll lose. I cannot perform both tasks, nor can I ignore both, nor even one of them. For if I could, I wouldn't be worrying. So I don't know what to do. The way things stand now, I am dishonored if I leave and disgraced if I stay. I cannot fight both battles and I dare not abstain from either. May God, who has guided me this far, give me good counsel, helping me pay heed to both alternatives and act correctly. I really don't want to desert her whom I first made a promise to, whose fear and suffering are completely my fault. How can deserting her befit an upright man? If I hadn't given my word, though, the mourning for the girl's death would be quick and easy in contrast to the harm that happens here. This lord here, as well, who wants my help, is surely worthy of it, as are Sir Gawein's sister and her daughter, who touch me deeply not only on their own account but also for the sake of him to whom I owe so much that I would never refuse to be of service to him. If I have to desert them, they will always imagine that I'm a coward.

[4914] Iwein's doubts and lamentations were dissipated by the arrival of the giant they were waiting for, who came riding up to the castle with his prisoners in tow. He had treated them in the crudest way. The sons were without any kind of clothing, except for the worst shirts ever worn by a scullion. They were driven by a dwarf who kept beating them with his whip, so that they were covered with blood.[35] The sons were riding barefooted. Their miserable shirts were made of frayed, coarse,

---

35. Compare two similar scenes in *Erec*: lines 44–58 and 5335–428.

black sackcloth, while their arms and legs were bare. Sir Iwein felt pity for them because of the privations they were suffering. The sick horses they were riding were mere skin and bones, stumbling about loose-reined and lame. The sons' feet were tied under the horses' bellies, and their hands were tied with bast behind their backs. The tails of the nags were plaited together, so that they could not get apart from each other. The sons looked so pitiful that I'm surprised their noble father's heart didn't break when he saw them come riding up, for it was truly a terrible sight.

[4951] The giant led them up to the castle gate, shouting that he would hang all four of them unless they were quickly ransomed by giving him their sister. The knight with the lion, the hope of those who counted on him, said to his host, "Sir, I shall indeed free our friends if I can. God will strike down this brutish man. The complete justice of your cause, together with his boundless arrogance, give me strength. He can't even manage to be ashamed of the crime of failing to respect their noble birth and name, no matter what they may have done to him. I shouldn't be berating a knight, but still he has to pay for being so benighted. I'll really make him suffer if I can."

[4973] It took him but a few moments to tie on his helmet and prepare for combat. Experience had taught him this. He saw to it that his horse was brought forward and he ordered the drawbridge lowered. "This," he said, "will bring pain and disgrace for one or even both of us; I'm confident in my ability to extinguish his threats. For sure he'll either be obliged to return your sons alive or he'll take my life too. And which it will be, will soon be evident." He then charged the giant, his lion following right behind him.

[4991] When the giant saw him approaching, he mocked him, saying, "Oh, stupid man! What presumption has overcome you, that you are courting death? That's not bright. Whoever counseled you to do this doesn't want you to live and—count on it—only wants to exact revenge on you for something you did to him. And he's getting a good revenge, because I'll soon fix things so that you'll never again do him either evil or good."

[5007] Sir Iwein answered, "Knight, what's the point of these threats? Skip the malicious talk and get down to business, or I'd be more likely to fear a dwarf, for all your huge size. Leave the scolding to ill-bred women, who aren't able to fight. If God wants to support what's right and proper, you'll soon be dead."

[5017] The giant's strength and boldness had taught him which weapon worked best for him and who would be able to harm him. He thought he was armed amply with the staff he carried. Sir Iwein was glad that his opponent seemed all but unarmed. Resolutely clapping his lance under his arm, he spurred his horse, took aim at the giant's chest, gave him such a thrust that the iron lance-tip broke from the shaft and lodged in his body. In return the giant landed such a blow that, I declare, if Iwein's horse hadn't borne him forward, another blow like it would have been enough to kill him. But his horse did carry him far enough away that he could draw his sword. Then, suddenly turning around, Iwein charged his foe again. Aided by his skill, strength, and valor, he inflicted another wound. But while his horse was bearing him away, the giant landed such a blow on him that he lay flattened out on his horse's neck, as if dead.

[5050] The lion, seeing the peril he was in, rushed fiercely at the uncouth giant and tore open his clothing and his flesh the whole length of his back, from his shoulders on down. Roaring like a bull, the huge fellow swung the staff that he carried to defend himself. But when he swung, the lion evaded him, and he made contact with neither the lion nor the man. He swung so hard that he bent forward with the blow and came very close to falling. Before he could take another swing, though, Sir Iwein got his revenge on him by inflicting two deep wounds and then thrusting his sword through his heart. That ended the fight; the giant toppled to the ground as if he were a tree.

[5075] A loud cry of joy arose from all those who benefited from the giant's defeat. They had found good fortune in the knight with the lion, and with the giant dead, they lived from then on free of fear and distress. They were exceedingly grateful to Sir Iwein for having killed the giant. Quickly saying good-bye, he didn't dare delay any longer, if he was going to preserve his honor with her who lay imprisoned because of him and to whose aid he was supposed to come around noon. His host urged him to get some rest, but he might as well have saved his words, for Sir Iwein could not and dared not stay. The host and his wife, placing themselves and their possessions at his disposal, jointly thanked him in every possible way.

[5102] Sir Iwein said, "If I have been of service, and you wish to repay me, do this thing that I ask, and I am well rewarded. I am very fond of Sir Gawein and I know he is fond of me. If ours is not a true friendship, then such has never existed. Whenever I can, I want to renew the strength of our friendship. Ride to him, sir, and give him my greetings. Take your sons along, who have been set free, their sister too, and also the dwarf, whose master lies dead here, and thank him for the service I have rendered you, for I did it for his sake. If he should ask you who I am, inform him that a lion is with me. By that he will know me when we meet."

[5127] The lord promised to do so and urged him to come back after the battle at the spring, and he would be provided with every comfort. "My return is doubtful," Sir Iwein replied. "I'd like to, if I'm allowed to by those whom I must fight. But

I really doubt they will let me ride away, if they can vanquish me." They all then prayed that God would preserve and protect both his honor and his life, declaring that they and their possessions were at his disposal. He commended them to God.

[5145] Knowing the roads, he arrived quickly at the chapel. Since it was already noon, the girl had been taken out of the prison. They had tied her hands and taken off her clothes, leaving just her chemise on. The pyre was ready, a fire set beneath it, and Lady Lunete was kneeling in prayer, praying God to care for her soul, because she had settled her accounts with life.

[5161] She had despaired that anyone would free her; then her defender arrived, pained at the wretchedness and woe she was suffering on his account. Sir Iwein had complete confidence that God and her innocence would not permit such a violent act or let him fail in any way. He also believed that his companion the lion would avail him in saving the girl. Spurring hard, he raced forward, for if he had come a moment later, she would have been lost. "Scoundrels," he cried out. "Leave this girl alone. Whatever she is charged with, I will answer for, and if she needs a champion, I will fight for her." Upon hearing that, her three antagonists felt nothing but contempt for him. They yielded to the stranger, though, making way for him. He looked around carefully, trying to catch a glimpse of her whom his secret heart always looked upon and acknowledged as its mistress. Soon he saw her sitting there, and as earlier, he just about lost his senses. For they say it hurts to be near one's heart's delight while in the guise of a stranger.

[5199] Looking around further, he saw many noble ladies of her retinue and he heard them lamenting bitterly as they prayed to almighty God. "Lord God," they said, "we pray with all our hearts that You will avenge us on him who would take our dear comrade from us. We shared in her accomplishments and honor. Now we have no one in the ladies' quarters who dares speak for us, so that our lady will favor us. This office was performed, at every opportunity, by our dear comrade, the faithful Lunete."

[5217] These words fortified Sir Iwein's zeal for combat. He rode over to Lunete, asked her to stand up, and said, "Lady, show me your tormentors, if they are here, and tell them to set you free immediately, or else they'll learn at first hand what kind of fight I can put up." His protector, the lion, quickly noting his anger, moved up closer to him. The good, innocent girl was so daunted by fear that she hardly raised her eyes. But she took courage and spoke up, "May God reward you, sir. He knows I've suffered this scorn and this disgrace through no fault of mine. And I pray to God to let them succeed in opposing you only commensurate with my guilt." With that, she pointed out all three of her antagonists.

[5341] The seneschal said, "Whoever comes to die for your sake is a complete imbecile. It is fitting enough that he who wants to die should be accommodated and that even he who is in the wrong should be entitled to fight. The whole country is familiar with her treachery, with how she betrayed her mistress, causing the latter to lose honor. Truly, sir, I advise you to reconsider. I would certainly like to spare you our taking both your life and your honor for the sake of such a disloyal woman. You can see there are three of us, and, if you're not a child, you might well stop supporting a cause that will cost you your life."

[5263] "No matter how much you threaten," said the knight with the lion, "you'll still have to fight me or let the girl go. The innocent girl swore an oath to me that she was not guilty of any betrayal of her mistress and that she never gave her false advice. So what if there are three of you? Do you imagine I am alone? God always stands by the truth. I am here with these two others, who I know will stand by me. So there are three of us, too. I suspect we are stronger than your team."

[5281] "If I should presume to oppose our God," said the seneschal, "I would reap only injury and scorn. Sir, you are threatening me with God, but I'm confident He'll help us more than He will you. I see you have a companion. You must tell your lion standing nearby to go off farther away, because no one is about to fight both of you. The other helpers are no problem."

[5292] "The lion is always with me," answered Sir Iwein. "I didn't bring it just for the fight, so I won't drive it off, either. If it makes a move on you, defend yourself." At that, they all shouted together that if he didn't send the lion away, no one would fight him, and he would soon see the girl burn. "That will not come to pass," said Iwein. So the lion had to withdraw farther. But as it went, it could not refrain from looking back over its shoulder at its master.

[5307] As the adversaries made ready for battle, words were put aside. The four quickly mounted and rode off in opposite directions, so that they would have room to charge. All three of Iwein's opponents charged at the one man as fast as their horses could run. As a smart man who knows his profession and cleverly saves his strength for the right moment, this is how Sir Iwein was obliged to defend himself. All three broke their lances on him, while he kept his undamaged. Turning his horse away from them, he ran it the length of the field with reins hanging loose. Swiftly he whirled around, fixed his lance firmly against his chest, as he always did, and charged back at them. The seneschal, who had eagerly peeled away from his brothers, came at him with his sword. But Iwein's lance caught him under the chin, sending him flying over his saddle.

[5337] He lay stretched out on the sand, abandoning any further attempt to harm

Iwein. His colleagues had no opportunity to receive assistance from him, because he lay there unconscious for quite a while. The two who were left rode at Sir Iwein again, wielding their swords as good knights should. They got their comeuppance, for each of Iwein's blows was like two of theirs. He still needed a lot of strength as well as defensive capability, because two men are generally superior to one.

[5351] The ladies of the court were all praying to God, in His grace and power, to come to their aid, to confer victory on their champion, for raising their spirits and saving their companion. God is so merciful and kind, and of such pure heart, that He could never refuse a proper prayer from so many sweet lips. The knights who were fighting Iwein were not cowards, and they had put him in grave danger. Although they failed to kill him, they pressed him hard. Still, they were unable to gain honor at his expense. The seneschal now regained his senses, got to his feet, picked up his sword and shield, and ran to help his worthy brothers.

[5375] The lion thought this was the right moment to intervene in the fight. Suddenly it charged the running man, tearing at his armor relentlessly. The rings of his armor went flying, as if they were bits of straw. The lion dismembered the seneschal, rending him whenever it could get at him. By the lion's command Lady Lunete was freed from the seneschal. That command was, precisely, death, and with compelling reason she was happy about it.

[5389] Here lay the seneschal; now the lion was enraged at the seneschal's companions, who had already taken and given many hard blows. They were now fighting for their very lives—in mortal danger. It was now two against two, for Sir Iwein, unable to drive the lion off, had to let it stay. Willing though he had been to do without its help, he was not exactly angry that it had jumped in to help him; he neither thanked it nor reproved it. They attacked from two directions, the lion here, the man there. Their adversaries were physically and mentally courageous. If they could have been protected by bravery alone, they would have been effectively defended. Each of them succeeded in dealing a wound to the lion. But when the lion felt the wounds, it fought back even more fiercely. Sir Iwein's distress at seeing the lion's wounds was manifest, for he abandoned all restraint. He was so enraged by the lion's own suffering, that his fury drained his enemies of their strength, and they lost the will to continue.

[5423] Thus they were conquered—not, however, before they had wounded Iwein four times. But no one heard him bemoan his own wounds, just those of the lion. Now in that period it was the custom that the accuser suffer the same death as that person was to suffer whom he had challenged to a trial by combat, if it turned out that the combat proved the accused to be innocent. That practice was observed now: Sir Iwein's enemies were put on the gridiron. The ladies of the court were ready to serve Lady Lunete. Falling at Sir Iwein's feet, they thanked him profusely, showing him every honor he could have expected, and beyond what he sought. Lady Lunete was very happy, as was to be expected. She regained her mistress's favor, who from then on made amends to her for Lunete's having endured misery and wretchedness, even though innocent.

[5451] It was easy for Iwein to leave, because no one knew who he was, except Lady Lunete, who at his behest remained silent. It was very strange that she who carried his heart with her did not recognize him. Still, she urged him to stay, saying, "Dear sir, for God's sake, stay here with me, because I know that you and your lion are badly wounded. Let me cure you."

[5465] The nameless knight replied, "I will never be comfortable or happy until the day comes when I regain my lady's favor, of which I am unjustly deprived." She said, "I can praise neither the heart nor the person of her who withdraws her favor from such a brave man as you have shown yourself to be. Unless you have caused her a lot of grief, she isn't acting wisely." "May help never come to me," he said, "if her wish was not always my command. May our Lord God grant that she will soon reflect on me. Christ knows, I'll never tell anyone of the misery that is my close companion, except the one who already knows how deeply it pains me." "Does anyone but you two know about it?" she asked.

[5490] "No, lady," said Sir Iwein. "Why don't you tell me her name?" she asked. "Lady, I can't do that either," he replied. "I must regain her favor." "At least," she said, "tell me who you are." He replied, "I want to be recognized by the lion that travels with me. If she never shows me mercy, I will always be ashamed of my life and of my own name and I will never be happy. I am called the knight with the lion. From this day forward, when anyone tells you anything about a knight whose companion is a lion, you will recognize me."

[5507] "How does it happen," the lady asked, "that I have never seen nor heard of you before?" The knight with the lion replied, "You have heard nothing about me because I am unworthy. I ought to have devoted my aspirations, my life, and my wealth to making myself better known. But if my luck is as good as my spirit and my mind, I am sure I will deserve your knowing me better." "If you are no worse a man than I have seen," she said, "you are worthy of every honor. And if it would help any, I would repeat the request that I made. I don't think I could stand the shame and the disgrace if someone should see you leaving my land so badly wounded." "God protect you," he said, "and give you happiness and honor, but I can't stay here any longer." The lady replied, "Since you decline my aid and com-

Iwein + lion leave, wounded

fort, I commend you to God's blessing. He can care for you better than I. And may He in His kindness allow you soon to transform your tribulations into happiness and honor."

[5541] Departing in sadness, Iwein said to himself, Lady, how little you know that you yourself have the key! You are the lock and the chest enclosing my honor and my happiness. Now it was time to ride off. No one accompanied him except Lady Lunete, who went with him for quite a distance. She made him a promise, which she later kept, giving her word that she would always remember him and would see to some resolution of his sorrow. The good Lady Lunete was so loyal, so trustworthy, that she was glad to do this. Iwein thanked her a thousand times.

[5564] The lion was so badly wounded that it had great trouble in following Iwein along the road. When it couldn't walk any farther, he dismounted, gathered moss and whatever soft plant material he could find, and lined his shield with it. He then put the lion on it and lifted it onto the horse in front of him. He, too, was in misery, suffering great pain, until the road took him to where he saw a castle. Needing rest and recuperation, he turned toward it, found the gate closed, and in front of it a squire, who well understood his lord's mind. Reflecting that good and noble disposition, the squire, the very image of his master, welcomed Iwein, offering him food and lodging. *Arrived at castle !*

[5586] Iwein, exceedingly travel-weary, was more or less obliged to accept the hospitality offered him. A guest who wants to stay with you is amenable to an invitation. When the gate was opened for him, he saw knights and servants approaching him. They received and greeted him courteously. They were glad to minister to his misery and pain, as their lord had ordered. The lord himself came and received him cheerfully, providing such comfort for him that you could see that his will and his disposition were unblemished and good. A private room was quickly appointed for him, and his lion reposed by him. They took his armor off there. His host sent for two of his daughters, very beautiful girls, and he ordered them to salve and bind Iwein's wounds. They were so kind and skillful that they quickly cured both him and his companion. He stayed here for two weeks before leaving, his body having fully regained its strength.

[5625] At this time, Death brought suit against a Count of Blackthorn, forcing him to suffer great distress in a lawsuit of which he was the loser, because to meet the judgment he had to give up both his health and his life. He left behind two beautiful girls. The older wanted to forcibly seize the inheritance designed to serve them both. At this, the younger said, "Sister, God forbid you from injuring me like that. I had hoped to enjoy a more affectionate relationship with you. You are too unkind, sister, and if you try to rob me of my property and my honor, I'll put up a struggle. As a woman, I cannot fight, but you won't get any advantage from my being a noncombatant, because I will surely find a man who will not refuse me a courtly response in defending me against you. Sister, you must let me have my share of our inheritance or else get yourself a champion, because I am going to King Arthur's court to find a champion who will bravely protect me from your arrogant misbehavior."

[5663] The evil sister took note of this and pondered what to do about it. Maintaining a deceptive silence, she arrived at the court first, soon enough to enlist Sir Gawein in her cause. The younger sister arrived later. Her naïveté was responsible for her having already revealed her plan. When she arrived, she found her older sister already there. The latter was well pleased with her champion, even though Sir Gawein had promised his aid only on the condition that she tell no one. This was at the time of the queen's return, whom Meljaganz had boldly abducted. It was also when the story was first bruited about that dwelled on the giant and how he had been killed by the knight with the lion. The good Sir Gawein expressed his sincere thanks that it had been done for his sake. After all, the unknown knight had asked that Gawein be informed, and Gawein's niece had done so. When she told him, how bitterly he complained he didn't know who the man was! For the man had not given his name. Only through the report did Gawein know of him, but not who he was.

[5699] When, as I told you, the girl came to court seeking a champion, nobody took up her cause. She complained vehemently about her property and her honor, because the knight she had counted on said, "Lady, I cannot serve you because I am very busy with other things that I have to do. If you had come to me sooner, before I had taken on a different task, my help would have been at your disposal."

[5715] Unable to find a champion, she went immediately to King Arthur. "Even though I could not find a champion here," she said, "I didn't want to leave without saying good-bye to you. But I will not forfeit my inheritance because I failed to find anyone here. I have heard of the great bravery of the knight with the lion. If I can find him, I will be helped. If my sister does the right thing by me, I'll be satisfied. With affection, she can get whatever of mine she wants, as long as she does so properly. But if she goes beyond that, I shall challenge her."

[5737] But since the older sister knew that the best knight at court would defend her, she took a solemn oath that she never would share the inheritance. To this the king replied, "The custom here is that whoever brings suit must wait forty days for a combat." She answered that anyone wanting to fight on her behalf should do so right away, because she wouldn't wait any longer. But when that seemed like a bad idea to the king, she changed her mind, for she was not worried that her sister would come up with anyone who could defeat her champion, even if she had to wait a year. King Arthur arranged for the fight to take place in six weeks. The younger sister, having said good-bye, went to look for her champion, praying that God would lend His assistance.

[5761] She rode far and wide, through many lands, finding neither the man nor news of where he might be found. Her fruitless search exhausted her and finally made her sick. Still on the lookout, she came to one of her relatives, to whom she described her journey and bemoaned her grief and her sickness. Perceiving her wretched state, he detained her to care for her and, at her request, sent in her stead his own daughter, who continued the search, suffering great difficulties in the process.

[5778] She rode all day long all by herself and at nightfall took a road that led into a wood. The night grew dark and cold, and a wind came up, bringing rain. It was an ordeal that would have frightened a brave man, not to mention a child who had never been exposed to danger. So unused was she to the distress she was suffering that she became terrified. The way grew dark and densely enclosed, and she called on God to consider her need and guide her to an inhabited place. After she had given herself up for lost, she heard a horn blowing in the distance. Our Lord arranged for her to change direction to where the sound of the horn was guiding her.

[5802] A valley led her to a castle. The watchman on duty quickly caught sight of her. A stranger who rides up, so late and so tired, is easily persuaded to spend the night if she has the time. She didn't need to be asked twice. After everything possible had been done for her comfort, and she had received everything she needed, and had finished eating, her host marveled at her journey and inquired what her mission was.

[5819] The girl replied, "I am looking for a man I've never seen and don't know. I don't know how I can tell you his name, because it was never told to me. All I know about his identity is that he has a lion. I need him badly. People speak of his courage. If I am ever to overcome my travail, I have to find him."

[5831] "You have not been deceived," said the host. "The person who told you of his bravery did not lie to you, for his valor saved me from great misery. God sent him to help me. How gratefully I bless the path that brought him to me! For he killed a giant who had desolated and burned my land. The giant killed two of my children. And the four who are still living he captured and would have hanged. I

Girl goes to the castle from the giant episode

was just an object of scorn to him. Then God sent this knight to avenge me. While I watched, he killed the giant, right in front of my castle gate. The bones are still lying there. He brought me great honor. May God protect him wherever he goes."

[5855] The girl, happy to hear this, said, "Dear sir, tell me, do you know where he was heading when he left you? Please inform me." The host replied, "Lady, I'm very sorry, but I don't. In the morning, though, I'll show you the road he took. Maybe God will help you from there on." It was now time to go to bed.

[5867] The next day at dawn the girl set out on the road after the knight, in the direction that had been pointed out to her. It was the right road, and it took her to the spring, where he had killed the seneschal and vanquished his brothers. People she met there told her about it, advising her that if she wanted to know where he had gone, the person for whom he had slain the seneschal and his brothers could probably tell her. She said, "Tell me who that is." "She is nearby," they answered, "a girl named Lunete. She is praying in the chapel there. Ride over and ask her. If she can't tell you, no one else here can either."

[5891] When asked if she knew where the knight was, Lady Lunete, who liked to act in a courteous way, sent for her horse and said, "I'll ride with you to the place he asked me to accompany him to. That was when he was leaving the country, after having fought for me here." So she led her there and said, "Here it is, lady; I left him at this spot. He wouldn't tell me where he intended to go. One thing I lament to God: he and his lion were so badly wounded that they couldn't have gone very far. May our Lord protect him from death! He is everything a knight should be. I wish you both well and hope you find him in good health, because with his help you will prevail over all your troubles. God knows, lady, I would be dead if he hadn't come to my aid. May you similarly be freed from your burdens. I will be happy to hear good news from you." With this they parted, and the girl hastened to resume her search. Following the right road, she saw the castle where Sir Iwein was being well cared for until he could recover from his wounds.

[5931] As she rode up to the castle gate, she noticed such a retinue of knights and ladies that it did honor to the host. Turning quickly to them, she asked if they had any information about the knight she was seeking. The host was kind enough to approach her pleasantly and offer her lodging. She replied, "I am looking for a certain man, and until I find him I must dispense with favors and relaxation. I was directed here." "What is his name?" asked the host. "I was put on his trail," she answered, "and was told no more about him than that a lion is with him." "At this moment," said the host, "he has just taken leave of us. I couldn't persuade him to stay any longer. He and his lion have completely recovered from their severe wounds. They left happy and healthy. If you want to catch up with them soon, you ought not to wait. Keep on the right track and stay on the right road. Then you will quickly catch up with him."

[5964] There was no further delay. Unable to keep to an ambling gait, she galloped and trotted until she caught sight of him. May you and I be as happy to see each other as she was then. "Good and powerful God," she reflected, "what will happen to me now that I have found this man? I have suffered great hardship during this search. I thought only of how happy I would be if I found him, and that I had overcome my troubles. But now that I have actually found him, I am very worried about how he will act toward me. If he declines to help me—what good are all my efforts then?" She spoke this silent prayer: "Lord God, teach me the words that will benefit me the most, so that he won't be put off by me and won't refuse me. If my bad luck or his anger causes me to lose what I want, then my finding him will have been in vain. God give me good luck and good sense."

[5996] She swiftly rode up alongside him and said, "God's greetings, sir. I have come a long way to seek a favor of you. May God persuade you to grant it." He replied, "It's not a question of doing a favor. I never refuse my help to any good person who really needs it." Because he could see that she had endured hardship while searching for him, he wished her well, saying, "Lady, I am sorry about all that you have been through, but if I can be of help, you don't need to worry anymore."

[6013] Bowing in acknowledgment to him and God, she thanked him abundantly, saying, "Dear sir, the request is not for me but for another, far worthier than I am, who sent me after you. I'll tell you about her situation. She has been victimized. Her father died recently, and her sister, who is a bit older, aims to disinherit and ruin her. She was barely able to gain a delay of five and a half weeks, after which a trial by combat is scheduled to decide between the two. By this means her sister wants to deprive her of her inheritance, unless the lady is fortunate enough to bring a champion to protect her from such a power play. Because everyone praises you, she indicated that she had chosen you to aid her. It was neither pride nor laziness that prevented her from riding after you herself. She started out but was truly afflicted by distress, for while under way she had the bad fortune to become sick from traveling and had to stop at my father's and go to bed. He sent me on in her place, and now I am asking you as she asked me. She told me, sir, to implore you with all my might. Since God has so honored you that you are more famous than many other knights, please honor God and women by being both courtly and wise. Please expand your fame for both your sake and hers; yours by adding to your honor, hers by saving her property. In God's name, please tell me how you feel about it."

[6062] "The messenger," he replied, "hasn't forgotten a thing. The old saying holds true: whoever sends a good messenger achieves his goal. From the messenger I can judge that the lady should be defended. As far as my strength permits, I will gladly do what she wants. Ride ahead and show me the way. Where you show me, that's where I'll go."

[6073] Thus was the messenger received; her doubts and fears had vanished. As they rode across the heath, they passed the time by telling each other stories, as well as the latest news. Then they saw ahead a castle by the road, well suited for people in need of lodging like themselves. The castle lay apart on a height, with a market town[36] down below, into which they rode. But everyone who was standing or sitting by the road received them rudely. They were almost frightened by the sidewise glances and the backs turned on them. The people said, "You're here at the wrong time. No one needs you here. If you knew what's going on here, you would ride on. You're not going to get any respect here. Who do you think is going to welcome you? Why did you presume to come by here? Who here wants you? You'd be better off elsewhere. You have been sent here by God's wrath, to your misfortune. You are not welcome here."

[6108] After they had heard this, the knight with the lion said, "What is the meaning of these reproaches and threats? How have I deserved this? If I ever reaped your anger, it was done unwittingly. I want to assure you of the real truth. I did not come here to harm you. If I can, I will leave here with the affection of all of you. My dear people, if you receive all strangers the way you received me, that can only be discouraging to someone coming here who needs your help."

[6125] As he struck out on the road to the castle, he rode right by a townswoman who had heard his angry outburst. She motioned to him from a distance. "Dear sir," she said, "don't get so angry. The people here say what they say for your own good. They feel empathy for your honor and for this noble lady. If you go up to the castle, you will lose your life.[37] The people don't talk like this because they dislike you but because they would prefer that you avoid the castle and ride on. A law has been foisted on us, prohibiting all of us, on pain of loss of life and property, from taking in any guest outside the castle gate. You cannot obtain lodging here. May God protect you. I know very well that if you proceed, you are risking your life. My advice is to turn around and keep riding."

[6154] "Perhaps it would help," Sir Iwein replied, "if I followed your advice. But

---

36. See *Erec*, note 7.
37. Compare *Erec*, lines 8086–169 and 8660–79.

it's too late. Where would I go? I have to spend the night here." "By God," said the lady, "it would make me happy to see you ride away from there with honor. But unfortunately that cannot be." So he rode on until the gatekeeper caught sight of him. The former gestured and said, "Come on, knight, come on! I assure you that the people will be glad to see you here—but that won't help you."

[6171] After this greeting he promptly opened the gate and received him with many a threatening word, to which Iwein paid no attention. Looking at the knight with the malice appropriate to a traitor, the gatekeeper said, "I took care to get you in here; now let's see how you are going to get out." And he barred the gate behind Sir Iwein.

[6183] Seeing nothing to be afraid of either in the castle or in front of it, Sir Iwein ignored what the gatekeeper had said. From inside the gate he noticed a big workhouse, whose architecture resembled that of a dwelling for poor people. Peering through a window, he saw a good three hundred women working; they were young, miserable, and poorly clad. Many of these poor women were weaving such articles as are made of silk and gold. Others were busy at an embroidery frame, producing high-quality needlework. Of those not skilled in either art, some sorted thread, others wound it, some beat flax, some scraped it, others combed it. Some were spinning, some sewing. All suffered from need, for their work hardly brought them more than constant hunger and thirst. They got just enough food and drink to permit them to survive in weakened condition. Haggard and pale, they suffered extreme want in both body and dress. Meat and fish were strangers to their cook-stoves. They were obliged to dispense with food and drink as well as with their honor, and they struggled with want.

[6221] The women were aware of the knight, and that threw them into still greater depression. Their suffering was now much greater, for they felt such shame that their arms fell, and tears welled up in their eyes and fell onto their clothing. So acute was their pain that a stranger had seen their poverty, that their heads sank, and without exception they forgot the work in their hands.

[6234] Iwein, seeing no one else around, was about to ask the gatekeeper about these wretched women. But when he turned toward the gate, the malicious fellow greeted him in a threatening way and said as cunningly as he could, "Do you want out, Sir Stranger? No way. The gate is bolted. We have other plans for you. Before the gate is opened for you, you will get your proper comeuppance in here, and you will make your exit under quite different conditions. All kinds of infamy are being prepared for you, and you will be taught appropriate courtly behavior. How completely God abandoned you when I got you inside here! You will depart in dishonor."

[6257] The knight with the lion replied, "You can be as menacing as you like, but if I'm exposed to no greater danger than that, I shall live forever. Why do you bolt your gate fast? If I were on the other side of it, I'd still come back in because I want to ask a question. Tell me, dear friend, what is the story of these poor women? Their behavior and their appearance suggest that they would be very beautiful if they were happy and rich."

[6272] The gatekeeper declined to answer, saying, "I'll tell you nothing. Do you imagine, Sir Stranger, that I am amused by your tiresome questioning? You're wasting your effort." "I'm sorry about that," the knight answered, laughing as he turned away, as one will do who doesn't want to get involved in an argument with a boor. He took the gatekeeper's words as a joke. He checked out all the walls until he located the doorway, which he entered. However much the women had been burdened by poverty, they were not frightened. They bowed to him all around and let their work lie untouched while he sat by them. This was required by their upbringing. He also noted that there was no superfluous talking, such as commonly occurs when women are in large groups. For here poverty was accompanied by modesty and propriety. They often blushed with shame when he offered them his service; their eyes grew sad and damp while he sat among them.

[6303] Profoundly affected by their plight, he said, "If it's all right with you, I'd like to ask about your social status and family. Because, unless I've lost my mind, you were not born to poverty. I can see that you are ashamed of your poverty. I get this impression because those used to poverty from childhood are not so ashamed of it as you seem to be. Tell me neither more nor less than just what the case is. Is it birth or misfortune that has brought you to this place?"

[6319] One of the women answered, "We will be glad to tell you of our origin and our present life. We lament to God and to good people everywhere about how we came to be deprived of our honor and brought to this wretched condition. Our country, sir, which is called the Island of Maidens, lies far away. The lord of that country conceived the rash idea of riding forth in search of adventure. Unhappily, his way, like yours, led him here, where the same thing happened to him as will happen to you. Refusal is out of the question, and tomorrow you will have to fight two minions of the devil. They are so strong that even if you had the strength of six men, it would be nothing compared with them. Only God can help you if He exerts Himself, for nothing is too hard for Him and nothing can happen without Him. Without His intervention, we must see you tomorrow in the same mortal peril encountered till now by many others.

[6349] "Thus my lord came riding up and had to fight them. His will and his

They are ransom for deters to two giants.

courage were steadfast and strong, but he was only eighteen years old and lacked the necessary strength. So, without wanting to, he had to forsake victory and yield without much of a fight. He would have been killed, except that he was released from these evil giants, as I will describe to you. They would have killed him, except that he swore an oath to give hostages and a guarantee in order to ransom himself. Every year he has to give them thirty girls as tribute for as long as he and the giants live. If, however, anyone should defeat the two giants, we would be freed. That agreement is unfortunately of no avail, because in addition to their strength they are so courageous that no one will ever gain victory over them.

[6377] "We are the tribute and we have a terrible life, a miserable youth, for those to whom we are subject are thoroughly corrupt, refusing to let us keep any profit at all from our work. We have to put up with whatever is imposed on us. With gold and silk we make the best clothes in the world, but what good does it do us? We don't live any better because of it. Laboriously we must strain our arms and hands just to earn enough to keep ourselves from starving. I'll tell you what we are paid, and you tell me who could get rich from pay like that. We get just four pennies out of each pound. That is not enough to buy food and clothing, both of which we are always in need of. They have gotten rich from our earnings, while we live in misery."

[6407] Sympathizing with their sad plight, Iwein sighed deeply and said, "May our dear God reward you ladies for your hard lives and grant you good fortune and honor. I am sorry about your misery, so sorry—of this I assure you—that I would gladly liberate you if I could. I'll go and find the people of the castle and see how they act toward me. No matter how fearful the matter is, if God is merciful, I hope to prevail easily." And he commended them to God, and they in return offered many prayers on his behalf.

[6425] Looking farther, he saw a beautiful big hall, which he and the girl inspected without finding a soul there. He followed a side path leading to a road that went past the hall. Searching carefully, he noticed some stairs. They took him to a huge park, more beautiful than any he had ever seen. There he saw an old knight lying comfortably on a couch, with which the goddess Juno,[38] in her greatest splendor, would have been pleased. The beautiful flowers, the fresh grass enveloped him in a sweet aroma—it was a pleasant place for the knight to be lying. He was handsomely mature, and in front of him sat a lady who was doubtless his wife. For all their advanced years the pair could not have been more handsome nor

Nice Park, living in free

38. In mythology, Jupiter's wife, thus queen of the gods, and goddess of marriage.

have acted with greater dignity. In front of them, in turn, sat a girl who, so I've been told, could read French very well and was entertaining them by doing so. Often she made them laugh. Because she was their daughter they thought whatever she read was fine. It is right to praise a girl who has good manners, beauty, noble birth, youth, wealth, modesty, kindness, and good sense. She had all this and everything else one could wish for in a woman—besides which she could read very well.

[6471] Upon noticing the stranger, the lord and the lady promptly got up and approached him while he was still some little distance away, receiving him as cordially as a host is expected to receive a welcome guest. The girl quickly relieved him of his armor. Hospitable treatment like this was more than welcome to a stranger. She then clad him in pure white: finely pleated linen and an ermine-lined velvet cape, which looks nice over a shirt. Since the evening was warm, he didn't need a coat. Taking him by the hand, she led him to the most attractive grassy place in the park, where they sat down together. He thereupon discovered that she was as kind and talented as she was youthful and charming. He was certain that a more virtuous or better-spoken girl could never be found. Given her fine qualities, she could have perhaps persuaded an angel to reject heaven on her account. She struck such an amorous blow at the constancy he had in his heart that his constancy would have been extirpated, had any woman's kindness been capable of effecting such a thing. Had he never seen her, it would have been far better for him—for parting hurt him so. Except for his own wife, he had never, neither before nor since, met a woman of greater beauty or more charming speech.

[6517] When the four of them spontaneously split up, they grouped themselves according to spirit and age. I have the impression that their wishes and thoughts were different. The two young people secretly yearned in their hearts for true love, rejoiced in their youth, spoke of the joy of summer and of how they both wished to lead happy lives, if that were possible. The old people, though, talked of how they were both the same age and said that since the winter would likely be cold, they should protect their heads from colds by wearing fox-fur caps. They discussed finances to cover their needs and comforts and considered their household situation. It had grown late when a messenger came to announce that the evening meal was ready.

[6545] When they sat down to eat, they made a point of showing conspicuous honor to their guest. And never did a host offer greater honor to his guest. He was worthy of it, though, and it was proper for him. Both honor and hospitality were in great abundance. But meanwhile he was thinking: everything is still going all right. Yet I am very much afraid that I'll have to pay dearly for the honor accorded me here. The reception is just too sweet, just as was promised me by that evil fellow, the host's gatekeeper, who let me into the castle, and also according to what the ladies told me. Be courageous and undaunted; what is supposed to happen will happen, and nothing else, as I well know.

[6569] After finishing their meal, they sat talking for a little while. The three travelers were then shown to their beds, prepared for their comfort in a separate room. Whoever thinks it odd that an unrelated girl lay so close to him at night without being touched by him, doesn't know that a proper man can restrain himself from everything that he should. Still, God knows there are not a lot of such men. The night passed quietly. In the morning may God grant them better news than Iwein expected.

[6587] When dawn came, he first heard a mass to the Holy Spirit[39] and then he wanted to depart. His host, however, said, "All the knights who have come here like you have complied with a custom of mine that invariably exposed them to great danger. Two giants live here, and each of my guests is required to fight them. If only someone would conquer them! The rule is as follows: to the man fortunate enough to defeat both of them, I will give my daughter. If he should outlive me, he would gain great power, and the whole country would be his, because I have no other children. It's too bad that up till now they have remained undefeated, so I haven't been able to give my daughter to anyone. Risk your life, knight. Surely you can use the booty. Get rich or die. Maybe you alone above all others will win the prize. It often happens that one man defeats two." *Lord wants Iwein to defeat giants*

[6620] Giving the impression of being afraid, Sir Iwein replied, "Your daughter is a beautiful girl, noble and rich as well, but I am not of such rank that I would be suitable for her. A lady should marry a lord. I'll find a wife all right, and when I do, she'll be suitable to my station in life. I don't want your daughter and I don't ever want to risk my life for any woman in such a reckless way that I shamefully let myself be killed, defenseless. For two contestants are always the master of one. I'd be afraid of fighting even one giant."

[6639] The host said, "You are a coward. I know why you have disclosed your pusillanimity to me. You refuse my daughter only because of your cowardice. Now fight! That is your only recourse. They'll kill you even if you don't try to defend yourself." The knight replied, "Sir, I'm bothered by the idea of having to pay for your hospitality with my life. But since I'm going to have to fight anyway, I may as well do so now as to keep putting it off."

---

39. Compare *Erec*, line 665.

[6654] Hesitating no longer, he put on his armor and sent for his horse, which had been well cared for overnight—in fact, it had never been better fed. May God not reward him who acted so diligently in feeding the horse, for it was not done at the guest's request. Things often get turned around, so that when one person aims to harm another, he actually helps him. The reward for any good deed performed against one's will should be small. The knight doesn't need to offer any thanks to anyone for ministering to his horse's well-being, because it was done in the expectation that the horse would be staying there with them. And if they were wrong about this, I'm not inclined to feel sorry for them.

[6676] The guest was ready as the giants approached, well prepared for battle. Heavily armored, they were capable of striking fear in a whole army. Only their heads, arms, and legs were uncovered. They carried clubs that wreaked destruction wherever they landed and that had already killed many people. But when the giants saw the great lion standing by its master, jaws agape and long claws tearing up the ground, they said, "Sir, what's the meaning of this lion? He seems to be threatening us with his ferocity. No one is going to do any fighting here unless the lion is confined. If he were to fight on your side, that would be two against two."

[6700] "My lion is always with me," Sir Iwein replied. "I like to see it standing near me and I'll never order it to leave. I didn't bring it here to fight, but since you are so angry at me, I would be glad to see you injured, whether by man or beast." They quickly decided they wouldn't fight him unless he took his lion away. So he had to leave the lion, which was put into an enclosure. But through a crack in the wall it could see the fight about to start in the courtyard.

[6717] The two uncouth fellows launched their attack. May God protect the stranger, because it was an uneven fight. He had never been in greater peril. The shield he held before him was quickly smashed to pieces. Against the clubs nothing he had on for protection did him much good. His helmet fell apart, his other armor was dealt with as if it had been made of straw. It was his courage and skill that enabled the noble and fearless knight to survive for quite a while, and he occasionally got in an effective sword-blow.

[6737] When his companion, the lion, heard and saw the hard blows its master was taking, it was troubled by his plight but it could find no way to get out. It searched everywhere until it located a rotten foundation beam by the wall. The loyal companion scratched and bit both wood and earth until it had made a hole big enough to effect an escape. That was very quickly the undoing of one of the giants. May God destroy them both! The lion then repaid its master for the risk he had once taken for his comrade. Fastening its sharp claws in the giant's back, it sent him sprawling violently to the ground. Divine judgment on him was fulfilled as the lion bit and tore his flesh where he was uncovered, until he screamed for help. His confederate delayed no longer. Abandoning his human adversary and charging the lion, he would gladly have killed it if its master had allowed him to. In the same way that the lion had saved Iwein, Iwein now came to the lion's aid, which was as it should be.

[6772] As soon as the minion of the devil turned his back to him, he inflicted on him, with God's assistance and in short order, many wounds. He administered many blows to his arms and wherever he was not armored. The other giant, lying on the ground, could not come to help his confederate because the lion had robbed him of his strength and his wits so completely that he lay in front of them as if he were dead. Both the lion and the man attacked the other giant and quickly killed him. He did not die like a coward, though, because he struck many hard blows, even after he stopped getting help from his fellow giant. The latter, still alive, had to give himself over to Iwein's mercy, who, for the sake of God, spared him. May God be praised that the gatekeeper's threats and mockery were thus turned into joyfulness.

[6799] After Iwein's victory the host offered him his daughter and his country. But Iwein replied, "If you knew how totally the love for another woman has overwhelmed my heart, you would be glad that I could never marry your daughter. For I can never be faithful to any woman other than to her whose absence deprives my heart of joy." "You have to marry my daughter," said the host, "or else become a prisoner. You're lucky I'm so accommodating. If you had the good sense to realize your good fortune, you would be asking me for her rather than me asking you to marry her."

[6818] The knight replied, "I'll tell you why you'd be cheated on such a deal. Very shortly I have to fight a combat that I've agreed to do in the presence of King Arthur; it will be at his court. If your daughter were my wife then, and I should lose my life, she would be disgraced." The host said, "Wherever you go, it's all the same to me. I'm sorry I ever offered you my daughter. I won't pressure you about her anymore, for as long as I live." Iwein was cool in the face of such anger.

[6835] "Dear sir," he said, "I seriously urge you to reflect on your preeminence and to keep your knightly vow. Since I have been victorious here, you are obligated to let all of your prisoners go free." Assenting "That is right," the host speedily freed them all. He put his guest up for another week, so that the ladies could be well taken care of, so that fine clothes could be readied for them, as well as mounts for them to ride. In this short week they completely recovered, becoming the most beautiful group of women he had ever seen. That is what the brief period of recuperation had done for them.

[6855] He then rode off with them, escorting them to safety as a courtly man would. When he finally left them, they prayed earnestly, which was right and proper, that God would grant His realm to their lord and friend in need, who had saved them from great misery, together with good fortune, honor, and a long life. As he emerged from the fight, with his lion uninjured, who could possibly be a menace to him now? He promptly resumed his journey to find the girl for whom he had pledged to fight and who had been left behind, ill, by her cousin. The cousin showed Iwein the right route, and they found the girl in the care of the cousin's father. The girl and her champion did not want to linger there, because the day appointed for the combat was so close that they had no leeway in setting out on their trip. Arriving at the appointed time, they found the girl's sister, her antagonist, already at the site. Sir Gawein, who had asked to remain undercover, had stolen away and concealed himself after telling everyone that he was unable to witness the fight, owing to another commitment. Thus he had withdrawn, but then he had stolen back with different armament, so that he went about unrecognized except by the older sister, to whom he had told his plan.

[6895] King Arthur was seated there with all his retinue, who wanted to see how the fight would go, when Sir Iwein and the girl came riding up. The lion did not come with them, having been left behind because Iwein didn't want it to be present at the fight. Thus no one there knew who he was. As Iwein and his opponent rode into the ring, everyone agreed that it would be very sad if no way could be found to keep one of them from getting killed. Such a loss would be long lamented, for they all declared that they had never seen two knights of such incomparable perfection in appearance and demeanor. They asked the king to request that the older sister share with the younger, for God's sake. She, however, rejected the king's request with such vehemence that he didn't pursue it. She was certain that her champion would prevail because she knew how strong he was and she was confident that he would win for her.

[6929] When King Arthur saw that reconciliation was out of the question, he ordered the ring cleared. It was hard to watch combat between two such excellent knights. For a proper man does not enjoy seeing a man die, although that is to be expected if another is to live.

[6939] If I were to describe with artistic words the combat between these exemplary knights, what good would my elevated style do? You have already heard so much about the valor of each, you will easily be persuaded that on this day they did not act like cowards and that, as before, they proved that there have never been two better contenders for earthly reward. That is why they wore the crown of knightly honor, which each wanted to increase at the other's expense. So I complain bitterly to God that the best comrades living at that time should fight each other. If either kills the other and later finds out whom he has killed, that will be to his eternal lament. If both could win, or both lie vanquished, or, without destroying each other, they both could abandon the fight upon recognizing each other, that would be the best thing for their enmity. They were not strangers to each other in spirit, but only by sight. It was concealed from each that his opponent was the best friend he ever had.

[6977] Since the combat must be, it is good for both that it begin quickly. Why wait? This is the place, they have the will. The horses were also in good shape—no need to wait on that account. They were to begin the fight mounted. To make room for his opponent's charge, each rode to the perimeter of the circle, which was a hundred yards or more in diameter.

[6988] They knew how to fight a combat; at that point they were not exactly beginners. How well they knew how to fight, both mounted and on foot! From childhood on, combat had been their occupation—they demonstrated that fact here. Let it be truly said that practice teaches even a coward to fight better than a bold hero who has not practiced. The skill and strength evident in the combatants would have enabled them to give classes in knightly practice. One must concede them the highest honors in knightly practice. They were better than any knights then living. Waiting no longer, they spurred their horses, and the two who were in fact comrades clashed with each other like bitter enemies.

[7015] It seems more or less impossible to me—and not only to me—that one vessel could contain both love and hate, that love could reside alongside hate in a single vessel. But even if love and hate never before occupied a single vessel, in this particular vessel love did dwell alongside hate, and neither love nor hate was in any hurry to vacate the vessel.

[7027] "Friend Hartmann, I think you are wrong about that. Why do you say that love and hate both inhabit one vessel? Think it over. Love and hate would be crowded in a single vessel, for hate, upon perceiving true love, abandons the vessel in favor of Lady Love, and where hate dwells, love leaves."

[7041] I'll explain it clearly to you how true love and bitter hate occupied a single crowded vessel. Each of the combatants' hearts was a very crowded vessel, in which love and hate dwelled together. But a wall separated them, you see, so that hate did not know about love. Otherwise love would have made life so miserable for hate that hate would have had to abandon the vessel in disgrace. And if hate finds Lady Love close by inside the vessel, he will leave in any case.

[7055] Ignorance was the wall that divided their hearts, so that, though seeing, their eyes were blind. Even though they were close friends, ignorance wanted one comrade to vanquish the other. If the one had done so and then later found out whom he had vanquished, he never would have been happy again from that time forward. His success, having been realized, would have turned into a curse, and his pain would have no end, even when fortune smiled at him. He who had gained the victory would have been the loser in the victory. All his hopes of happiness would have turned into unhappiness. What he loved he would have hated, and what he gained he would have lost.

[7075] Their horses ran swiftly. At just the right instant the adversaries lowered their lances, bracing them against their chests so they wouldn't wobble. They neither raised them nor lowered them, with the result that the lances were neither too high nor too low but just the way they should be as each combatant aimed to unhorse the other. Both lances struck the area between shield and helmet, targeted by the man who knows how to unhorse his opponent. That was evident, because each contender was jolted backward so hard that he came closer than ever before to falling. That each remained in his saddle was owing only to the fact that their lances broke. They had clashed with such a shock that the shafts broke into hundreds of pieces. To a man everyone claimed never to have seen a more beautiful joust. A large group of squires shouting encouragement quickly came running up, each carrying two or three lances.[40] All that could be heard was the cry: "A lance! A lance! This one is broken. Bring another!" The combatants thrust and thrust again, shattering all the available lances. If they had then fought with swords while on horseback, which neither wanted to do, it would have meant the death of the poor horses. And so both felt constrained to avoid such crudity and to fight on foot, for the horses hadn't done anything to them. They were fighting each other to the death.

[7125] I'll tell you what the two experienced fighters did when they came together. They spared the armor that protected their bodies. Their swords were busy, though, and they were not exactly easy on each other's shields. The fighters hated the shields, each of them reflecting, What good are my exertions? As long as he keeps a shield in front of him, he is safe. So they chopped up the shields with their swords but were careful not to strike blows below the knees, where their legs

40. See *Erec*, note 84.

were not protected by shields.[41] Without guarantor and without guaranty they lent each other more powerful blows than I can describe—and they were promptly repaid.

[7147] It is a good idea to repay loans promptly, because when one wants to borrow again, he can easily do so.[42] They had to pay attention to this, for he who borrows and does not repay is most likely punished. They feared punishment if they borrowed without repaying, because he who borrows and fails to repay is often punished. If the loans had not been repaid, they would have been punished. It was therefore important to each not to be deprived of credit. They had to pay in full to avoid both the censure of death and the reputation of being deadbeats. They both paid generously. They did not, however, need to send for more money because, having brought both principal and interest to the field, they repaid on the spot, more and sooner than they were asked to. Worthless idleness distresses both God and the world. No one gets into such a state except someone without ambition.

[7175] He who likes to acquire honor has to direct all his thoughts to some type of livelihood, so that he can achieve something and pass the time acceptably. They had done so. They had not spent their lives in idleness. Both were unhappy when days passed without their finding any profit in the trade to which they had devoted themselves. The two, well known as clever moneylenders, made loans from their stock in trade in a strange way. They made a profit from it, like two entrepreneurs. Their orientation to gain was very odd. If any merchant had used their method, it would have ruined him. But these two grew rich from it. They made loans, all right, but repayment would have distressed them. Just look, though, how one can be enriched by such earnings. With swords and lances they lent thrusts and blows of which nobody could repay even half. This increased their fame and honor. Their banking services were so readily available that they never turned down anyone's proposal for them to exchange their risky labor for fame and honor. But never before had they received such prompt and full payment as now. They lent no single blow that wasn't instantly repaid. Their shields, offered up as pledges for their lives, were quickly hewn out of their hands. Then, having no other pledge but their metal armor, they pledged that. Finally their bodies were not spared but were also pledged as security and rapidly paid. Several places on their helmets were severely cut up. Their coats of mail were growing red with blood, because within a very short period the combatants had received a lot of wounds, none of which was fatal.

41. That is, they disdained to take unfair advantage of each other. But observe, line 6777, that no such chivalrous restraint applies when one's opponent is a giant.
42. Compare *Erec*, lines 850ff.

[7235] This fearful fight, with its claims to valor, had started sometime in the morning and it lasted a long time. By mid-afternoon neither of the contenders could strike any more damaging blows. Exhaustion had so completely robbed them of their strength that they felt their deeds were not redounding at all to their honor, and so they stopped fighting. Parting amicably, they sat down to rest until their strength returned.

[7251] After resting briefly, they jumped up and charged at each other again. As to both desire and strength, they were two reinvigorated men. Their earlier combat was nothing compared with the one that began now. If their earlier blows had been powerful, now they were even more powerful, and more numerous as well. Although many battle-tested men were watching the fight, no one's eye was so experienced or so penetrating that he would have been able to say for certain, under oath, which champion had fought better by a hair's breadth on this day. It was not possible to attribute superiority to either. A more equal battle had never been seen.

[7273] Everyone now began to worry about the lives and fame of the champions. If the two could have been honorably parted, the other knights would have liked to do so. They started discussing this because they would have regretted it if either had been killed or had his honor compromised. Alternately pleading and reasoning, the king tried to stir some spirit of conciliation in the older girl who had refused to share the inheritance with her younger sister. His pleas were fruitless; she refused him so rudely that he did not ask her further.

[7291] But when the younger sister saw the discomfiture of the good knights, she was deeply troubled. When no one was able to part and conciliate the combatants, she did what she could. The noble and beautiful, thoughtful and modest, sweet and admirable girl, the sweet-spirited girl, who could act only in a sweet way, smiled with sweet red lips at her sister and said, "It would be better if both my life and our land went up in flames than that such an honored man should meet death or lose his honor on my account. Take my inheritance with my good wishes. I cheerfully grant you the land as well as the victory. Since I cannot have it, I truly would rather let it go to you than to anyone else. Tell them to stop fighting; their lives are worth more than mine. It is better for me to be a poor woman than for either of them to lose his life on my account. I will renounce my claim in your favor."

[7321] No one beheld her intent without praising her goodness. Counseling the king, they all begged him for God's sake to take action and ask the older girl to give her sister a third or even less of her inheritance, for it was a question of the life of one or both champions, if they were not separated. The older sister would perhaps have done so, had the king followed through on the knights' advice. But he was so angry at her because of her hard heart that he wouldn't pursue the proposal. He deemed the younger sister such an excellent person that he was reluctant to reject her request. She had, after all, put herself at the disposal of his court. The two champions had fought honorably, landing many knightly blows, till the end of the long day. Their lives were still hanging in the balance when night fell and darkness put an end to things.

[7349] So it was night that parted them. By now each knew well his opponent's strength, and had had enough of his opponent, and was amenable to taking a break without incurring dishonor. They called a halt until the next day. They acted as right-minded men have always done: whatever pain a virtuous man suffers at the hands of another, if the pain does not come from the other's wantonness in trying to kill him, he will not hate that opponent but will like him better than he would a worthless man who never harmed him. That was more than evident with these two.

[7371] Sir Iwein, exonerating his battle comrade, would have thought it a great boon if each of them knew who the other was. So he started a conversation with him. "Now that we have stopped our hostile game," he said, "I can say what I feel like saying. I have always loved the bright day more passionately than the night. Many of my joys were closely associated with daytime, as is true with everyone. Day is happy and clear, while night is dreary and oppressive, making hearts sad. Day favors weapons and valiant deeds, while night favors sleep. Until now I have loved the day above all. But you, good and noble knight, have completely changed my opinion about that. Down with the daytime! I shall hate it forever, because it came very close to stripping me of all my honor. God bless the night!

[7401] "If I grow old honorably, I shall owe it to night. Don't you think I have good reason to feel oppressed and aggrieved about the day? If the day had lasted three blows longer, those blows would have brought you victory and deprived me of life. This dear night saved me from that. Rest will bring me renewed strength, so that on the hard day that follows I will be able to fight again. Still, however, I have to worry about tomorrow. If God doesn't release me from my obligation, I again have to confront the very best knight I ever knew. God knows that that involves worry. The knight I refer to is you. May God be merciful. May He save my life and my honor! Never before have I feared for them so much. And you should know that I never had to do with any man whom I wanted to know as much as I do you. It would be no disgrace if you were to tell me your name."

[7430] "It would not disgrace me to tell it to you," said Gawein. "We are in agreement. Sir, you have anticipated me in this. If you had been silent, I would have said what you have just said. What you love, I love. What you fear, I fear. Today is a day I will always hate, because it brought me the kind of danger that I have always been exempt from. For sure, no one ever stripped me so completely of my strength to fight. Had you been able to see well enough to land two more blows before nightfall, I would have been obliged to affirm your victory. I could scarcely wait for night to fall. As much fighting as I have done, I have never been exposed to greater danger. I fear disgrace or death at your hands tomorrow. We do have similar concerns. Let me assure you that, owing to your valor, I will grant you every honor that does not cost me too dearly.

[7459] "My heart is overburdened with grief that I must keep trying to wound you. Just as long as it doesn't disadvantage me, I wish you everything you want. God knows you deserve it. I wish these two girls had what they wanted, so that we might be of service to each other. I'll tell you my name: Gawein."

[7472] "Gawein?" "Yes." "That explains the hard day I just had! You gave me many an unfriendly blow. You vented your anger on your true servant. I don't doubt you would have spared me the beating I took if I had told you beforehand who I was. In earlier times we were better acquainted. Sir, I am Iwein."

[7484] The two of them were joyful and sad at the same time. They rejoiced at finding each other. They grieved at having caused each other such pain—which they together regretted deeply. Sadness and anger quickly left their hearts, and joy and love reigned there. They showed that by throwing their swords away and running to each other. No one ever had a happier day, and I don't know whether anyone else can experience such happiness as God gave them there. A thousand times they kissed each other on eyes, cheeks, and lips.

[7505] The king and the queen were both greatly surprised to see the mutual love and the friendly embraces. Hesitating no longer, they rushed forward, because they were pleased both at seeing such gestures of friendship and at seeing who the two knights were—which nobody else knew, although they soon found out. At first, though, their helmets and the darkness hid their faces, and the ferocity of the fight had distorted their voices such that they would have remained unidentified if they had not spoken their names.

[7523] "Alas," said Sir Iwein, "may both this day today and the sword with which I struck you be dishonored. Sir Gawein, my dear lord, what can I say except that I honor you as your knight and your servant? That is my intention, and by rights I ought to do so. You have honored me so often and have managed my affairs so well and so thoroughly, that in many countries I have been credited with more excellence than would have been the case without you. If I in return could fittingly honor you, I would be happy forever. But all I can do is be your Iwein, as I have always been and will be—except only for this day, which I can surely call the bitterest of the year, because truly neither my hand nor my sword was ever equal to the arrogance of striking you. I curse this sword and this day; and my hand—ignorant of what it was doing—shall be its own pledge that in atonement I will serve you as long as I live. Sir Gawein, you could not inflict better punishment on me, for this hand has dishonored me and increased your glory. It has defended itself in such a way as to give you the victory. Because God knows I was defeated, I surrender and swear my allegiance to you. I leave here as your prisoner."

[7567] "No, dear comrade and lord," said Sir Gawein. "My fame shall not increase at your expense. I'll gladly forgo the glory that comes at my friend's expense. What's the point of deceiving myself? Whatever honor I might presume to, everyone saw quite well what happened between us. I surrender and I submit to you because I was the one defeated."

[7579] Sir Iwein replied, "You may think I surrendered just for your sake. If you were the most remote stranger who ever dwelled in Russia, I would still swear allegiance to you before engaging in combat with you again. So it is right and proper for me to submit to you." "No, lord and comrade," said Sir Gawein. "I submit to you." This friendly but earnest quarrel between them persisted for a long while. The king and his people asked each other what the meaning could be of the love between these two knights, following so closely after the enmity that had just been witnessed.

[7599] The situation was quickly made clear to the king when his nephew Sir Gawein said, "We would like to tell you about it, sir, so that you don't take us for cowards, and so that nobody gets the notion that with this accommodation we are trying to avoid further combat. We used to be comrades. Unfortunately, neither of us knew that today, until this moment. There is no hostility between us now. I, your nephew Gawein, fought against him to whom I owe more service than to anyone in the world, until he asked me my name. Upon hearing it, he told me his; our hostility vanished, and from now on we are in accord. It is my friend Iwein. Believe me when I tell you that if he had had more daylight at his disposal, his valor and my unjust cause would have put me at risk.

[7625] "The girl people see me fighting for here is in the wrong, and her sister is in the right. Because God has always helped the person who is in the right, I would have died at Iwein's hand if night had not intervened. Since this misfortune has happened to me, I'd much rather that my friend defeated me than killed me." Sir Iwein did not like these words, and blushing painfully at Gawein's praising him so excessively, he declined to put up with the flattery. If Gawein spoke well, Iwein spoke better. This was anger without enmity.

[7643] There was a lot of talking, each striving to increase the other's fame at the expense of his own. The king liked this, declaring, "Both of you must let me settle your quarrel. I will make a decision that satisfies both of you and is advantageous for me as well."

[7653] So the whole matter was turned over to the king. He sent for the two girls and asked them, "Where is the girl who, owing simply to arrogance, denied her sister her share of the inheritance that their father had left to both?" The older sister hastily declared, "Here I am." Because of this slip of the tongue with which she proclaimed her wrong, King Arthur was delighted and he called on everyone present to be witnesses. "Lady," he said, "you have confessed. And it happened before so many people that you cannot renege. If you are to comply with the decision of this court, what you have taken from your sister you must give back to her."

[7671] "By God, no, lord," she said. "One's property and life are subject to your command. But a woman can easily say something she shouldn't. Whoever uses what we women say to punish us will have a lot of punishing to do. We women need indulgence every day for the stupid things we say, which are sometimes harsh, but without guile, spiteful, but without hostility. The sad truth is we don't know any better. However I may have erred verbally, you should proceed according to your law and not expose me to arbitrary power."

[7688] The king replied, "I will leave you what is yours, and your sister may have what is hers. The decision about the combat has been left to me, and your good sister has turned her whole case over to me, with simple nobility of heart. She must by rights have her share. If she and I are in agreement, you will emerge from the lawsuit disgraced and dishonored, because my nephew Gawein asserts he was defeated. But if you willingly give your sister her share, it will enhance your fame and fortune forever."

[7703] He said this because he knew she was so hardhearted and harsh that she would be moved neither by a sense of justice nor by kindness, only by power and fear. And so, afraid of his threat, she said, "Do neither more nor less than what seems right to you. Since you won't desist from the case, I must and shall yield to her. I'll share both land and people with her, and you can be the guarantor."

[7717] The king replied, "Let it be done." Because the case had been remanded to him, it ended well, with the giving of a guaranteed pledge that the younger sister would receive her inheritance. When this was completed, the king said, "Nephew Gawein, take off your armor, and let Sir Iwein do so, too, for you both need rest." They did as he ordered.

Dispute settled [handwritten marginal note]

[7726] The lion, which, as you have heard, had been locked up, now emerged, following its master's trail. When the people saw it running across the field in their direction, they were so afraid that they backed away. Everyone was fleeing for his life, when Sir Iwein said, "It won't harm you. It is my friend and is looking for me." Only then did they understand that he was the famous hero with the lion, who had killed the giant and, so they had heard, had done other marvelous deeds.

[7745] "Friend," said Sir Gawein, "I'll always be unhappy at having given you poor thanks for the favor you did me. You killed the giant for me. About that my niece sang your praises when she came to me with your message. She told me that the knight with the lion had done it for me but that he would not tell her his name. I bowed in every direction, not knowing where or to whom, because I wanted to show my appreciation to him who had faced danger for my sake. And unless death prevents me, I shall pay him proper homage. I recognized you by the lion." At that the lion ran up to its master and showed him its happiness and devotion as intensely as a dumb beast can.

[7769] A place to rest was promptly set up for the two knights, where their wounds were alleviated by doctors whom Sir Gawein had sent for to treat them. Moreover, the queen and King Arthur consistently saw to their good care. So they were not in the infirmary very long before they were healed.

[7781] After Sir Iwein was restored to strength and good health, his spirit in many respects was still suffering from mortal wounds because of his love for his wife. He thought he would soon die if his wife did not quickly save him, with her special kind of help. This idea was abruptly forced on him by the sufferings of love. "No matter what I do, I don't know how I can ever win her love except by going to the spring and pouring water on it again and again. If I reap pain from it—well, I'm quite familiar with pain and would rather suffer in the short run than to bear pain forever. But I shall suffer forever unless she also suffers so deeply that I can force her to return my love."

[7805] Accompanied by his lion, he stole away—of which no one either at court or elsewhere was aware—and caused such a terrible storm that no one within the walls expected to survive. Everyone was crying out, "Damn the first settler of this land! This suffering and disgrace is striking us at his whim. This world has a lot of worthless places, but this is the very worst place ever to have a castle built on it."

[7821] So many trees toppled to the ground, and the roaring and tumult continued so long, that everyone grew desperate. At that, Lady Lunete said, "Mistress, you must quickly find out where you can get a man who can help you overcome this misery and disgrace. God knows, no one here is about to help, so you'll have to search abroad. You could not incur a greater disgrace than to allow the man who has offered you this insult to depart, without having to engage in combat. If you don't take steps in this matter, it will happen again tomorrow. You won't ever be allowed to live in peace." Her mistress asked, "Can you help me? To you I lament my misfortune because you know my situation better than anyone else."

[7849] "Lady," the girl replied, "you have a more suitable source of advice. I am a woman, and if I should presume to dispense advice like a wise man, I would be more foolish than a child. Like the others here, I'll suffer whatever I have to until the day comes when we see who of your retinue comes to your aid, takes this burden on himself, and proves equal to the task of protecting us. It may come to pass, but I wouldn't bet on it."

[7863] Her mistress replied, "Don't talk like that. I have no hope, no expectation of finding such a man among my retinue. So what is your best advice?" The girl answered, "If only someone knew where the knight is who killed the giant and rescued me from disgrace and death by freeing me from the stake before your very eyes. If that knight could be located and would agree to come, then things could not be better. But one thing I know quite well: as long as his lady is unkind to him, no one will manage to persuade him to go anywhere unless one gives him a pledge—in return for helping you—to exert one's entire effort and resources to help him regain his lady's love." The lady replied, "I'll use all the wisdom God grants me, plus my life and property, to drive away her anger, if I can. Shake hands on that."

[7895] But Lady Lunete said, "You and your request are both charming. What noble lady would be disposed to refuse such charming lips, if you plead earnestly with her? If you are really serious and forthcoming about it, he will definitely win her favor. But before I leave you, I must insist that you promise under oath to provide such help." Lady Lunete administered the oath she had ready. It put special emphasis on many things that could benefit the man whom she was going to search for. "Lady," she said, "I must fortify the oath with such wisdom in order that no one can accuse me of deception. He whom I am riding out to look for is a very straightforward man, who will require firm words. If you want to send for him and will fulfill by deeds the words I put into the oath, then, lady, repeat after me."

[7923] Her mistress, placing her fingers on a shrine,[43] swore, "If the knight who travels with the lion comes and helps me out of my need, I, renouncing all deception, shall devote my power and my mind to regaining for him his lady's

---

43. A reliquary or receptacle containing relics of a saint or saints. Note that Laudine uses the plural of saint.

Lunete finds Iwein

love. May God and these good saints help me achieve eternal happiness." Nothing was left out that was apt to prove needful for him whom the girl intended to bring back.

[7939] Lady Lunete undertook her journey gladly, riding off in a happy frame of mind, even though at the moment when she started her trip she didn't have a clue as to where she would find the knight. She was, however, soon blessed by luck, for, recognizing him by the lion, she found him near the spring. Her lord recognized her when she was still a long way off. Responding to his friendly greeting, she said, "Thank God I found you so close at hand."

[7956] "Lady, you must be joking, or were you actually looking for me?" "The latter, lord, if you don't mind." "What is your wish?" "You have endured a long travail, owing in part to your own misdeeds and in part to the disfavor of her through whom you became ruler of this land and who sent me to search for you. If she who sent me does not break her oath, then I have brought things to the point where you will soon be my lord again, just as she is my mistress."

[7973] They were both very happy. Sir Iwein, in fact, had never in his life been so happy. He kissed the girl's lips, hands, and eyes a thousand times, as he said, "You have proved how much you think of me. I deeply fear and regret that my wealth or my life or both will run their course before I can suitably reward you for your great love in a way befitting the service you have rendered me." "Don't worry," she replied. "You will have enough years and wealth to show your kindness to me—if I have deserved it—and to whomever else you wish. Even if you are fully gratified, I have not done more for you than would a debtor who is ready to repay what he has borrowed. You lent me the great accomplishment of rescuing me from being burned at the stake. You risked your life for my life, restoring my life. A thousand women would not deserve the favor you did me." "Don't talk that way," he replied. "You have more than repaid it. I have been repaid a thousandfold for whatever I may have done for you. Now tell me, dear Lady Lunete, does she know who I am?" "That," Lunete replied, "would be bad. Believe me, she knows nothing at all about you except that you are the knight with the lion. She'll find out the rest in good time."

[8017] No one met them as they rode to the castle. And, as it happened, by a miraculous stroke of luck they reached Lunete's room without anyone's seeing them ride up. Lunete went to her mistress, whom she found quite alone, at prayer. She immediately told her mistress that the knight with the lion had come. The lady had never heard such happy news. She said, "He is welcome. I would be very happy to see him, if it can be properly arranged. Go and ask him whether he wants to come here or whether I should go to him. That is to say: because I need him, I can go to him. If he needed me, he would come to me."

[8037] Lady Lunete fetched him without delay, and he appeared as she had advised him to, in full armor. Her mistress received him who was actually lord there as if he were a guest. At her initial greeting he fell at her feet but made no request. "Mistress," said Lady Lunete, "tell him to stand up. And redeem your oath as I promised him you would. I'll tell you the plain truth: the help he needs depends on you alone." Her mistress replied, "Just tell me. For his sake I'll do anything I can." "Lady," said Lunete, "you phrase it well, for no one is in a better position to help him. His mistress dislikes him. If you command it, her anger will be allayed. If you command differently, he is lost—which could be to your own great sorrow. For truly you have no better friend than him. It was the wish of our Lord Christ, Who pointed out the way to me, that he was so quickly found, in order that the separation between you two might be resolved into union. From now on no affliction short of death shall ever part you. So keep your promise and fulfill your oath. Forgive his misdeed, for he never loved and never will love another woman. This is Sir Iwein, your husband."

[8075] These words startled her. Taking a quick step backward, she said, "If what you say is true, your wiles have simply handed me over to him. Am I supposed to live from now on with someone who has no respect for me? I can gladly do without that. The storm never harmed me so much that I wouldn't rather endure it than give myself forever to a man who had no respect for me. I tell you truly, I wouldn't do it if I weren't compelled by the oath. The oath has trapped me into forsaking my anger. I must strive to deserve that he love me more than he has up till now."

[8097] When Sir Iwein heard and saw that the matter was turning out well, and that his pain would end, he said joyously, "Lady, I did wrong and I am truly sorry. A repentant sinner is generally forgiven everything—no matter how severe the offense—if the sinner repents conscientiously and makes amends, promising never to repeat his offense.[44] That is exactly the situation now. If I receive your mercy now, I'll never lose it again through any fault of mine." "I took an oath," she replied, "and whether I like it or not, I can't renege on my pledge." "This is the moment," he said, "that I will always call the Easter—the peak—of my happiness."[45]

---

44. For an analogous situation, a juxtaposition of Iwein's "venial, secular sin" and Gregorius's "mortal" sin, compare *Gregorius*, lines 35ff.
45. Easter was the principal holiday in the medieval church.

[8121] "Sir Iwein, my dear lord," said the queen, "be merciful to me. You have suffered greatly on my account. I ask you for God's sake to please forgive me, because for as long as I live I must regret it from the bottom of my heart." With that she fell at his feet, imploring him passionately. "Stand up," he said. "You are not to blame. For I lost your affection only because of my own willfulness." And her anger was mollified.

[8137] Lady Lunete took solace in their reconciliation. When a man and a woman whose health and wealth, fine thoughts and youth are free of any dishonor become companions who can and will hold to each other—and if God lets them live long lives—they will have many a sweet moment. Such was to be hoped in this instance. And Lady Lunete's helpful nature contributed greatly. Cleverly she transformed Iwein's and Laudine's mutual antipathy into love, as she had long hoped to do. Her services were well worth a reward, and I think she was so generously rewarded that she did not regret her efforts. A good life was to be expected at this court, but I don't know the what or the how of what happened to everyone afterward. That was not imparted to me by him from whom I got the story. So I can't tell you any more. All I can say is may God grant us honor and good fortune.

BIBLIOGRAPHY

Critical Editions of the Works of Hartmann von Aue

Hartmann von Aue: Das Büchlein. Edited by Arno Schirokauer and Petrus Tax. Berlin: Schmidt, 1979.

Hartmann von Aue: Lieder. Edited, translated into modern German, and with commentary by Ernst von Reusner. Stuttgart: Reclam, 1985.

Erec. Edited by Albert Leitzmann. Fourth edition edited by Ludwig Wolff. Tübingen: Niemeyer, 1967.

Gregorius. Edited by Friedrich Neumann. Wiesbaden: Brockhaus, 1968.

Der arme Heinrich. Edited by Hermann Paul. Thirteenth edition edited by Ludwig Wolff. Tübingen: Niemeyer, 1966.

Iwein. Edited by G. F. Benecke and Karl Lachmann. Seventh edition edited by Ludwig Wolff. Berlin: Walter de Gruyter, 1968.

Works in English Translation

Collections

Fisher, R. W., trans. *Narrative Works of Hartmann von Aue*. Göppingen: Kümmerle, 1983.

Erec

Keller, Thomas L., trans. *Hartmann von Aue: Erec*. New York: Garland, 1987.

Resler, Michael, trans. *Erec by Hartmann von Aue*. Philadelphia: University of Pennsylvania Press, 1987.

Thomas, John Wesley, trans. *Erec*. Lincoln: University of Nebraska Press, 1982.

Gregorius

Bühne, Sheema Zeeban, trans. *Gregorius*. New York: Ungar, 1966.

Zeydel, Edwin H., trans. (with Bayard Quincy Morgan). *Gregorius: A Medieval Oedipus Legend by Hartmann von Aue*. Chapel Hill: University of North Carolina Press, 1955.

Iwein

McConeghey, Patrick M., trans. *Iwein*. New York: Garland, 1984.
———. "A Translation of Hartmann von Aue's *Iwein* with Introduction and Interpretive Commentary." Ph.D. diss., Stanford University, 1978.
Thomas, John Wesley, trans. *Iwein*. Lincoln: University of Nebraska Press, 1979.

The Lament

Hornung, Rolph, trans. "The Lament." Ph.D. diss., Rice University, n.d.
Keller, Thomas L., trans. *Hartmann von Aue: Klagebüchlein*. Göppingen: Kümmerle, 1986.

Lyric Poetry

Thomas, John Wesley, trans. *Medieval German Lyric Verse in English Translation*. Chapel Hill: University of North Carolina Press, 1968.

Poor Heinrich

Bell, Clair Hayden. *Peasant Life in Old German Epics: "Meier Helmbrecht" and "Der arme Heinrich."* 2d ed. New York: Columbia University Press, 1965.
Thomas, John Wesley, trans. *Poor Heinrich*. In *The Best Novellas of Medieval Germany*. Columbia, S.C.: Camden House, 1984.
Tobin, Frank, trans. *Der arme Heinrich* (medieval text with facing literal English translation). In *McGraw-Hill Anthology of German Literature*, vol. 1, *Early Middle Ages to Storm and Stress*, ed. Kim Vivian, Frank Tobin, and Richard H. Lawson, 69–104. New York: McGraw-Hill, 1993. This anthology has been reprinted as *Anthology of German Literature: Vom frühen Mittelalter bis zum Sturm und Drang* (Prospect Heights, Ill.: Waveland Press, 1998).
———. *The Unfortunate Lord Henry*. In *German Medieval Tales*, ed. Francis G. Gentry, 1–21. New York: Continuum, 1983.

Selected Secondary Works in English

General Works

Clark, Susan L. *Hartmann von Aue: Landscapes of Mind*. Houston: Rice University Press, 1989.
Combridge, Rosemary. "The Uses of Biblical and Other Learned Symbolism in the Narrative Works of Hartmann von Aue." In *Hartmann von Aue: Changing Perspectives, London Hartmann Symposium*, 271–84. Göppingen: Kümmerle, 1988.
Gibbs, Marion E., and Sidney M. Johnson. *Medieval German Literature: A Companion*. New York: Garland, 1997.
Gillespie, George T. "Real and Ideal Images of Knightly Endeavour and Love in the Works of Hartmann von Aue." In *Hartmann von Aue: Changing Perspectives, London Hartmann Symposium*, 253–70. Göppingen: Kümmerle, 1988.
Hasty, Will. *Adventure as Social Performance: A Study of the German Court Epic*. Tübingen: Niemeyer, 1990.

————. *Adventures in Interpretation: The Works of Hartmann von Aue and Their Critical Reception.* Columbia, S.C.: Camden House, 1996.

Jackson, Timothy R. "Paradoxes of Person: Hartmann von Aue's Use of the *contradictio in adiecto.*" In *Hartmann von Aue: Changing Perspectives, London Hartmann Symposium,* 285–311. Göppingen: Kümmerle, 1988.

Jackson, William Henry. *Chivalry in Twelfth-Century Germany: The Works of Hartmann von Aue.* Cambridge: Brewer, 1994.

————. "The Tournament in the Works of Hartmann von Aue: Motifs, Style, Functions." In *Hartmann von Aue: Changing Perspectives, London Hartmann Symposium,* 233–52. Göppingen: Kümmerle, 1988.

McFarland, Timothy, and Silvia Ranawake, eds. *Hartmann von Aue: Changing Perspectives, London Hartmann Symposium.* Göppingen: Kümmerle, 1988.

Mills, Mary Vandegrift. *The Pilgrimage Motif in the Works of the Medieval German Author Hartmann von Aue.* Lewiston, N.Y.: Mellen, 1996.

Tobin, Frank. "High Middle Ages." In *A Concise History of German Literature,* ed. Kim Vivian. Columbia, S.C.: Camden House, 1992.

Erec

Boggs, Roy Amos. "Hartmann's *Erec.*" In *Innovation in Medieval Literature: Essays to the Memory of Alan Markman,* ed. Douglas Radcliff-Umstead, 49–62. Pittsburgh: University of Pittsburgh Press, 1971.

Clark, S. L. "Hartmann's *Erec:* Language, Perception, and Transformation." *Germanic Review* 56 (1981): 81–94.

Firestone, Ruth. "Boethian Order in Hartmann's *Erec* and *Iwein.*" *Essays in Literature* 15 (1988): 117–30.

Green, D. H. "Hartmann's Ironic Praise of Erec." *Modern Language Review* 70 (1975): 795–807.

Hatto, A. T. "Enide's Best Dress: A Contribution to the Understanding of Chrétien's and Hartmann's *Erec* and the Welsh *Gereint.*" *Euphorion* 54 (1960): 437–41.

Heine, Thomas. "Shifting Perspectives: The Narrative Strategy in Hartmann's *Erec.*" *Orbis litterarum* 36 (1981): 95–115.

Jackson, William Henry. "Some Observations on the Status of the Narrator in Hartmann von Aue's *Erec* and *Iwein.*" *Forum for Modern Language Studies* 6 (1970): 65–82.

Jacobson, Evelyn M. "The Unity of *wort* and *sin:* Language as a Theme and Structural Element in Hartmann's *Erec.*" *Seminar* 27 (1991): 121–35.

Lewis, Robert E. "Erec's Knightly Imperfections." *Res Publica Litterarum* 5 (1982), 151–58.

McConeghey, Patrick. "Women's Speech and Silence in Hartmann von Aue's *Erec.*" *Publications of the Modern Language Asssociation* 102 (1987): 771–83.

McMahon, James V. "Enite's Relatives: The Girl in the Garden." *Modern Language Notes* 85 (1970): 367–72.

Palmer, Nigel F. "Poverty and Mockery in Hartmann's *Erec,* ll. 525 ff.: A Study of the Psychology and Aesthetics of Middle High German Romance." In *Hartmann von Aue: Changing Perspectives, London Hartmann Symposium,* 65–92. Göppingen: Kümmerle, 1988.

Pickering, F. P. "The 'Fortune' of Hartmann's *Erec.*" *German Life and Letters* 30 (1977): 94–109.

Ranawake, Silvia. "Erec's *verligen* and the Sin of Sloth." In *Hartmann von Aue: Changing Perspectives, London Hartmann Symposium,* 93–115. Göppingen: Kümmerle, 1988.

See, Geoffrey. "An Examination of the Hero in Hartmann's *Erec.*" *Seminar* 27 (1991): 39–54.

Sterba, Wendy. "The Question of Enite's Transgression: Female Voice and Male Gaze as Determining Factors in Hartmann's *Erec.*" In *Women as Protagonists in the German Middle*

Ages: An Anthology of Feminist Approaches to MHG Literature, ed. Albrecht Classen, 57–68. Göppingen: Kümmerle, 1991.

Tobin, Frank J. "Hartmann's *Erec:* The Perils of Young Love." *Seminar* 14 (1978): 1–14.

Willson, H. B. "Sin and Redemption in Hartmann's *Erec.*" *Germanic Review* 33 (1958): 5–14.

———. "*Triuwe* and *untriuwe* in Hartmann's *Erec.*" *German Quarterly* 43 (1970): 5–23.

Gregorius

Carne, Eva-Marie. "Trust and Confidence in Hartmann's *Gregorius.*" *Proceedings of the Pacific Northwest Conference on Foreign Languages*, ed. Ralph W. Baldner, 21 (1970): 49–55.

Christoph, Siegfried. "Guilt, Shame, Atonement and Hartmann's *Gregorius.*" *Euphorion* 76 (1982): 207–21.

Dickerson, Harold D. "Hartmann's *Gregorius:* An Alternate Reading." In *Wege der Worte: Festschrift für Wolfram Fleischhauer*, 178–88. Cologne: Böhlau, 1978.

Duckworth, David. *Gregorius: A Medieval Man's Discovery of His True Self*. Göppingen: Kümmerle, 1985.

Fisher, Rodney. "Hartmann's *Gregorius* and the Paradox of Sin." *Seminar* 17 (1981): 1–16.

Harris, Nigel. "The Presentation of Clerical Characters in Hartmann von Aue's *Gregorius.*" *Medium Aevum* 64, no. 2 (1995): 189–204.

Herlemprey, B. "Guilty or Not Guilty, That Is Often the Question: A Critical Discussion of Guilt as Portrayed in Hartmann von Aue's *Gregorius* and in the *Vie du pape Saint Grégoire.*" *Germanisch-Romanische Monatsschrift* 39, no. 1 (1989): 3–25.

Kalinke, Marianne E. "Hartmann's *Gregorius:* A Lesson in the Inscrutability of God's Will." *Journal of English and Germanic Philology* 74 (1975): 486–501.

King, Kenneth Charles. "The Mother's Guilt in Hartmann's *Gregorius.*" In *Medieval German Studies Presented to Frederick Norman*, 84–93. London: University of London Institute of German Studies, 1965.

McCann, W. J. "Gregorius's Interview with the Abbot: A Comparative Study." *Modern Language Review* 73 (1978): 82–95.

Murdoch, Brian. "Hartmann's *Gregorius* and the Quest of Life." *New German Studies* 6 (1978): 79–100.

Picozzi, Rosemary. "Allegory and Symbol in Hartmann's *Gregorius.*" In *Essays on German Literature in Honour of G. Joyce Hallamore*, ed. Michael Batts et al., 19–33. Toronto: University of Toronto Press, 1968.

Plate, B. "Grégoire and Gregorius—From Legend to Epic-Poem Embodying Criticism of the Nobility (Hartmann von Aue's *Gregorius* and the Anonymous 12th-Century French Poem *Vie du Pape Grégoire*)." *Colloquia Germanica* 19, no. 2 (1986): 97–118.

Rocher, D. "The Motif of Felix-Culpa and of the Deceived Devil in *Vie du Pape Grégoire* and in *Gregorius* by Hartmann." *Germanisch-Romanische Monatsschrift* 38, no. 1–2 (1988): 57–66.

Schwarz, Werner. "Free Will in Hartmann's *Gregorius.*" In *Beiträge zur mittelalterlichen Literatur*, ed. P. Ganz, 25–44. Amsterdam: Rodopi, 1984.

Tobin, Frank. "Fallen Man and Hartmann's *Gregorius.*" *Germanic Review* 50 (1975): 85–98.

———. *"Gregorius" and "Armer Heinrich": Hartmann's Dualistic and Gradualistic Views of Reality*. Stanford German Studies, 3. Bern: Lang, 1973.

Wailes, Stephen L. "Hartmann von Aue's Stories of Incest." *Journal of English and Germanic Philology* 91 (1992): 65–78.

Walshe, M. O'C. "The Prologue to Hartmann's *Gregorius.*" *London Medieval Studies* 2, no. 1 (1951): 87–100.

Wells, D. A. "Gesture in Hartmann's *Gregorius.*" In *Hartmann von Aue: Changing Perspectives, London Hartmann Symposium,* 159–86. Göppingen: Kümmerle, 1988.

Willson, H. Bernard. "*Amor inordinata* in Hartmann's *Gregorius.*" *Speculum* 41 (1966): 86–104.

———. "Hartmann's *Gregorius* and the Parable of the Good Samaritan." *Modern Language Review* 54 (1959): 194–203.

———. "A 'New Order' in Hartmann's *Gregorius* and *Der arme Heinrich.*" *Nottingham Mediaeval Studies* 18 (1974): 3–16.

Iwein

Batts, Michael. "Hartmann's *humanitas:* A New Look at *Iwein.*" In *Germanic Studies in Honor of Edward Henry Sehrt,* ed. Frithjof Andersen Raven et al., 37–52. Coral Gables: University of Miami Press, 1968.

Clifton-Everest, J. M. "Christian Allegory in Hartmann's *Iwein.*" *Germanic Review* 48 (1973): 247–59.

Clark, S. L. "Changing One's Mind: Arenas of Conflict and Resolution in Hartmann's *Iwein.*" *Euphorion* 73 (1979): 286–303.

Curschmann, Michael. "*Der aventiure bilde nemen:* The Intellectual and Social Environment of the Iwein Murals at Rodenegg Castle." In *Chrétien de Troyes and the German Middle Ages,* ed. Martin H. Jones and Roy Wisbey, 219–27. Cambridge: Brewer, 1993.

Firestone, Ruth. "Boethian Order in Hartmann's *Erec* and *Iwein.*" *Essays in Literature* 15 (1988): 117–30.

Gellinek, Christian J. "Iwein's Duel and Laudine's Marriage." In *The Epic in Medieval Society: Aesthetic and Moral Values,* ed. Harald Scholler, 26–39. Tübingen: Niemeyer, 1977.

Hart, Thomas Elwood. "The Structure of *Iwein* and Tectonic Research: What Evidence, Which Methods?" *Colloquia Germanica* 10 (1976–77): 97–120.

Hasty, Will. "The Natural Order of Things in Hartmann's *Iwein:* The Adventure of Paradox." In *Adventure as Social Performance: A Study of the German Court Epic,* 17–37. Tübingen: Niemeyer, 1990.

Hatto, Arthur T. "*Der aventiure meine* in Hartmann's *Iwein.*" In *Medieval German Studies Presented to Frederick Norman,* 94–103. London: University of London Press, 1965.

Heinen, Hubert. "The Concepts *hof, hövesch,* and the Like in Hartmann's *Iwein.*" In *The Medieval Court in Europe,* ed. Edward R. Haymes. Houston German Studies, 6. Munich: Fink, 1986.

Jackson, William Henry. "Some Observations on the Status of the Narrator in Hartmann von Aue's *Erec* and *Iwein.*" *Forum for Modern Language Studies* 6 (1970): 65–82.

Keller, Thomas. "Iwein and the Lion." *Amsterdamer Beiträge zur älteren Germanistik* 15 (1980): 59–75.

———. "*MF* 205, 1: 'Sit ich den sumer truoc' as Microcosm of *Iwein* of Hartmann von Aue." *Germanic Notes* 11 (1980): 5–7.

Kratins, Ojars. *The Dream of Chivalry: A Study of Chrétien de Troyes's Yvain and Hartmann von Aue's Iwein.* Washington, D.C.: University Press of America, 1982.

Lewis, Robert E. *Symbolism in Hartmann's "Iwein."* Göppingen: Kümmerle, 1975.

McFarland, Timothy. "Narrative Structure and the Renewal of the Hero's Identity in *Iwein.*" In *Hartmann von Aue: Changing Perspectives, London Hartmann Symposium,* 129–57. Göppingen: Kümmerle, 1988.

Milnes, Humphrey. "The Play of Opposites in *Iwein*." *German Life and Letters* 14 (1960): 241–56.

Mowatt, D. G. "Irony in Hartmann's *Iwein*." In *Deutung und Bedeutung: Studies in German and Comparative Literature Presented to Karl-Werner Maurer*, ed. Brigitte Schludermann et al., 34–53. The Hague: Mouton, 1973.

Pearce, L. "Relationships in Hartmann's *Iwein*." *Seminar* 6 (1970): 15–30.

Robertshaw, Alan. "Ambiguity and Morality in *Iwein*." In *Hartmann von Aue: Changing Perspectives, London Hartmann Symposium*, 117–28. Göppingen: Kümmerle, 1988.

Sacker, Hugh. "An Interpretation of Hartmann's *Iwein*." *Germanic Review* 36 (1961): 5–26.

Salmon, Paul. "'Ane zuht': Hartmann's von Aue Criticism of *Iwein*." *Modern Language Review* 69 (1974): 556–61.

————. "The Wild Man in *Iwein* and Medieval Descriptive Technique." *Modern Language Review* 56 (1961): 520–28.

Werbow, Stanley Newman. "Queen Guinevere as a Pedagogue: Pronominal Reference and Literary Composition in Hartmann's *Iwein*." *Modern Language Notes* 80 (1965): 441–48.

Willson, H. Bernard. "*Inordinatio* in the Marriage of the Hero in Hartmann's *Iwein*." *Modern Philology* 68 (1970–71): 242–53.

————. "Kalogrenant's Curiosity in Hartmann's *Iwein*." *German Life and Letters* 21 (1968): 287–96.

————. "Love and Charity in Hartmann's *Iwein*." *Modern Language Review* 57 (1962): 216–17.

————. "The Role of Keii in Hartmann's *Iwein*." *Medium Aevum* 30 (1961): 145–58.

The Lament

Seiffert, Leslie. "On the Language of Sovereignty, Deference and Solidarity: The Surrender of the Accusing Lover in Hartmann's *Klage* and *Der arme Heinrich*." In *Hartmann von Aue: Changing Perspectives, London Hartmann Symposium*, 21–52. Göppingen: Kümmerle, 1988.

Lyric Poetry

Heinen, Hubert. "Irony and Confession in Hartmann's 'Sit ich den sumer' (*MF* 205, 1)." *Monatshefte* 80 (1988): 416–29.

————. "'Mit gemache lân': A Crux in Hartmann's 'Maniger grüezet mich alsô' (*MF* 216, 29)." *Studies in Medieval Culture* 12 (1978): 85–90.

Keller, Thomas. "*MF* 205, 1: 'Sit ich den sumer truoc' as Microcosm of *Iwein* of Hartmann von Aue." *Germanic Notes* 11 (1980): 5–7.

Salmon, Paul. "The Underrated Lyrics of Hartmann von Aue." *Modern Language Review* 66 (1971): 810–25.

Sayce, Olive. *The Medieval German Lyric, 1150–1300: The Development of Its Themes and Forms in Their European Context*. Oxford: Clarendon, 1982.

————. "Romance Elements in the Lyrics of Hartmann von Aue." In *Hartmann von Aue: Changing Perspectives, London Hartmann Symposium*, 53–63. Göppingen: Kümmerle, 1988.

Seiffert, Leslie. "Hartmann von Aue and His Lyric Poetry." *Oxford German Studies* 3 (1968): 1–29.

Poor Heinrich

Anderson, Philip. "Court and Anti-Court in Hartmann von Aue's *Der arme Heinrich*." *New German Studies* 7 (1979): 169–87.

Blamires, David. "Fairytale Analogues to 'Der arme Heinrich.'" In *Hartmann von Aue: Changing Perspectives, London Hartmann Symposium*, 187–98. Göppingen: Kümmerle, 1988.

Buck, Timothy. "Hartmann's *reine maget.*" *German Life and Letters* 18 (1964–65): 169–76.

———. "Heinrich's *Metanoia*: Intention and Practice in *Der arme Heinrich.*" *Modern Language Review* 60 (1965): 391–94.

Duckworth, David. "Heinrich and the Godless Life in Hartmann's Poem." *Mediaevistik* 3 (1990): 71–90.

———. *The Leper and the Maiden in Hartmann's "Der arme Heinrich."* Göppingen: Kümmerle, 1996.

Heinen, Hubert. "The World and Worldliness in Hartmann von Aue's *Der arme Heinrich.*" In *Languages and Cultures: Studies in Honor of Edgar C. Polomé*, 260–68. New York: Walter de Gruyter, 1988.

Jones, Martin H. "Changing Perspectives on the Maiden in *Der arme Heinrich.*" In *Hartmann von Aue: Changing Perspectives, London Hartmann Symposium*, 211–31. Göppingen: Kümmerle, 1988.

Margetts, John. "Observations on the Representation of Female Attractiveness in the Works of Hartmann von Aue with Special Reference to *Der arme Heinrich.*" In *Hartmann von Aue: Changing Perspectives, London Hartmann Symposium*, 199–210. Göppingen: Kümmerle, 1988.

McDonald, William C. "The Maiden in Hartmann's *Armen Heinrich*: Enite *redux?*" *Deutsche Vierteljahrsschrift für Literaturwissenschaft und Geistesgeschichte* 53 (1979): 34–48.

Rose, Ernst. "Problems of Medieval Psychology as Presented in the *klein gemahel* of Heinrich the Unfortunate." *Germanic Review* 22 (1947): 182–87.

Seiffert, Leslie. "The Maiden's Heart: Legend and Fairy-tale in Hartmann's 'Der arme Heinrich.'" *Deutsche Vierteljahrsschrift für Literaturwissenschaft und Geistesgeschichte* 37 (1936): 384–405.

Snow, Ann. "Heinrich and Mark, Two Medieval Voyeurs." *Euphorion* 66 (1972): 113–27.

Swinburne, Hilda. "The Miracle in *Der arme Heinrich.*" *German Life and Letters* 22 (1969): 205–9.

———. "Some Comments on the Language of *Der arme Heinrich.*" *German Life and Letters* 24 (1971): 303–15.

Tobin, Frank. "*Gregorius*" and "*Armer Heinrich.*" In *Hartmann's Dualistic and Gradualistic Views of Reality.* Stanford German Studies, 3. Bern: Lang, 1973.

Wailes, Stephen L. "Hartmann von Aue's Stories of Incest." *Journal of English and Germanic Philology* 91 (1992): 65–78.

Wallbank, Rosemary E. "The Salernitan Dimension in Hartmann von Aue's *Der arme Heinrich.*" *German Life and Letters*, n.s., 43, no. 2 (1989–90): 168–76.

Willson, H. Bernard. "*Der arme Heinrich*'s 'Confession' and Guilt." *Journal of English and Germanic Philology* 78 (1979): 469–84.

———. "'Marriageable' in *Der arme Heinrich.*" *Modern Philology* 64 (1966–67): 95–102.

———. "New Light on *Der arme Heinrich* from Variant Readings." *Modern Language Review* 74 (1979): 335–50.

———. "A 'New Order' in Hartmann's *Gregorius* and *Der arme Heinrich.*" *Nottingham Mediaeval Studies* 18 (1974): 3–16.

———. "*Ordo* in the Portrayal of the Maid in *Der arme Heinrich.*" *Germanic Review* 44 (1969): 83–94.

———. "Symbol and Reality in *Der arme Heinrich.*" *Modern Language Review* 53 (1958): 526–36.

Wynn, Marianne. "Heroine Without a Name: The Unnamed Girl in Hartmann's Story." In *German Narrative Literature of the Twelfth and Thirteenth Centuries*, ed. Volker Honemann et al., 245–59. Tübingen: Niemeyer, 1994.